STRATEGY AND TACTICS
OF
SOVIET FOREIGN POLICY

John Malcolm

J. M. MACKINTOSH

LONDON
OXFORD UNIVERSITY PRESS
NEW YORK   TORONTO
1962

Oxford University Press, Amen House, London E.C.4

GLASGOW NEW YORK TORONTO MELBOURNE WELLINGTON
BOMBAY CALCUTTA MADRAS KARACHI LAHORE DACCA
CAPE TOWN SALISBURY NAIROBI IBADAN ACCRA
KUALA LUMPUR HONG KONG

© Oxford University Press 1962

PRINTED IN GREAT BRITAIN

CONTENTS

I

THE FOUNDATION OF SOVIET POST-WAR FOREIGN POLICY: 1944–47

THERE have been, roughly speaking, two themes in Soviet foreign policy since the Revolution in 1917: the drive for the revolutionary conquest of the world, expressing itself in attempts to break up by violence the nearest ring of non-Communist states bordering on the Soviet Union; and the 'active defence' of the Soviet base, the protection of the heartland of Communism from destruction by war or economic pressure, which expressed itself in the diplomacy of Soviet alignment with different groups of capitalist states, according to the international situation. Both approaches had been tried before 1944, the first from 1917 until the emergence of Stalin as dictator of Russia, and the second during the late 1920s and 1930s. Both are now part of the Soviet tradition in foreign policy, and both contributed to the Soviet attitude to the outside world in 1945, as can be seen from a brief glance at Soviet policy since the Revolution.

In the year 1917 a group of Russian political thinkers and men of action known as the 'Bolsheviks', who had evolved a plan for organizing society along the lines first publicized by the mid-nineteenth-century thinker Karl Marx, made their way to the Russian capital Petrograd, heart of an empire foundering as a result of defeats in war. In a situation of great confusion, they seized power in the city on 7 November 1917, but were forced to spend their first four years in government prosecuting an exhausting civil war against rival claimants to power. By 1921–22 they had extended their rule over the greater part of the old Russian Empire, and were generally recognized in the course of the next few years as the *de facto* rulers of Russia. During the early years much of what the Bolshevik leaders said and wrote concerned the export of their Master Plan to every country in the world. Organizations such as the Third International were set up in Moscow to co-ordinate the activities of those who supported the Plan in other countries. The Bolshevik Government declared 'war' on all non-Communist governments, parties or groups, proclaiming their belief that workers everywhere were part of the Communist movement, and that all existing governments and parties were usurpers. In the years which followed the end of the First World War revolutions did, in fact, break out in Germany and Hungary, and one attempt was made, in the course of a war with Poland, in 1920, to send the Red Army with an imported Communist government in its baggage train, into a neighbouring country. The weakness of Russia in 1917–21 proved a fatal obstacle to expansion; but great attention was paid to the needs of the Communist parties in other countries, many of whose leaders attended conferences in Moscow and debated with Lenin almost on equal terms.

However, early failures in missionary activity—the collapse of the German and Hungarian revolutions and the major defeat of the Red Army before Warsaw in 1920, brought a halt in the expansionist trend. And in spite of attempts to create revolutionary situations in various parts of the world, the first decade of Soviet power failed to produce a second Communist State, if one excludes the armed columns of nomadic Chinese followers of Marx and Lenin who fought a fierce but sporadic civil war against the Central Government of China from 1927 onwards, and ultimately created an autonomous Communist region in north-western China. The Communist failure was partly due to a reluctance of the Western industrial proletariat to abandon traditional Social-Democratic guidance in favour of the untried inflammable leadership offered by the Communists, and partly to the reaction of established governments everywhere to Moscow's 'declaration of ideological war', Under the leadership of Josef Stalin, who emerged as dictator of Russia in the 1920s, a new concept of Soviet foreign policy emerged. Stalin maintained that the time was not ripe for the Soviet Union to adopt the role of operational headquarters of a world-wide revolution against the established order, because the country was isolated, and encircled, particularly after the failure of revolutionary movements in Western Europe and the rise of rival dictatorships in Italy, Germany, and Japan. The prime task of Soviet foreign policy should therefore be the defence of the territory of the Soviet Union, that is, the protection of the home of Communism. The fate of other Communist parties faded in importance compared with the security of the frontiers of the Soviet Union. The German, Italian, and Japanese Communist parties were wrecked under the rigorous suppression carried out by rival totalitarian régimes, and no Soviet move was made to save them. In fact, in 1939 the Soviet Government entered into a solemn

alliance with the Nazi Government of Germany which had destroyed
the German Communist party, but which was ready to acquiesce in
the extension of the Soviet frontiers. Moscow therefore abandoned
short-term preparations for proletarian dictatorship in the world's
major industrial centres, and concentrated upon the military, political, and economic strengthening of the Soviet Union as a State.
This was the period when Stalin put into effect his plans for industrialization of the Soviet Union and the collectivization of its
agriculture, plans which brought much suffering to the Russian
people, but at the same time created the basis of a Soviet State able
to play its part in the struggle for power in Europe and the Far East.
In 1938 and 1939, for example, the Soviet Union was able to defend
its own and its ally Outer Mongolia's territory against Japanese
incursions. In November 1939, in search of military security, the
Soviet Union embarked upon an open war of aggression against her
small neighbour, Finland, to gain possession of seventy miles of
fortified territory, sacrificing in doing so all possibility of making the
Finnish Communist party the leader and inspiration of the Finnish
working people. *Frontier Hill No. 209*, commanding river crossing
X, became more important in Soviet foreign policy than the goodwill of millions.

Yet by 1945 the goodwill of millions had been secured for the
Soviet Union, thanks to the wartime achievements and sacrifices of
the peoples of Russia, and the efficiency with which the Soviet leaders
organized their vast country for total war. But Soviet military success
in 1945 brought more than goodwill to the leaders in the Kremlin.
It brought a possibility of reconsidering their previous approach to
foreign policy. The victorious march of the Soviet Army into Eastern
Europe, Manchuria, and Korea, gave the Soviet leaders an opportunity to resume the export of Communism, which had been abandoned in the 1920s. The Soviet victory also increased the influence
and prestige of Communist parties all over the world, particularly
in France and Italy, where membership figures approached or passed
the two-million mark, and improved the position of the Chinese
Communist party in its armed camp in north-west China,

In theory, wartime conquests presented the Soviet leaders with an
ideological dilemma. They could have regarded the victory over Nazi
Germany, Fascist Italy, and the Japanese Empire, in alliance with
the non-dictatorial capitalist countries of Western Europe and
America, as removing once and for all the danger of lawlessness and

aggression in international affairs. They could have interpreted the situation as calling for the maintenance of the alliance with the countries of the West in order to concentrate all their efforts on the rehabilitation of devasted Russia and the development of the economic power of the Soviet State. On the other hand, the Soviet leaders could interpret their position of tremendous strength as the vindication of all that Lenin and Stalin had prophesied. They could argue that Marxism-Leninism was proving a true guide to the future in that the Soviet Army had paved the way for the establishment of Communist régimes in a number of former capitalist countries. The point at issue, in fact, was whether or not the dream of world revolution had been revived in Moscow by the arrival as conqueror of Soviet armies in Berlin, Vienna, and Port Arthur.

There does not seem in practice to have been much hesitation in resolving this problem. Even before the war against Japan was over, Soviet party and state leaders were telling the Soviet people that the war they had just won was by no means the end of their struggle. The Soviet people should remember that their mission was the overthrow of capitalism, not merely the defeat of this or that national enemy. In August 1945 the Soviet President, Mikhail Kalinin, addressed a conference of party propagandists on this subject. After complaining that Soviet troops returning from Germany had developed a 'superficial admiration for German culture', which must be 'uncrowned', Kalinin went on:

Even now, after the greatest victory known to history we cannot for one minute forget the basic fact that our country remains the one socialist state in the world. You will speak frankly about this to the collective farmers. The victory achieved does not mean that all dangers to our state structure and social order have disappeared. Only the most concrete, most immediate danger, which threatened us from Hitlerite Germany, has disappeared. In order that the danger of war may really disappear for a long time, it is necessary to consolidate our victory.[1]

In his report on the 28th anniversary of the October Revolution on 6 November 1945 the Soviet Foreign Minister, Vyacheslav Molotov, said:

As long as we live in a system of states, and as long as the roots of fascism and imperialist aggression have not finally been extirpated, our

[1] *Propaganda i Agitatsia*, Leningrad, No. 18, p. 3, quoted by Frederick C, Barghoorn: *The Soviet Image of the United States*, Harcourt, Brace and Coy. New York, 1950, p. 107. This key article was also reprinted in *Bolshevik*, an important journal of political theory.

vigilance in regard to possible new violators of peace should not slacken. . . .[1]

On 1 June 1945 another Soviet political journal, *New Times*, adopting the new line, explained that those who wished to provoke new conflicts were still active all over the world. From these quotations it is clear that in the year in which the world celebrated victory over Germany and Japan the Soviet leaders decided to use their share in that victory to continue the struggle against capitalism in general, even against their own wartime allies.

Victory in war and the occupation of wide areas of Europe and the Far East extended the physical frontiers of the Soviet heartland, and provided bases from which a policy of expansion could be carried on. With renewed confidence in Communist theory and the prophetic qualities of Marxist analysis, the Russians treated Europe and Asia not as a sphere for rehabilitation but as an area in which some of the basic characteristics of a revolutionary situation were clearly apparent, and in which Soviet territorial security could be achieved once and for all. The Soviet leaders demanded a safe and secure protective belt of countries unquestionably loyal to themselves to cover their vulnerable Western frontier. They were clearly aware of the potentialities of the atomic bomb, and the power which it put into the hands of the United States, power which, it was probably feared in Moscow, might be used to effect an American presence in Europe so strong that it might penetrate to the very borders of the Soviet Union.

At the same time, it is more than likely that Stalin regarded the position of strength won by Soviet arms as his hour of destiny. Previous leaders of the Soviet State, he probably argued, had abandoned the spread of Communism only because of the isolation and weakness of the Soviet Union, and now, after years of struggle, he had power at his command such as no one before him had ever held. To shrink from turning Lenin's prophecies into history probably seemed to Stalin little short of treachery. True, Stalin was not reckless in foreign affairs, and his knowledge of the outside world was limited; but by 1945 his mind was made up, and he pursued his chosen course with the same relentless persistence that had characterized his own rise to supremacy in the Soviet Union and throughout the Communist world.

[1] Royal Institute of International Affairs, *Survey of International Affairs 1939–46*, Pt. III, *America, Britain and Russia 1941–46*, pp. 653–4.

As the full implications of their position of strength became clear to the Soviet leaders one of the earliest tasks of Soviet foreign policy was to secure Communist political control of areas under Soviet military occupation, particularly those areas which protected the frontiers of the Soviet State.

This process began even before the end of the war. In Poland, for example, in spite of the existence of a Government in exile in London, with which the Russians had broken off diplomatic relations in 1943, the Soviet Government set up its own administration, known as the Lublin Committee, named after the first major Polish city to be captured by the Soviet Army in July 1944, and signed an agreement granting the Committee legal powers to govern Polish territory conquered by the Soviet Army. On 31 December 1944 this Lublin Committee declared itself the lawful Government of Poland, and on 5 January 1945 was recognized as such by the Soviet Government. Under the Yalta Agreement of 11 February 1945 the Soviet Government undertook to establish a new and broader Polish Government with representatives of the Polish underground resistance movement and the Polish Government in London. Within a month of giving this pledge, the Soviet authorities arrested the main leaders of the resistance movement, an act which ensured that they at least could not take part in the new Government. They were later tried and imprisoned on charges of sabotage against the lines of communication of the Soviet Army, and their leader, General Okulicki, died in prison.

In the Coalition Government which was formed on 23 June 1945 from elements of the London and Lublin governments, the Communists secured the key Ministries of Public Security, Defence, and Information. In May of the following year, despite protests from the Western powers based on the Yalta Agreement, the Polish Communists opened their campaign to destroy all other political parties, particularly the Peasant and Socialist parties, alleging 'fascist tendencies'. In February 1947, after a Communist-organized general election, the Peasant party was expelled from the Government, and in August many of its most prominent figures were imprisoned. In October, Stanislaw Mikolajczyk, the Peasant party leader, who had returned to Poland to try to make the Yalta agreement work, fled to the West and the party, whose branches all over the country had been raided and closed by the Communist-dominated police, disintegrated. In March 1948 the Socialist party virtually disappeared when its leader, Jozef Cyrankiewicz, agreed to merge it with the Communist party. And finally, 1948 witnessed a big Army purge, in which officers who had served under Western command during the war were dismissed and replaced by Soviet officers. Many of the dismissed officers were arrested and several generals, whose sympathies were supposed to have lain with the West, were tried and imprisoned. By 1949 all non-Communist political activity in Poland had ceased and the country was in the hands of a régime which owned allegiance only to the Soviet Union. Attempts by Poland's Western allies to intervene or halt the process through normal diplomatic channels were ignored or blocked by the Soviet Government—just as if Poland were *de jure* and *de facto* part of the Soviet Union.

The process of integrating the countries of Eastern Europe into the Soviet base began first in Poland, an ally, but moved more speedily and ruthlessly in Rumania and Bulgaria, whose ex-enemy status made Soviet actions less accountable. The Rumanian Government had broken with Germany on 23 August 1944. On 11 February 1945 Rumania's future was discussed at the Yalta Conference by the leaders of Britain, the United States, and the Soviet Union, who pledged themselves to 'act in concert in assisting the peoples liberated from the dominion of Nazi Germany and the peoples of the former Axis satellite states of Europe to create democratic institutions of their own choice'. [1] Sixteen days later, on 27 February 1945, the Soviet Deputy Foreign Minister, Andrei Vyshinski, arrived in Bucharest and, without informing his allies, gave the King of Rumania a four-and-a-half-hour ultimatum to form a new government according to a list of personalities approved by Moscow. On 6 March a Government dominated by the Communists was formed, and on 8 May, the very day of victory over Germany, the Soviet Government, without consultation with its allies, signed a five-year treaty with the new Government under which many of Rumania's natural resources were placed under joint Soviet-Rumanian control, with Soviet chairmen and managing directors of the companies concerned. After an inter-allied commission had made recommendations on the re-constitution of the Government on a broader basis on 8 January 1946, general elections were held in November. But this apparent Soviet concession had no substance, for, contrary to the pledges given by the Soviet representative at the January meeting, only the Communist-dominated Coalition was allowed to put

[1] Text of the Yalta Agreement.

forward candidates. The result was, therefore, a foregone conclusion. On 30 January 1947 the Rumanian Peasant party caused to exist, and in July its leader, Ion Maniu, was imprisoned. In December 1947 the King abdicated, and on 13 April 1948 Rumania became officially a People's Democracy under a constitution modelled on that of the Soviet Union.

The story in Bulgaria was similar. The country was occupied by the Soviet Army without resistance in September 1944, and for the first few months was governed by a Coalition in which the Communist, Peasant, and Republican [1] parties shared the portfolios, with the Communists holding the key Ministry of the Interior. The Communists' campaign against their coalition allies began early in 1945, with the enforced flight to the protection of the American political representative of the Peasant party leader, Dr. Dimitrov, in January. Later in the year the campaign was personally directed by his namesake, Georgi Dimitrov, formerly head of the Third International, the Comintern in Moscow. The Opposition was led by Nikola Petkov, the new leader of the Peasant party, and Kosta Lulchev of the Socialists, who refused in December 1945 to join the Government on Soviet terms. In July 1946 the Communists purged the Army; the Minister of Defence was forced to resign, and leading generals were sentenced to imprisonment. On 27 October, a Communist-organized general election placed Parliament in the hands of the veteran Communist, Georgi Dimitrov. However, the Communists' main opponent, the Peasant party, under Nikola Petkov, still commanded the allegiance of the vast majority of the farming population—75 per cent of the country's total—and the Peasant party had to be crushed without delay. First, Opposition newspapers were suppressed by decree. Then, in June 1947, Petkov was arrested and brought to trial for high treason. After a judicial farce in which prosecution witnesses contradicted each other and the prepared indictment, Petkov was executed on 23 September 1947. Thereafter the remnants of his party were merged with the Communists. In 1948 the Republican group *Zveno* and the Socialist parties were abolished, and Bulgaria, too, became a People's Democracy—a one-party dictatorship.

The turn of Hungary came a little later. Although occupied by the Soviet Army in the spring of 1945, Hungary enjoyed the peculiar privilege of a free election in November of that year. The Hungarian Communist party polled only 17 per cent of the votes cast and the

[1] Known as *Zveno* (the Link) in Bulgarian political history.

formation of a Government was entrusted to Ferenc Nagy, the leader of the Smallholders' party, which had won the elections. But defeat at the polls in a Soviet-occupied country did not mean respect for the will of the people on the part of the Hungarian Communist party. It brought home to the Communists the need to organize the next election. In December 1946 the Communist party exploited judicial proceedings against certain deputies belonging to the Small-holders' party to vote for removing their mandates, and thus cut down the Smallholders' parliamentary majority. On 25 February 1947 the Soviet Army took a hand: it ordered the arrest of Bela Kovacs, Secretary-General of the Smallholders' party, and in May the Communist party forced the Premier to resign. The Small-holders' party was broken up into tiny groups, and over the rem-nants the Communist party organized another general election. By prior disenfranchisement of part of the electorate—officially ad-mitted at 500,000 voters—the Communists succeeded in gaining a small lead over their opponents.[1] This lead was increased by further *post-factum* disqualifications and re-counts, and by 1948 was large enough to enable the Communists to take full control of the country, which they did by the proclamation of a People's Democracy and a Soviet-type constitution ensuring the indefinite continuation in office of the Hungarian Communist party.

While Poland, Rumania, and Bulgaria were being turned into Soviet satellites, the new frontiers of the Soviet base were being tested for soft or undefended spots where further penetration might suc-ceed or protective zones set up. In Northern Persia, which had been under Soviet occupation since August 1941, an attempt was made in November 1945 to separate the northern province, Persian Azer-baijan, from the rest of the country. In November 1945 a 'Demo-cratic' Government of Azerbaijan suddenly appeared in Tabriz, and the Soviet Army of Occupation barred the way to Persian Govern-ment troops sent from Teheran to investigate the situation. In March 1946 a 'Kurdish Republic' was proclaimed, professing separatist aims. However, when the Persian Government brought the question of the prolonged stay of Soviet troops in Persia before the United Nations on 19 March 1946 the Soviet Government decided to with-draw its troops. But in June Soviet pressure increased, and succeeded

[1] As admitted by the Hungarian Premier Dinnyes at a Press Conference, quoted in Paul Winterton, *Inquest on an Ally*, London, The Cresset Press, 1948, p. 66.

in forcing the Persian Government to recognize the 'Democratic Government of Azerbaijan' as an autonomous administration, and to include pro-Communist politicians from the Tudeh party in the Cabinet in Teheran. This arrangement proved short-lived, the new Government fell apart, and gave way to a Cabinet without Tudeh representation. In December 1946 the Premier ordered the Persian Army to re-enter Azerbaijan and Kurdistan. There was no resistance. The two régimes collapsed at once and their leaders fled to the Soviet Union. Although the Soviet Government from time to time threatened Persia, no further attempt at physical penetration was made during Stalin's lifetime. Persia could not apparently qualify as a 'soft spot' and active operations to extend the Soviet base in this direction were called off. It is worth noting that the Soviet attempt on Persia began before the United States had put forward any plans for economic or military aid to Western Europe or the Middle East, or had taken any stand against Soviet expansion. The Persian case is, therefore, a clear example of the strategy of selecting a potential weak spot on the frontier of the Soviet heartland and attempting to incorporate a border province into the Soviet bloc of countries.

Persia, however, was not the only country to be marked down for experimental pressure. The revival of Soviet and Communist interest in Greece and Turkey, both bordering on the Soviet base, engendered the belief that these countries, too, were ready for penetration. Within months of achieving the partial encirclement of Turkey by the occupation of Bulgaria late in 1944, the Soviet Union began to make territorial and other claims upon her. On 19 March 1945 the Soviet Union denounced her treaty of friendship with Turkey, and accompanied this move by a demonstration of military strength in south-east Bulgaria. On 7 June in an interview with the Turkish Ambassador in Moscow, Mr. Molotov declared that the areas of Kars and Ardahan would have to be returned to Russia before a new Soviet-Turkish Treaty could be signed.[1] On 24 June 1945 the Soviet Government suggested to Turkey that the defence of the Straits should be a joint Soviet-Turkish responsibility, a proposal which would have involved the stationing of Soviet troops on the Bosphorus and the Dardanelles. Soviet territorial claims against Turkey were extended during the next year by articles in the Press calling for the transfer of part of the province of Trebizond and Kerasund to

[1] Royal Institute of International Affairs, *Survey of International Affairs 1939–46: The Middle East 1945–1950*, p. 20 n.

the Georgian Soviet Socialist Republic, and also by attempts, linked with the campaign to detach northern Persia, to focus attention on a 'Kurdish question'.

However, Turkey, like Persia, stood firm, and the Soviet attempt to extend its frontiers in this direction failed to gather momentum, especially when a situation with greater possibilities appeared to be developing in Greece later in 1946.

There is insufficient evidence to determine the degree of Soviet responsibility, if any, for the opening of guerilla operations in northern Greece by bands led by the Greek Communist party in the late summer and autumn of 1946.[1] But there can be no doubt about the Soviet attempt to exploit the situation or about the part played by the Soviet Union's Balkan allies to hasten the victory of the rebels. Greece appealed to the United Nations on 3 December 1946 and her complaint was heard by the Security Council on the 19th. The reports of the United Nations' Special Committee on the Balkans, the organization set up in Salonika on 1 December 1947 to investigate Greek complaints against her northern neighbours Yugoslavia, Bulgaria, and Albania, were unanimous in their findings of direct help to the Greek Communists. Albania, Bulgaria, and Yugoslavia were found to have sheltered Greek guerillas, trained them for military operations, secured their entry and re-entry into Greece, supplied them with ammunition and weapons, and nominated their tasks inside Greece. All these countries, according to the Report, had allowed their territory to be used for tactical operational purposes, especially Albania, along whose border lay the biggest Greek guerilla concentration. They had also protected defeated guerilla bands from pursuit by the Greek Army. The three countries were involved in the large-scale settlement and indoctrination of Greek

---

[1] Certain events in Bulgaria in 1946 may have had some bearing on a decision to encourage the resumption of the Civil War broken off in 1945. In July 1946, immediately after a prolonged visit to Moscow of the Soviet Commander-in-Chief in Bulgaria, the Soviet military authorities in Bulgaria created a 25 kilometre forbidden zone along the whole Greek-Bulgarian frontier. About the same time there were persistent reports of supplies of arms being sent from Bulgaria into southern Yugoslav Macedonia, and even across the Yugoslav frontier again into Albania. Both the Soviet and Bulgarian authorities began to show sensitiveness about the area of Berkovitsa in north-west Bulgaria, which later became the main centre for the training and rehabilitation of Greek guerillas in Bulgaria. See also General Markos's alleged letter to Zahariades, in Royal Institute of International Affairs, *Documents 1947–48*, pp. 318–20, which claims a Soviet origin for the fighting.

children kidnapped by the Communists.[1] In some cases, the armed forces of these countries engaged the Greek Army either from their own territory or on Greek soil in order to cover the retreat of a guerilla band into Albania, Bulgaria, or Yugoslavia.[2] The evidence presented by the United Nations' agencies proved that, however the revolt started, its leadership was rapidly assumed by the Soviet Union, acting through its Balkan allies and that the guerilla activity, was exploited in an attempt to bring the territory of Greece into the Soviet bloc.

However, the Communist attempt to conquer and absorb Greece failed, thanks not only to the operations of the Greek Army, and American economic and military help, but also to the defection of Yugoslavia from membership of the Soviet bloc.

The Soviet decision to take coercive political and economic action against Yugoslavia in 1948 belongs to the period after the foundation of the Cominform, and will be dealt with in a later chapter. However, much of the material published in letters exchanged by the Central Committees of the Yugoslav and Soviet Communist parties which led up to the Soviet break with Yugoslavia refers to Soviet strategy and tactics during the period between 1945 and 1948. It is appropriate, therefore, to include the main points here, because they provide a remarkably clear illustration of what the Soviet Union demanded of its junior partners during the campaign to spread its influence over Eastern and Central Europe.

The Soviet Union was faced with a unique situation in Yugoslavia in 1945. She could not import a Communist-controlled coalition as in Poland, for Yugoslavia already had a revolutionary Communist Government. She could not use the privileged status of the occupying power which she had in the ex-enemy countries Bulgaria, Rumania, and Hungary to impose a Communist régime, for Yugoslavia was an ally, without a Soviet army of occupation. Yugoslavia was a country geographically within the Soviet orbit in which a Communist Government had already installed itself without Soviet assistance. Soviet strategy demanded that this Government should be brought under the same degree of control as the Polish or Bulgarian Govern-

---

[1] Tacit admission of this accusation and of the detention of captured Greek Army soldiers was made when the East European governments agreed to the return of Greek children and soldiers to Greece in 1956 and 1957.

[2] Full details can be found in the reports of the United Nations Special Commission on the Balkans.

ments. The ineptitude of Soviet tactics ensured Yugoslav resistance to this strategy, and led to her defection from the eastern bloc.

How did the Soviet Government approach the Yugoslav problem? Experience of the other East European countries showed that absolute Soviet control was secured, among other methods, by penetration of the police and security forces, by intervention in the country's economic life, and by dominating the machinery for choosing leading party and government officials. The exchange of letters between the Central Committees of the Yugoslav and Soviet Communist parties and subsequent speeches by Yugoslav spokesmen show exactly how Soviet penetration was attempted as soon as the war was over. In the Yugoslav letter dated 13 April 1948 Marshal Tito and Edvard Kardelj complained:

> We regard it as improper for the agents of the Soviet Intelligence Service to recruit in our country, which is going towards socialism, our citizens for their intelligence service. . . . We have proof that certain agents of the Soviet Intelligence Service in recruiting our party members cast doubts on our leaders, sought to ruin their reputation, showed them as inefficient and unreliable. For example, Colonel Stepanov did not hesitate in 1945, in recruiting one of our good comrades who was working in the Central Division of Coding and Decoding in UDBA (the Security police) to blacken and cast doubts on all our leaders, stating 'for the present Marshal Tito works as he should'. Such cases are still occurring today.[1]

On the economic side, the speech made by Dr. Vilfan, the Yugoslav delegate to the Economic Committee of the United Nations, on 7 October 1949 was particularly revealing.

> In 1946 [he said] the Yugoslav Government and the Government of the Soviet Union signed agreements by which two companies were formed, a shipping company and an air transport company. . . . Half of the shares of those two companies belonged to the Yugoslav Government and the other half to the Government of the Soviet Union. The active management was in the hands of a director appointed by the Soviet Government, while the assistant director was a Yugoslav. The Government of the Soviet Union did not invest the capital which it had undertaken to invest. Thus, in 1948, it had invested in one of the companies only 9.83 per cent of its share, while the Yugoslav Government had invested 76.25 per cent of its share; nevertheless, the director appointed by the Soviet Government directed the activities of the company in a manner which served primarily the interests of the economy of the Soviet Union. . . . Yugoslavia paid 0.4 dinar per ton-kilometre of transportation expenses, the U.S.S.R. 0.19

---

[1] Royal Institute of International Affairs, *Documents on International Affairs, 1947–48*, Oxford University Press, 1952, p. 364.

dinar, and the other countries 0.28 dinar. Under those conditions, Yugoslavia preferred to wind up these two companies.[1]

. Even much-publicized aid was used to try to bring the Yugoslav
economy, including national defence, under the control of the Soviet
Union. Marshal Tito himself referred to this in a speech on 28
December 1950:

It is true that we received some army equipment, but this cost so much
that if we had continued to buy from Russia our workers and peasants
would have had to devote most of their work to paying for this brotherly
aid. Of the 220 guns which the Soviet Union should have sent us, 85 were
obsolete but repainted, some of the tanks were worn out, and 30 mobile
tank repair shops were incomplete. The field telephone units were and still
are unworkable. Other supplies were equally worn, rusty and useless.[2]

The Soviet Union demanded the right to call for the dismissal of
senior Yugoslav Government officials. 'We cannot understand,'
wrote the Central Committee of the Soviet Communist party on
27 March 1948, 'why the English spy Velebit still remains in the
Ministry of Foreign Affairs of Yugoslavia as the First Assistant
Minister. The Yugoslav comrades know . . . that the representatives
of the Soviet Government consider Velebit a spy. Nevertheless,
Velebit remains in the position of First Assistant Foreign Minister
of Yugoslavia.' And in a later letter, the Soviet Government wrote:

Velebit is not the only spy in the Ministry of Foreign Affairs. The
Soviet representatives have many times told the Yugoslav leaders that the
Yugoslav Ambassador in London, Leontić, is an English spy. The Soviet
Government is aware that besides Leontić three other members of the
Yugoslav Embassy in London, whose names are not yet disclosed, are in
the English Intelligence Service. . . . It is clear that since the Yugoslav
Government persistently refused to purge its Ministry of Foreign Affairs
of spies, the Soviet Government is forced to refrain from open corres-
pondence through the Yugoslav Ministry of Foreign Affairs.[3]

From this correspondence emerges the full range of Soviet
demands on those small countries which fell within the Soviet orbit
at the end of the war. Not content with the installation of a Communist régime, the Soviet Government demanded the right to exploit
the country economically, to choose its leading personalities, and to
have its own views on any subject unquestionably accepted.

So far, this brief survey of Soviet post-war strategy and tactics has

---

[1] Royal Institute of International Affairs, *Documents 1949–50*, p. 485.
[2] Royal Institute of International Affairs, *Documents 1949–50*, p. 506.
[3] Royal Institute of International Affairs, *Documents 1947–48*, p. 354.

covered only nations in the Soviet Union's 'operational area' in Europe and the Middle East, comprising Soviet-occupied countries and provinces bordering on the Soviet bloc.

At the same time, the Soviet Union took stock of its political allies in Western Europe, the major Communist parties which had emerged in a strong position from the Resistance, and had to decide upon the strategy and tactics most likely to further Soviet plans. Take, for example, France. France had a long revolutionary tradition and a history of friendship for the Russian State, and this helped to build the French Communist party into one of the two largest in Europe. In the French general elections of October 1945 the Communist party won 25 per cent of all votes cast, a figure which was increased to 28 per cent a year later, on 10 November 1946. At the end of the war the Communist party had considerable influence over other left-wing groups and controlled the Central Trade Union Organization, the *Confédération Générale du Travail*. Moreover, the party's Resistance record during the latter part of the war weighed heavily in its favour. In the general atmosphere of resentment at defeat in 1940, and the material and psychological damage done by the four years of German occupation, there might have been a case for direct action by the French Communist party to establish a Communist Government in Paris. Indeed, if the charges made against André Marty after his expulsion from the party are correct, namely, that he favoured such action in 1945, then a considerable body of opinion in the French Communist party probably rated the chances of success high. Nothing, however, was done, and there is excellent evidence that Stalin was against an attempt to seize power.[1] Instead, the French Communist party entered the post-war governments, and agreed to the appointment of the party leader, Maurice Thorez, as a Vice-Premier in a *bourgeois* coalition. Some attempt seems to have been made to create a centre of Communist strength inside the administration by widening the powers of certain offices hitherto regarded as largely formal.[2] Similar action in entering coalitions was taken by

[1] Stalin specifically referred to this decision in the correspondence between the Soviet and Yugoslav Central Committees in 1948. In the letter sent by the Soviet Party Central Committee, Stalin wrote: 'The reason why there is now no Communist government in Paris is because in the circumstances of 1945 the Soviet Army was not able to reach French soil.'

[2] See discussion in Seton-Watson, *The Pattern of Communist Revolutions*, p. 293, on the role in this direction of the 'Cabinet du Ministre' of the Communist Ministers.

leaders of the Italian and Belgian Communist parties and the evidence seems to point to a general strategic decision against attempts to seize power in countries beyond the reach of the Soviet Army. Communist parties in these circumstances were recommended to join popular coalitions.

The winter of 1946–47 represented the end of the first stage of Soviet foreign expansion, a stage in which the Soviet Government concentrated on digesting politically areas in Europe already under their military occupation, creating a protective zone around their frontiers, while probing experimentally a number of 'soft' spots along the Soviet borders. It is important to note that the expansion was carried out at a time when the Western powers were concentrating on rehabilitation and demobilization of their armed forces. The process of installing Communist-controlled governments in Poland, Rumania, Hungary, and Bulgaria was complete or well under way before either the Truman Doctrine or the Marshall Plan ever saw the light of day. It was already far advanced before the American loan to Britain in 1946. The Soviet attempt to set up a Communist state in northern Persia in 1945 was certainly not caused by any action taken by Britain and America in that area. Nor could the Soviet attempt to gain control of the state and party machine in Yugoslavia be described in any way as an 'answer' to an earlier Western initiative. In fact, in the United States immediately after the war, there was still support for President Roosevelt's reported view that British imperialism was more dangerous than Soviet expansion. American criticism of Britain's action in using British troops in Greece to block a Communist-led assault on Athens in December 1944 and after the outbreak of the second Communist rebellion was widespread, and opposition to British and Dutch policy in Indonesia and French policy in Indo-China often appeared to be in line with that expressed in Soviet circles. At the same time, Britain's official attitude to Russia was summed up by the Secretary of the Labour party, Mr. Morgan Phillips, in 1946 when he addressed a goodwill mission about to set off on a visit to the Soviet Union: 'It seems to me to be the most natural thing in the world that the peoples of Britain and Russia, now both governed by socialist administrations, should wish to understand each other more thoroughly. Our approach to the final objective may be different, but we hope and believe that we are both striving towards the realization of the world of the common man.'

The direction of Soviet foreign policy in the years 1944 to 1947 cannot therefore be attributed to any influence exerted by the Western Powers. It is, of course, just possible that at some stage in the immediate post-war years there existed inside the Soviet leadership a group which may have preferred a policy of collaboration with the Western Allies, but of this there is no evidence available. Soviet policy appears to have been a planned initiative in its own right. It can justly be described as an example of the strategy and tactics of a Soviet Government acting unfettered and unhindered in this first stage by any opposition from the non-Communist world. And the evidence points to a strategy of territorial extension of the Soviet heartland by gaining control of countries and provinces bordering on the Soviet Union, whether allied (Poland, Yugoslavia, and Greece), ex-enemy (Bulgaria, Rumania, and Hungary) or neutral (Persia and Turkey), but to adopt a more cautious attitude in countries out of reach of Soviet military power. In the period from 1944 to 1947 Soviet policy was single-minded, if not always successful, in its pursuit of the aims laid down by Stalin: to exploit the Allies' victory to bring the world nearer to Soviet Communism, a task in which force and threats clearly had a place alongside propaganda, subversion, and the Soviet interpretation of international treaties.

II

WESTERN REACTION AND THE SOVIET
REPLY: 1947–53

IT is now time to consider the second stage of Soviet policy in Europe, which was dominated by the Soviet reaction to the slow but profoundly significant change of policy towards Russia undertaken by the West in 1947 in answer to the Soviet threat. In 1946 the United States had agreed upon a substantial loan to Britain to help the British economy, and while this loan could not be said to have been an answer to Soviet threats, it set a pattern afterwards to be followed when countries menaced by post-war difficulties appealed for help. The first step on the part of the United States to help countries directly threatened by Communism was President Truman's acceptance of a plea for help made by the Greek Government on 3 March 1947, at a time when the British Government had found aid to Greece an increasingly heavy burden. This plea was subsequently approved by Congress and put into practice under a treaty between America and Greece on 20 June 1947. American help was also made available to Turkey under the same law, the whole policy being known as the Truman Doctrine on Aid to Greece and Turkey.

American readiness to help Greece and Turkey was swiftly followed by the offer of financial and economic assistance to all countries which were struggling to rehabilitate their economies after the war. It was made in a speech by the United States Secretary of State, General Marshall, on 5 June 1947, and warmly welcomed in Britain, France, and other countries.[1] The Soviet Union agreed to discuss the offer, in which Czechoslovakia and Poland were especially interested. On 27 June the Foreign Ministers of the United States, Britain, France, and the Soviet Union met in Paris to work out a plan of action, but the conference quickly ran into heavy weather when it became clear that the Russians were only interested in General Marshall's offer if the United States' aid took the form of an outright gift to each country, to be used entirely at the discre-

[1] Royal Institute of International Affairs, *Survey of International Affairs, 1947–48*, pp. 23–25.

tion of its Government. This conception of American assistance for rehabilitation was entirely contrary to that of its authors, for it was implicit in the Soviet plan that American aid to East European countries would be acceptable only if it fell under the control of governments amenable to Soviet influence. In this way, American aid could be used to strengthen the position of the East European Communist governments, who would dispense or withhold it according to the political needs or requirements of the ruling party. From the Soviet point of view, American aid would be unacceptable if it helped to strengthen non-Communist elements or governments in any country, no matter how badly that country needed help. No United States Government could accept this concept of economic aid, and the Soviet withdrawal from the conference and rejection of the plan put an end to the hopes of the Eastern European countries which needed help most. Even the provisional acceptance of the Plan by Czechoslovakia, and strong Polish desire to accept were brushed aside by Moscow, who saw the plan as an attempt to establish American influence in the protective zone in East and Central Europe which the Russians were determined to keep for their own.

In the face of Soviet opposition, the Western Powers went ahead with their plans, and a working agreement was concluded between the United States and her European partners. In reply the Soviet Union took steps to tighten her own party and administrative control over the borderlands of the Soviet base in preparation for the next phase in European strategy. It is indeed at this point, the spring and summer of 1947, that Soviet policy underwent a major tactical change.

The origin of the new tactical approach was the final and firm decision by the Soviet leaders in 1946–47 that the United States, the only rival to the Soviet Union in the world, had decided to use its strength to defend the 'capitalist' system in Europe; that the Soviet Union and the Communist parties in Europe, in their campaign to exploit allied victory in the war, would have to face not only war-weary Britain, France, and Italy, but the tremendous power of the United States. The evidence on which the Soviet leaders relied was based on Marxist-Leninist theory that the Americans would ultimately have to act in order to prevent Western Europe falling to Communism. This evidence was gathered gradually during the years 1945–47, and included the retention of even small numbers of United States troops in Germany after 1945, the United States loan to Britain in 1946, the American-Soviet clash in the Four-Power Government in Germany over reparations from current production in May 1946, American aid to Greece and Turkey, and finally, the Marshall Plan.[1] Seen from Moscow, the Marshall Plan, which would seriously reduce the likelihood of economic collapse in Western Europe, put an end to the period of American disinterestedness in Soviet or Communist expansion.[2] It seems that Mr. Winston Churchill's famous speech in Fulton in the United States in March 1947 played a part in clinching Stalin's argument that he now had to face a united Anglo-American front in the pursuit of his plans in the field of foreign strategy.

This interpretation did not suggest to the Soviet leaders that they should abandon their decision to expand. It only meant that new tactics and methods were to be worked out so that the strategic decision to expand could be continued unchanged in the face of American opposition. The tactics were probably worked out in detail in the summer of 1947, and were given ideological blessing by the foundation of the Cominform in September of that year.[3]

Roughly speaking, the new Soviet tactics followed three main lines. First in timing was the Western Communist parties' abandonment of their support of the 'bourgeois' coalition governments which they had joined in 1944 and 1945. Once in opposition the Communist parties adopted a policy of organizing labour unrest, wherever possible in a political context. The French Communist party brought about the dismissal of Communist ministers in the French Government in May 1947, Communist deputies in the National Assembly voted against the Government on a major

[1] Stalin told the American Ambassador in Moscow on 4 April 1946: 'The United States of America has definitely aligned itself with Britain against the U.S.S.R.' W. Bedell Smith, *Moscow Mission*, p. 40.

[2] It should be remembered that Soviet home and foreign propaganda at this time discussed economic problems in Britain and Western Europe in terms of almost imminent overthrow of the existing régimes. The 'squatters' and the 1946–47 fuel crisis in Britain were treated by Moscow Radio in terms of 'rebellion' and 'economic collapse'.

[3] It has been suggested that the Cominform represented the influence of Zhdanov, the arch-priest of anti-Western thought in literature and the arts and senior Soviet representative on the Cominform. While there is evidence that Zhdanov headed a faction in internal Soviet politics, it is not certain that he was anything more than Stalin's mouthpiece in foreign affairs. There was no move away from Cominform policy after his death in August 1948—indeed, pressure on Tito increased, and the Korean war broke out. It is probable that in foreign affairs the personal role of Zhdanov has been exaggerated.

economic issue, and the first big post-war strikes occurred in November 1947, after the 11th Congress of the French Communist party. In Italy, the Premier, Signor de Gasperi, formed his first Government without Communist participation on 31 May 1947. In Austria, Communist participation lingered on till the autumn, but in Belgium it ceased in March 1947. The timing of these moves clearly reflected a Communist policy decision taken in Moscow.

The Soviet Union's second tactical move involved the tightening of Soviet control over the area it already occupied. This led to the foundation of a new Communist organization to bind the East European parties together and the French and Italian Communist parties to Eastern Europe.

In September 1947 representatives of the Communist parties of the Soviet Union, France, Italy, Poland, Bulgaria, Rumania, Czechoslovakia, Hungary and Yugoslavia met at Wiliza Gora in Poland to set up an organization ostensibly for the exchange of information between the member parties but possessing, as the speeches of the Soviet delegates Andrei Zhdanov and Georgi Malenkov revealed, a much deeper purpose. The Cominform declaration and the speeches of its founders reaffirmed the Communist parties' belief in their faith, and of their readiness to accept Soviet leadership in the struggle for its fulfilment. The declaration firmly divided the world into two camps—the 'imperialist', headed by the United States, and the 'peace-loving', headed by the U.S.S.R.—and foretold the decline and destruction of the former. Among measures to hasten the achievement of this aim was the re-establishment of direct operational contact between Communist parties, interrupted, according to Georgi Malenkov, in 1943.[1] 'Experience has shown,' Mr. Malenkov declared, 'that the absence of contact between the Communist parties is a hindrance in co-ordinating the action of Communists in various countries . . . in our opinion it is necessary to put into effect definite measures designed to eliminate the present abnormal situation in this respect.'[2]

The foundation of the Cominform and the division of the world into two warring camps was, of course, a declaration that the Soviet Government regarded itself as engaged in a major struggle against the non-Communist world in both Europe and Asia. At once the Soviet Union took the offensive in three European areas on the

---

[1] This was the year in which the Third International dissolved itself.

[2] Royal Institute of International Affairs, *Documents 1947–48*, p. 141.

frontier of the Communist bloc: Czechoslovakia, Berlin, and Yugoslavia. The Czechoslovak Government, by indicating initial agreement to the Marshall Plan, had revealed dangerously independent tendencies and had shown signs of permitting a weakening of Communist party influence within the Cabinet. The Western enclave in Berlin, tolerated so long as the United States, Britain, and France had not seriously opposed Soviet plans, might become a Western spearhead in Soviet Eastern Europe. Yugoslavia, of whose sins of independence Moscow had already complained, certainly could no longer be tolerated in its existing heretical form. It seems likely that as well as increasing the degree of Soviet control in Eastern and Central Europe, these operations contained an element of 'reconnaissance-in-force' of the Anglo-American-French will to resist further Soviet expansion.

In the case of Yugoslavia, the Soviet Union tried to insist upon certain key privileges, which were commonplace in Poland, Bulgaria, Rumania, and Hungary, but were denied to Soviet representatives in Yugoslavia. These were privileges which, like control of intelligence, recruitment of Soviet agents, access to secret information and freedom of movement for representatives of the Soviet Communist party, could have turned Yugoslavia into a satellite like her neighbours. When these demands were rejected, politely and with some bewilderment by the Central Committee of the Yugoslav Communist party, it seems likely that Stalin and his advisers viewed Yugoslav opposition in the context of American 'intervention' in Europe, and decided to bring about Belgrade's submission by threats, if arguments failed. They therefore rushed into their ill-considered attempt to browbeat the Yugoslav Communist party into acceptance of satellite status. We have already noted some of the tactics employed by the Soviet party leadership to bring about Yugoslavia's submission, but the last act is particularly revealing. It appears that in February 1948 Stalin made a dramatic attempt to bring Yugoslavia under his control—by ordering immediate federation with Bulgaria. The Bulgarian Prime Minister, Georgi Dimitrov, had broached the subject of an economic and customs union between Bulgaria and Yugoslavia in January 1948. He was immediately called to order by the Soviet newspaper *Pravda*, and bowed his head in acceptance of the rebuke. Marshal Tito revealed what followed in his speech on foreign affairs in the Yugoslav National Assembly on 27 April 1950: [1]

[1] Royal Institute of International Affairs, *Documents 1949-50*, pp. 199-200. See also Dedijer, *Tito Speaks*, p. 330.

I should like to say a few words on the so-called Balkan Federation, because today we are accused of wishing to incorporate not only Albania, but Bulgaria by means of such a federation. . . . When our comrades Kardelj, Djilas, Bakarić, and others were in Moscow during February and March 1948 there was present in the same city a Bulgarian delegation consisting of Dimitrov, Kolarov, and Kostov, who are no longer alive. In the presence of this delegation, Stalin himself imperatively demanded the immediate federation of Yugoslavia and Bulgaria, but declared that he was opposed to federation with Albania. As relations with the Soviet Union were already strained, when our comrades returned from Moscow and told us of this proposal, it seemed suspect to us, and we came to the conclusion that its aim was the subjection of Yugoslavia. We therefore rejected it. The rulers of the Soviet Union have not brought up the question of the federation of Yugoslavia and Bulgaria as a problem affecting these two countries, but solely in the interest of their own plans and schemes.

Taken in conjunction with Moscow's criticism of Dimitrov less than a month earlier for suggesting only an economic and customs Union, it is clear that Stalin's sudden reversal of policy towards Balkan Federation was made in the hope that the loyal satellite Bulgaria would be the dominant partner—a convenient way of bringing Yugoslavia into the Soviet bloc. As Marshal Tito explained, Yugoslavia refused to agree and the Soviet plan failed. Four months later the Cominform met in Bucharest to announce Yugoslavia's expulsion.

The Cominform's action against the Yugoslav Communist party did not immediately involve America or Britain; but the overthrow of the existing Government of Czechoslovakia and its replacement by one readily accepting satellite status certainly came much nearer to doing so. It is not suggested that the Soviet Government simply and artificially created the crisis in Czechoslovakia just in order to reduce the country to satellite status in accordance with an approved timetable. Nevertheless it seems true that without Soviet intervention, the local crisis which developed in Prague in 1948 might well have brought Czechoslovakia out of the Communist camp and left her in a position similar to that of Finland.[1]

Czechoslovakia's experience of Communism since 1945 was much more like that of France than of her Eastern neighbours, Poland, Rumania, or Hungary. The Czechoslovak voter had given the Communist party a strong parliamentary position in 1946 in free elections,

[1] In a similar crisis in Finland in May 1948 the non-Communist parliamentary majority forced the Communist Minister of Interior, Leino, to resign—a unique case.

partly out of gratitude to Russia for her wartime achievements, and partly because of a distrust of Britain and France based on bitter memories of Munich. The Government of Czechoslovakia during this period was a coalition of democratic parties with the Communist party, whose representatives held the Premiership and controlled the police. But two years' experience of the régime was beginning to turn the people against the Communist party. News of Communist brutality in the provinces, of cases of bribery and corruption hushed up when leading Communists were involved, and Communist attempts to interfere in university and school education antagonized large sections of the population; had there been a free general election early in 1948, according to an unofficial poll taken in Czechoslovakia at the time, the Communist party would have lost ten per cent of its parliamentary strength.[1]

The immediate crisis arose when the Communist Minister of the Interior replaced eight Prague police chiefs by Communists. When, on 13 February 1948, the Cabinet instructed the Minister to cancel the order and to stop the constant change of personnel in his Ministry the Minister, backed by the Politbureau of the Communist party, refused to obey. Thereupon some non-Communist Ministers, excluding the Social Democrats, offered to resign, and were accused by the Communists of setting up a rival non-elected government 'with the help of foreign reaction'. Under this slogan, the Communists delcared their intention of falling back on 'the support of 'the people'; they armed the workers' militia, called out factory workers and organized several noisy demonstrations in the streets of the capital and other cities.

On 19 February the Soviet Deputy Foreign Minister, Mr. V. A. Zorin, arrived unexpectedly in Prague, and is generally credited with responsibility for guiding the Czechoslovak Communist party in the days which followed. With workers' militia, Communist-controlled police, and armed factory workers in the streets, in control of the radio and Press buildings, the struggle was transferred to the palace of the ailing President Beneš. The Communists, led by the Prime Minister, Klement Gottwald, pressed the President to accept the resignation of the non-Communist Ministers; the latters' supporters called on him to uphold their views, to support them against Communist lawlessness as the only alternative to complete Communist

[1] See *Who's Next? The Lesson of Czechoslovakia*, by John Brown, Hutchinson & Co. Ltd., 1951, p. 141.

dictatorship, and to take a firm stand for democracy. This was on 20 February. For six days the fate of the country hung suspended, while the Communists increased their violent activity through the Communist-controlled militia and 'action committees' and also tried, with some success, to split the anti-Communist groups.[1] On 23 February the Communist party placed Prague under police rule and raided the headquarters of the non-Communist parties. Everywhere Communist-inspired lawlessness was on the increase, and the tension began to tell on the President. After several interviews with Gottwald, in which the Communist leader threatened civil war if his demands were not met, the President capitulated. He accepted the resignations of twelve non-Communist Ministers on 25 February and agreed to leave the formation of a new Government to Gottwald. On 4 May Beneš resigned as President; he died on 3 September 1948. His colleague and Foreign Minister, Jan Masaryk, was found dead on 10 May. Many non-Communist leaders fled abroad and the way was cleared for Czechoslovakia to become a Communist dictatorship. The frontier of the Soviet heartland reached out to the Sudeten mountains.

The consolidation of Communist and Soviet power in Czechoslovakia came as a profound shock to the West, particularly to Socialist parties in France and Britain, where many Czechoslovak left-wing non-Communist politicians had close and admiring friends. For this reason, Communist methods in the Czech coup, though no worse than those used in Rumania, Bulgaria, or Hungary, aroused strong anti-Communist sentiments in Socialist circles. Yet even while the outcry against the 'February coup' in Czechoslovakia was at its height, a more direct Soviet assault on the West was in preparation: the attempt to force the Western Powers out of their position in West Berlin, to which they were entitled under wartime and post-war agreements between the victorious allies.

By the spring of 1948, as a result of the growing disagreements which marred the four-power administration of Germany from 1945 to 1948, four-power government had come to a standstill.[2] The Soviet Government refused to co-ordinate any major act of the

[1] For example, the Communists secured control of the left wing of the Social Democratic party, and compelled its representatives to remain in the Government.

[2] Royal Institute of International Affairs, *Survey of International Affairs, Germany and Austria* and *1949–50*, pp. 149–79, give the full story of these disagreements.

government of Germany with its Western allies, who were expected to supply the reparations demanded by the Russians from current industrial output in Western Germany (since the Russians had already taken everything they could lay their hands on in the East), thus forcing the West either to let Western Germany starve, dissolve into political chaos, or be kept alive by the British, American, and French taxpayers.

On 20 March 1948 the Russians withdrew from the Allied Control Commission on the grounds that the Western Powers had discussed Germany at a meeting of Foreign Ministers in London without Russian participation. The actual crisis which the Soviet Government decided to exploit was a currency reform in the Western zones. The three Western Powers informed the Russians in advance of their plans, and specified that the reform did not apply to their sectors in Berlin. The Russians responded by introducing their own currency reform, and by applying it to the whole of Berlin, stating that the city as a whole was economically part of the Soviet zone.[1] This the Western Powers could not accept, and introduced the West German currency into their sectors in Berlin. Meanwhile on the technical grounds that the railways and roads leading into Berlin were in need of repair the Soviet authorities began their blockade of the Western sectors of the city. All rail, road, and river traffic was halted and the the city authorities, faced with the alternatives of accepting an alarming threat to food and fuel supplies or capitulating to the Soviet demands, turned to the Western Powers for help. Thus began the remarkable Berlin air-lift, undertaken by the Royal Air Force and United States Air Force, which brought food, fuel, and other necessities of life to Berlin, and kept the Western Zones alive for nearly a year.

Whatever the validity of technical reasons advanced for the blockade may have been, the Soviet position was clearly stated by the Soviet Commander-in-Chief, Marshal Sokolovski, when he said:

The agreement concerning the four-power administration of Berlin is an inseparable component part of the agreement for the four-power administration of Germany as a whole. After the United States of America, Great Britain, and France, by their separate actions in the Western zones of Germany had destroyed the system of four-power administration, they

[1] See the letter from Marshal Sokolovski to General Clay, 20 June 1948, Royal Institute of International Affairs, *1947-48*, pp. 579-80.

thereby undermined the legal basis which assured their right to participation in the administration of Berlin.[1]

There can be no doubt that the Soviet Government hoped for a Western capitulation and agreement to withdraw from Berlin based on the expected reluctance of Britain and America to face the consequences of opposing the Soviet Union on her own ground. But as it turned out the struggle was not conducted on Soviet ground, but in the air, with two decisive factors in Western favour: their superiority in civil and military air power in Europe, and the enormous quantity of food, fuel, and other goods available to the Americans for transport to Berlin. The West, through intelligent use of air power, was able to feed, clothe, and warm West Berliners and to keep their industry alive. Later they introduced their own counter-blockade of East Germany, and eventually succeeded in making the Soviet Government realize that as a tactical move in the cold war the blockade was a failure. On 12 May 1949 the railways and roads which had been 'closed for repairs' for nearly twelve months reopened, and all Europe realized that Soviet tactics had failed.[2]

The year 1949 thus began badly for Soviet foreign policy in Europe and the Soviet Government set about recouping its losses in other ways. The Soviet Government transferred the struggle for Germany to the council table—this time in Paris on 23 May 1949, and engaged the Western Governments in lengthy and on the whole fruitless discussions on the German problem.

Berlin was not the only setback to the Communist cause. In the late summer of 1949 Greek Government forces finally succeeded in clearing the mountainous strongholds in northern Greece of Communist rebels, and on 4 November 1949 the Greek rebel radio finally admitted defeat. Moreover, in spite of a virulent propaganda campaign and economic blockade against Yugoslavia, the Soviet Government failed to overthrow Marshal Tito, or to make Yugoslavia into a satellite state. Indeed, Tito's resistance had far-reaching effects in East Europe itself. Soviet energy was directed to destroying real or imaginary 'Titoist' fifth columns in the Communist-ruled countries of Eastern Europe, including that attributed to Laszlo Rajk in

[1] Royal Institute of International Affairs, *Documents of International Affairs, 1948–49*, p. 580.

[2] It is interesting to note that just before the blockade was lifted Marshal Sokolovski and his political adviser, General Makarov, were replaced in Germany and recalled to Moscow.

Hungary (executed on 15 October 1949), to Traicho Kostov in Bulgaria (executed on 19 December 1949), to Wladyslaw Gomulka in Poland (disgraced in 1948 and arrested in 1950), and to Koci Xoxe in Albania (executed in the autumn of 1948). These activities, which involved the disgrace or disappearance of many of the remaining native Communist leaders associated with the Resistance movements during the war, led to the imposition of closer and more thorough Soviet control of these countries, in which Government and party leadership was increasingly entrusted to men who had spent decades in the Soviet Union. There was also an increase in the number of Soviet citizens appointed to key posts in Eastern Europe.[1] The latter included factory directors, economic planners, and Army commanders. These measures increased tension within the East European states, and led to a dissipation of Soviet energies, which in turn affected the vigour and single-mindedness of their approach to expansion in Europe.

Meanwhile, Soviet policy in Europe led to a reaffirmation of solidarity between the Western countries, particularly in defence matters. Britain and France came together in the Treaty of Dunkirk, signed on 4 April 1947. On 17 March 1948 this treaty was expanded by the adherence of Belgium, Holland, and Luxembourg into Western Union. After the Communist seizure of power in Czechoslovakia and the Soviet blockade of Berlin, the countries of the Western Union and the American and Canadian Governments began to plan how to associate the vast potential strength of North America with the new alliance of Western Europe. After some months of diplomatic activity, a North Atlantic Treaty was signed by twelve Western Governments in Washington on 4 April 1949 and in the course of that summer ratified by all the parliaments concerned.

The next step was to provide the means for making the Treaty an effective instrument of defence, and this was done through the American Mutual Defence Assistance Programme, put forward by the Truman Administration on 25 July. After a full debate in Congress it was finally signed by the President on 28 October 1949. This led to the establishment of an Atlantic Treaty Headquarters,

---

[1] Examples were Vulko Chervenkov in Bulgaria, appointed Prime Minister in February 1950, who had been in the Soviet Union from 1925 to 1944; Matyas Rakosi in Hungary; and a group of leaders in Poland, including Army commanders, who were former Soviet citizens. In addition, Poland received a Soviet Minister of Defence, in the person of Marshal Rokossovski, one of the outstanding leaders of the Soviet Army in World War II.

'SHAPE', in Paris to co-ordinate the military strength of the North Atlantic powers under the direction of General Eisenhower, who took the title of Supreme Allied Commander, Europe.

Yet another result of the breakdown of four-power government and especially of the Soviet failure to drive the West out of Berlin, was the impetus given to the emergence of a sovereign German State in the West. There was only one practical alternative to four-power government in Germany in 1948–49—the gradual transfer of power to the Germans themselves, and on 8 April 1949 the Foreign Ministers of America, Britain, and France reached agreement on how this should be achieved in Western Germany. Six weeks later, a Basic Law on the first stages of the transfer of power was approved by the West Germans' elected representatives. The Russians replied by setting up their own Government controlled by the Communists in East Germany, and by organizing an East German armed force which had reached a strength of 50,000 by 1949.[1] The zonal frontier across Germany became a rigid state frontier, and Europe settled down to a period of stalemate marked by a violent propaganda war and dwindling contacts between the two parts of the Continent.

After the situation in Eastern Europe had been consolidated politically, the Soviet Union set up an organization through which the economic resources of the area could be controlled and co-ordinated. This was the Council for Mutual Economic Assistance, which came into being in January 1949. However, in its early years, very little use seems to have been made of the organization; it met twice in 1949, once in 1950, and after that not until 1954, after Stalin's death. It is true that in 1949–50 decisions were announced on an increase in intra-bloc trade and on the exchange of scientific information, but while Stalin was alive the organization existed as a potential instrument of economic control and integration, which was not, however, fully exploited. The real Soviet control over the economies of the East European countries was effected through the bi-lateral treaties which the Soviet Government had signed with each country, and through the joint stock companies which existed in Hungary, Rumania, and Czechoslovakia.

But a stalemate after the events of 1944 to 1949 had some advantages, and it is a fact that no further Soviet expansion occurred in Europe from 1949 to Stalin's death in 1953. True, the struggle

[1] Statement in the House of Commons by Mr. Anthony Nutting on 12 May 1952.

between East and West continued, particularly on Germany and Austria. But the fact is that the Soviet strategy on which the direction of Communist expansion had been based had resulted in a number of failures, and was reconsidered in Moscow. Out of four operations undertaken by Moscow since the foundation of the Cominform in 1947, namely in Czechoslovakia, Greece, Yugoslavia, and Berlin, only in one, Czechoslovakia, was the strategical choice correct or the tactics successful. Soviet tactics, moreover, produced a reaction which severely limited the Soviet Union's freedom of action in Europe, for in driving the Western countries to unite in their own defence, the Soviet leaders found themselves faced by a situation in which further expansion might well mean total war. Areas in Europe in which Soviet expansion could be attempted without danger of war were almost non-existent by 1950.[1]

This stalemate from 1949 to 1953 provides an opportunity to trace the pattern of Stalin's strategy and tactics in Europe since the war. The Soviet Government clearly believed that it had the right, because of its war victories and in the interests of its national security, unilaterally to decide the future of the small countries of Eastern Europe along the Soviet frontier. Without brooking any interference from its wartime allies, the Soviet Union proceeded to impose, first a Communist-controlled coalition, and then a fully-fledged Communist régime upon each country in turn. At all costs, Western influence had to be kept out of the Soviet protective zone. It was a characteristic of this process that it was never attempted beyond the reach of the Soviet Army. No plans for the conquest or subversion of any major Western country were put in hand, notwithstanding the fact that in two of them, France and Italy, the local Communist parties were the largest single political parties. This was partly due to the need to keep within the reach of the Soviet Army, and partly a genuine strategy of piecemeal conquest. Thus, while absorbing Eastern Europe, the Soviet leaders revealed no specific strategic plan for establishing Communism in France or Italy. They clashed with these countries if they attempted to interfere actively in areas in which the Soviets were operating—Eastern Europe, Greece, Persia, Germany, or Austria—but until the Soviet frontier had been pushed

[1] In the summer of 1952 there were some slight signs of a re-shaping of Soviet policy in Europe towards a relaxation of tension: a general change-round of Soviet ambassadors took place, which often heralded a new line; little, however, was accomplished before Stalin's death, but compare with the situation in Asia Ch. V, p. 57.

westwards so that it marched with that of France or Italy or Britain, the struggle would be waged against them on the level of propaganda and the activity of the local Communist parties.[1] Even when, in Soviet eyes, the United States aligned itself with the defence of Western Europe, the Soviet policy planners dealt with United States' military and political commitments in Europe in a territorial, European context, without altering their general approach to the United States as a state in North America.

Soviet policy in Europe from 1944 to 1949 can thus be seen as a methodical attempt, more successful in its initial than its later stages, to extend the area of Soviet control by military force or the threat of force, by subversion, and political, economic, and psychological methods. Where it failed, the reasons included incorrect strategic assessment of suitable areas for penetration, inept tactics, ignorance of Western Europe on the part of Stalin and his colleagues, and the excessive emphasis laid on military factors in planning a policy which might have been more successful if it had relied mainly on political, economic, and psychological factors. When the threat of military power failed (as in Greece, Yugoslavia, and Berlin) the Soviet machine ground to a halt. It had no flexible alternative policy and had to dig in its heels and rely on wearing down its opponents in a diplomatic or political stalemate. Its victories were won against small and powerless states, countries whose geographical position was awkward, or whose wartime activities made it difficult to rouse public support for them, where leading statesmen faltered in the face of the military threat, or where there were no leaders capable of organizing opposition. Finally, it must not be forgotten that many crucial positions in Eastern Europe were already in Soviet hands before the end of the war against Germany and therefore the Soviet Union had an important advantage in the reluctance of her Western allies to split the fighting alliance by questioning the political actions

---

[1] While it would be quite wrong to describe Soviet strategy during this period as a continuation of pre-revolutionary Russian policy, there is an element of similarity with pre-revolutionary Russian history. Russia's expansion in the nineteenth century was a piecemeal advance, and her clashes with other great powers usually took place when she crossed paths with them in areas where she was extending her boundaries and not near their own territory. Thus, Russo-British rivalry in the nineteenth century developed in the area of Turkey, Central Asia, Persia, and India; there were no direct problems concerning Russia and the British Isles, and therefore when agreement was reached in the early part of the twentieth century on the areas of expansion in the Near and Middle East, nothing stood in the way of a Russo-British rapprochement.

of a government which had borne the brunt of the land fighting against the German Army. This was particularly true of the Soviet political conquest of Poland, most of which had been accomplished by the end of the war in 1945. Soviet strategists got off to a good start, particularly in the establishment of a protective zone covering Russia's western frontiers, but certainly failed to reach their main objective in Europe: the creation of a strong Soviet bloc in the East, facing disunity and weakness in the West, and an isolationist United States.

III

SINO-SOVIET RELATIONS AND THE
PROSPECTS IN THE FAR EAST: 1945–50

THE year 1949 brought a strategic stalemate in Europe: no further Soviet territorial advance could be made without risking retaliation under the terms of the North Atlantic Treaty Organization, or collective resistance under the United Nations Charter. However, in the Far East an entirely new set of circumstances, bound up with the conquest of the Chinese mainland by the Chinese Red Army, and the establishment of a Central Chinese Communist Government in Peking on 1 October 1949, opened up great possibilities for Soviet strategy. From 1949 to 1953 it was the Far East that claimed priority among the planners of Soviet strategy in Moscow.

The history of Soviet relations with her Far Eastern neighbours and with the Chinese Communists who moved from southern China to the north-west in the period from 1934 to 1936 was marked by periods of advance and retreat similar to those of Soviet policy in the West. During World War II, when Russia was fighting for her life in the West, Soviet influence in the Far East was in eclipse, and in 1941 the Soviet Government signed a non-aggression Pact with Japan. But after the turn of the tide on the German front and the failure of the Japanese to press home their early military and naval successes against Britain and America in the Pacific and south-east Asia, the Soviet Union re-entered the Far Eastern area.

In 1943 the Soviet Union, in consultation with her Western allies, had undertaken to enter the war against Japan after victory in Europe had been won, and from 1944 began to build up her military strength in the Far East. This decision was not surprising, for prospects for Soviet intervention in the Far Eastern war must have appeared excellent in Moscow in 1944–45. Any military offensive by the Soviet Army against Japan would inevitably bring Soviet troops into Manchuria, Korea, or North China—or all three. Wherever Soviet troops established themselves, as in Eastern Europe, they would be likely to remain until they had furthered the political aims of the Soviet Government. If the Japanese strenuously resisted the

Soviet invasion and a long campaign developed, the firmer would become the Soviet right to the occupied territories; if the Japanese capitulated quickly the possibilities for extensive bloodless conquests by fast-moving Soviet columns would be limitless. Secondly, the Chinese Communists controlled an important area in north China within easy reach of advancing Soviet armies. There was, however, one question which had to be answered in Moscow if the Soviet Union entered the war against Japan: would Soviet prospects be improved by collaboration with the Chinese Nationalist Government (whose military fortunes in 1944–45 were at their lowest ebb) or with the Chinese Communists in their virtually autonomous area in north-west China?

In the later stages of the war, from 1943 onwards, Soviet Press treatment of Chinese affairs had shown a definitely pro-Communist and anti-Nationalist bias.[1] These articles continued in the same vein until April 1945 when attacks on the Nationalist Government ceased. The Soviet Government made up its mind as a result of the Yalta Conference that it would gain most by public collaboration with the Nationalist Government.

On Far Eastern questions, the Soviet Government's proposals put forward at the Yalta conference indicated that priority was given in Moscow to the satisfaction of Soviet territorial ambitions. Stalin called for recognition of the *status quo* in Outer Mongolia,[2] the annexation by Russia of the southern part of Sakhalin Island and the Kurile Islands, the lease of Dairen (as a commercial port) and Port Arthur (as a military and naval base), and joint Chinese-Soviet management of the main trunk railway across Manchuria. These proposals were accepted by Mr. Churchill and President Roosevelt, and the latter undertook to persuade the Chinese Government to accept them and to agree to negotiate a Treaty of Alliance and Friendship with the Soviet Government.

The advantages of dealing with the Nationalists and ignoring the Chinese Communists in this context were obvious to the Soviet

---

[1] See *Moscow and the Chinese Communists*, by Robert C. North, p. 202 and note. It is interesting to note that, when allowance has been made for Communist terminology, many of these quotations are remarkably similar to the views transmitted to the United States Government by its officials in China in 1943–44 (see State Department, *U.S. Relations with China*, pp. 64–65).

[2] Outer Mongolia, which had been legally part of China, had had a Soviet-supported Communist régime since 1922, and in 1942 had been proclaimed as an independent People's Republic.

leaders. The Chinese Nationalists could agree to the immediate and legal transfer of Japanese-occupied Chinese territory to the Soviet Union, while the Communists could not. The Nationalists were, moreover, weak politically, militarily, and economically and, since their greatest fear was of their Communist rivals in North China, they were psychologically ready to grant concessions to Russia in return for a Soviet undertaking not to recognize or help the Communists. This the Soviets agreed to do in a solemn undertaking written into the Sino-Soviet Treaty signed on 14 August 1945.

Meanwhile, events in the war in the Pacific were moving swiftly to a climax, thanks mainly to the American employment of the atomic bomb against Japan on 6 and 8 August. At the Potsdam Conference, the Soviet Union had indicated that the timing of its entry into the war against Japan depended on the conclusion of a Sino-Soviet treaty.[1] However, two days after the first atomic explosion over Hiroshima on 6 August the Soviet Union declared war against Japan, although negotiations for a treaty with China were not yet complete, and this represents a clear refutation of the Soviet contention that the atomic bomb had no bearing on the Japanese decision to surrender. Soviet troops entered Manchuria on 9 August and by the 21st had occupied the whole province. Farther south, Soviet troops entered Korea, and reached the 38th parallel, which had been agreed upon as the temporary dividing-line between Russian and American units chosen for the purpose of organizing the surrender of the Japanese garrison.

In the period of confusion which inevitably followed the surrender of Japan two important points of Soviet strategy and tactics emerged. The first was the priority given by Stalin to the military occupation of the territories allotted to Russia at Potsdam and Yalta, and the seizure and transfer to the Soviet Union of as much of Manchuria's industrial equipment and machinery as possible. The Soviet Command also removed to the Soviet Union all available Japanese prisoners of war as a cheap labour force.[2] The second point concerned the Soviet Government's relations with rival Chinese administrations. Under the treaty of 14 August 1945 the Soviet Government had undertaken to recognize and deal only with the

[1] Royal Institute of International Affairs, *Survey of International Affairs, America, Britain and Russia, 1941–46*, p. 633.
[2] The United States Economic Mission under Edwin W. Pauley put the damage to Manchurian industry at 858 million dollars.

Nationalist Government in Chungking, and this Moscow proceeded to do—on the surface. But it seems clear that the Soviet Union also maintained relations with the Chinese Communist authorities, whose forces had fought against the Japanese, and who demanded the right to be represented in the negotiations for the surrender of Japanese forces in Northern China. Two views of the policy of the Soviet Government have been put forward: first, that the Russians secretly and consistently plotted the overthrow of the Nationalist Government with the Communists in North China; this is the view advanced by the Nationalists themselves. And second, that Stalin miscalculated Communist strength, and against Mao Tse-tung's advice recommended a policy of initial Communist collaboration with President Chiang Kai-shek and the Kuomintang.

The evidence quoted in support of the latter interpretation is to be found in the presentation of Stalin's views by the Yugoslav leader, Vladimir Dedijer in his book *Tito Speaks*.

> . . . after the war [Dedijer wrote, quoting Stalin] we invited the Chinese comrades to come to Moscow and we discussed the situation in China. We told them bluntly that we considered the development of the uprising in China had no prospect, and that the Chinese comrades should seek a *modus vivendi* with Chiang Kai-shek, that they should join the Chiang Government and dissolve their army. The Chinese Communists agreed here with the views of the Soviet comrades, but went back to China and acted otherwise.
>
> They mustered their forces, organized their armies, and now [1948—author], as we see, they are beating the Chiang Kai-shek army. Now, in the case of China, we admit that we were wrong. It proved that the Chinese comrades and not the Soviet comrades were right.[1]

This quotation, together with accounts of Stalin's interviews with American officials in 1944–45 in which the Soviet leaders spoke lightly of the strength of the Chinese Communists, have been used in support of the theory of Stalin's miscalculation of Communist strength and capabilities.[2] A report in the *New York Times* of 30 October 1945 quoting a Nationalist Government source, to the effect that the Soviet Command in Manchuria refused to allow the Chinese Communists into the province as armed units but only as civilians, has also been cited in support of this belief.[3]

---

[1] *Tito Speaks*, by Vl. Dedijer, Weidenfeld & Nicholson, London, 1953, p. 33.
[2] See I. Gluckstein, *Mao's China*, for a presentation of this view.
[3] See F. C. Jones, *Manchuria Since 1931*, Royal Institute of International Affairs, p. 231.

There seems, however, to be another possible interpretation of the evidence which is consistent with Soviet strategy and the situation of the Chinese Communist party. As far as Stalin's repeated criticism of the Chinese Communists in 1944-45 is concerned, it would be natural for him to try to allay American suspicions on this score at a time when he was preparing to enter the Far Eastern War as an ally of the United States. As for Soviet reluctance to admit even Communist armed units into Manchuria, experience in Eastern Europe showed that the Soviet Army rarely accepted assistance freely offered by regular or irregular forces, Communist or non-Communist, and were particularly sensitive about the activities of even Communist partisans in the rear of their troops.[1] But when operations in Manchuria were over, the evidence shows that the Soviet Army did allow the Communists to take over quite important outlying towns from which the Russians made an early withdrawal.[2]

Certainly it is a fact that large numbers of Communists did penetrate into Manchuria in August–October 1945, and at the southern end of the Soviet zone of occupation—in Jehol and north Hopei—towns of some importance fell into their hands at this stage. It is difficult to believe that this penetration or seizure of towns could have been carried out against the wishes of the Soviet Union.[3]

But the most impressive evidence in favour of the theory of

[1] The Soviet Army was ruthless in bringing to heel and even disbanding Communist-led partisans in Slovakia, Bulgaria, Eastern Serbia, and in parts of the Baltic States.

[2] This evidence is obtained by a comparison of Soviet and Chinese Communist military communiques. On 10 August 1945 the Communist Commander-in-Chief, Chu Teh, issued an order to his troops to advance to areas where they could take the surrender of Japanese troops, and instructed units in Hopei, Jehol, and Liaotung provinces to move 'without delay to recover the whole of north-east China, in co-ordination with the Soviet Army'. (Quoted in a Chinese Communist publication *From Yenan to Peking* by Liao Kai-lung, Peking, 1954, pp. 8–9). Soviet military communiqués and historical surveys of operations in Manchuria in 1945 claimed the capture by the Soviet Army and by Mongolian cavalry under Soviet command of the main centres of Jehol and northern Hopei, including Kalgan and Zhekhe (Chende) and the coastline south of Chinchow. (*Ocherki istorii velikoi otechestvenoi voiny*, Moscow 1954, pp. 500–1). Yet when in September and October 1945 Nationalist armies marched north to take over Manchuria, they found not Soviet troops in these towns, but Chinese Communist forces. To give one example: the Soviet communiqué claimed the capture of Kalgan on 19 August 1945; on 10 September the Chinese Communists claimed to have defended this town against the Nationalists. The same is true of the coastal strip occupied by the Soviet Army on 19 August.

[3] See F. C. Jones, *Manchuria Since 1931*, pp. 232–3, for details of the Communist migration.

miscalculation is undoubtedly Stalin's self-criticism on China, as reported by Vladimir Dedijer. Yet it seems that on the political front the Chinese Communists did at least make an attempt to carry out Stalin's directive.

Although they had spent eighteen years in guerilla warfare against Generalissimo Chiang Kai-shek's régime, the Chinese Communists agreed to go to Chungking to discuss the future government of China with the Nationalists. On 28 August 1945 Mao Tse-tung and Chou En-lai arrived in the wartime capital, and began negotiations which ended on 10 October 1945 with partial agreement on the convocation of a political consultative assembly. The Communist delegates agreed to major reductions in their armed forces, and withdrawal and demobilization of Communist units in Central and Southern China. Later, in January 1946, when a truce was arranged under American auspices after fighting had broken out in Northern China, the Communists agreed to take part in a joint Communist-Nationalist-American Executive Headquarters in Peking. Of course, none of these agreements went as far as Stalin is alleged to have suggested, but they do imply a certain degree of readiness—however doubtful the Chinese Communists may have been about Stalin's knowledge of the situation on the spot—to follow the Soviet lead at this time.

The whole question of Soviet strategy in China in 1945–46 is complicated by the fact that each side was dealing with the problems on several levels. Thus, the Soviet authorities were in touch with the Nationalist Government under the terms of the treaty of 14 August 1945, and at the same time allowing the Communists to migrate into Soviet-occupied Manchuria. The Nationalists, while negotiating with the Soviet authorities for the introduction of Nationalist civil and military power into Manchuria, were taking their own military measures against the Communists whom those same Soviet authorities appeared to be protecting. Paradoxes of the most startling kind arose in this situation; early in 1946 the Nationalist Government, which had been pressing for the evacuation of Soviet forces from Manchuria, had to ask the Soviet Government to delay its withdrawal in order to prevent Manchurian cities from falling into Communist hands.

There is, however, evidence that a clearer decision on Soviet strategy in China was taken early in 1946 after Chinese Nationalist troops, which had been transported by air and sea by the Americans to north China, forced their way through Communist-held Jehol and advanced on Mukden, which they took from a small Communist force in March. Perhaps impressed by the scale of American support for the Nationalists, or by the failure of the Communist forces in Jehol and Mukden to halt the Nationalist advance, the Soviets announced that their troops would leave Manchuria in April 1946. As they withdrew the Russians handed over the main cities of Northern Manchuria, Harbin, Tsitsikar, and Kirin, to the Communists, and a provisional Communist administration was set up in those areas. On 14 April the Russians evacuated the capital of Manchuria, Changchun, ahead of schedule, and the city was immediately seized by the Communists. The Nationalists, however, advanced from Mukden and drove the Communists out of Changchun on 23 May; and a sort of 'frontier' between the two administrations was formed along the Sungari river. The conception of a Communist zone or base, in which a regular administration functioned is very like the conception of a Communist zone in North Korea, 1945–48, in Persian Azerbaijan in 1945–46, and in northern Greece in 1946–47, and is consistent with the whole development of Soviet expansion in Europe by creeping forward across frontiers. This interpretation of the appearance of a type of Communist zone along the Soviet frontier is supported by an interview given to a correspondent of the *New York Times* by the senior Chinese Communist adviser to the Communist régime in Northern Manchuria, Li Li-san. Li Li-san, who had lived in exile in Moscow since 1931, returned to China in 1946, and told his interviewer that he advocated the severance of relations with the Nationalists, and the establishment of a Communist régime in Northern Manchuria.[1]

The parallel with Soviet policy in Eastern Europe, Greece, and Persia is indeed striking. In Europe the Soviet Government satisfied Russian territorial claims against Poland, Rumania, Finland, and Germany as first priority.[2] There followed a strategy aimed at depriving non-Communist governments of effective authority over areas bordering on the Soviet Union, and the creation of Communist bases, zones, or areas of guerilla activity there. In China too, Soviet strategy led to the acquisition of Port Arthur, Darien, and the Manchurian railway, but avoided committing the Soviet Union or

---

[1] *New York Times*, 11 October 1946, as quoted by F. C. Jones, op. cit., p. 235.
[2] The Soviet Government demanded and received confirmation of the incorporation of Eastern Poland, Bessarabia, and the Karelian isthmus, and annexed the area round the city of Königsberg in East Prussia.

the Chinese Communists to full-scale revolutionary war to overthrow major non-Communist governments if the areas of conflict would be beyond the reach of the Soviet Army. The Soviet strategists probably hoped at first that the Chinese Communists could have held their own over the whole of Manchuria and in this case the Soviet Government might have looked forward to a Chinese Communist state covering everything north of the Great Wall. Direct Soviet support to the Communists to do this was discreetly concealed, because the Soviet Government was also engaged in securing as many concessions as they could from the Nationalists, such as the legal transfer of Chinese territory to the Soviet Union and the securing of economic and transport advantages. Perhaps partly because Soviet help to the Communists was thus restricted, the latter were unable to hold all China north of the Great Wall, and Soviet strategy crystallized early in 1946 in favour of a base in northern Manchuria of smaller dimensions, from which, it was probably hoped, the Communists would ultimately break out and spread their influence southwards.

It was perhaps at this point that the disagreement to which Stalin referred occurred—in the Chinese decision to press on in 1946 with the civil war, and not to pause for reorganization and rehabilitation within their area. We cannot be certain. The fact is, however, that the war did go on, and that after initial successes in the autumn of 1946 and the early part of 1947 the Nationalists were forced on the defensive, driven out of Manchuria, and faced by internal collapse. Peking fell to the Communists in January 1949, and by the summer, practically the whole of the Chinese mainland was in their hands. Naturally, when the Chinese Communists' military and political victory was complete, the Soviet Union was the first to recognize this tremendous addition to the Communist camp, and to invite the Chinese Communist leader Mao Tse-tung to a lengthy and much-publicized conference in Moscow, which lasted from December 1949 to February 1950.[1]

In a treaty signed on 14 February 1950 the Soviet Union undertook to return to China after a fixed period many of the concessions

---

[1] Recognition of the Chinese Communist victory did not prevent the Soviet Union from exploiting its relations with the Nationalists up to the last minute to obtain concessions. As late as 1948, when the Communist armies were already approaching the Yangtse river, the Soviet Ambassador to the Nationalist Government was exercising pressure to obtain concessions in Sinkiang—concessions which the Communists agreed to endorse in 1949–50. (See Gluckstein, op. cit., pp. 408, et seq.).

wrung from the Nationalists in 1945—Port Arthur, Dairen, and the
Manchurian railways, formalized a close military alliance, and
granted China a credit of 300 million dollars. The treaty was followed by a series of trade and economic agreements on 20 April
1950 under which China was to supply Russia with raw materials in
exchange for arms, machinery, and the services of Soviet technicians
and advisers. Joint Sino-Soviet companies, modelled on those in
Eastern Europe, were set up to exploit China's mineral wealth and
natural resources.

The outbreak of the Korean war in June 1950, and the involvement of Communist China in continuing warfare in the interests of
a policy which originated in Moscow meant that the dominating
influence in Sino-Soviet relations was bound to be the need to retain
unity in the face of United Nations' military power in the field, and
of the possibility that the war might spread. Indeed, while Stalin was
alive, it seems probable that the major factor in Sino-Soviet relations
was Chinese military and economic dependence on Moscow. The
deeper problems of long-term Sino-Soviet relations remained beneath
the surface, a state of affairs which prevented Soviet strategy and
tactics towards China from experiencing the kind of challenge which
had developed between the Soviet Union and Yugoslavia. Sino-
Soviet relations, therefore, entered the post-Stalin period relatively
undisturbed and, on the surface, characterized by identity of interest.

IV

KOREA: EXPANSION BY LIMITED WAR
1950–52

THE victory of the Chinese Communists was not the only situation in the Far East which attracted Moscow's attention in 1949 and 1950. Developments in the two parts of Korea, divided since the military demarcation agreement of 1945, aroused the interest of Soviet strategists anxious for a new outlet for Communist expansion after their recent disappointments in Europe.

Both Soviet and American troops took part in the post-war occupation of Korea, their forces, by mutual military agreement, being halted along the 38th parallel. Immediately, attempts were made to unify the country with the advice and help of America, Russia, Britain, and China, but it soon became clear that the Soviet Union was, in fact, intent on making a small satellite state out of her zone of occupation.[1] The Soviet Commander in North Korea would discuss only postal and other communications with his American opposite number; deadlock arose over the interpretation of the phrases 'a democratic party' and 'social organizations' which were mentioned in the directive on Korea issued by the Foreign Ministers' conference in Moscow in December 1945. Further attempts to discuss the future of Korea on a Four-Power basis were made in 1946 and 1947, but by the latter year Soviet influence in the northern zone had reached the stage at which the Korean Communist party, known as the 'Democratic' Front, could emerge with a monopoly of Soviet favour and political power. The Korean problem was referred back to the Foreign Ministers time and again but without success. In August 1947 the American Government proposed early elections in both zones to elect a provisional government, which with the advice of the Four Powers should move towards political independence. This, once achieved, would be followed by the withdrawal of Soviet and American forces. The American proposals were accepted by Britain and China, and rejected by Russia.

[1] A detailed study of Korean problems 1945–50 can be found in Goodrich, *Korea: a study of United States policy in the United Nations.*

This was the end of serious direct negotiations among the Great Powers on Korea. While the American Government brought the Korean question before the United Nations, Russia pressed on with the creation of a Communist state north of the 38th parallel. In 1948, after United Nations efforts to find a solution had failed, the Americans followed the Russian lead and two rival governments appeared in the Peninsula. In the south, Dr. Syngman Rhee, the veteran Korean statesman who had spent years as an anti-Japanese exile in America, formed a Government after a general election held under the auspices of a United Nations Commission. In the north the Soviet authorities handed over power to a 'People's Democracy' on the East European model, headed by a former anti-Japanese Resistance leader, Kim Il Sung. The United Nations agreed to admit the Republic of Korea, as the southern part of the country was styled, to membership on 12 December 1948. At the end of 1948 all Soviet troops left North Korea, and the United States forces evacuated the country six months later, on 29 June 1949.

It was after about a year of this kind of split existence of Korea, in which each part was governed by a native régime representing the Communist and anti-Communist ideologies, that the Soviet Union resumed a strategic interest in Korea. The outbreak of war in Korea in June 1950 is of special importance as the only case in which we can study the military aspect of Soviet strategy and tactics, and can learn when and in what circumstances Stalin was ready to embark on limited warfare. 'Soviet' strategy and tactics is a phrase used deliberately, because any conception that the North Korean régime would have taken military action on its own responsibility without the prior approval, or against the instructions of the Soviet Government, flatly contradicts all that is known of the behaviour of countries in the Communist camp. It is particularly important, therefore, to study how the decision was taken to resort to limited war in Korea in 1950.

It must be pointed out first of all that the North Korean régime was a purely Soviet creation. Its governmental structure was already in being before the Communists came to power in China. Its advisers and technicians were Russian, and some of the North Korean Communist party and Government officials had been Soviet citizens or served in the Soviet Army during the war. The North Korean Army, which was founded on 8 February 1948, was organized and trained on Soviet lines without the help of the Chinese Communists.

Responsibility for final decisions acted upon by the North Korean Government must be laid at the door of the Soviet Government. One point is of primary importance in any study of the outbreak of war in Korea in June 1950: the relationship between the growth of the North Korean Army after 1948, and policy declarations on the strategic importance of the Korean peninsula made by American statesmen. It is now known that as long ago as 26 September 1947 the United States Joint Chiefs of Staff had prepared a memorandum (which was not made public till 1952) that the United States of America had little strategic interest in Korea. It was no doubt this military appreciation which prompted Mr. Acheson, then American Secretary of State, to declare on 12 January 1950 that Korea would have to depend for its defence on its own efforts, subject always to the help it could obtain from the United Nations. On 2 May 1950 Mr. Acheson followed this up with the suggestion that South Korea was militarily untenable, and confirmed that this view had been made known to Congressional Committees.[1] While Mr Acheson and his American military advisers were probably thinking of the military risks of locking up American troops in the Korean Peninsula when he made these statements, there can be no doubt that his declaration of the American position on the defence of South Korea made a profound impression in Moscow, for there is a direct relationship in timing between it and the preparatory mobilization of the North Korean Army.

At the end of 1949 North Korea had four infantry divisions and a number of Border Guard brigades; of these, only one infantry division had been formed in the last half of the year. After the Korean War had been in progress for some time, the American military authorities released to Press correspondents in the Far East details of the build-up of the North Korean Army since February 1950—that is, since Mr. Acheson's first declaration on the defence of Korea. This information showed that a 5th infantry division was activated in the town of Wonsam in north-east Korea on 1 March 1950, and a 6th division was formed in Sariwon on 17 April 1950, two regiments of which were composed of Korean soldiers who had served in the Chinese Communist Army.[2] On 29 March 1950 the

[1] See Royal Institute of International Affairs, *Survey of International Affairs, 1949–50*, p 480 and note.
[2] According to the *Military Situation in the Far East*, hearings before the Committee on Armed Services and Committee on Foreign Relations, U.S. Senate,

North Korean Radio at Pyongyang inaugurated a 'voluntary' savings campaign to buy arms. On 19 May, the South Korean Government formally reported to the United Nations the moving of North Korean troops to the 38th parallel. When the attack came on 25 June 1950 the 1st, 2nd, 3rd, 4th, 5th, and 6th North Korean infantry divisions and three Border Guard brigades took part in the crossing of the frontier. By 20 July 1950 the United Nations Command had further identified the 7th, 8th, 9th, 10th, 12th, 13th, and 15th infantry divisions in action.[1] The implication is clear. Up to the time of the American statement on the defence of South Korea, the North Korean Army was neither organized nor mobilized for aggression; from February onwards, when Koreans were released from the Chinese Communist Forces, the North Korean Army began its transformation to a war footing. With an initial striking force of six infantry divisions and three border brigades, the North Korean Army clearly had not less than seven infantry divisions forming between April and June 1950. The American declaration that South Korea would have to defend itself, subject to United Nations commitments, clearly played an important part in influencing the Soviet strategic decision to use limited war to try to extend the frontiers of the Soviet bloc to include the whole of the Korean Peninsula.

We must assume, therefore, that the Soviet Government came to believe in early 1950 that the military invasion of South Korea by the North Korean Army would not provoke intervention by the United States. There were other factors supporting this view. The Soviet Government probably argued that the Security Council would be unlikely to act either in the absence of the Soviet delegate, or against his veto, for unanimity was believed to be essential for action in collective defence.[2] South Korea itself was believed to be in a state

---

82nd Congress, Part 5, p. 3403, the Chinese military authorities began releasing men of Korean origin from their Fourth Field Army (then in Southern China, but originally recruited in Manchuria) in February 1950. The release of Koreans from the Chinese Army was admitted by Radio Peking on 22 September 1950.

[1] *Military Situation in Far East*, op. cit., Part 5, p. 3389. It is interesting to note that on 10 March 1950 General MacArthur's Headquarters in Japan told Washington that the North Korean Army had mobilized sixteen divisions, and planned to invade South Korea in mid-June. See *MacArthur 1941-51*, by Charles A. Willoughby and John Chamberlain, McGraw-Hill Book Coy. Inc., 1954, pp. 350 et seq.

[2] The Soviet delegate to the Security Council had walked out in protest against the Council's refusal to recommend the admission of Communist China.

bordering on internal collapse. Communist-led partisans were active in the south-west of the country, where elements of two or three South Korean divisions were operating against them. This left only parts of five under-strength infantry divisions along the frontier with North Korea. During the spring of 1950 the North Korean Army had made several incursions into South Korean territory, testing, no doubt, the degree of resistance of the South Koreans. Raiding units crossed the parallel, skirmishing with South Korean outposts, and withdrew after a few hours. It was therefore only too easy for the Soviet authorities to convince themselves that limited war could safely be launched in Korea, that the South Koreans were in no state to resist a Northern invasion, and that the United Nations would be powerless to act, especially in view of the Americans' views on the defence of the peninsula.

The invasion of South Korea began at dawn on 25 June 1950 with a rapid advance by North Korean regular troops on Seoul, the capital, in the centre of the peninsula, and along the east coast, where landings from the sea took place. The South Koreans were taken by surprise and withdrew in disorder.[1] However, the South Korean Government did appeal to the Security Council, which met on 26 June, and within a matter of days American aircraft, ships, and later ground troops were in action in Korea. A United Nations Command under General MacArthur was formed, and a call went out from New York to all members of the United Nations to send troops to halt aggression in Korea. After an impressive forward rush southwards the impetus of the North Korean advance faltered, and by September 1950 the United Nations forces had established a firm defence line in the south-east corner of the peninsula. On 11 September a United Nations force landed from the sea behind the North

---

[1] The official Soviet version of the beginning of the war is to be found in Kravtsov *Aggressia Amerikanskikh Imperialistov v Koree* Moscow, 1951, pp. 302-5. According to Kravtsov, seven South Korean infantry divisions and one mechanized division attacked the North after an artillery and air bombardment at dawn on 25 June. They advanced only two kilometres before being defeated and hurled back 10 kilometres south of the 38th parallel. According to North Korean communiqués in June 1950 North Korean troops were already in Kaesong, south of the parallel at 0700 hrs, and a landing was in progress on the east coast. If the South Koreans had attacked at dawn, it is difficult to see how this amphibious landing could have been prepared, the troops embarked, moved by sea to their destination and landed all in about two hours. Moreover, according to United Nations reports on Korea before the outbreak of hostilities, the South Korean Army had no heavy weapons, no tanks, only sixteen obsolete training aircraft, and certainly no mechanized division.

Korean lines at Inchon, reoccupied Seoul, and cut the North Korean
Army off from its homeland. A general United Nations offensive
from the south-east drove the North Korean Army in headlong
flight over the 38th parallel, which was reached by United Nations
forces along its whole length at the end of September.

Before this point had been reached, however, it was clear that the
original Soviet strategic decision to attempt the conquest of South
Korea by force had been rendered obsolete by the North Korean
failure on the battlefield, and the problem facing the Soviet planners
was no longer the extension of their frontiers, but the protection of
an integral part of their heartland—North Korea. This change
probably impressed itself on the Soviet leaders in three stages: first,
the intervention of United States ground forces in Korea in July;
secondly, the successful United Nations defence of the Pusan perimeter in south-east Korea in August; and finally, the sea-borne
landing at Inchon and the break-up of the North Korean Army in
September.

There were in theory two courses of action open to the Soviet
Union. She could cut her losses in Korea and authorize the North
Korean Communists to make what peace terms they could with the
United Nations in the hope of restoring the *status quo* north of the
38th parallel. This course had two serious objections: to admit
defeat in Korea so soon after the Soviet failure to subdue Yugoslavia
and to drive Britain, America, and France out of Berlin would have
been humiliating. Secondly, with no army, and smarting under its
military defeat, could the North Korean régime subsequently maintain itself in power unaided? There must have been serious doubts
on this point in Moscow and therefore all the more weight was
probably given to the second possible course of action: to continue
the war. This meant foreign Communist intervention—in practice,
either by Soviet or Chinese forces, since there were few North Korean
troops left to fight.[1] Intervention by Soviet troops might have turned
a limited war into a global one; the choice therefore fell upon the
Chinese.

There is some evidence that the Chinese Government had advance

[1] See United Nations fortnightly summaries of Korean operations. No. 11,
1950, printed in *Military Situation in Far East*, op. cit., Part 5. No regular North
Korean forces took part in the fighting in November–December 1950. Their
reconstituted army reappeared in strength only after 4 January 1951. *Summary
No. 13*, pp. 3444 and 3451–2.

knowledge of the general intention to launch limited warfare in Korea, although the actual date of the attack may have taken Peking by surprise.[1] The release of soldiers in the Chinese Army of Korean origin in February 1950 followed closely on the lengthy conference in Moscow between Stalin and Mao Tse-tung, and soon after the war began the Chinese propaganda machine swung into full-scale action against the United Nations and the United States for 'aggression in Korea'. Nevertheless, it seems to have been the case that the Chinese Government had decided upon a considerable reduction in their Army in the summer of 1950 after the capture of Hainan island and completion of operations in southern China. Early in June 1950 Mao Tse-tung spoke on demobilization, the return of troops to their peacetime stations, and their transfer to work on land reclamation, railway building, and agriculture.[2] This particularly applied to the Fourth Field Army, most of whose units had been formed in Manchuria and north China, but which had moved south in 1949 for the campaign against Canton and Hainan island. According to Press reports, the units of the Fourth Field Army stationed in Canton began to pull out before 18 July 1950,[3] and the 38th and 39th Armies of this Field Army reached their home stations in Manchuria before the end of August. It was not until the beginning of October, however, that these troops, which were the first to cross into Korea (on 14 October) moved from their Headquarters in Manchuria to the Korean frontier.[4] The implication is that the move of the Fourth Field Army northwards in July and August was connected with Mao's demobilization policy rather than with the Korean war. While it is true that some Chinese troops moved into Korea as early as 14 October, after South Korean troops (but no other member of the United Nations' forces) had crossed the parallel, subsequent military moves showed that this was to a certain

---

[1] See C. P. Fitzgerald, *China in Revolution*, p. 200.

[2] See the article on Chinese Armed Forces by Richard Harris in *Brassey's Annual*, 1951, p. 123.

[3] *New York Times*, 18 July and 25 August 1950. At this time the Chinese Communist Army was organized in four Field Armies, each of from two to six Army Groups. Three or four armies of three infantry divisions each made up an Army Group, so that a Chinese 'army' was equivalent to a Western 'corps'. The 38th and 39th Armies were part of the 12th Army Group of the 4th Field Army.

[4] According to information released in Tokyo by the United States Far Eastern Command to the Press dated 29 November 1950, the 39th Army Headquarters moved from the Mukden area of Manchuria about 20 October, and the 38th Army Headquarters from Changchun, farther north, on 18 October 1950.

extent a holding operation.[1] The sign that the Chinese Communists were prepared for serious military operations in Korea came between 30 September and 10 November 1950, when the first indications reached the United Nations Command that units of the Third Field Army, until that moment detailed for the invasion of Formosa, had begun a move northwards to Manchuria.[2]

The movement to Korea of this Field Army containing China's most experienced troops indicated that the Chinese Government was prepared to go farther than merely defending China's frontier on Korean soil. That could have been done by the Fourth Field Army already deployed in Manchuria. But the employment of another Field Army meant that China had undertaken to protect the North Korean Communist régime and to restore and perhaps improve the original Communist perimeter as a major commitment.

The Chinese offensive in North Korea which began in November 1950 drove the United Nations Army south of the 38th parallel, but was halted by a series of counter-attacks in January 1951 during which Seoul was re-taken by the United Nations. A line was established roughly along the 38th parallel. At the end of April 1951 the second Chinese Communist offensive opened, but failed to achieve a major break-through and the line was stabilized once more near the parallel. At this point, when two major Chinese offensives had failed to destroy the United Nations forces, the first suggestions for a cease-fire came from the Communist side.

Significantly, it was a Soviet move. On 23 June 1951 Mr. Malik, the permanent Soviet representative in the United Nations, stated in a United Nations broadcast:

> The Soviet people believe that, as a first step, discussions should be started between the belligerents for a cease-fire and an armistice providing for the mutual withdrawal of forces from the 38th parallel.

On the 25th, the Chinese Press endorsed this proposal, and the United Nations Command decided to take it up at once. On 8 July

---

[1] Chou En-lai was reported to have told the Indian Ambassador in Peking on 2 October that China would intervene in Korea if non-Korean troops entered North Korea, but not if only South Koreans were involved. In fact, Chinese troops crossed the Yalu ten days before MacArthur lifted the ban on non-Korean troops in North Korea.

[2] *General MacArthur 1941–51*, op. cit., pp. 378 and 401. See also *The U.S. Marines in Korea*, Volume 3, for the movements of the 9th Army Group of the Third Field Army, which attacked the 1st Marine division in North-East Korea on 28/29 November 1950.

1951 the first meeting between the two sides took place at Kaesong. The negotiations were slow and difficult, and more than once were suspended or interrupted by the resumption of large-scale fighting at the front; particularly difficult was the attitude of the Communists over prisoners of war who did not wish to be repatriated. And, in fact, no armistice was signed while Stalin was alive. The North Korean and Chinese authorities resorted to tactics similar to those which had been used after the failure of the blockade of Berlin when the struggle was transferred to the council table. This type of negotiation therefore must be classified as a basic tactical weapon in the Soviet armoury to be used to extricate Communists from defeat or miscalculation.[1]

One lesson to be learnt from Soviet policy in the Korean war was that pronouncements by Western Governments implying that an area bordering on the Communist bloc was no longer considered as a defence commitment were taken literally in Moscow, and helped to influence a strategic decision to pursue the policy of expansion by limited war. Another was that the defeat of the Soviet auxiliary army concerned on the battlefield did not induce the Soviet Government to cut its losses, but led to the intensification of the war until the territory of North Korea was once again firmly in the military and political control of the Communists. Only then did the Communist side agree to a cessation of military operations, and the ensuing negotiations were used by the Communists to continue the struggle on a different level. The case of Korea proved that in Soviet eyes, if a country or part of a country which had been firmly in the hands of an established and orthodox Communist party slipped from the Communist grip, all methods, including military action, should be taken to restore it to Soviet or Communist control. On this, there could be no compromise with the non-Communist world. The Soviet Union's obligation to maintain Communist régimes in power by all means, including limited war, was certainly in Stalin's day a cornerstone of Soviet strategy.[2]

[1] An exactly similar case of the employment of delaying tactics with the help of propaganda was the Palais Rose Conference in 1951, during which the representatives of the Big Four discussed European problems. The Soviet delegate spun out the discussions on the agenda alone to seventy-four meetings.

[2] The one possible exception to this rule was the abandonment of the pro-Soviet régime in Persian Azerbaijan in 1946. It may be argued, however, that Communist power was not as firmly entrenched in Tabriz as it was in Pyongyang, and did not constitute an established régime.

V

SOUTH-EAST ASIA: THE SEARCH FOR A POLICY OF REMOTE CONTROL: 1945–53

So far, this study has covered Soviet strategy and tactics in Europe, Persia, and in the Far Eastern areas bordering on the Soviet Union —China and Korea. It is now time to look at south-east Asia, an area where the war had opened the floodgates of nationalism, where old régimes were disappearing and new powers were in the making, some of them bearing names not to be found on pre-war maps— Pakistan, Indonesia, and Vietnam. And like the other Powers with world-wide commitments, the Soviet Union had to work out a policy for the unstable yet vigorous nationalism of this vital area.

The initial approach by the Soviet Union to south-east Asia after the Second World War bore a strong resemblance to the pattern laid down for countries beyond the reach of the Soviet Army. No direct attempt was made to seize power for the Communists, but the local parties strove to enter national coalitions, to obtain possession of key posts and to consolidate and widen party influence by supporting nationalist propaganda among the population and in trade union organizations. In Indonesia, for example, where a group of nationalist leaders had proclaimed the country's independence of Holland on 17 August 1945 sporadic fighting developed between the nationalists and British troops who had been landed to accept the Japanese surrender until the Dutch Army arrived. The Indonesian Nationalists, broadly united on national issues, contained right- and left-wing elements. The centre groupings of both wings on the whole favoured negotiations with the Dutch Government (except at the time of the two Dutch military actions against Republican-held territory in May 1947 and December 1948), and it is significant that at this period the Indonesian Communist party, along with the Socialists, aligned themselves with the moderates.[1]

In Burma the Communist party also emerged from the war as a member of a nationalist coalition, the Anti-Fascist People's Freedom

[1] See *The State of Asia*, by Lawrence K. Rosinger and Associates, Alfred A. Knopf, N.Y., 1951, p. 422.

League, formed in 1943-44 by a group of young Burmese nationalists who had originally taken service under the Japanese but who had repudiated their allegiance to Tokyo during the Japanese occupation of their country in 1942. After the war the Communist party at first remained within the ranks of the Anti-Fascist People's Freedom League, and when the League took part in forming an Executive Council to advise the Governor in September 1946 a Communist received the portfolio of Agriculture and Rural Economy.

At this point occurred one of those deviations from orthodoxy so distressing to Moscow, and yet so characteristic of the fluid and complicated conditions of post-war Asia. The Burma Communist party split into two parts after a quarrel over personalities; one became known as the White Flag Communists and the other the Red Flag Communists. The White Flag remained for the time being in the Anti-Fascist People's Freedom League, but the Red Flag, whose leaders were expelled from the Burma Communist party, left the League, and attacked their White Flag rivals with accusations of anti-Marxism and secret wartime collaboration with the Japanese. Even after the final break between the Burma Communist party (the White Flag) and the League in October 1946 (over the League's decision to negotiate with Britain for independence), when both branches of the Burma Communist party took to the mountains and forests as partisans, Red and White Flag Communists remained bitter enemies, fighting each other as they fought the League. Meanwhile, the anti-Fascist People's Freedom League, increasing its strength and influence, negotiated Burmese independence with Britain in 1947 and formed a Government which elected to leave the British Commonwealth.

In Indo-China, after the Japanese surrender in August 1945, the Communist parties of the various states emerged as members of nationalist coalitions, of which the most prominent was that in the northern part of the country, the Viet-Minh. The Japanese-sponsored administration voluntarily dissolved itself in August, and on 2 September 1945 a Democratic Republic of Vietnam was proclaimed, led by the Viet-Minh National Liberation Committee, including a nucleus of Communists under Ho Chi Minh. This Committee claimed authority over Annam, Tonkin, and Cochin China, but not the separate states of Cambodia and Laos.[1] There followed

---

[1] The situation *vis-à-vis* the Communists was complicated by the existence and activities in Cochin China of a Trotski-ite group (see *The State of Asia*, p. 235).

an Anglo-Chinese military occupation of Indo-China for the purpose of accepting the surrender of the Japanese Army, and early in 1946 the French administration returned to the southern part of the country. During this period the Communists remained in the Viet-Minh coalition, and along with other parties represented in the Committee agreed not to oppose the return of French troops to the northern part of the country after the withdrawal of the Chinese. But when fighting broke out in December 1946 in the north between the French and the Viet-Minh the situation of the Communists became unbelievably complicated. They occupied a leading position in the Viet-Minh coalition, but their leader, Ho Chi Minh, had taken up a moderate position in relation to the French, in which he seems to have been influenced by his own links with the French Communist party in Paris. The French Communist party, which still had members in the French Government in December 1946, tried hard not to commit itself on Indo-China and it is hardly surprising that the Soviet Union, which had taken a vigorous part in criticizing Britain and Holland in the United Nations on the Indonesian case, remained silent when Indo-China was discussed. It was not until 1947-48, when circumstances in Europe had altered the position of the French Communist party, that the situation of the Communists in Indo-China was clarified, and they were fully able to align themselves with the nationalist opposition against which the French Army fought until 1954.

In India the situation developed somewhat differently. After some years of suppression, the Indian Communist party was legalized in 1942 and, while supporting the war effort, attempted to spread its influence in labour movements and among intellectuals. Individual members joined the Indian Congress party, but many of the latters' leaders found Communist support an embarrassment, and a movement within Congress to force the Communists out succeeded in the autumn of 1945. In February 1946 considerable Communist influence was detected in a mutiny in the Indian Navy, but the Communists as a political party continued to offer their co-operation to the Indian Congress both before and after the achievement of independence in August 1947, until a change of policy in 1948 brought a more militant party leadership to the fore.

Malaya was another Asian country which followed a similar pattern. Although no coalition emerged from the war, the Communist party had taken a leading part in resisting the Japanese, and entered the post-war period with the publication of a 'popular front' type of programme, aimed at uniting nationalist and left-wing elements in the country. But the tactics of the Malayan Communist party towards the population appear to have been hasty and ill advised, and lost them much support. In January 1946 they organized a general strike which lacked popular sympathy, and as a party they all too readily resorted to the traditional habit of demanding protection money by threats and blackmail. In spite of this they tried to cling to their position within the country's constitutional framework until the force of events drove them into violent opposition.

A similar picture appeared in the Philippine islands, where American forces landed in October 1944, and after a bitter campaign wrested the islands from the Japanese. A resistance movement, the Hukbalahap (known as Huks, for short), partly agrarian in character, and including Socialists and other left-wing elements under the leadership of the Communist party, emerged from the occupation as a political and military factor. After the war they refused to disband and for the first few years an uneasy truce existed between them and the United States military and Philippines civil administration.

In Japan the Communist party, which was founded in 1921, had been outlawed after a short period of legality, but the release of political prisoners in October 1945 under the Allied Occupation brought the party back to life. At first the Communists concentrated with some success on a parliamentary struggle and attempts to gain influence in workers' organizations, and in the elections of 1946 the party polled 2,135,000 votes, or 3.8 per cent of the total. This gave them fifteen seats in a Parliament of 450. Support for them declined in 1947 but rose again in 1948–49, when no less than thirty-five candidates were returned, thanks mainly to the defection of certain leaders of the Social Democratic party who brought their followers into the Communist party. This increase in numbers put the Japanese party in a relatively favourable position at a time when what appeared to be a new directive from Moscow reached Asian Communists in 1948.

The evidence is as follows: in Europe, the foundation of the Cominform in September 1947 led to the cessation of co-operation between Communist parties and non-Communist Governments in France, Italy, Belgium, and Austria, and the adoption of more militant and vigorous policies against Western states and their influence in Communist-held countries. It seems very likely that this change in Communist tactics was also reflected in directives to the Asian Communist parties in 1948, probably transmitted during the Conference of 'Progressive Youth of Asia', and the Congress of the Indian Communist party, both of which were held in Calcutta early in 1948. After these meetings, the tactics of the Communists in all Asian countries changed from co-operation with the non-Communist nationalists to extreme and often violent opposition, sometimes culminating in armed uprisings.[1]

In Indonesia, after the arrival of a Moscow-trained Communist, Musso (who had been active in the Communist movement in the 1920s), in the summer of 1948, the Communist party organized and led an armed rising in western Java in September 1948. It was crushed by the Government, and many leading Communists were caught and executed. Seriously weakened, the Indonesian Communist party relapsed into a state of bitter, though passive, opposition to the Government, failing to regain any significant portion of its strength while Stalin was alive.

In Indo-China the new directive not only made relations between the local Communist party and the French Communist party easier, but coincided with the final break with the French authorities in Indo-China itself. Partisan warfare was intensified, and grew into the formidable struggle which culminated in the long siege and fall of the French base at Dien Bien Phu in 1954.

Partisan warfare also became the order of the day in Burma, Malaya, and the Philippines. In 1948 the two branches of the Burma Communist party widened their areas of operations, and on more than one occasion fighting with Government forces took place within the suburbs of Rangoon. Gradually, however, the Government began to win back key points, to reopen roads and railways, and generally to gain the upper hand, in which task it was assisted by the internal dissensions of the Burmese Communists themselves.[2]

[1] The new line was much in evidence at the Conference of the World Federation of Trade Unions held in Peking in November 1949. Speakers emphasized: 'It is necessary to set up wherever and whenever possible a national army, led by the Communist party . . . armed struggle is the main form of struggle for the national liberation of many colonies and semi-colonies.' There is some evidence that this Chinese conference was held against the advice of the Soviet Government and was an independent Chinese initiative.

[2] These few lines on civil disturbances in Burma are of necessity restricted to the Communists, and cannot take into consideration non-Communist and separatist opponents of the Government, such as the revolt conducted by the Karens.

In Malaya the abandonment of the constitutional struggle and the Communists' return to jungle warfare occurred in June 1948. The same date is significant in the Philippines, for it was in that month that the final break-down in negotiations between the Huks and the Government over the disposal of arms took place and guerilla warfare was resumed on a large scale. Even in Japan, under the eye of the American military authorities, the year 1948 witnessed a sharp move away from parliamentary activities, and the adoption by the Japanese Communist party of tactics of violence. A wave of destructive strikes swept Japanese industry, which together with riots, acts of sabotage, and attacks on United States soldiers led to the curtailing of its activities.

Finally, in India the year 1948 was associated with a change of leadership in the party, and a move towards a policy of riots and unrest. At the party conference held in Calcutta in March 1948 the Secretary-General, P. C. Joshi, was forced to give up his post, and was replaced by B. T. Ranadive, who embarked upon a policy of opposition to the Indian Government and to the Congress party. Communist methods of promoting civil disorders and riots led to the outlawing of the party in Bengal, Madras, and other provinces, and by 1949–50 it seemed clear that they were losing support. Ranadive was dropped from the party leadership in 1950 and the party began to plan new and less violent policies.

This premature exhaustion of several of the Asian Communist parties resembled, though in a more extreme form, the sense of frustration which crept into several of the older Communist parties in Western Europe when their political strikes against American aid, economic recovery, and Western defence failed.[1] It seems that the Soviet Union attempted to apply the same directive to the fluid situations in south-east Asia as it had worked out for European Communist parties in countries beyond the reach of the Soviet Army. From 1945 to 1948 the Communist parties collaborated with non-Communist national régimes and movements, a policy which

[1] In Italy major political strikes were organized by the Communist party in July 1948, in September and November 1951, in February and March 1952, and March 1953. In France the Communist party brought out two million workers in November 1947, and in October 1948, and in 1949 and 1950 (against the war in Indo-China). On several occasions the Government was compelled to bring troops to keep essential services running. Feeling ran high when clashes occurred between strikers and the troops or police, but the movement of supplies, arms, and economic aid was never in danger from Communist activity.

in some Asian countries appeared to bring the Communists some success.[1] In 1948 all south-east Asian Communist parties turned abruptly away from collaboration, and each embarked on a policy of violence. Only in Indo-China, and to a lesser extent in Malaya, did this policy bring the Communists any degree of success, and in Indo-China ultimate success was probably due to external factors, namely the victory of the Communists in China, which provided the Communist forces with a common frontier with the Sino-Soviet bloc.

Viewed from Moscow at the time of Stalin's death in March 1953, the Communist situation in south-east Asia was not an encouraging one. Too many national Communist parties were exhausted or labouring under legal handicaps; too many had forfeited popular support by violence, apparently decreed by Moscow in 1948; and too many had been called upon to make a maximum effort while they were, relatively speaking, in their infancy. Probably the most important factor working against the new directive of 1948 was that it forced the local Communist parties into opposition not only against Western 'colonialism', but against local nationalism. The Communist parties were thus divorced in the public mind from the nationalist cause at a time when nationalism was stronger than ideology. Stalin underestimated the hold of nationalism on the Asian mind. There is some evidence that by the autumn of 1952 he was beginning to learn this lesson, and that a new phase of Soviet policy was in the making for south-east Asia. A change was noticed, for example, in the resolutions put forward at the Communist-sponsored 'Asia and Pacific Area Peace Conference' in Peking in October 1952. The eleven-day conference, unlike that in November 1949, passed without one reference to the need for armed struggle. The Chinese delegate spoke of a peace in south-east Asia which could raise the standard of living throughout the area, and his Soviet colleague declared: 'Each people here represented should have freedom to choose their own way of life, their own political system, and their own ideology.'

This was a reversal of a policy which had failed. Nationalism,

---

[1] Exceptions were India and Burma; India, because of the all-powerful Congress leadership, which actively rejected the Communists' advances, and in Burma, because of the split in the Communist party itself. In Malaya, too, Communist tactlessness and lawlessness alienated much sympathy at a time when by following the directive more closely they might have achieved results.

properly handled, could help Communism, Stalin had discovered.
It is interesting to note that the change of line on Asia made its
appearance while Stalin was still alive, and was to prove of great
importance to Stalin's successors when they faced the task of formu-
lating their own foreign strategy towards underdeveloped countries
after 1953.

VI

STALIN'S STRATEGY AND TACTICS
THE BALANCE SHEET: 1945–53

THE study of Soviet strategy and tactics from 1945 to 1953 in parts of the world where the Soviet Union or the Communist party were active allow certain general conclusions to be drawn. Communist ideology coupled with a new position of strength and fear of America's potential power reinforced the move to exploit the wartime achievements of the Soviet Union, to expand the territory of the Soviet Union, to increase the number of its dependent territories, and to raise the power and influence of the Communist parties throughout the world. Stalin's problem was to choose the correct strategy. It seems clear that at first he decided upon a strategy aimed at securing a protective belt of states on the periphery of the Soviet Union, and a policy of collaboration with local nationalist forces for countries outside the reach of Soviet land power. In Eastern Europe, already under Soviet military occupation, Communist Governments subservient to the Soviet Union were set up in the period 1944 to 1948, so that each country became, in effect, politically, economically, and socially part of the Soviet heartland. Each had to be protected on the same terms as the actual territory of the Soviet Union. In certain other areas bordering on the Soviet Union, which were selected by Soviet strategic planners as potential fields for expansion, attempts were made to build an enclave or base under the control of the local Communist party, with the idea either of separating that enclave from its parent country, or of using it as an area from which to expand at some later date. Examples of this strategy were the attempt to detach Azerbaijan from Persia in 1945–46, the exploitation of the civil war in Greece in 1946–49, the establishment of a Chinese and Communist base in Manchuria in 1945–46. The first two attempts failed: the third led ultimately to success, although the full story of the relationships between the Soviet and Chinese Communist parties is not easy to establish. It seems clear, however, that the Chinese Communists made an effort to fit in with Soviet plans and only diverged when they saw their chance to seize power over the whole country by means of a full-scale civil war.

It was only at the very end of Stalin's life that the strategy of expansion was reviewed by the dictator himself. At no time from 1944 to 1953 was there any suggestion that Stalin considered the ideological decision a wrong one, even though practical effort in most directions had come to a standstill by 1952. It merely seemed that certain strategic and tactical conceptions such as that adopted towards Asian countries from 1948 to 1952 had been misapplied or had outlived their usefulness.

Soviet tactics, however, changed frequently, both in the peripheral area of operations and beyond it. From 1945 to 1946 operations were carried on in the peripheral area apparently on the assumption that the United States of America was not prepared to use its great potential strength to lead the non-Communist world, and that Britain, immeasurably weaker than America, would be the only opponent of Soviet expansion. Tactically, therefore, the Soviet Union believed that the best policy for the Communist parties in the non-Communist world would be to nullify British or French opposition by entering national coalitions in Europe and Asia so that they could veto or sabotage anti-Soviet policies from the inside.

In the course of 1946 and 1947, however, it became clear that American strength would be employed in leadership of the non-Communist world. As the Russians saw it, the appearance of America as a champion of the Western world was a serious step backwards. America was the world's most powerful State, and possessed the means to make her influence felt all over the globe. Moreover, America possessed a monopoly of the atomic bomb, although the process was known in Moscow by 1947. By all the laws of power politics, the United States should have striven to force Russia to her knees. To meet the new situation the Soviet Union changed its tactics. In 1947 the Cominform was founded, a tactical move designed to tighten discipline within the Communist camp and to clarify and simplify the ideological position by defining the division of the world into two camps. Communist parties in Western countries forsook government coalitions, and launched offensives on the industrial and political front. In the following year the Soviet Union proclaimed Yugoslavia a heretic, organized the seizure of power in Czechoslovakia, and attempted to drive the Western Powers out of Berlin. In Asia the Communist parties' contribution to the struggle against America's assumption of leadership of the non-Communist world was to embark on the path of violence in circumstances which compelled the Communists to pit their strength against the forces of nationalism which were sweeping the area from Pakistan to the Philippines.

By 1950, it was clear that these tactics had brought no success to the Soviet Union in Europe. However, the military and political successes of the Chinese Communists and developments in divided Korea attracted the attention of Soviet strategists to possibilities of expansion in the Far Eastern peripheral area. The tactics chosen were those of limited war conducted by a Communist State, North Korea, against its non-Communist neighbour in the south. This gamble also failed, thanks to prompt action by the United Nations, and the Soviet Government changed its tactics yet again. From 1950 in Europe, and from 1952 in Korea, the Soviet Union waged a campaign of continuous pressure against the non-Communist world, using wearing-down tactics, without attempting to select a strategic soft spot for territorial penetration. Sometimes this pressure took the form of a guerilla movement designed to sap the strength of the country concerned, as in Malaya and Burma. Sometimes it took the form of endless obstruction and wrangling at the conference table—over Korea, the German problem, Austria, or Trieste. Sometimes pressure was restricted to propaganda, subversion and the activities of local Communist parties. It was an unrewarding struggle, yet the very fact that stalemate had been reached can only be interpreted as a defeat for Stalin. He had roused the non-Communist world to look to its defences, he had made a success of the United Nations' security organization, and he had opened the eyes of the vast majority of people in Europe and America to the realities of Soviet power and Soviet strategy. To be forced to adopt tactics of slow pressure in pursuing a strategy of peripheral expansion only five or six years after overwhelming military victory in Europe and the Far East could only be the result of faulty strategic decisions and tactics on Stalin's part.

Indeed, by the early 1950s the Soviet leaders appeared to have convinced themselves that the United States was seeking to block the Soviet Union's expansion or threaten its security, perhaps even exclude Russia from her place in world affairs. A good example was the Soviet attitude to the proposals put forward in 1950–51 by the American Government for a Japanese Peace Treaty. An American draft, prepared under the pressure of the war in Korea, claimed trusteeship of Okinawa and the other Ryukyu Islands, and allowed for a security treaty between the United States and Japan. Soviet amendments put before the Conference in San Francisco in September 1951 aimed at removing American power from Formosa, the Ryukyus and Japan itself. Deadlock was reached, but the treaty was signed by forty-nine out of fifty-five countries on 8 September, the absentees being Russia, China, Poland, Czechoslavakia, India, and Burma. There can be little doubt that the Soviet leaders regarded this treaty as a successful unilateral exercise of American power, and therefore as in some degree a failure in Soviet foreign strategy.

In fact, Stalin's successes came where the Soviet Army was in a position to lay a firm foundation for Communist political domination, and his failures occurred in areas where the case for Communism had to be put by persuasion, propaganda, and example. Why was Soviet propaganda so unsuccessful outside the reach of the Soviet Army, when the Soviet Union enjoyed a degree of popularity in Western Europe at the end of the war unequalled in Russian history?

First of all, as early as 1945, the Soviet Union returned to the full rigidity of Communist ideology concerning the inevitability of struggle between the Communist and non-Communist worlds. A prerequisite for action along these lines was the insulation of the Soviet people from the outside world. The Soviet people had to be convinced that there could be no relaxation of effort, for the war had weakened the capitalist system not only in Germany, Italy, and Japan, but in Russia's allies, Britain and America, as well. A few more crises, and capitalism would be destroyed. Soviet propaganda attempted to prove that economic disaster in the West was imminent, that the workers were in revolt, and that the colonial peoples of Asia and Africa were driving out their European masters. Coupled with this approach was a campaign of extreme nationalist chauvinism designed to prove that the Soviet Union and Imperial Russia had been the home of all significant scientific and military discoveries, and of culture and art.

The myths and legends about the Western world transmitted by radio, Press, and books to the unsuspecting Soviet people cannot be described in detail here,[1] but what is important is the Communists' colossal blunder in passing them on to the Western peoples them-

---

[1] Some of the more fantastic and ludicrous verbatim quotations from the Soviet Press and radio can be found in Paul Winterton's *Inquest on an Ally*. For example, discussing British general elections, the Moscow Youth paper *Moskovski*

selves, apparently unaware that such distortions of Western life
could only bring resentment and ridicule down on the head of the
Soviet Government. Of course, a relatively small proportion of the
people in the Western countries actually listened to Moscow Radio
in English or French, but the contents of Soviet 'isolationist' propaganda did filter through. For example, consider the damage done to
the Soviet cause by the Government's ban on marriages between
Soviet citizens and foreigners, which was brought home to the
British people by the Soviet refusal to allow the Russian wives of
British subjects to join their husbands in Britain. The short-sighted-
ness, for example, of broadcasting to Britain, only two years after a
war in which aerial bombardment had destroyed hundreds of houses
in London alone, the comments of a visiting Soviet professor who
described the British housing programme and the temporary pre-
fabricated houses on bombed sites as 'pitiful', is extraordinary.[1] So
was the claim that the British Admiral Lord Nelson had learnt his
seamanship from a Russian admiral, that the convoys on the Arctic
run from Britain to Russia, which had suffered such severe losses,
had been of little importance.[2] The sustained effort of the Royal Air
Force's Bomber Command against German war potential was dismissed as having had no influence on the outcome of the war. On
13 June 1944 Stalin had described the crossing of the Channel on
D-day as 'one of the greatest military operations in history', but a
few years later his propagandists were writing about it as the 'so-
called invasion of Western Europe', and announced that it had only
taken place after the German forces defending the Channel coast
had been withdrawn to the Russian front. In 1941 and 1942 Britain

---

Komsomolets referred its readers in January 1947 to the *Pickwick Papers* and
wrote: 'Eatanswill is an imaginary place, but what Dickens wrote correctly
describes English reality' (p. 211). On the transfer of power in India, a radio
commentator said: 'It is symptomatic that though the British Government has
declared itself ready to make India independent, the proposals do not proclaim
even dominion status for India, let alone independence. At the same time the
police in India have been reinforced, the prisons are being enlarged, and the
enormous British Army maintained.' A month after independence, in September
1947, Moscow Radio said: 'The Indian Army will remain under the British.
Large British forces will remain in India' (p. 205).

[1] Professor Palladin, who was invited to Oxford University in 1947 to read a
scientific paper.

[2] As late as 1957 the Soviet Army paper *Red Star* awarded a prize to a Soviet
naval officer for a short story on this theme, in which he described how a British
Arctic convoy had been saved from destruction only by decisive action by the
Soviet Navy.

sent numbers of her latest tanks which she could ill spare to Russia;
in September 1947 the British audience was informed by Moscow
Radio that they proved to be useless compared to Soviet tanks.

Much of this short-sighted and malicious abuse sailed harmlessly
through the ether, but enough reached the British public to lower
Soviet prestige and ruin the Soviet attempt to pose as the friend and
ally of this country.[1] It was not, of course, confined to Britain:
France, the United States of America, Italy, Holland, Belgium, and
Scandinavia all received their share of lectures on Soviet superiority,
in a stream of propaganda compiled and presented in blind ignorance
of the national feelings or sympathies of the intended audience. It
was a glaring psychological error which did much to turn public
opinion away from whatever genuine merits a Soviet case may have
had.

Another reason for the failure of Soviet propaganda in Western
Europe was its hypocrisy, an outstanding example of which was the
'Peace Campaign'. This was launched in 1949 at a time when Soviet
prestige was low after the failure to drive the West out of Berlin, to
win the civil war in Greece, and to stamp out heresy in Yugoslavia.
It was mainly directed to the populations of Western Europe who
had suffered most from two world wars, and it was a kind of psychological rearguard action to cover a Soviet retreat.[2] It is interesting to
note that at first the campaign seems to have been less interested in
appealing to Asian opinion, perhaps because in 1949–50 war was
bringing good results in China, Burma, Malaya, Indo-China, and
Korea.

The object of the Soviet 'Peace Campaign' was to convince the
peoples of the world that America and Britain were preparing for
war against the Soviet Union, while the Soviet Union was pursuing
only a policy of peace. In 1949, a 'World Peace Council' was set up
at a meeting which was the precursor of a series of Peace Congresses
in various countries. One of these Congresses, in 1950, produced the
Stockholm Peace Appeal, to which millions of signatures were sup-

[1] It is possible that the cumulative effect of such propaganda was one of the
factors leading to the rejection by the British public at the general election in
1950 of practically every candidate who had been vociferous in supporting the
Soviet point of view in Parliament since 1945.

[2] Soviet ideologists were careful to point out that the Peace Campaign was
only an auxiliary, and should not be confused with the struggle for Communism.
In the Soviet journal *Bolshevik*, 1952, Stalin wrote: 'Under certain circumstances,
the struggle for peace may develop in one place or another into a struggle for
socialism.'

posed to have been affixed. Soviet and Communist propaganda media publicized its activities with all the means at its disposal, but the effect was negative. The Council praised the peaceful nature of Soviet policy, but it failed to explain why the Soviet Union maintained the largest army in the world. The sincerity of the main sponsors of the World Peace Council, the Communist parties in Western Europe, was called in question when, at the height of the Peace Campaign, each party was called upon to make a formal pledge to support the Soviet Army if the latter reached its territory. And the Soviet decision to use limited warfare in Korea in 1950, followed by the lengthy and complicated arguments used by Soviet spokesmen in the United Nations and elsewhere to prove that war to unite a divided country was in fact justifiable, destroyed any lingering impression in Europe that the Peace Campaigners were interested in peace as such.[1] But the main reason for its failure to further the aims of Soviet foreign policy was that its target was that part of the population most able to measure it against Soviet deeds, particularly Soviet readiness to use armed force when circumstances permitted.

Another field where Soviet argumentation and behaviour failed to convince the non-Communist world was the United Nations. At first, Soviet policy in the United Nations was apparently based on the belief, with which the Soviet Government was in general agreement, that the United States and Britain intended it to be a kind of twentieth-century Holy Alliance, a Supreme Council by which the four or five Great Powers could rule the world. The original United States' suggestion of a veto for the Great Powers in the executive organ, the Security Council, as embodied in Article 27 of the United Nations Charter (which was due to the rights of the United States Congress to control American participation in the kind of action which the Security Council might authorize), as well as President Roosevelt's readiness to discuss the Far Eastern settlement bilaterally with the Soviet Government, without Britain or China at Yalta in February 1945, probably appeared to Stalin as proof of this view of the United Nations. The shock to the Soviet Government when it was realized that this was not the Western intention, that the United Nations was to be among other things a forum in

---

[1] The definition of 'pacifism' to be found in the Soviet *Dictionary of Foreign Words*, edited by Lekhin and Petrov, reads: 'Hypocritically hiding behind the slogan "pacifism", reactionaries oppose all liberation, revolutionary, civil, and other just wars. Pacifists deceive the workers and conceal the preparations for the imperialist wars of the bourgeoisie.'

which the Soviet Union, along with any other country, could be censured, was all the greater, and the Soviet reaction all the more vigorous and resentful.

The Soviet Union first encountered the true Western conception of the United Nation's task during the Soviet-Persian crisis of 1945–46. Soviet actions in setting up a pro-Communist Government in Persian Azerbaijan were widely criticized in the United Nations, and the Soviet reaction was awaited with particular interest. This came in March 1946 when, after the failure of the Soviet delegate's attempt to delete the Azerbaijan question from the agenda of the Security Council, the delegate and his staff walked out rather than listen to the speech of the Persian delegate. This action, which was followed by the Soviet Union's use of the veto to screen Albania's guilt in the Corfu Channel dispute, gave a preview of the Soviet attitude to the United Nations, particularly the Security Council.[1] If the matter under discussion could be exploited to further Soviet foreign policy, or to bring discredit on the United States, Britain, or France, no delegation was more forward in referring it to the United Nations. But if the subject concerned Soviet policy, particularly if criticism of Soviet actions was made or implied, the Soviet delegation would not co-operate;[2] it either withdrew from the debate or applied the veto in the Security Council. If the Soviet Government did initiate a proposal, it was usually found to contain provisions against its exploitation to the detriment of the Soviet Union. Thus the Soviet Union vetoed all suggestions for the modification of the use of the veto, although the other permanent members of the Council were ready to restrict its use. When the creation of a United Nations force was discussed between 1946 and 1948, the Soviet delegate proposed that members' contributions should be no more than those of its weakest member.[3] A force to which all contributed as many troops as, say, Holland or Belgium could hardly be effective in opposing any action undertaken by the Soviet Union.

[1] Britain accused Albania of responsibility for the sinking of two British destroyers with the loss of forty-four lives as a result of striking mines in the Corfu Channel in 1946. Britain's case was upheld, but the Soviet veto prohibited action.

[2] A Radio Moscow commentator confirmed this in July 1946: 'Unanimity' (i.e. the veto) 'is a safeguard against the danger that certain reactionary groups would use the organization as a means of isolating socialist or new democratic régimes', quoted in Winterton, op. cit., p. 223.

[3] See *United Nations Yearbook 1948*, 'Report of Military Staff Committee', issued on 30 April 1948.

Soviet tactics in the United Nations over the question of the Greek Civil War made a profound impression. At first the Soviet delegate vetoed a proposal to hold a United Nations inquiry at Greece's request into allegations that the Communist states on Greece's northern border, Albania, Yugoslavia, and Bulgaria, were helping Greek rebels to overthrow the legal Government. In December 1946, however, the Soviet Union agreed to take part in such an inquiry, but her delegates did all they could to render it ineffective. The Soviet delegate in the Security Council vetoed an Australian motion merely calling on the parties involved to 'cease provocation and enter into direct negotiations', and vetoed a suggestion to transfer discussion to the General Assembly.[1] Three years later, when war broke out in Korea, there was little doubt that aggression conducted under Soviet auspices might have gone unpunished if the Soviet delegation had been in its place in the Security Council when the latter met to consider the Communist invasion of South Korea.

Disarmament and the control of atomic energy was another vital subject raised both within and outside the United Nations on which the Soviet attitude ran counter to Soviet propaganda, and therefore had a damaging effect on her international reputation. As soon as the Second World War was over, the United States of America, the only country which had constructed and used an atomic bomb, submitted a plan on atomic energy to the United Nations, drawn up by Mr. Baruch, the veteran American statesman. It proposed an international authority to own all uranium mines and plant capable of being used to produce atomic weapons, with powers of inspection of these plants in whatever country they might be. In cases where action by the Security Council would be necessary, the veto would not apply. This plan was rejected by the Soviet Government, which brought the full weight of its propaganda machine to bear against it and its American authors. Instead, the Soviet Union suggested the banning of the atomic bomb, and the destruction of all existing stocks of such weapons—in other words, the Russians asked the Americans to give up unilaterally the only weapon which they had capable of matching the vast army of the Soviet Union. In March 1947 the Soviet delegate at the United Nations, Mr. Gromyko, declared categorically that the Soviet Union would never agree to any plan giving an international body the right to interfere with Soviet industrial production.

[1] See *United Nations Yearbook 1947–48*, pp. 348–50.

Meanwhile, the Soviet Union was making progress towards the manufacture of its own atomic weapons.[1] In October 1948, when a successful explosion of an atomic bomb was probably in sight, the Soviet Government put forward new proposals, one for atomic weapons, and one for conventional weapons. The first contained the declaration that atomic weapons should be eliminated and banned, but that plants capable of manufacturing them should remain under national control, and only subject to periodic inspection, while the control system would be subject to the veto in the Security Council. On conventional armaments, the Soviet plan envisaged a reduction in the armed strength of each major power by one-third, without disclosing the number of troops or establishments to be dealt with in this way. It was not difficult to see how this plan would leave the Soviet Union, relatively, in the same position of superiority in conventional forces as before.[2] Deadlock was reached on both subjects, and although in 1952 the United Nations set up a new Disarmament Commission, in which the Soviet delegates agreed to serve, the Soviet refusal to consider any effective system of international inspection with sanctions against offenders remained the main stumbling-block to agreement during Stalin's lifetime. In fact, until his death the Soviet attitude throughout was so clearly dependent on Soviet progress in arming the country with atomic weapons that public opinion in Europe and America became accustomed to regard Soviet pronouncements on disarmament, nuclear or conventional, as part and parcel of Soviet foreign policy planning.

The foregoing study of the reasons why Soviet propaganda in Western Europe and America failed to create a favourable atmosphere for Soviet expansion, when taken together with the strategical and tactical errors already outlined, provide the back-

[1] The Soviet policy on atomic disarmament has to be studied against the background of her own search for atomic weapons. Documents published during the Canadian spy trial in 1946 show that the search was in full swing as early as March 1945 (see *Report of the Royal Commission*, Ottawa, 27 June 1946, pp. 447–57). The first Soviet explosion of such a weapon came in 1949. While the Russians were relatively far from this achievement, their main disarmament theme was the destruction of American stocks; as they approached their goal, the theme changed to one aimed at preventing international control or inspection of Soviet plants.

[2] The Soviet Union reorganized its Army after the war into 175 line divisions and forty artillery and A.A. divisions; of the former total, sixty-five were armoured, with eighteen armoured and four infantry divisions in East Germany

ground to Stalin's last major pronouncement on foreign affairs. This took the form of an article entitled 'Economic Problems of Socialism in the U.S.S.R.' in the magazine *Bolshevik* published in September 1952, just before the Nineteenth Congress of the Soviet Communist party. The main theme of this article was an attack on Soviet economists who had lost their sense of proportion and of reality, and had come to believe that Soviet society could change the laws of nature, of economic progress and could even make new laws of science and economics. Stalin advised caution and realism. He maintained that the struggle between America, Britain, France, and Italy, and later Germany and Japan, for what remained after the Second World War of the pre-war world market upon which 'capitalist' economics depended, would sharpen and become more bitter because the total area was getting smaller and smaller. And Stalin concluded that in these circumstances, the outbreak of wars between individual capitalist countries was still likely; as he put it:

The capitalist countries' struggle for markets and the desire to drown their competitors turns out to be stronger than the contradictions between the camp of capitalism and the camp of Socialism. The question is, what guarantee is there that Germany and Japan will not rise again to their feet, that they will not try to wrest themselves from American bondage and live their own independent lives? I think there are no such guarantees. And it follows that the inevitability of wars among the capitalist countries remains.

Stalin's article, which was published in time for the opening of the Nineteenth Party Congress in October 1952, was treated as a new directive by all speakers at the Congress, and particularly by Mr. G. M. Malenkov, who read the main report on behalf of the Central Committee of the party. Referring to foreign policy, Malenkov said:

It would be wrong to think that war can be launched only against the Soviet State. It is common knowledge that the imperialists unleased the First World War long before the U.S.S.R. came into existence. The Second World War began as a war between capitalist states, and it inflicted severe damage on the capitalist countries. The antagonisms which

---

—a total of 2,800,000 men. At the same time, in 1949–50, the United States active army had a strength of 596,000, organized in twelve divisions, only one of them in West Germany. For details see *Brassey's Annual 1951*, pp. 250–51 and 260. The advantage of Soviet 'one-third' plan from their point of view is not hard to appreciate.

now rend the imperialist camp may lead to a war of one capitalist state against another.[1]

Owing to the peculiar circumstances of the last five months of Stalin's life, it is difficult to say what this directive might have led to in Soviet policies in Europe had he lived to put it into effect. Stalin was clearly preoccupied with the fabrication of the 'Doctor's Plot', of which Mr. Khrushchev spoke so vividly at the Twentieth Party Congress in 1956.[2] But in Asia the new line decreed by Stalin was evident in the resolutions of the Asian and Pacific Peace Congress,[3] which predicted a rejection of a policy of armed struggle, and encouraged all classes in small nations to combine against the United States. He might well have initiated a period of tactical collaboration with non-American capitalist states, using his influence to weaken their ties with the North American Continent. The fact remains, however, that his new policy hung fire in Europe, and we are left with only the directive itself, which he handed on to his successors unfulfilled.

Stalin himself made only one brief public appearance at the Nineteenth Party Congress, but his speech was relevant to foreign policy. It was addressed to the foreign Communist delegates present at the Congress. Stalin encouraged them with promises of an expected split in the Western camp, and chided them gently to spur them on to greater efforts. But one wonders if, as he surveyed them, he recalled how their public support had shrunk compared with 1945. In Europe only Signor Togliatti could boast of an increase in membership. In Britain the Communist party had fallen from 45,000 members to 33,000, and lost its only two members in the House of Commons. In France membership fell from 907,000 in 1947 to 506,000 in 1953. In Denmark the party membership dropped from 45,000 to 16,000; in Norway from 40,000 to 7,000; in Western Germany it dropped from 200,000 to 75,000, and was halved in Holland, Sweden, and Switzerland.

Indeed, the verdict on Stalin's conduct of foreign strategy and his tactics in Europe must be this: wherever the Soviet Army set foot,

---

[1] G. Malenkov: *Report to the Nineteenth Party Congress on the work of the Central Committee of the C.P.S.U.(R.)* on 5 October 1952: Foreign Languages Publishing House, Moscow, 1952.

[2] Certain Jewish doctors were accused on 13 January 1953 of causing or plotting the death of leading Soviet military figures; the charges dating back to 1945. After Stalin's death, the whole affair was exposed as having no foundation.

[3] See above, p. 57.

it usually succeeded in establishing a Communist régime. In Asia, Communism scored a great success in China, though the effort was Chinese, not Russian. In areas where new nations were appearing, Stalin's premature use of the Communist parties against the local forces of nationalism after 1948 proved to be a blunder. But although he attempted to make a last-minute adjustment in his strategical and ideological approach in 1952, ignorance, obstinacy, and an unrealistic reliance on the threat of force seem to have been Stalin's major failings as a planner of foreign policy: the Twentieth Congress of the Soviet Communist party in 1956 showed that Mr. Khrushchev thought so, too. The new leaders who succeeded Stalin in 1953 inherited a new directive on foreign policy; they also came to the conclusion that if they were going to avoid many of Stalin's mistakes, they would have at least to be well informed on the areas in which they intended their foreign policy to operate.

VII

THE FOREIGN POLICY OF THE MALENKOV
GOVERNMENT: 1953-55

STALIN died on 5 March 1953. His powers in the Soviet Union were divided between the leading members of his entourage with a sense of urgency which underlined the new leaders' need to survive the shock of his death without disturbance among the Soviet population. Within twenty-four hours Mr. G. M. Malenkov assumed the premiership and the post of First Secretary of the Communist party. L. P. Beria, V. M. Molotov, N. A. Bulganin, and L. M. Kaganovich became Deputy Premiers, each taking charge of a vital part of the State machinery—internal security, foreign policy, the armed forces, and industrial production. This 'collective leadership' carried the State and party without untoward incidents through the period of Stalin's funeral, and helped to ensure that the régime survived the transfer of power to the oligarchy which succeeded the solitary rule of the aged dictator.[1]

Soon afterwards the emergency structure of power began to shift and show signs of breaking up. First, Mr. N. S. Khrushchev, the party's second-in-command and Party Secretary in Moscow, was admitted to the oligarchy, succeeding Mr. Malenkov as the First Secretary of the Soviet Communist party on 25 March.[2] Soon afterwards, on 5 April, Mr. Beria used his authority in matters of security to release from custody the doctors arrested on charges of treason in January, a move generally interpreted as designed to increase his own prestige and popularity. Mr. Beria also promised the Soviet people an end to arbitrary arrest, and a return to 'socialist legality and justice', and forthwith proclaimed an amnesty for many types

---

[1] Although widely attributed to Lenin and Stalin, the modern conception of oligarchic rule by 'collective leadership' was explained in detail in an article in *Kommunist*, No. 11, July 1953, by F. Yakovlev. For English translation see Meissner and Reshetar, *The Communist Party of the Soviet Union*, pp. 203-22.

[2] Mr. Malenkov's readiness to hand over the key post of First Party Secretary is one of the most puzzling acts of his brief career as Premier. There is no evidence that he was under pressure from his colleagues, and yet his experience with Stalin must have made him aware of the great power of the party post. If it was a miscalculation on his part, it led straight to his downfall in 1955.

of prisoners. It seems that these acts alarmed Beria's colleagues in the oligarchy; they suspected a plot on his part to seize power, and on 26 June, they ordered his arrest on charges of trying to overthrow the Government. The speed with which the rest of the oligarchy acted, and the support they won from the leaders of the armed forces have been interpreted as indicating that a *coup d'état* by Beria and the N.K.V.D. Generals of the Moscow Garrison was, in fact, a possibility.[1] One contributory factor to the decision to arrest Beria may have been his fall in prestige due to the failure of his colleagues in the East German police to suppress the rising of the East German workers on 16-17 June. The Germans' inefficiency may have helped to convince Beria's colleagues that his actual power was less than had been feared. Beria was tried and executed at the end of the year, and with his death and that of the N.K.V.D. Generals Abakumov and Ryumin, the security apparatus which Stalin had created was split up and brought under party control. During the next few years the concentration camp population in the Soviet Union was gradually reduced, and the general fear of the 'State Security' which had been so marked a feature of Stalin's rule faded considerably.

This was the first great change of 1953; but there were others, equally important, in home and foreign policy.[2] When Stalin died the Soviet Union's foreign policy was in a state of stagnation, largely due to the failure of many of Stalin's strategic decisions for Europe and Asia. On many important issues between East and West the Soviet Government had either broken off contact or was locked in stalemate. Four-power government of Germany hardly existed, and only the most superficial formal contacts continued between the Allied representatives in Berlin. Both sides were engaged in building up separate German States along Western or Communist lines. In Korea, although armistice negotiations were in progress, most of the committees were in a state of permanent suspension—mainly on the issue of the future of those Chinese and North Korean prisoners of

---

[1] The crisis surrounding Beria's arrest is one of the most intriguing mysteries of recent Soviet history. Up to 1953 the key posts in the Moscow Garrison had been held by Generals not of the Army, but of the N.K.V.D., who were responsible to Beria, i.e. the C.-in-C. of the Moscow District and of the city's garrison, the Commandant of Moscow City, and the Commandant of the Kremlin; there was also a division of N.K.V.D. troops in the capital. After Beria's arrest, these officers were replaced by Generals from the Regular Army, and in 1954 the command of the N.K.V.D. Army itself was entrusted to an Army officer, General Perevertkin.

[2] For a discussion of Mr. Malenkov's economic policies, see Ch. VIII.

war who did not wish to be repatriated.[1] Negotiations for an Austrian State Treaty had continued fruitlessly for years, and the Foreign Ministers' Deputies appointed to work out an agreed draft had suspended their meetings. Contacts between the Soviet Union and Yugoslavia and Greece were minimal, and the Soviet Union had broken off relations with Israel during the crisis which followed the arrest of the Jewish doctors in January 1953. There was even deadlock over the nomination of a successor to Mr. Trygve Lie as Secretary-General of the United Nations; moreover, the Soviet Union took an active part in only a few of the Organization's scientific or technical committees.

Russia was, in fact, so isolated by lack of contacts with other countries that it was practically impossible for its Government to have a positive policy in international affairs. It is not surprising, therefore, that the new leadership showed itself interested in restoring some of the contacts broken needlessly by Stalin, without prejudice to future strategy or tactics. Restoration of contacts could have the additional advantage of reducing tension between the great powers during a period of transition at home.

This was the motive underlying Soviet foreign policy in the months following Stalin's death. An early opportunity for the Soviet leaders to put it into effect occurred on 12 March 1953, when Soviet and British aircraft became involved in a collision over the Soviet zone of Germany. The Soviet reaction, which was conciliatory in tone, contained a suggestion for a three-power conference on air safety over Germany. In New York, the Soviet Government withdrew its objections to the appointment of Mr. Dag Hammarskjöld as Secretary-General of the United Nations, and Mr. Malenkov offered to resume diplomatic relations with Israel, a proposal which was accepted in Jerusalem. In Eastern Europe abuse of Yugoslavia by the Soviet Union began to dwindle, and in June the Soviet Government proposed the re-establishment of full Soviet-Yugoslav diplomatic representation. The East European governments who were members of the Cominform began to follow suit, toned down their anti-Yugoslav propaganda, and offered to make amends over frontier disputes.[2] On 30 May the Soviet Government withdrew all

[1] The Communist negotiators, largely from motives of prestige, refused to accord prisoners of war the right to determine their destination on release and demanded that they should all be returned to China or North Korea, if necessary, by force. The U.N. Command, on humanitarian grounds, refused to consider this.

[2] In Hungary a slightly more liberal and less anti-Yugoslav Government came

her territorial claims against Turkey, and suggested a new approach to the problem of the Straits.

Perhaps even more interesting than these diplomatic moves was evidence of a new departure in the Soviet attitude to publicity for the Western point of view. On 25 April 1953 the Soviet newspaper *Pravda* published a speech by President Eisenhower, objectively and without accompanying abuse. More encouraging still was a Sino-Soviet initiative which gave new life to the Korean armistice talks in Panmunjom. The leaders of the Chinese Communist Government had visited Moscow for Stalin's funeral in March, and shortly after their return to Peking it was announced in Panmunjom that the North Korean and Chinese Army Commands had found themselves able to agree to a United Nations' proposal on the immediate exchange of wounded prisoners of war. Two days later, on 30 March, the Chinese Government agreed to discuss the repatriation of all prisoners without consideration of the use of force against those unwilling to return to their homelands.

This declaration was the first move in a slow, difficult, and tortuous advance towards agreement which led first to an exchange of prisoners, and later to an Armistice which put an end to the Korean fighting. In spite of the delays and interruptions inherent in negotiating with the Communists, it became clear that both Chinese and Russians had decided to put an end to the war, while insisting, for reasons of prestige, that North Korea and her 'volunteer' allies from China had been the ultimate victors in the struggle. When a renewal of fighting was threatened in July 1953 by the South Korean Government, the Chinese Communists launched a powerful offensive against a Korean-held sector of the line and inflicted a tactical defeat upon the South Koreans which had the desired effect of modifying the belligerency reigning in Seoul.[1] The Armistice was signed on 27 July

---

into being on 30 June 1953 when Mr. Imre Nagy was appointed Prime Minister, and introduced plans for the reorganization of industry and agriculture.

[1] This reason for the offensive was confirmed by Peking Radio on 21 July 1953. In the context of the South Koreans' reluctance to sign an Armistice while Chinese troops remained in North Korea, it is interesting to note that within two weeks of the Armistice, on 7 August, an extensive purge was carried out in the North Korean Government and Communist party. The victims included a Vice-Premier, a former Foreign Minister, and seven members of the North Korean Communist party's Central Committee. It has been suggested that this purge represented the Communist reaction to a parallel opposition in North Korea to an Armistice while United Nations forces still remained on South Korean soil. (Royal Institute of International Affairs, *Survey, 1953*.)

1953, and among its accompanying provisions was a proposal for a new conference on the political reunification of Korea.

The signature of the Korean armistice marked the end of the first series of Soviet initiatives to restore contacts with the outside world. When Mr. Malenkov addressed the Supreme Soviet on 8 August 1953 the Soviet Government was no longer isolated from the rest of the world by severed diplomatic relations and suspended negotiations. By the end of July the Soviet Union and China were in formal contact with the Western Powers in Korea, and were free once again to seek advantages for the Communist cause in negotiations denied to them in a military stalemate. The Soviet Government had re-established contact with Yugoslavia and with Israel, and had made a new approach to Turkey. Diplomatic discussions on specific Anglo-Russian problems had opened in Moscow, and an inter-allied conference on Air Safety over Germany had been summoned. Encouraged by the hope that these Soviet moves might be the prelude to a more realistic approach to the major problems facing the Great Powers, Western leaders began to consider a high-level exploratory meeting with the new Soviet leadership. The initiative came from the British Prime Minister, Sir Winston (then Mr.) Churchill in speeches to the House of Commons on 20 April and 11 May. The idea gained ground in France and later in the United States; after a preliminary Anglo-French-American meeting in Bermuda, the Western Powers sent an invitation to Moscow on 10 July 1953 proposing a conference on outstanding problems at the end of September.

In Moscow the Western offer was not, however, accepted. When Mr. Malenkov did put forward his interpretation of the international situation—in his speech to the Supreme Soviet on 8 August—it was not regarded as encouraging in the West. In his attempt to separate the United States from its allies, the Soviet Premier appeared to be influenced by Stalin's last pronouncement on foreign policy in September 1952.

France, Britain, and Japan, singled out by Stalin in this connexion, were described as seeking ways to escape from their existing dependence on the United States. While the Soviet leader spoke of the possibility of normalization of Soviet-American relations—as Stalin had often done—the United States was harshly attacked as a war-mongering, war-profiteering state, as the organizer of subversion against the Soviet Union and other Communist countries, and as a self-appointed guardian of the world. Some non-Communist countries like Persia, Turkey, Afghanistan, Pakistan, and India were praised by the Soviet Premier, and in one brief but significant phrase Mr. Malenkov made an oblique reference to Stalin's theory of the divisions within the 'capitalist' camp:

'One of the decisive advantages of the democratic camp, which is its principal point of difference with the imperialist camp, is that it is not torn by internal contradictions and struggles. . . .'[1]

The speech, with its open attempt to concentrate the world's anger against the United States, seemed to offer little hope of a new Soviet approach to foreign policy. One reason for the Soviet Premier's attitude was not difficult to find, for he was speaking only a few weeks after the first attempt by a nation ruled by a Communist party to rise in active demonstration against the régime. This had occurred in East Germany in June 1953, and may well have shaken the confidence of the new leadership to its foundations. The East German Communist régime had run into difficulties in its industrial and agricultural plans which were partly due to the economic demands of the Soviet Union. On 28 May 1953 the East German Government, in an attempt to cut its wages bill, raised industrial norms in a number of industries, and this led to demonstrations of protest by East Berlin workers in the streets of the city on 16 June. Official spokesmen were shouted down, and a delegation called on the Government to reduce the cost of living and agree to free elections. A hurried decree restoring the cuts in wages came too late to be effective and on the following day, in a series of mass demonstrations, Berlin's industrial workers became virtual masters of the city. Communist officials were attacked and manhandled, the red flag was torn from public buildings and Communist propaganda material was burnt, while Government leaders took refuge in buildings guarded by Soviet troops. At midday on 17 June 1953 the Soviet Army moved in. Three mechanized divisions blockaded Berlin itself and, in taking up positions at key points, clashed with demonstrators, some of whom were killed and injured. The Soviet Commandant, General Dibrova, declared a state of emergency and forbade all street demonstrations. Within two hours of this order a West Berlin resident, Willi Goettling, was executed under martial law as a 'provocateur'. In view of the obvious determination of the Soviet High Command to crush the strike by force, the workers'

[1] *Pravda*, No. 221, 9 August 1953, p. 3.

leaders, while repudiating their own Communist régime, advised against a head-on clash with the Soviet Army, and cleared the Berlin streets.

Meanwhile, news of the workers' protest spread throughout East Germany, and in Magdeburg, Leipzig, Dresden, and other cities, the workers seized control, and set up their own committees. Here again the Soviet Army intervened, though in many places with less effect than in Berlin, for the workers in the provincial factories went on strike, barricading themselves in their factories, from which the Russians were reluctant to force them out by military action. Relative calm was restored when the East German régime confessed its mistakes and failures, and agreed, temporarily, at least, to many of the demands of the strikers. For their part, the strikers saw little hope of dislodging a régime so firmly entrenched behind the Soviet Army. But the suddenness and widespread success of the workers' action, coupled with the evidence it provided of the nation-wide hatred of the Communist régime, must have come as a great shock to Mr. Malenkov and his colleagues, and doubtless made them less ready to depart from the orthodox methods used by Stalin. And this probably contributed to the disappointing contents of his speech on 8 August.

However, in September, the Western Powers renewed their invitation, proposing a meeting at Lugano on 15 October to deal with Germany and Austria; but the Russians called for concessions involving Western defence measures as a prior condition to the solution of the German problem. The exchanges continued throughout the winter, until hopes were raised again when the Soviet Government agreed to a meeting of Foreign Ministers in Berlin to begin on 25 January 1954.

To many diplomats and journalists who covered the Berlin Conference on Germany and Austria in 1954 the Soviet approach appeared to be the same as that used at all previous conferences on this thorny subject. As in the past, Mr. Molotov presented the Soviet case, which amounted to rejection of Germany's freedom to choose her own future, and accompanied his presentation by distorting Western motives in drawing together for defence. Britain, France, and the United States proposed to solve the German problem beginning with free all-German elections, leading to the formation of an all-German Government and the convocation of a Peace Conference. Mr. Molotov proposed a merger of the existing Governments of East and West Germany, a Peace Conference at which Germany should be represented by this joint Communist-Western coalition Government, and finally, free elections. The Western Powers refused to put the Communist régime in East Germany which had not been elected by the people it claimed to represent and had called in foreign troops to put down a rising of its own workers—on the same level as the elected Government of Western Germany. From this it became clear early in February 1954 that the Soviet Government would not agree to free elections in Germany until the two halves of the country had been artificially united by placing the Communist leaders of the East side by side in one Cabinet with the elected representatives of Western Germany. Furthermore, the Russians demanded the subsequent neutralization of Germany, and the abandonment of N.A.T.O. and the Western Alliance, as an integral part of their price for agreement on the German problem.

Once again, therefore, the discussions on the future of Germany reached deadlock, where they were soon joined by those on Austria. In order to reach a quick decision on an Austrian State Treaty, the Western Allies had proposed to the Soviet Government in March 1952 a simple joint declaration that Austria was a sovereign state, and that all foreign troops should be evacuated. The Soviet Government refused to discuss this project, or even to resume talks on the Austrian problem until this suggestion was withdrawn. This the West agreed to do, but found that their concession merely led to new and more complicated conditions added by Mr. Molotov. He declined to fix a date for the withdrawal of Soviet troops on the grounds that evacuation would lead to a new *Anschluss* with Western Germany, and insisted on linking Austria with an agreement on Trieste.

On 18 February 1954 the Berlin Conference came to an end with the publication of a communiqué stating that the four powers had been unable to agree on Germany, Austria, or European security.

One result of the discussions on these subjects was clarification of the unwillingness of the Soviet Government to submit the Communist régime in East Germany to the test of public opinion. The question, therefore, which caused surprise was not that there was no agreement, but why Mr. Molotov came to Berlin at all. The publicity surrounding his Government's fear of free elections could only damage Russia's reputation, and the haggling over Austria emphasized the Soviet refusal to give up a profitable military occupation of a rich and valuable corner of Europe. It is, in addition, very un-likely that so experienced a negotiator as Mr. Molotov expected the Western Powers to discuss seriously the disbandment of N.A.T.O. and a merger of the East and West German Governments. It is probable that the Russians came to Berlin first and foremost to make their new Government's position on Germany clear, particularly with the memory of the Berlin rising so fresh in their minds. It is also possible that the Russians had another motive for stalemate in Europe which may have been connected with events taking place in the Far East.

It appears possible that the Soviet leaders decided to turn their attention to the situation in Indo-China, where there was some danger of the war spreading. Mr. Malenkov and his colleagues had learnt from Stalin to concentrate their full attention on one strategic area in foreign policy at a time, and if the Far East was to be the centre of attention, it would be most wise to see that the situation on the other main fronts, particularly Europe, was stable, or at least in a state of deadlock. A conference which reaffirmed the Soviet intention to maintain the *status quo* in Germany and Austria would be likely to discourage new initiatives in Europe during a crisis in the Far East.[1]

No one would deny that the situation in the Far East was critical in the spring of 1954, and attention was particularly directed to the north-western corner of Indo-China, where an important battle was raging between Communist-led Viet-Minh forces and the French Army in Indo-China for the possession of an earth-work defence position, not far from the Siamese and Chinese frontiers, named Dien Bien Phu.

By the end of 1953 the Viet-Minh forces in Indo-China, which had risen in rebellion against the French in 1946, were in control of most of the northern part of the country except for the Red River

---

[1] On 16 February 1954 Mr. Molotov suggested that Soviet and Western diplo-matic representatives should be instructed to resume discussions of the Austrian Treaty in the series of meetings which had gone on since 1945. On 25 March 1954 the Soviet Government declared East Germany a sovereign state, and among the effects of this move was the refusal of the Soviet Ambassador, Mr. Semenov, to discuss technical measures to ease the division of Germany, on the grounds that they were in the competence of the East Germans. Both moves helped to ensure the *status quo*. This is, naturally, only one explanation of Russia's agreement to attend the Berlin Conference. It is also possible that the new leader-ship, involved as it was in internal problems, had simply not considered practical alternatives to the standard policy on Germany and Austria.

delta and Dien Bien Phu. This village had been reoccupied and fortified by the French Army in November 1953 in order to help in the defence of Laos, one of the Associated States in the French Union. Although the main battlefront was in the north of Indo-China, Viet-Minh troops and partisans were active in Central Annam, in Cochin China—and in the capital, Saigon, itself. The large numbers of men engaged on both sides made the war in Indo-China more than a struggle to put down an outbreak of partisan warfare. By 1954 some 200,000 French troops and about 300,000 South Vietnamese troops and militia, faced about 335,000 Viet-Minh regulars and guerillas. But what really riveted attention on Dien Bien Phu was that since the end of the war in Korea the war in Indo-China had acquired the proportions and some of the characteristics of an East-West clash in which intervention by the United States and Communist China could lead to the outbreak of a third World War.

It was in this situation that the Soviet Government announced on 18 February 1954, the final day of the Geneva Conference on Germany and Austria, that it was ready to take part, along with the Chinese Communist Government, France, Britain, the United States, and the Associated States of Indo-China, in a conference on Korea and Indo-China, also to be held in Geneva. But before the Conference met changes occurred in the military situation. First, the Viet-Minh Army launched an assault on Dien Bien Phu, and by the middle of March had achieved some important successes in breaching the French defences. At about the same time the Chief of the French General Staff, General Ely, arrived in Washington after a tour of Indo-China, with news of the gravity of the military situation there which reversed the more optimistic reports then current in the American capital.[1] These two events, when seen in the context of France's apparent readiness to discuss a settlement of the problem of Indo-China with the Communist powers gave many Americans a feeling that a new Far Eastern 'Munich' was being prepared which would lead to the abandonment to the Communists of an important area in south-east Asia without a struggle. The French Government naturally wanted to save Dien Bien Phu and were not averse to a certain degree of American help in this respect. The Americans, however, regarded Indo-China as possibly the next testing-ground in the struggle between Democracy and Communism, and were

[1] See footnote, p. 83.

ready to consider action along with their allies to hold the anti-Communist front on this sector.[1] In the first week of April some Americans in authority contemplated an air strike by carrier-based aircraft against the Viet-Minh army at Dien Bien Phu, and there was some talk of land intervention either by American or allied ground forces as well. The American Government attributed the successes of the Viet-Minh to the military and political influence of Communist China, and suspected the Chinese of exploiting the war in Indo-China to compensate for their failure to drive the United Nations out of Korea. In the words of Mr. Dulles on 5 April, 'China was saving herself from the charge of aggression only by technicalities.'

Neither France, who was directly involved, nor Britain saw the situation in Indo-China in the same light. Unless Communist China openly and aggressively intervened in the war, they saw little hope of persuading their peoples that the issue between Communism and Democracy was being fought out in Indo-China. Public opinion in Western Europe was centred upon the Far Eastern Geneva Conference which opened on 25 April. Until 8 May the Conference dealt only with Korea, and failed to make progress. But on that day, twenty-four hours after the fall of Dien Bien Phu, the Ministers turned to the subject of Indo-China.[2] Progress was slow, but by 29 May the participants had authorized the opening of military discussions by local commanders in Indo-China on regrouping of forces, and the first meeting took place on 2 June. Soon afterwards, however, the French Government fell, and the new Premier, M. Mendès-France, introduced a new element of drama into the Conference by undertaking to achieve a settlement in Indo-China by 20 July or to resign. After a recess of three weeks to allow the local talks to proceed, the Foreign Ministers reassembled on 12 July, and after eight days of feverish activity, and within minutes of the time-limit, agreement to end the war was reached and an armistice signed.

The settlement, generally speaking, was based on the principle of partition of the State of Vietnam, and the establishment of four States in Indo-China; Laos, Cambodia, and South Vietnam remained with the French Union, while a Communist-organized

---

[1] See Royal Institute of International Affairs, *Survey 1954*, pp. 21–42, for detailed account of the moves apparently contemplated by the U.S.

[2] It would have been consistent with Communist tactics to have extended discussion of Korea until the fall of Dien Bien Phu, in order to place France and her allies at a disadvantage during the negotiations.

People's Democracy was established in North Vietnam with its capital at Hanoi. The United States declined to accept responsibility for the settlement, although it declared that it would not upset it by force.

One important fact which emerged from this Agreement was that the Soviet and Chinese Governments must have taken a critical decision to assist in putting an end to the war in Indo-China at a time when a complete military victory over the French seemed to be in sight for the Viet-Minh Army. Indeed, there were suggestions that the Viet-Minh were displeased with the Geneva terms.[1] There are, in general, two possible interpretations of this decision. One is that put forward by the then Secretary of State, Mr. Dulles, who claimed in a newspaper interview that the United States Government's readiness to intervene against the Communists in Indo-China prevented war and convinced the Communist powers of the need for a settlement.[2]

This interpretation depends on the assumption that the Soviet Union and China wanted to press on with the war, and changed their views only when the United States Government made public its readiness to intervene. But this readiness was first mentioned by Mr. Dulles in his speech on 29 March 1954, and was urged by leading figures in America, including the Vice-President, only in the latter part of the month. It was underlined by subsequent declarations and movements of air and naval forces in late March and the early part of April. Yet the Soviet Union had agreed to discuss Korea and Indo-China as early as 18 February, that is, before official American spokesmen had talked of intervention, and at a time when American political and military leaders still took an optimistic view of France's military prospects in Indo-China. Throughout February, indeed, U.S. leaders specifically denied any intention to intervene or threaten armed support for France.[3] In fact, the Soviet Government, carrying with it the Chinese Government, may have taken the decision to stop the war in Indo-China at a time when American intervention seemed

[1] See the *New York Times*, 25 July 1954, and the account of the French Commander in the Red River delta, Gen. Cogny, of Viet-Minh prospects in that area. The Viet-Minh campaign in Laos in November–December 1953 gave some indication of the mobility and striking power of the Communist Army.

[2] Mr. Dulles' case was put in an interview in *Life* magazine on 16 January 1956.

[3] See statements by President Eisenhower on 12 February, of Mr. Wilson, Secretary of Defence, on 9 February, and Admiral Radford on 18 February. All assessed the chances of France favourably, and denied the need for U.S. ground or air intervention.

unlikely, because in these circumstances the creation of a new Communist State seemed to be a practical possibility.

This interpretation is based on the assumption that Mr. Malenkov's Government was guided in its foreign policy by Stalin's strategy, if not always his tactics. We have seen how on many occasions since 1944 Stalin attempted to create a Communist-controlled enclave in a country bordering on Soviet territory as a first stage to the ultimate absorption of the whole state by the Communist bloc. It was attempted in Korea, in Persia, in Manchuria, and in Greece. Now the situation of the Viet-Minh Communist forces in northern Indo-China probably suggested to the Soviet leaders that as soon as the last French outpost of Dien Bien Phu could be captured the whole area would be ripe for the establishment of an enclave bordering on Communist China. To extend Viet-Minh conquests southwards might increase the risk not so much of U.S. intervention, but of defeat by the French Army, as it fell back on more secure bases, a defeat which might deprive the Viet-Minh of some of its existing achievements. A halt in February 1954 would enable a compact Communist State to be set up, which, in fulfilment of Stalin's strategy, could later, perhaps, be used as a base for a further advance. It seems probable, therefore, that the motive behind the Soviet proposal for the Geneva Conference was one of timing: to choose the best moment in the development of the Viet-Minh movement to turn it from a partisan army into a Communist State. The subsequent American belligerency served, no doubt, to hasten Soviet readiness to agree, but was not the prime motive behind the negotiations.

If this was Mr. Malenkov's plan, then it succeeded, for a new Communist State—North Vietnam—appeared on the map of the world in 1954. This success in the Far East was, however, the only one registered by Mr. Malenkov's régime, for after the crisis in Indo-China had been settled, attention turned once again to Europe. Having secured stalemate on Germany and Austria in February 1954, the Soviet Government devoted its efforts towards the rejection of the European Defence Community, through which Western Germany was expected to contribute to the defence of the West. Throughout the summer of 1954 the debates in the Western parliaments on the Community rose to a climax in Paris on 28 August, when the French Assembly refused to ratify the agreements.

Soviet Press and Governmental reaction was, of course, jubilant, and on 9 September hailed the French decision as 'an important event in the political history of Europe'. But the rapid conclusion of the Paris and London Agreements in October, which brought Western Germany into N.A.T.O. as a sovereign state, overwhelmed Soviet policy by its speed and completeness. Earlier in the year, after the failure of the Berlin Conference, the Soviet Government had made efforts to summon a meeting on European Security by suggesting that Russia and some of the East European countries should join N.A.T.O. This had been rejected in the West, but the Soviet Government now submitted another proposal in more specific form. On 23 October 1954 it proposed a new four-power Conference on the re-unification of Germany and free all-German elections; the four powers should then call an all-European Conference on European Security, and should, in the meantime, reopen discussions on Austria. The Soviet Government followed this Note with an invitation on 13 November to twenty-three European States to attend a conference on European Security, at which the United States and China should be represented as observers. The Conference, it was suggested, should begin on 29 November, so that it could precede the parliamentary debates on ratification of the Paris and London Agreements. The Note also carried the kind of threat on German re-unification which, it was probably hoped, would secure the rejection of the Nine-Power Agreements, as the E.D.C. had been refused. The Note said:

The realization of the London and Paris Agreements would mean that the unification of Germany by means of free all-German elections would fall victim to present plans for restoring German militarism.[1]

On 20 November, Mr. Molotov added a further warning in an interview with *Pravda*. He stated:

Therefore, if it comes to the point of ratification and implementation of the Paris Agreements . . . a new situation will arise in Europe which will only aggravate the threat of a new war. In such circumstances, the peace-loving European States will have to give thought to new measures to guarantee their security.

Nine days later, on 29 November 1954, the Western Powers replied to the Soviet invitation, declining to attend the European

[1] Text of Soviet Note of 13 November 1954. It was noted in the West that this reference to 'Free all-German elections' for the unification of Germany had not, apparently, appealed to the Soviet Government at the Berlin Conference in February, when the entry of West Germany into N.A.T.O. was not an issue.

Security Conference, and confirming their determination to press on with the ratification of the London and Paris Agreements. On the same day the Conference, attended only by the eight countries of the Soviet bloc and an observer from China, opened in Moscow. On 2 December the participants issued a communiqué declaring their readiness to take part in a European Security organization if the Paris Agreements were abandoned; otherwise they would set up their own defence headquarters to safeguard their security. At the same time, Mr. Malenkov's Government threatened to denounce the Anglo-Soviet and Franco-Soviet Treaties of 1942 and 1944 respectively as incompatible with the entry of West Germany into N.A.T.O.

There can be no doubt that the Western plans for the association of Western Germany with the defence of the West introduced a new sense of urgency into Soviet policies. Perhaps the Soviet leaders genuinely feared a new German Army allied to N.A.T.O., and the influence which the German Government might have on the Western Alliance. But undoubtedly their greatest fear was the increased strength such an acquisition would give to N.A.T.O., and thus first and foremost to American military and political power in Europe.

This happened at the end of December 1954, and already Mr. Malenkov's days as Soviet Premier were probably numbered. His dispute on internal economic policy and defence with Mr. Khrushchev was certainly in its final stages, and the visit of a Soviet delegation to China led by Mr. Khrushchev and Marshal Bulganin probably provided an occasion for securing Chinese approval of the decision to replace Mr. Malenkov at the earliest opportunity.

Mr. Malenkov's handling of the situation which arose after the signing of the London and Paris Agreements was negative, and characteristic of Soviet reaction when the initiative lies, even temporarily, in the hands of the Western Powers. In view of the fact that Mr. Malenkov's successors reversed some of his decisions on foreign policy in 1955, it is possible that his conduct of strategy and tactics also came under fire from his rivals in the party, and added reasons for his removal. Yet Mr. Malenkov did take two major strategic decisions with regard to the wars in Korea and Indo-China, of which his detractors could not complain. His Government used its influence to bring these two wars between Communist and non-Communist forces to an end, and to restore political or diplomatic contact between the belligerents. The Malenkov régime added a new Communist State to the Sino-Soviet bloc, the first since 1948. It also successfully abandoned certain of Stalin's tactics in East-West relations and adopted a more reasonable attitude towards the non-Communist world in diplomatic and social matters. On the other hand, the new leadership showed itself as inflexible as Stalin on the future of Germany and Austria and on the political reunification of Korea. In each case the stumbling-block to progress in the Western sense was the already traditional Soviet unwillingness to submit Communist régimes to the test of public opinion through free elections. Moreover, Mr. Malenkov proved during the East German rising that any attempt by the peoples of the countries of Eastern Europe to throw off the Communist régime by popular revolt or strikes would be thwarted by all available means, including the use of the Soviet Army.

We must conclude, therefore, that Mr. Malenkov was not an initiator of foreign policy in 1953 or 1954. His policy was based upon Stalin's post-war strategy, with the modifications introduced in the autumn of 1952, but never put into effect by Stalin, largely because of the distractions of internal affairs. In negotiations over Germany and Austria—and above all, in dealing with the East German rising—Mr. Malenkov acted in the spirit of the decisions of Stalin's later years. It was left to those who overthrew Mr. Malenkov in 1955 to make a major break with Stalin's legacy in strategy and tactics in the field of foreign affairs.

VIII

THE SOVIET DEFENCE DEBATE
1953–56

IN the preceding chapter we traced briefly the foreign policy conducted by the collective leadership under Mr. Malenkov up to his resignation as Premier on 9 February 1955. One reason for Mr. Malenkov's fall was certainly a personal struggle for power between himself and Mr. Khrushchev. These two men, so different in temperament and background, had crossed swords before, and were to do so again.[1] Each knew that Stalin had put through his policies by fear, and that this had had ill effects on progress in industry, agriculture, military doctrine, and social life. Each recognized the need for change. As their views diverged on the nature of the changes required, the two leaders found themselves involved in a struggle for supremacy, which was resolved in Khrushchev's favour first in February 1955 and, more dramatically, in June 1957.

In 1953 both Mr. Malenkov and Mr. Khrushchev realized that agriculture and the standard of living had to be improved and raised, but later came to differ on the degree of relaxation which the country could afford to achieve it. Mr. Malenkov appeared to believe that the Soviet Union, having achieved wonders in heavy industry, could afford to produce more consumer goods upon the basis of existing industrial power. He declared the Government's intention of raising the standard of living in two or three years, and of supplying the shops with 32,000 million roubles' worth of goods, an increase of ten per cent over the original target of the 1950 Plan. It is important to note that at this stage the Government's plans were not directed against heavy industry. Mr. Malenkov said:

> In the future we will develop our heavy industry—our metallurgy, fuel, energy, chemical, forestry, machine-building, and construction industries. We must always remember that heavy industry is the basic foundation of our socialist economy, for without its development, the future growth of

[1] In his 'secret' speech to the Central Committee in February 1956, Mr. Khrushchev revealed that Mr. Malenkov had opposed him at a critical time in the battle for Kharkov in May 1942.

ight industry, of agriculture, and of our country's defensive strength is
impossible.[1]

It was only after making this proviso that Mr. Malenkov went on:

It is on the basis of successes already achieved in the development of
heavy industry that we now have conditions in which to organize an important rise in the production of consumer goods.[2]

At first it seems that Mr. Malenkov and Mr. Khrushchev did not
differ basically on what ought to be done to rescue the Soviet
economy from the stagnation of Stalin's later years.[3] But in the
course of 1954 serious differences of opinion developed between
them on the actual priorities in the allocation of resources to the
producer and consumer industries, and Mr. Khrushchev, backed by
a strong element in the party and by the armed forces, led a movement whose interpretation of the needs of the situation differed from
that of the Premier, and gradually found its way into the public
mind. By the autumn of 1954 the official Soviet Press was stressing
once again the unique importance of priority for heavy industry, and
of its further development. In October 1954 Mr. Khrushchev himself
spoke on this subject, significantly enough just after a visit to China.
On 24 January 1955 *Pravda* severely criticized those who advocated
priority for consumer goods, and Mr. Khrushchev described such
people in a speech on the following day as resembling the 'right'
deviation of Rykov and Bukharin—two of Stalin's victims of the
purge in the 1930s. This accusation pointed straight at Mr. Malenkov,
and on 9 February 1955 he resigned. He was succeeded as Premier
by Marshal Bulganin, and the Marshal, with Mr. Khrushchev at his
side, took over direction of affairs.

It should not be assumed, however, that the producer-consumer
controversy was the only motive behind the clash between Mr.
Malenkov and Mr. Khrushchev. Together with the struggle of personalities for leadership it played a great part; but at the same time
an equally significant debate was going on in Party and military
circles on defence, the hydrogen bomb, and military doctrine, in
which the two leaders found themselves on opposite sides. This

---

[1] See the Soviet journal *Komunist*, No. 8, April 1954, for an early attack on
those who advocated the consumer goods at the expense of heavy industry.

[2] Translated from *Pravda*, No. 21, 9 August 1953, p. 1.

[3] See A. Bergson, 'The Russian Economy Since Stalin's Death', in *Foreign
Affairs*, January 1956. 'In 1953 the new Government reduced little, if at all, the
share of this investment going to heavy industry' (p. 215).

debate had a great effect on the Soviet attitude to disarmament and foreign policy, and also undoubtedly played a part in the fall of Malenkov himself. In order to understand what happened, it is necessary to look back to Stalin's lifetime to see where Soviet military thought stood before the debate began.

As far as atomic energy was concerned, Soviet official interest in the first atomic bombs dropped on Japan in August 1945 has been described as 'limited'. On 24 September 1946, after the first series of major United States tests at Bikini, Stalin, in answer to a question, said:

I do not believe the atomic bomb to be as serious a force as certain politicians are inclined to regard it. Atomic bombs are intended to intimidate the weak-nerved, but they cannot decide the outcome of a war, since atomic bombs are by no means sufficient for this purpose.

Nevertheless, Soviet scientific investigation proceeded rapidly, and on 6 November 1947 Mr. Molotov declared that for the Soviet Union the secret of the atomic weapon had ceased to exist long ago. On 23 September 1949 the Soviet Union exploded its own atomic bomb.[1] Even so, the explosion had little effect on Stalin's military thought which was condensed, as far as publicity was concerned, in an Order of the Day issued in his name on 23 February 1942. Stalin maintained that there were five constant factors which win wars, listed in this order: first, the stability of the home front; second, the morale of the armed forces; third, the quantity and

---

[1] The Soviet Union's policy over atomic weapons was double-edged. In propaganda to the West the Soviet Government emphasized the inhuman nature of atomic weapons, the awful destruction they caused and the horror of atomic radiation. During debates in the United Nations the Soviet delegate frequently called for the unconditional banning of all atomic weapons on those grounds (which would have left the conventional Soviet military force unsurpassed in the world). But in the Soviet Union itself the destructiveness and efficiency of the weapon was played down. A typical example of the line taken by the Soviet military-political Press as late as 1955 was the following extract from an article in *Red Star* by Major-General B. Olisev, on 3 August 1955: 'There are reliable ways and methods of protection from an atomic bomb. Troops well-prepared and trained for action can . . . fulfil any tasks. One thing is clear: the blanket of secrecy has been torn from atomic weapons. Their effective characteristics and real potentialities have been greatly exaggerated by the enemies of peace for the purpose of blackmailing world public opinion, of intimidating people with the "horrors" of atomic war.' The author went on to give some very optimistic advice: 'Having seen the flash of the explosion, one has time to lie down on the ground, or, if there is a shelter nearby, to hide in it, because the shock wave travels from the point of explosion at a distance of 1,000 metres in approximately two seconds. . . . This is time enough for taking measures of protection.'

quality of the divisions; fourth, the armament of the armed forces, and fifth, the abilities of the commanders.[1]

Stalin also maintained that other factors, such as surprise, climate, and natural and geographical features were only temporary in modern war. They could prolong a war and influence its course, but not change its outcome.[2] Again, Stalin laid down that Western military thought was developing in the context of capitalism, which cannot possess the five contant factors, and therefore was not capable of progress.[3] Capitalist armies, therefore, had to rely on surprise and other temporary factors to bring them victory. Thus, Western countries were doomed in advance in any war against the Soviet Union. Finally, Stalin believed that the correct defence policy for the Soviet Union in peacetime would be to prepare the country for a planned retreat into the great spaces in the interior of the country, wearing down an advancing enemy. Once full mobilization had been achieved, all five constant factors would come into play and the enemy would be destroyed in a massive counter-offensive.[4]

The implications of this overall military doctrine are easily seen. While the basic principles of the five constant factors appear to be orthodox military thought, the consequences of accepting *automatic* and *exclusive* Soviet superiority in these factors could be highly dangerous for the defence of the Soviet Union in an age of atomic weapons. Soviet soldiers and politicians brought up to rely on the superiority of the Soviet political system to defeat any enemy, no matter how well armed and experienced he might be, would be unlikely to press for imaginative modernization of the fighting forces or of the home defence of the U.S.S.R. They would, of course, work hard to bring their existing land, sea, and air forces to the highest pitch of efficiency, but their overall belief in the inevitability of Soviet victory could prevent full consideration of the implications of atomic and nuclear weapons. This is exactly what happened under Stalin, and is the background to—and the reasons for—the big debate on defence which began in 1953.

Very little of the early stages of the debate, which was apparently conducted in the restricted Soviet military Press, has become

---

[1] *Large Soviet Encyclopaedia*, 2nd Edition, Vol. 34, p. 255.
[2] See Colonel I. Mariganov: *The Principles of Soviet War Science*, 1951, and *Large Soviet Encyclopaedia*, 2nd Edition, Vol. 8, 'Surprise (military)'.
[3] Stalin's letter to Colonel Razin, *Bolshevik*, Moscow, 1947, March issue.
[4] See *Large Soviet Encyclopaedia*, 2nd Edition, Vol. 8, 'Art of War', by General N. V. Pukhovski.

available to the non-Soviet reader.[1] It was only after the fall of Mr. Malenkov in February 1955 that the subject came under public discussion. From the evidence available it became clear that a group of Soviet military thinkers, in investigating the effect of atomic and nuclear weapons on modern war, put forward a set of entirely new tasks for the armed forces, which could have a significant implication for home and foreign policy.

These military thinkers, many of whom came to occupy high positions in the defence establishment after 1955, drew attention to the danger that a nuclear attack could paralyse a country before the constant factors had time to come into play. Thus, on 24 March 1955, the Soviet Marshal of Armoured Forces, P. A. Rostmistrov, published an article (probably written much earlier), in the daily newspaper of the Soviet Army, *Red Star*, which was the signal for the presentation of the new line to the public.[2] Rostmistrov was careful to uphold the continuing validity of the five constant factors: he wrote:

> It can easily be understood that the growing importance of surprise in no way diminishes the importance of the constant factors in deciding the outcome of a war. What is more, the role and significance of these factors is increasing.

But he went on to bring in the added dangers created by nuclear weapons in these words:

> It is necessary to state clearly that in certain cases a surprise aggression with the use of atomic and hydrogen weapons may appear to be one of the decisive conditions for the achievement of success, not only in the initial period of a war, but in the war as a whole.

This modestly-worded deviation from Stalinist military doctrine opened the way for other Soviet military leaders to add their support and to draw the logical conclusions. Marshal I. K. Bagramyan, one of the Deputy Defence Ministers, wrote:

> From the history of wars and the art of war it is clear that the element of surprise in striking a blow at an adversary ensures considerable advan-

---

[1] This point is discussed in an article by N. Galai: 'New Trends in Soviet Military Doctrine', in the *Bulletin of the Institute for the Study of the U.S.S.R.*, Vo.. 3, No. 6, 1956, p. 9. It may also be significant that in early 1953 the Chief of the General Staff, General Shtemenko, was replaced by Marshal Sokolovski, who held the post till 1960. But see the interesting account in *War and the Soviet Union*, by H. S. Dinerstein (Atlantic Books), pp. 37 et seq.

[2] *Red Star*, 24 March 1955: 'For a creative solution to the problems of Soviet military science.'

tages to the aggressor in war. The importance of the surprise element increases with the contemporary development of armed forces and military techniques, as an unexpected blow may be struck not only at the forces deployed at the front, but also at strategic objectives—important political and economic centres situated far from the front line.[1]

Marshal S. S. Biryuzov, the Commander of the Air Defence of the Soviet Union, emphasized the difficulties his command faced owing to the rapid increase in the speeds of aircraft and the heights at which they fly. He went on:

> Jet-propelled aircraft, carrying atomic or thermo-nuclear weapons, are capable of covering great distances very quickly and striking a blow at a country's administrative, industrial or military centres situated well in the interior.[2]

It was left to a leading Soviet strategist and military historian, Major-General N. A. Talenski, to put the issue squarely before the Soviet military and political leaders. Writing in the journal of the Soviet General Staff, *Military Thought*, he explained:

> The problem is not merely one of explaining the surprise factor, or of studying facts and examples of the use of surprise in the last war. Our task is to work out a solution seriously, paying attention to methods, a system of advance warning of surprise aggression by an enemy, and of dealing him forestalling (*uprezhdayushchie*) blows at all levels—strategic, operational, and tactical.[3]

According to this body of military opinion, if immediate preparations for a nuclear strike against the Soviet Union were detected by Soviet intelligence, it would be the duty of the Soviet armed forces to forestall it by striking the first blow against the launching bases. For, as a well-known Soviet writer on military doctrine, Colonel V. Emelin, wrote:

> In order to deprive the enemy of the possibility of using his atomic weapons in a surprise capacity, it is essential to carry out ceaseless intelli-

---

[1] *Oktyabr*, No. 5 (May 1955).

[2] *Voennie Znanie* (Military Knowledge), *No. 8* (August 1956). The first reference to nuclear warfare in these terms appeared in an article by Marshal V. I. Chiukov in *Red Star* on 3 February 1955. He was followed by Marshal Sokolovski the Chief of the General Staff, and Marshal Vasilevski.

[3] *Military Thought*, No. 5 (May 1955). With this article—indeed this issue of *Military Thought*—the Soviet public debate had covered the ground in nuclear weapons' debates in the U.S.A. and Britain in 1954. For a summary of Western conclusions, see Royal Institute of International Affairs, *Survey, 1954*, Chapter 'Atoms and Strategy'.

gence of all kinds, and to keep all the enemy's activities under constant observation. This . . . will enable us to strike a powerful and immediate blow with our air force and long-range artillery against the enemy's means of atomic attack as soon as they are discovered, in order to disrupt or weaken his atomic strike.[1]

Articles published in 1955 also reversed Stalin's views on Western military science, and credited N.A.T.O. with an up-to-date and efficient doctrine of war, and great military strength. These articles revising military doctrine became available to the public immediately after the fall of Mr. Malenkov and the appointment of Marshal Bulganin as his successor (with Marshal Zhukov as the Minister of Defence), but they were written and debated in 1954. They represented the conclusions of a group of military thinkers with whom, it is fairly clear, Mr. Malenkov did not agree.[2] Indeed, there is good evidence that Mr. Malenkov and some of his colleagues had come to their own conclusions on the significance of nuclear weapons and their effect on defence and foreign policy soon after he announced, on 8 August 1953, that the Soviet Union possessed a hydrogen bomb. The first indication of these conclusions with which, as it later transpired, Mr. Malenkov was in sympathy, came in the November 1953 number of the theoretical party magazine *Zvezda*. A certain M. Gus mentioned that nuclear weapons opened possibilities of 'paralysing the law of the inevitability of war', and suggested that a foreign policy could be found which would involve compromises and wise concessions.[3] Gus's theory was, it is true, attacked by some party officials, but on Lenin's anniversary, on 21 January 1954, the speech was made by a senior member of the Presidium, Mr. P. N. Pospelov, who avoided the usual references to Lenin's views on war. A curious discrepancy appeared in the speeches of the leaders at the Supreme Soviet session in March 1954. The Premier, Mr. Malenkov, Mr. Pospelov, Mr. Pervukhin, and Mr. Saburov declared that the armed forces of the Soviet Union possessed everything they needed to carry out their tasks. The First Secretary of the party, Mr. Khrushchev, Marshal Bulganin, Mr. Molotov, Mr. Kaganovich, and President Voroshilov demanded the further strengthening of the Soviet forces.

[1] *Sovremennaya Voennaya Tekhnika* (Contemporary Military Technique), Moscow, 1956, p. 131.
[2] See Dinerstein, op. cit., p. 171, for an admission by the editors of a Soviet military journal that they had held back publication of an article on this theory.
[3] M. Gus, *Zvezda*, No. 11, 1953, as quoted by Dinerstein, op. cit.

In March 1954 Mr. Mikoyan, the Soviet Deputy Premier, speaking in Armenia, said that the danger of war had receded largely because the Soviet Union possessed atomic and hydrogen bombs.[1] On 12 March 1954 Mr. Malenkov himself made his position even more clear in terms which indicated that he agreed with the writer in *Zvezda*:

> The Soviet Government is resolutely opposed to the cold war, for this policy is a policy of preparation for another world slaughter, which, given modern methods of warfare, means the destruction of world civilization.[2]

Although these quotations are of necessity incomplete, they show that in 1953–54 Mr. Malenkov and some of his colleagues were prepared to look upon weapons of mass destruction as a deterrent to global war. This argument implied that neither the Soviet Union nor the U.S.A. would risk such destruction, and both sides could therefore manoeuvre *within* the limits of global warfare, which would enable the Soviet Government to readjust Russia's internal economy, and, if necessary, to use her armed forces in limited warfare. Further, it is possible that Mr. Malenkov may have been influenced in this respect by Stalin's prophecy (which he himself had quoted at the Nineteenth Party Congress in 1952) that a war between capitalist countries was more likely than one between the 'capitalist' and the Communist powers. The 'capitalists' would be even less ready to use nuclear bombs against each other, and such wars would probably be fought largely by conventional forces. If the Soviet Union were to intervene, it would be with conventional forces, and therefore priority in defence planning should go to their modernization. Those who adhered to this argument would be less likely to require a drastic revision of military doctrine, since they saw relatively little need to prepare for global nuclear war. At all events, while Mr. Malenkov was Premier the Soviet Marshals faithfully repeated the

[1] Speech by Mr. A. Mikoyan in Erivan, Armenia, on 12 March 1954. The disputed passages in this speech were not reproduced in the Moscow Press. (See Dinerstein, op. cit., p. 71.)

[2] It is true that on 26 April 1954, Mr. Malenkov reversed his position on the universal destructiveness of nuclear war, and publicly endorsed the orthodox view that it would inflict enormous damage to both sides, but that only capitalism would be annihilated. It is unlikely that Mr. Malenkov really changed his views so radically in six weeks, and he may have agreed to make this particular recantation purely on grounds of Communist orthodoxy. His earlier view regrettably placed capitalism and Communism on the same level—a disastrous error to those claiming the inevitability of Communist victory.

Stalinist formula in articles in the Press,[1] and their uniformity lends weight to the belief that Mr. Malenkov himself supported the 'mutual deterrent' theory of the hydrogen weapon, and was reluctant to publicize any divergent views.

Ranged on the other side was the main body of the professional service chiefs, whose views came to be shared by Mr. Khrushchev. To the military, as has been seen from their articles, the significance of the hydrogen bomb meant not so much its deterrent power, but the conditions in which it might have to be used, both by the Soviet Union and the United States. As soldiers, they tended to envisage situations in which the U.S.A. might attack the U.S.S.R. with nuclear weapons without warning, and they believed that this required a drastic reorganization of military doctrine. In reply to a question on the validity of the theory of 'mutual deterrence', two days before his assumption of the Ministry of Defence, Marshal Zhukov replied:

> I consider this to be an incorrect point of view . . . unfortunately, such irresponsible statements have been made by many prominent military leaders—for instance, Montgomery and Gruenther.[2]

These, then, were the opposing sides in the defence debate of 1953-54, and, as it turned out, Mr. Malenkov's views were overruled after he had resigned.

The professional soldiers, once their theories had been accepted by the new Government, demanded a military establishment capable not merely of preventing nuclear war, but of waging it.[3] Acceptance

---

[1] See Marshal Sokolovski's article in *Red Star* on 23 February 1954. Marshal Vasilevski's in *Red Star* of 9 May 1954. There was, however, after May 1954 a move away from attributing the constant factors to Stalin personally.

[2] Marshal Zhukov's interview with Hearst, Smith, and Conniff, Moscow, 7 February 1955, *Manchester Guardian*, 2 February 1955.

[3] A major reorganization of the Soviet Army in 1955-56 was undertaken along these lines, in the course of which the Air Defence Command of the Soviet Union was raised to the status of a fourth arm of service on the same level as the Land Forces, the Air Force, and the Navy. Part of the fighter strength of the Air Force was detached and placed under the Air Defence Command, and the Soviet forces began to consider the possibility of having to fight two kinds of war simultaneously: the defence of the Soviet Union as one commitment, and the defeat of the enemy's armed forces as an entirely separate operation, perhaps waged outside the borders of the Soviet Union in order to avoid the worst effects of atomic radiation. It can also be seen that such a defence programme would require full priority for heavy industry, and why the military chiefs were so opposed to Mr. Malenkov's ideas on this subject.

of this theory had one important implication for foreign policy. If the professional soldiers expected that hostile nuclear attacks could be made against industrial and administrative targets far in the interior of the Soviet Union, then there could no longer be any safe area into which the Soviet land forces could retreat in order to gain time to mobilize. The Army, therefore, could not be relied upon to 'buy time' by 'selling space' as it did in 1941–42, and should not be put in this position by the Government's foreign policy. Therefore, according to the military, the planning of foreign policy should be tied in very closely with the Army's readiness to forestall or parry a nuclear blow. It seems that Mr. Khrushchev agreed with the Generals that once a weapon had been invented in this world of strife it was the duty of statesmen and their military advisers not to rely on its deterrent qualities, but to prepare the country for its use, both defensively and in the context of a forestalling blow against an enemy about to strike. After all, a nuclear war, according to Communist orthodoxy, would be far more dangerous to the brittle society of capitalism than to Communism, and therefore a convinced Communist could think of war not only with horror at its destructiveness, but with a degree of confidence in the ultimate outcome denied to his capitalist opponent.[1] It can be seen, therefore, that Soviet military planners had come to the conclusion by 1955 that surprise long-range attack with nuclear weapons was the greatest threat to the security of the Soviet Union, and among the fields where this conclusion carried new weight was disarmament. Hitherto, Soviet disarmament proposals had aimed at forcing the United States to give up stocks of atomic and nuclear weapons, and to accept fixed cuts in conventional forces (for example, a cut of one-third in all national forces). Acceptance of this proposal would have left the Soviet Army unrivalled in strength anywhere in the world. This call for the abolition of nuclear weapons was repeated as late as February 1955, but on 10 May, the day on which the Communist-sponsored World Peace Council was to meet in Helsinki, the Soviet Government introduced a new proposal on disarmament which basically

---

[1] See, for example, Mr. Khrushchev's speech to the East German editors, 5 August 1959: 'You may say, but would the Soviet Union suffer no losses in the event of war? Yes, it would have losses, and great ones. But while we would suffer losses, the Western Powers would be literally wiped off the face of the earth.'

altered the Communist line and caused the hurried abandonment of the meeting of the Peace Council.[1]

Briefly, the essence of the Soviet proposals was that a two-stage disarmament programme should start in 1956 and be virtually complete by the end of 1957. From the moment of acceptance in principle to the beginning of 1956, there should be a 'freeze' of all armed forces, conventional armaments, and military expenditures at the level of 31 December 1954. Early in 1956 the five Great Powers would begin a programme of cutting down their armed forces which, by December 1957, would reach the following levels: for the U.S.A., the U.S.S.R., and China, 1 to 1½ million men each; for the U.K. and France, 650,000 men each, with corresponding reductions in armaments and defence expenditures. About one-half would be completed by the end of 1956.

After this had begun a world disarmament conference would be convened—not later than June 1956—which would debate and fix the disarmament obligations of all armed states, including a ban on tests of nuclear weapons, and negotiations for the gradual liquidation of military bases on foreign soil. All countries would undertake not to use nuclear weapons, even against aggression, except in execution of a decision of the Security Council.

This procedure, it was proposed, should be complete by December 1956. In 1957 the remaining reductions in conventional forces would be carried out, and all foreign bases would be given up. Half-way through this second stage, the production of nuclear weapons would cease, complete prohibition of their use ruled, and all stocks gradually eliminated. By the end of 1957, therefore, the plan envisaged the possession by each of the great powers of conventional armies of fixed size without nuclear weapons, stockpiles, or foreign bases.

The Soviet proposals envisaged certain measures of international control. In 1956 observers employed by an agreed control organ would be stationed at large ports, railway junctions, roads, and aerodromes, 'in order to prevent a surprise attack by one state on another'. The control organ would have the right to demand informa-

---

[1] The postponement of the Helsinki World Peace Council meeting from 10 May to 22 June is evidence of the suddenness of the change in Soviet policy, and implies close links between Soviet disarmament proposals and the advice of Soviet military chiefs on the defence of the U.S.S.R. When the Council did meet, its final report reflected the Soviet change of view in the following sentence: 'An effective abolition of nuclear weapons cannot be obtained as an isolated act, and must take place within the framework of a general disarmament scheme.'

tion on the progress of the plan in each country and have access to national records on military expenditures. In 1957 the control organ could 'inspect on a continuing basis to the extent necessary to ensure implementation of the convention', and have inspectors stationed in each country with unimpeded access to what the proposals called 'all objects of control'. Violations at all stages would be reported to the Security Council.

Let us leave aside for the moment the objection that recommendations for action against violators would be subject to the veto in the Security Council and concentrate on the proposals as they appeared to Soviet policy planners in May 1955, remembering as general background the research into the use and effect of nuclear weapons going on in the Soviet Army.

The new Soviet proposals went a considerable distance towards the acceptance of existing Western ideas on a disarmament programme. The Russians accepted the Western figures for the levels of forces to be permitted to the five Great Powers, the Anglo-French proposal of 19 April 1955 for beginning the elimination of nuclear stocks after three-quarters of the reductions in conventional forces had been completed, and the principle of setting up a single international control organ with expanding functions as the plan was put into operation. The Soviet proposals also omitted the rigid and automatic cut of one-third in all defence forces. For the first time the suggested control organ would be allowed to send international observers to selected points behind the Iron Curtain.

What would happen, in the Soviet Government's view, if these proposals were accepted and put into effect step by step? Marshal Bulganin threw some light on this in a speech in Warsaw on 11 May 1955.

It is difficult to imagine that states which do not trust each other and whose relations are strained, would admit controllers from other countries to their military plants and enterprises manufacturing atomic materials and atomic and hydrogen weapons. . . . Even if such control were possible, it would be ineffective, since, in the absence of mutual trust, avoidance of this control would be possible. This is all the more probable because the technology of atomic production makes it possible rapidly and without any particular difficulty to convert atomic materials earmarked for peaceful uses into atomic weapons by means of certain special devices. Thus, it is possible to have controllers but no control. How, then, should one act in these circumstances?

It is well known that modern war is inconceivable without the deployment and concentration of large land, air, and naval forces. Atomic weapons by themselves, without the active participation of all types of military forces, cannot be effective, in the sense that they alone do not decide the issue of a war. Atomic weapons cannot be used without means of delivering them to the target. Therefore, the Soviet proposals on control are based on the need for creating conditions in which the aggressive intentions of any state could be discovered and stopped in time. We propose to establish such a control as would give a timely warning of any dangerous concentration of land, air, or naval forces. For this, it is essential to have control posts in large ports, on aerodromes, and in centres of communication of strategic importance. The institution of such a control would fully preclude sudden attacks by one state on another.

The first stage of the Soviet plan would include the 'freezing' of the forces of all states (especially the five Great Powers) at the level of 31 December 1954. This would have left on the European Continent (excluding the main reserves of the Soviet Army in Western Russia) on the Soviet side twenty-eight Soviet line divisions (not counting artillery and A.A.), sixty-two East European divisions, and seven East German divisions, a total of ninety-seven divisions, or 350,000 Soviet troops and over 900,000 men in allied armies of lesser value. On the Western side, a 'freeze' in December 1954 would have left on the Continent six American divisions, four British, one Benelux, five French divisions (and two in North Africa) and no West German divisions, with a small number of Portuguese formations available only in Portugal itself.[1] In the European theatre the West would then have some sixteen operational divisions, a total of 240,000 men 'frozen', as opposed to ninety-seven operational divisions, approximately 1,250,000 men on the Soviet side during the initial critical period as far as Soviet defence planners would be concerned.[2] It should also be noted that a 'freeze' in forces and military expenditures would rule out the establishment by either side of new bases on foreign soil.

During this phase control observers would be stationed at ports, railway junctions, highways, and *aerodromes*, 'the places', according to Marshal Bulganin, 'where a surprise attack could be most easily detected'. The most significant point here was that the Soviet Government was ready to admit observers to its own long-range

[1] This estimate does not take into account the situation on N.A.T.O.'s south-eastern flank, where Greece and Turkey faced Soviet and Bulgarian forces in the Caucasus and the Balkans.

[2] We may take the average strength of a Soviet and East European division in 1954 as 12,000 men, and a N.A.T.O. division as 14,000, to which should be added headquarters staffs and supporting elements.

air bases in exchange for control at the headquarters of the much more dangerous American Strategic Command.

Thus, in 1955, Soviet military superiority in Europe would be ensured, while, in 1956 the use of nuclear weapons would be placed under the veto of the Security Council. When the arms reductions agreed upon were ready to be carried out—in 1956—the Soviet defence chiefs would already be secure both against surprise attack and against retaliation by the United States' Strategic Air Command and British Bomber Command using nuclear weapons, and against any operations by conventional forces in Europe, none of which could have increased their military striking power by the establishment of new bases. Seen through the eyes of Soviet planners, the danger period for nuclear damage to the Soviet Union would be over by 1957. U.S. air bases would be in process of being dismantled, nuclear bombs eliminated, and the retaliatory power of N.A.T.O. to answer any Communist use of conventional forces by nuclear weapons would have disappeared. By the end of 1957 the Soviet Government could confidently expect to choose the type and strength of its 'conventional forces' (taking manpower problems into account) without fear of any military power on earth.

It was largely on the grounds of the overwhelming advantage which this plan gave to the Soviet military machine that the Western powers felt unable to accept it. Yet it seems logical to assume that in May 1955 the Soviet Government sought an agreement with the Western Powers to provide security against surprise attack on the Soviet Union which would also rule out all possibility of Western nuclear retaliation should war break out in any other way. At the same time, the Soviet Government, presumably on the advice of its military advisers, re-started nuclear tests in August 1955 *before* the United Nations subcommittee on disarmament had met on 29 August on the recommendation of the Geneva Conference.[1] This decision was in line with the acceptance by the Soviet Government of the thesis that the adoption of weapons of mass destruction involved their testing and perfection, in order to be able to use them in war, and should be continued as required by the responsible military advisers.[2]

[1] See Ch. IX.

[2] See Mr. Khrushchev's answer to a Japanese question on 19 March 1957: 'Suspension of tests by the Soviet Union would delay the development of nuclear weapons, and might have serious effects on the forces of peace.' (Moscow Radio's Far Eastern Service.)

Simultaneously with the presentation of the disarmament proposals by the Soviet Government on 10 May 1955 certain other steps
were taken which were in line with the new approach to defence. In
1955 and 1956 a general reorganization of the Soviet and East European conventional forces was carried out, which involved re-
dispositions, reductions of top-heavy command structures, and the
raising of the Air Defence Command to the status of an arm of
service, which has already been mentioned. First, both as a political
and a military act, the Soviet Government decided to carry out its
plan to set up an East European Defence Pact. When the Paris
Agreements had been ratified on 26 March 1955 the Polish Government invited the Communist states to a conference in Warsaw on
11 May to set up a joint command for the East European armies.

The Conference was attended by the Premiers, Foreign Ministers,
and Ministers of Defence of the Soviet Union, Poland, Czechoslovakia, Hungary, Rumania, Bulgaria, and Albania, the Premier
and Foreign Minister of East Germany, and the Chinese Minister of
Defence, Marshal Peng Te-huai, as an observer. On 14 May the text
of the Treaty was published. After declaring their support for the
new Soviet disarmament proposals and attacking the Paris Agreements, the signatories announced the setting up of a joint command
and staff for their armed forces in Moscow under the Soviet Marshal
Konev. Each member would provide a senior officer as a deputy
commander-in-chief of the Joint Command and permanent staff
representatives for its General Staff. In the event of armed attack all
members, who agreed in advance to discuss arrangements for
stationing troops on each others' territory, would come to the help
of the victim of aggression. In a separate communiqué the Chinese
Defence Minister offered Chinese military help to the members of the
Pact in Europe.

This treaty had, of course, both political and military significance,
and its political importance was the most obvious. It was openly
declared to be an answer to a political 'threat', the adherence of
West Germany to N.A.T.O. West Germany had no Army, and
therefore could not in 1955 be regarded as an increase in Western
military strength. This point was emphasized by the exclusion from
the Warsaw Defence force of the seven East German divisions.[1] Had

---

[1] The East German Army was formally set up on 18 January 1955, but had
been in existence since 1948. The East German Army was admitted to the
Warsaw Pact forces in 1958. See U.K. Statement (Central Office of Information)

there been a military threat from Western Germany, there would have been no objection to including the East German Army in the Warsaw Pact. The exclusion of these troops was therefore a political move designed to expose the N.A.T.O. Alliance as the first group of states openly to admit the ex-enemy to its councils.

Politically, the new Pact was to prove useful in offering negotiations with N.A.T.O. on the basis of two 'equal' European Security organizations. It also provided the basis for requests by member-nations for the continued stationing of Soviet troops on their soil after the original conditions for their presence had lapsed. This was to have a particular application to Austria, for when Soviet troops were withdrawn in 1955, the Warsaw Pact enabled the Russians to continue to maintain garrisons in Hungary and Rumania, although the original conditions for their retention no longer applied.

The inclusion of Albania in the Warsaw Pact was a pointer to its political rather than its military character. Since 1948 the Soviet Union had carefully refrained from committing its armed forces to the defence of this isolated country, cut off from the rest of the bloc by Yugoslavia. There are no grounds for believing that the new trend in Soviet military thinking allowed the Soviet forces to give direct help to isolated Albania, or that, in a period of upheaval in military thought, they would be anxious to take on new responsibilities.

The Pact had also some military value to the Soviet Union. There is some evidence that it established a new and more realistic organization for military liaison and modernization of the East European armies, and enabled the Soviet High Command to put through its reorganization and its re-deployment in smoother collaboration with its allies than would have been likely without the Pact. For example, each Warsaw Pact ally received a new Soviet military mission in 1955 led by a senior General, and the ordinary military attachés were relieved of the responsibilities of training the East European armies.

The greater part of the reorganization of the Soviet forces which began in 1955 on the basis of the new line in military thought belongs

---

released on 2 December 1952 for details. By 1952 the first Corps had been established at Pasewalk, with three divisions at Eggesin, Prenzlau, and Prora. The Corps had 350 Soviet-type tanks and 200 guns up to 152-mm. howitzers. By 1955 a second Corps had been added. An Air Police Force came into existence in November 1950, and the nucleus of an East German Navy in June of the same year.

to a later period, but it is useful to note its main features by way of conclusion to discussion of the Defence Debate of 1953–56. Soviet troops were withdrawn from exposed salients and bases in Austria, Finland, and Port Arthur in 1955, and later some reductions were made in East Germany. In addition, manpower cuts were made, first on 13 August 1955 and later on 15 May 1956 which totalled 1,840,000 men. The main burden of these cuts fell on the land forces, where economies were made in the numbers of intermediate headquarters, and in the transfer of several formations from operational to training strengths, without, however, reducing the number of divisions.

Meanwhile, as we know now, and Mr. Khrushchev knew then, every month was bringing the Soviet forces nearer to the possession of operational medium-range missiles, and an experimental I.C.B.M., first tested in 1957. In fact, the importance to foreign policy of the outcome of the defence debate in Moscow in 1953–56 can hardly be exaggerated.

Its conclusion helped to determine the Soviet attitude to disarmament; it confirmed the Soviet leaders' existing ideological belief, based on the inevitability of Communist victory, that a nuclear war could break out, and could be won by Communism; and this caused them to reject the theory of mutual deterrence. The outcome of the debate was at the foundation of the Soviet military policy of building up a modernized conventional force, re-deployed for nuclear war, and a missile force capable both of defending the U.S.S.R. and of delivering a long-range strike against the United States. What is important to realize is that most of the groundwork for this defence policy had already been completed when the Soviet Government embarked on its approach to the Summit, in an atmosphere which became generally known as 'the Geneva Spirit'.

IX

SOVIET STRATEGY AND TACTICS IN EUROPE: THE GENEVA SPIRIT: 1955–56

AFTER the Soviet Government had settled the priorities in economic planning, and had adopted a defence policy for the nuclear age, evidence appeared of a new Soviet approach towards four-power relations in Europe. Much of this evidence indicated direct intervention in the conduct of foreign affairs by the indefatigable Mr. Khrushchev, for although as First Secretary of the Communist party of the Soviet Union he held no governmental post, he began to receive foreign diplomats and distinguished guests, to take part in delegations to foreign countries, and to make extempore pronouncements on international affairs at foreign embassies and legations.

One of the first moves of the new approach affected Austria, and appeared to be a hopeful break with past Soviet actions on this subject. For years the conclusion of an Austrian State Treaty had been held up by Soviet obstruction, sometimes on economic grounds connected with reparations, and sometimes because the Soviet Government insisted on linking an Austrian Treaty with a settlement in Trieste. Russian policy on Austria had given the impression that the Soviet General Staff had advised against giving up a forward military and air base in the heart of Europe, especially since, under the Peace Treaties with Hungary and Rumania signed in 1947, Soviet troops were only entitled to remain in those two countries to guard the lines of communication to the base in Austria.

In the spring of 1955, therefore, it came as a pleasant surprise to hear that the Soviet Government had invited the Austrian Chancellor to discussions in Moscow from 11–16 April. Hopes rose still further when the Austrian leader announced that agreement on the terms of a draft State Treaty had at last been reached with the Soviet Government. The Russians, he said, had abandoned a number of economic claims against Austria, had solved the problem of German assets in his country, and had agreed to return to the Austrian State the oil-fields and refineries in Eastern Austria which the Soviet Union had seized in 1945. A vexed point on the repatriation of Austria's large anti-Communist refugee population was also conceded by the Soviet Government, but the most striking agreement of all was the Soviet readiness to withdraw her forces from Austrian territory.[1] In return, Austria was to make a declaration of permament neutrality.[2]

Both Austria and the Western Powers readily agreed to a State Treaty on these terms, and on 15 May 1955 the four Foreign Ministers met in Vienna for the signing ceremony. From the Soviet point of view, the most important element of the treaty was Austria's promise of neutrality, for, if the Soviet Union was prepared to give up a military base, it had to ensure that no other great power established its forces there. This was made clear by Mr. Molotov in these words:

> The Soviet Union attaches great importance to the Austrian statement that she will not join any military alliance, and that she will not permit foreign military bases on her territory.[3]

The Soviet announcement on the value of neutral states quickly became one of the new themes in Soviet propaganda. Countries like Sweden, Switzerland, and Eire, which had long been criticized for the 'undemocratic' character of their political systems, became objects of praise for their foreign policy of permanent neutrality. It was claimed that these small countries had benefited economically from their neutrality, and that many of those now linked to the N.A.T.O. Alliance would be more prosperous if they either withdrew into neutrality or at least 'dragged their feet' in fulfilling their N.A.T.O. obligations.[4] As for security, such countries would be better served by membership of an all-European Security Pact along Soviet lines.

The example of Soviet co-operation with the West which provided a State Treaty for Austria, taken together with the generally more friendly tone of Soviet spokesmen when addressing the Western leaders, encouraged thoughts of a possible meeting of the

---

[1] The question of the future of Soviet troops in Hungary and Rumania was settled under the terms of the Warsaw Pact. Both Governments requested Soviet troops to remain as part of the East European Security Organization. In view of this arrangement, strategically speaking, the withdrawal from Austria took the form of the evacuation of a lightly held and exposed salient. The Russians had less than two divisions in Austria in 1954.

[2] It is possible an additional motive for the evacuation of Austria was Mr. Khrushchev's desire for a rapprochement with Marshal Tito. The Yugoslavs had long disliked the presence of Soviet troops in Austria.

[3] *The Times*, 16 May 1955.

[4] The phrase used in a Soviet reference to Denmark.

four Heads of Governments on European problems. Before the Austrian negotiations had been completed, both President Eisenhower and Marshal Bulganin had spoken in favour of the idea, and on 10 May 1955, the Western Powers suggested such a 'Summit' meeting in Switzerland in the early summer. On 13 June the Soviet Government agreed to the date of 18 July for the opening of a Four-Power Conference, but added the warning that the Soviet delegation would not agree to discuss either the régimes in Eastern Europe or the activities of 'international Communism', as suggested in some quarters in the West. Preparations went ahead, and during the celebrations of the tenth anniversary of the foundation of the United Nations in San Francisco, the four Foreign Ministers completed the arrangements for the meeting.

As the date of the Summit Conference drew nearer, the climate of cordiality developed still further. The Soviet Union agreed to hand back to the United States wartime vessels used by Russia under the Lend-Lease agreement, and admitted partial responsibility for an air accident involving an American plane. Marshal Zhukov, the Soviet Defence Minister, sent a friendly message to the Overseas Press Club in Washington, in which he expressed his admiration for President Eisenhower. The Soviet Government supported the creation of a special committee of the British Council in London to extend Anglo-Soviet contacts, and early in July the first major Soviet ministerial delegation, led by the Minister of State Farms, Mr. Benediktov, arrived in Britain for a tour of British farms and agricultural establishments at the invitation of the *News Chronicle*.[1] Invitations were extended to the leaders of many countries to visit the Soviet Union, including one to Mr. Nehru, and to the Swedish, Syrian, Greek, and Persian Governments. On 7 June the Federal German Chancellor, Dr. Adenauer, was invited to Moscow for talks aimed at establishing diplomatic relations with the Federal Republic as a separate State—a friendly gesture, yet with an ominous ring to it on the eve of a 'Summit' Conference with the reunification of Germany on the agenda.

Indeed, although tension during the summer was much relaxed, a study of Soviet pronouncements on the agenda of the Geneva Conference showed that the Soviet Government was not prepared to commit itself in advance to any concessions on European problems.

---

[1] The delegation, after a fortnight's stay, expressed the desire to prolong its visit, and a further invitation was extended by the Foreign Office.

Mention has already been made of the Soviet refusal to discuss international Communism or Eastern Europe, and Mr. Molotov, in his speech at the United Nations' anniversary meeting in San Francisco, repeated Soviet demands for the dismantling of foreign bases, the abandonment of embargoes on trade in strategic goods, and the withdrawal of forces from Germany.

Before going to Geneva, however, the Soviet leaders made an attempt to heal the breach between Russia and Yugoslavia. It is believed that in the first instance Mr. Khrushchev had tried to persuade Marshal Tito to come to Moscow, but the Yugoslav leader remained firm in his demand for a Soviet pilgrimage to Belgrade. Nor was this the only point on which Marshal Tito was adamant. He was ready to subscribe to the re-establishment of normal state relations between Yugoslavia and the Soviet Union, and to add his country's support to many Soviet proposals in world affairs. But not even the spectacle of an acutely embarrassed Mr. Khrushchev reading out at Belgrade airport an indictment of the late Lavrenti Beria for causing the rift between the Soviet Union and Yugoslavia could persuade him to agree to close liaison between the two Communist parties. Yet the visit to Belgrade would only be worth while in Mr. Khrushchev's eyes if Yugoslavia agreed to return to the Communist fold at the party level. Every ruse was tried to bring this about: Mr. Khrushchev, the First Secretary, acted as spokesman on the Soviet side rather than Marshal Bulganin the Premier, and he spoke continually of 're-establishing mutual understanding' between the two Communist parties. The Yugoslavs, on the other hand, ignored the party aspect of the talks, and emphasized their governmental nature. In the end, the Soviet delegation had to be content with the assurance—of considerable value in certain circumstances—that despite these ideological differences with the Soviet Communist party, Yugoslavia would support the Soviet line on German reunification, disarmament, the abolition of nuclear weapons, and a treaty to ensure European security.

The 18th of July 1955 found the Heads of Government of the four Great Powers, Britain, France, the United States, and the Soviet Union, in Geneva prepared to discuss the problems of Europe in an atmosphere more friendly and hopeful than at any time since the end of the Second World War. The new atmosphere was due to the action of the Soviet Government in abandoning, in certain of its dealings with the outside world, the attitude of xenophobia and suspicion, the officially inspired hatred towards anything non-Soviet, and the refusal to accept blame for any act of Soviet policy so characteristic of the Stalin era. On this unique occasion, President Eisenhower, Sir Anthony Eden, M. Mollet, and Marshal Bulganin (with Mr. Khrushchev at his elbow) seemed to be speaking something approaching a common language.

The agenda of the Conference was quickly agreed. It contained four items: the reunification of Germany, European security, disarmament, and means of improving contacts between East and West. In discussing these subjects, the four Heads of Government indicated that they did not intend to make detailed decisions, but to draw up a series of directives to be worked upon by their Foreign Ministers. In most cases, the views of all four leaders were included in the final directives.

At the request of the Soviet delegation, the Conference agreed to discuss the future of Germany and European security together. Marshal Bulganin produced a draft treaty (to which the United States would be a party), outlining progress towards European security by stages. At first the N.A.T.O. and Warsaw Alliances would remain intact, but by means of gradual reductions of troops, improved contacts, and solemn agreements on the renunciation of the use of force in settling international problems, both security organizations would be replaced by a single European Treaty. The three Western Governments maintained that the greatest single obstacle to European security was the existence in Europe of two Germanies, and suggested that the first stage should include the unification of this nation of 60 million people by free elections. A general treaty might then be signed by the Big Four together with the free-elected Government of a reunited Germany. Sir Anthony Eden added to this Western plan the conception of a demilitarized zone in the areas of physical contact between East and West, with control and inspection of armed forces in Germany and her neighbours as part of an agreement on the limitations of armaments.[1]

In his answering speech Marshal Bulganin politely expressed his disbelief in the Western proposals, though he did promise to give them further consideration. In return, he suggested an interim

[1] See Royal Institute of International Affairs, *Documents, 1955*, p. 43. The context of these proposals, which became known as the 'Eden Plan', is important, for during the 1957-58 public debate on disengagement they were often misquoted or taken out of context.

agreement between the N.A.T.O. and Warsaw Treaty Organizations. The Heads of Government then formulated their directive on this point: they called on the Foreign Ministers to draw up a Security Treaty for Europe, or part of Europe, whose signatories would undertake to renounce the use of force. The treaty area would be subject to limited control and inspection of armed forces, and should include a zone between East and West in which the disposition of forces would be subject to agreement. On the future of Germany, the directive stated that the 'reunification of Germany by free elections should be carried out in conformity with the national interests of the German people and the interests of European Security'.[1]

On disarmament, the United States took the initiative on 21 July in offering to make available to the U.S.S.R. on a reciprocal basis a blueprint of American military establishments, and to permit Soviet aircraft to fly over the United States for the purpose of aerial photography. The Soviet delegation did not make a direct reply to this offer, but instead repeated its disarmament proposals of 10 May. The Russians did, however, agree to a Western suggestion that both disarmament proposals should be handed on to a subcommittee of the United Nations disarmament commission, which was to meet in New York on 29 August. In the directive on disarmament, the Foreign Ministers were instructed to note the progress of this subcommittee.

Little disagreement was expressed when the Heads of Government came to discuss East-West contacts, except for sharp Soviet reaction to a mention by the American President of the status of the East European countries. In the directive the Foreign Ministers were instructed to study the progressive elimination of barriers which interfered with free communications and peaceful trade, and to examine 'such free contacts and exchanges as are to the mutual advantage of the countries and peoples concerned'.[2]

The four leaders concluded their discussions on 23 July and, after an invitation by Sir Anthony Eden to Marshal Bulganin and Mr. Khrushchev to visit Britain in 1956 had been extended and accepted,

[1] Royal Institute of International Affairs, *Documents, 1955*, p. 48. This text is extremely important, since its loose wording has frequently given rise to a misleading interpretation of the Soviet view on free elections for Germany.

[2] Royal Institute of International Affairs, *Documents, 1955*, p. 49. Observers have pointed out that the wording of this passage could allow Governments to justify the prohibition of free circulation of books, magazines or films, and the jamming of radio broadcasts.

they returned to their respective countries to present the results of the conference to their Parliaments and public opinion. All observers were agreed to one point: that the Soviet leaders had done their utmost to maintain the spirit of affability during the conference sessions, and were relaxed and friendly in official and unofficial contacts. When they disagreed with Western delegations, they did so with courtesy and consideration, where in the past their reaction would certainly have been abusive.[1]

The question asked by everyone was: what did the Conference achieve? It set a pattern, known as the 'Geneva Spirit' for a reasonable atmosphere in which governmental, diplomatic, and unofficial contacts could develop between East and West, and between the Soviet Union and the uncommitted countries of the world. On his return from Geneva, Marshal Bulganin took the unprecedented step of entertaining the diplomatic corps in Moscow at his country home in an atmosphere of informal and relaxed hospitality. Invitations to foreign statesmen to visit Russia were extended to the French and Norwegian Prime Ministers, as well as to the President of Finland, the Burmese Prime Minister, and to representatives from the Governments of the British Commonwealth. Soviet scientists were authorized to join the work of United Nations' technical committees, and also took part in an important conference on the peaceful uses of atomic energy. A Soviet textile delegation, led by a member of the Presidium, Mr. Kosygin, spent two weeks in Britain and placed a big order for textile machinery. The Royal Navy and the Soviet Navy exchanged visits to Leningrad and Portsmouth. The Soviet leaders themselves planned an extensive tour of Asia for the end of the year, and these, and other similar activities, gave a general impression that Soviet isolationism was a thing of the past, and that the Soviet Union was ready to come forward to solve world problems on the basis of normal and generally accepted procedure.

In fact, the Soviet Government had many reasons to be pleased with the practical results of the Summit meeting in Geneva. It had taken place largely on Soviet terms, for items which the Western

---

[1] One example may be cited. In the course of the discussions on European security, Sir Anthony Eden, acting in accordance with Western public opinion, offered the Soviet Union 'additional guarantees' against attack from a reunited Germany. To the Soviet leaders, who maintain, and teach their people that the Soviet Union won the war 'singlehanded' the idea that any smaller nation should help to 'guarantee' the U.S.S.R. against Germany might, in more normal times, have produced a reaction explosive enough to break up the Conference.

Powers had wished to discuss, such as Eastern Europe and international Communism, were not brought up during the Conference. The agenda had included only those European problems on which the Western Powers might be asked to make concessions, and agreements were so worded as to give 'escape clauses' to the Soviet Union should evasion become necessary. This point was made abundantly clear by Mr. Khrushchev himself within days of the end of the Conference. On his way back to Moscow, Mr. Khrushchev called in at East Berlin, where he gave his version of the meaning of the Four-Power directive on free elections as a means to reunite Germany, as follows:

> We are convinced that the workers in the German Democratic Republic will not agree to a solution which puts the interests of the Western groupings ahead of the interests of the German Democratic Republic.[1]

Since the directive had spoken of the carrying out of free elections 'in conformity with the national interests of the Germany people', Mr. Khrushchev, it is clear, was thinking only in terms of the *East* German 'people', of the Communist 'People's Government' of the Soviet zone. In other words, Mr. Khrushchev had already promised on 26 July 1955 that no free elections would be allowed in Germany which would result in the fall of the Communist Government there.

Mention has already been made of the vagueness of the wording even of the agreement of the Heads of Government on East-West contacts. The phrase 'such free contacts and exchanges as are to the mutual advantage of the countries and peoples concerned' could, of course, be used to rule out the introduction into the Soviet Union of any printed, filmed or broadcast material which, perhaps unintentionally, threw doubt on the infallibility of Communism or criticized the Soviet system. Disarmament was referred to a United Nations subcommittee and the Soviet Union postponed its reply to President Eisenhower's proposed scheme of aerial survey and exchange of military information. A somewhat sombre comment on the Soviet disarmament position came from the United States atomic authority on 4 August when it announced that the Soviet Union had resumed her tests of nuclear weapons.

The main achievement of the Geneva Conference, then, was a welcome relaxation of tension in international affairs. Its tragedy was that while the relaxation affected the methods of negotiation, it

[1] *Pravda*, 27 July 1955.

was rarely applied by the Soviet Government to the actual solution of the problems themselves. This became clear when, as arranged at the Summit Conference the four Foreign Ministers met in Geneva on 27 October 1955 to work out an agreement on the basis of the Heads of Governments' directives. Mr. Molotov opened the meeting with a departure from the directive by reversing Marshal Bulganin's position in July and insisting on discussing European security and the German problem separately. Instead of taking the Geneva directive as a whole, he extracted Marshal Bulganin's original draft treaty on security, and attempted to have it discussed in lieu of the directive which contained Western suggestions as well. Fortunately, this proved to be an 'expendable' manoeuvre, but it was an uncomfortable reminder of Soviet tactics in earlier conferences.

After Mr. Molotov had withdrawn this feeler, the Conference got down to serious work in an attempt to bring the two draft security treaties mentioned in the directive together. The Foreign Ministers reached tentative agreements on the principles of an inspection zone in Europe and on the continuing existence side by side of N.A.T.O. and the Warsaw Alliance. One point separated them: Western drafts included references to *one* German State (reunited through free, all-German elections); the Soviet plans spoke only of *two* Germanies.

On 31 October Mr. Molotov, pressed to clarify his position, produced his plan for German reunification. He suggested, first, the establishment of an all-German Council made up of the representatives of the East and West German Parliaments to co-ordinate the two parts of Germany and thus 'create the prerequisite for unification'. Unification in stages by formal act of this Council would be followed by the withdrawal of all foreign troops, and limitations on the strength of a future German Army.

Since the Western Powers could not place the elected Parliament in Western Germany and the nominated Chamber in the East on an equal footing in this way, they countered with a direct motion calling for free all-German elections in September 1956. To this, Mr. Molotov made his historic reply:

It has been suggested here that a plan should be adopted for All-German elections. . . . As I have already shown, such a plan ignores the real conditions in Germany, inasmuch as the question of holding such elections has not yet matured. Such a mechanical merging of the two parts of Germany through so-called free elections, held, moreover, in the presence of foreign troops as envisaged in the Eden plan, might result in the violation of the vital interests of the working people of the German Democratic Republic, and we cannot agree to that.[1]

In other words, the Soviet Government would not agree to any election or referendum as a result of which the people of Germany might vote to end the Communist régime in the Eastern part of the country. Mr. Khrushchev's assurance to the Communists of East Germany in July was formally repeated by Mr. Molotov in conference in October, and thus confirmed their continued acceptance of one if the cardinal elements of Stalin's strategy in Europe: that in present circumstances all plans involving the fall of an established and loyal Communist government in an East European country are doomed to failure in advance.

In fact, the Western Powers were mistaken in their appraisal of the Soviet attitude on this point. Believing that Marshal Bulganin had given his blessing to free elections in Germany at the Geneva Conference of Heads of Government, they now accused Mr. Molotov of evading a Soviet promise previously made. But the Soviet Government never promised to hold free elections in Germany; the wording of the directive was deliberately chosen to make free elections dependent upon the 'national interests of the German people', which, in the Soviet mind was, and is, identical with the existence of the Communist régime in East Germany.

However, the apparent breach of faith exacerbated the remaining negotiations at the Foreign Ministers' meeting on disarmament; both sides noted with regret the lack of progress made in the United Nations subcommittee which had met on 29 August, but each blamed the other for holding up proceedings. Once again Mr. Molotov took his stand on Marshal Bulganin's proposals on the prevention and detection of surprise attack, while the Western Powers concentrated their attention on inspection and control. Mr. Macmillan, the British Foreign Secretary, called for a 'confidence-building pilot scheme' for disarmament—some small sector of the vast disarmament field for which a foolproof inspection machinery could be set up. But it was without success. Not even a joint declaration could be phrased, and the Ministers were forced to hand the whole disarmament problem back to the United Nations.

The deteriorating climate of the Conference was most clearly visible in the discussions on East-West contacts which came later in

[1] *Pravda*, 9 November 1955.

the proceedings. Mr. Molotov understood the directive as referring to improving the machinery for the exchange of official parties and delegations. The Western Powers interpreted it as encouraging unofficial as well as official contacts between the peoples of East and West, and a free exchange of ideas in science, literature and politics. The Western delegations had prepared a list of seventeen ways of improving contacts along these lines, including an end to Soviet jamming of Western radio broadcasts, financial concessions for tourists, and the opening of Western bookshops and reading-rooms in the Soviet Union. Mr. Molotov denounced all these ideas, describing the reading-rooms, in particular, as 'centres of espionage'. Consequently, no progress was made towards bringing the two sides together, and this directive was referred back for further discussion through diplomatic channels.

Disappointing though the results of the second Geneva Conference were, they did not at once bring the relaxation of tension, the 'Geneva Spirit', to an end. International contacts continued in a relatively friendly atmosphere, and in the spring of 1956 Marshal Bulganin and Mr. Khrushchev carried out their projected visit to Britain, where they found readiness to meet the Soviet leadership half-way on as many points as possible. But it must be remembered that by the time of the Soviet leaders' visit to Britain, Mr. Khrushchev had already launched his campaign for the political and economic penetration of the Middle East, India, and parts of the Far East. This strategy will be examined in detail in the next chapter, but it is essential to bear in mind that shortly after the Geneva meeting of Heads of Government the first sales of arms to Egypt were being arranged, and that within days of the break-up of the second Geneva Conference, Marshal Bulganin and Mr. Khrushchev were on their way to India and Burma, about to embark on a fiery propaganda campaign against Britain in particular, and the West in general, in Asia.

Against this background, the negative elements in the Soviet approach to the West during the summer of 1955 achieved their true perspective as a part of a tactical holding operation, while a change in the 'direction of the main blow' was effected. This is not to imply that the Soviet approach was insincere. The mere fact that the Soviet Government took enormous pains to relax tension and to approach the Western Powers on their own ground and speaking their language, proves that the Soviet leaders certainly wanted to achieve some form of agreement with the West. But the Soviet proposals in practice offered no concession on any point which indicated a change of heart, for example, on the principle of free elections, particularly in Germany, effective disarmament inspection and control, or the free exchange of ideas. The Soviet leaders sought a genuine agreement on Europe with the West without abandoning any key Soviet positions or principles, which would leave their hands free for the main theatres of operations. And they probably believed that an agreement would be more likely in a relaxed and friendly atmosphere than in the icy conditions of Stalin's day. If the West could be persuaded to give up the accession of West Germany to N.A.T.O., or abandon its foreign bases and its persistent interest in Eastern Europe—so much the better. If not, then there must be no mistake about the firmness of the Soviet grip on the existing situation.

The latter is what the second Geneva Conference achieved.

X

THE APPROACH TO THE MIDDLE EAST
1953–56

WHILE Mr. Khrushchev was pursuing the policy of *détente* in Europe without giving way on any fundamental point of Soviet control in Eastern Europe, he was also developing plans for a major departure from Stalin's strategy in another part of the world. Mr. Khrushchev, perhaps adopting elements of a policy already broached by Mr. Malenkov, had decided to break into the uncommitted countries of the Middle East, Africa, and the Indian subcontinent and to turn this vast area into a battleground in a struggle against the West fought with political, economic, and propaganda weapons. The Soviet leader intended the struggle to be highly mobile, he expected to open up territories hitherto considered without prospects for the Soviet cause, and he confidently hoped, by seizing and maintaining the initiative, to force the unsuspecting Western Powers on to the defensive, and ultimately drive them first economically, and then politically from the whole area.

In official Soviet and Communist eyes, the countries of the Middle East and North Africa presented targets for a struggle of the 'anti-colonial' type.[1] As long ago as 1924, Stalin had described the case for the 'anti-colonial' struggle in a lecture in Moscow in these words:

Formerly it was tacitly assumed that the victory of the proletariat in Europe was possible without a direct alliance with the movement for emancipation in the colonies. Leninism has proved that the road to victory in the West lies through a revolutionary alliance with the liberation movements of the colonies and dependent territories. This does not mean that the proletariat must support every national movement. Cases occur when national movements in certain oppressed countries come into conflict with the interests of the proletarian movement. In such cases, support is, of course, entirely out of the question. For national movements must be

[1] One element in the Marx-Leninist approach to the problems of struggle against capitalism in the underdeveloped countries of the world was the prediction that if the capitalists were deprived by Communist successes in these areas of their source of raw materials and of their markets, their whole economic system would be dangerously weakened and collapse would be brought nearer.

examined concretely from the point of view of the interests of the revolutionary movement, and not from the point of view of abstract rights.[1]

The quotation guided Soviet policy towards the Middle East and Africa during Stalin's lifetime. In 1945-46 the Soviet Government made one attempt to use its troops stationed in Northern Persia to detach a province from the Persian State, but it resulted in failure and Stalin appeared to be reluctant to interfere in the Middle East and Africa except in the field of propaganda against the established Governments and their alliances. Each of the Middle Eastern Governments was bitterly attacked in this way—including, strange to say, the anti-Western Government of Dr. Mossadeq in Persia.[2] The Arab League was described as '. . . an instrument for the enslavement of the peoples of the Arab East by the British imperialists. The British and American imperialists are jointly exploiting the League's leaders, who are obedient to them, for the realization of a further war and for the suppression of the progressive forces of the countries of the Middle East.'[3] The military *coup d'état* carried out by General Neguib in Egypt in June 1952, which forced King Farouk to abdicate, nevertheless, 'aimed at establishing a fascist military dictatorship to stifle the growing anti-imperialist movement in Egypt. General Neguib's bloody reprisals against the working class show his fear of the growing power of the Egyptian masses.'[4] Social and economic proposals worked out in the Middle East itself were denounced by the Soviet Union. In May 1954 *Pravda* denounced a suggestion to build a railway linking Iraq and Persia, and on 8 May 1954 *Tass* attacked a general proposal to improve road communications between the Middle Eastern countries.

In many ways the problem faced by the Soviet Union in the Middle East after 1947 arose from the collapse of British and French power in the area. Britain found herself opposed to the establishment of the State of Israel and at the same time faced the rising tide of nationalism in Israel's most bitter enemies, the Arab countries. The Soviet Government had itself taken a stand against Zionism inside the Soviet Union, and could hardly give unqualified support to the State of Israel. Yet the vacuum left by British and French power

---

[1] From a lecture by Stalin at the Sverdlov University, April 1924.

[2] By the Azerbaijan 'Democratic' Radio on Soviet territory in the Caucasus on 30 January 1952.

[3] *Red Star* (the Soviet Army paper), Moscow, 29 April 1950.

[4] Polish Press Agency, 20 August 1952.

created a situation which it was very difficult for the Soviet Union to exploit. The established Middle Eastern Governments were strongly anti-Communist, and so were many of the nationalist groups, particularly in the armed forces, who were preparing to take over power in Egypt, Syria, and other countries. In most Arab countries the Communist party was banned or in its infancy, and it was hard to see to whom the Soviet Union could appeal in this situation.

For some years the problem appeared to have remained unsolved in Moscow, until just before Stalin's death there were signs that a decision in principle to approach the nationalist groups in the Arab countries had been taken. Communists like Khalid Bikdash, the Syrian party leader, appeared as candidates in Parliamentary elections and Communist propaganda talked of the need for 'broad, popular fronts uniting all national forces'.

It was left to Mr. Malenkov, in his speech to the Supreme Soviet on 8 August 1953, to make the earliest favourable references to established Middle Eastern Governments, as well as to those of India and south-east Asia. At the end of the year it was noted that Cairo radio had begun to make friendly comments on Soviet policy, and to use the word 'neutrality' as a possible foreign policy for countries like Egypt. Early in 1954 an Egyptian trade delegation appeared in Eastern Europe, and a number of barter agreements were concluded with countries of the Soviet bloc for the purchase of Egypt's cotton, the sale of which is so essential to her economy. In September 1954 the Soviet Government opened a cultural centre in Cairo, and it was reported that the Egyptian Tourist Agency was negotiating for an office to be opened in Moscow. In fact, even before the dismissal of Mr. Malenkov, the first steps had been taken by the Soviet Government to formulate a policy of economic and political penetration of the Arab countries of the Middle East.

This was, of course, the policy also adopted towards India and south-east Asia, and it is difficult to say, even in retrospect, whether Soviet policy would have continued to develop smoothly along these lines in the Middle East during the years ahead. For where Soviet policy in the Middle East differed from that towards India was in the decision by Mr. Khrushchev and his colleagues to sell arms to Egypt and Syria, and thus to upset the military balance between the Middle Eastern states themselves. It is possible to argue that because of the strategic importance of the Middle East, and its relative nearness to the Soviet Union, the Soviet planners had always envisaged a more active policy of driving Western influence out of the area by exploiting rivalries and differences between the Arab states, raising tension by supplying the more turbulent among them with arms. On the other hand, the evidence of timing suggests that the Soviet decision to arm the anti-Western group of Arab states, Egypt, Syria, Saudi Arabia, and Yemen, may have been prompted, or at any rate brought forward, by the creation of a Middle Eastern defence organization associated with the Western Powers.

The evidence is as follows. The origins of the defensive grouping of those countries in the Middle East near to the Soviet frontier can be traced to the year 1950. In their Declaration of 25 May 1950 the Western Powers offered to sell arms to the Middle Eastern states for purposes of internal security and external defence on condition that the recipient undertook not to use them for aggression.[1] The offer was not followed up by the Arab countries largely because many Arab Governments wanted arms to use against Israel, and also because of deadlock in the Anglo-Egyptian negotiations over the future of the British military base in Suez.

In 1953, however, the American Secretary of State, Mr. Dulles, toured the Middle and Far East, and drew attention in a speech to the 'vague desire' which he found among countries near to Russia for a collective security system.[2] Mr. Dulles went on: 'While awaiting the creation of a formal Security Association, the United States, I am convinced, can usefully help strengthen the interrelated defences of these countries if they want strength, not against each other or against the West, but to resist the common threat to all free peoples.'

This implication of American interest in a Middle Eastern defence arrangement was first taken up in Turkey and Pakistan, whose Governments announced in February 1954 that they had agreed to study ways of closer collaboration in defence, and a few days later the United States made public its intention to grant military and economic aid to Pakistan. Egypt, which was then in the throes of an internal crisis arising from the struggle for power between General Neguib and Colonel Nasser, was assured of Pakistan's continued support for the Arab cause against Israel and for Egypt's demand for the evacuation of British forces from the Suez base. Likewise India was given assurances by America that arms supplied to Pakistan were for defence only. There were, however, reports that the British Government did not welcome this American

[1] Text in *The Times*, 26 May 1950.   [2] *New York Times*, 2 June 1953.

initiative, particularly because of its effect on Egypt and India, whose reaction was severely critical.[1] In addition, Moscow sent notes of protest to both Turkey and Pakistan, and the Egyptian Government informed the United States that Egypt would do all in its power to prevent an extension of the pact.

Nevertheless, the Turkish-Pakistani defence pact was signed on 2 April 1954, and its text did contain an invitation to neighbouring countries to join. The Prime Minister of Iraq, General Nuri es-Said, thereupon declared himself willing to buy arms from the West, accepting the conditions of the 1950 proposals. On 19 May 1954 Pakistan signed her own defence treaty with the United States. At the same time it was reported that Britain still had reservations on the wisdom of these pacts and was understandably reluctant to enter into new defence commitments in the Middle East at a time when she did not know whether or not her armed forces would have a firm land base within reach of the area of possible conflict.

By the summer of 1954, therefore, elements of a defence agreement with general American approval between certain of the countries situated on the Soviet Union's southern frontier were beginning to appear.[2] Turkey was already a member of N.A.T.O.; she was now linked to a Pakistan which had a defence treaty with the United States, while one of the countries which divided them geographically, Iraq, had agreed to accept Western arms. The next step was taken by the Iraqi Government. In August 1954 Nuri es-Said put forward proposals for a wider defensive grouping, including Egypt, and held discussions with Egyptian representatives first in Baghdad, and later with Colonel Nasser himself during a visit to Cairo. The Egyptians, however, were at this stage energetically opposed to the Iraqi idea of turning the Arab League Collective Security Pact of 1950 into a regional defence alliance under article 51 of the United Nations' Charter. The old rivalry between Iraq and the Egyptians for supremacy in the Arab world re-emerged to prevent the creation of a single organization to which all Arab states could adhere.[3]

[1] See the *New York Times*, 29 January 1954, for reports of Britain's objections.
[2] Britain made it clear that she had been informed, but not consulted about these American plans. (*New York Times*, 29 July 1954.)
[3] Some months later, in an interview with the *New York Times* of 4 April 1955, Colonel Nasser claimed that the Western Powers, in supporting Nuri es-Said's initiative, had broken faith with Egypt, to whom had been promised leadership in an Arab defence arrangement free from formal links with the Great Powers.

Independently of the 'Northern Tier' negotiations, Britain and Egypt finally concluded an agreement on the future of the Suez military base on 19 October 1954. British forces were to be withdrawn, but had the right of re-entry in the event of an attack on any member of the Arab League or on Turkey. This agreement led to a slight improvement in relations with Britain, and occurred at a time when Colonel Nasser had aroused anger among some sections of the Arab world by his ruthless suppression of the extremist Muslim Brotherhood. And it is interesting to note that one of Colonel Nasser's arguments against an Iraqi-Turkish alliance was that it was unnecessary since Iraq's security was already covered by her treaty with Britain.

After the breakdown of the Iraqi Prime Minister's mission to Egypt, Iraq joined the Turkish-Pakistani Pact on 24 February 1955 and Britain, now that the future of the Suez base had been decided, joined the Treaty on 5 April 1955. The whole defensive agreement became known as the Baghdad Pact, and a Secretariat to co-ordinate the new alliance was set up in the Iraqi capital. Egypt, meanwhile, had made two moves. She applied for arms to the Western Powers, but formally refused to adhere to the Western conditions restricting their use to internal security and defence. Secondly, Colonel Nasser brought negotiations for a defence pact with Syria to a successful conclusion in March 1955, and the two countries invited Jordan, Lebanon, and Saudi Arabi to take part. Saudi Arabi agreed to align herself with the new grouping, but Jordan and Lebanon preferred to remain neutral in the power struggle between Egypt and Iraq.

This, then, was the situation in the Middle East which faced the new Soviet leadership early in 1955. As part of its campaign of economic and political penetration of the Middle East, the Soviet Government had already begun to take sides in the dispute between Egypt and Iraq, and also in the Arab-Israeli quarrel, supporting Egypt and Syria against Iraq, and the Arabs as a whole against Israel.[1]

About ten days after the British decision to join the Baghdad Pact was made public, the Soviet Government made its first major pronouncement on the situation in the Middle East. On 16 April

---

[1] An early indication that Soviet policy towards Israel had changed came in the United Nations' debate on the Gaza incident (which involved an Egyptian-Israeli armed clash) when the Soviet Union appeared among the most vigorous critics of Israel.

1955 the Soviet Foreign Ministry declared that under 'Western pressures and threats' aggressive military blocs were being formed in the Middle East, and alleged that efforts were being made to force Syria into the Baghdad Pact. Middle Eastern countries were warned against being drawn into alliances of this nature. At first, since the Soviet Union had not shown great eagerness in the recent past to involve herself directly in the Middle East, it was widely believed that this statement was designed to influence the Bandung Conference of Asian and African States then about to begin in Indonesia. But, in fact, it seems much more likely that the statement represented a warning that a new strategic approach to the Middle East was under consideration in Moscow, for it is virtually certain that within two months a decision had been taken to supply arms to Egypt and Syria.

This decision to arm Egypt without guarantees against aggression is so important for a study to Soviet foreign policy that it requires the closest investigation.[1] We cannot be sure on the evidence as to whether Colonel Nasser took the first step in asking for arms, or whether the Soviet Government preceded his request by offering an arms deal. But it is known that in June 1955 Colonel Nasser told the United States Ambassador in Cairo that he was making inquiries from Russia about the purchase of arms.[2] And it is safe to assume, therefore, that the subject was up for discussion as early as June. It is reported that Colonel Nasser made his final decision on 25 August,[3] and we do know that Mr. Dulles was aware of the existence of a deal of some sort on the 31st.[4] The sale of arms to Egypt, allegedly by Czechoslovakia, was finally made public in Cairo on 27 September 1955, on the day on which an exhibition of Czechoslovak aircraft opened in the Egyptian capital.

From the Egyptian point of view, the acceptance of Communist arms by a Government which had outlawed the local Communist party can be explained in terms of prestige, particularly a desire to turn the tables on the Western Powers who had refused to give arms

---

[1] Although the sale of arms was officially arranged between Egypt and Czechoslovakia, Colonel Nasser revealed on 26 July 1956 that it was the Soviet Union which had concluded the deal, and it will be therefore referred to here as the Soviet decision to supply arms to Egypt.

[2] Royal Institute of International Affairs. Information Department Memorandum: *The Baghdad Pact*, February 1956, p. 8.

[3] The *Sunday Times*, 6 November 1955.

[4] *New York Times*, 31 August 1955.

to Egypt on the latter's terms, and had set up a defence organization in the Middle East which included Iraq, Egypt's main rival for Arab leadership. At the same time it should not be forgotten that Egypt did not consider the arms deal with the East as committing her to the Soviet bloc. For the same reasons of prestige she was buying arms from other quarters as well; on 25 July, for example, Britain sold two destroyers to the Egyptian Navy. Egypt clearly regarded the purchase of arms from wherever she pleased as a sign of political independence and as a means of satisfying her national pride. But for the Soviet Union more than prestige was involved, although in the context of serving notice on the Western Powers that Russia intended to act as a Great Power in the Middle East, prestige was certainly important. She had not offered arms to India or Burma as part of her new policy in the Asian world, nor was she to do so when the first steps were taken to found the South-East Asia Treaty Organization. From the Soviet point of view, the events of 1954–55 had brought into existence a new military alliance along the southern borders of the Soviet Union, which included among its members one of the Great Powers, equipped with atomic weapons and the means of delivering them, and two members of N.A.T.O. Until the conclusion of the Baghdad Pact, the only act of Soviet policy in the Middle East which would have led to the outbreak of a third World War would have been an attack on Turkey. Now, any attack on Iraq or Pakistan would involve Britain, and through her, might ultimately involve the United States. Moreover, the Pact might bring N.A.T.O. bases even nearer to the Soviet southern border, with all their modern equipment; probably Persia would agree to join, and thus the Pact could lead, in Soviet eyes, to the creation of a great armed camp stretching from Turkey to the Indian frontier.

Such an expansion of pro-Western military power had to be prevented, and yet there was no comparable military counter-weight which could be built up in the short term easily and quickly. However, as the Soviet Government probably saw it, the Baghdad Pact had only one Arab member—Iraq. If the loyalty of the people of Iraq could be transferred from their own Government to that of Egypt, and if all other Arab states could be discouraged from joining the Pact, its central pillar could be seriously weakened. If Iraq's leaders became doubtful of the loyalty of their Army and people, the country's actual value to the Alliance would be considerably reduced. So what Soviet policy had to do was to raise Egypt's prestige among the Arabs, and to ensure that no other Arab state joined the Pact, thus maintaining Iraq's isolation. The Soviet planners shrewdly calculated, no doubt, that nothing would raise Colonel Nasser's and Egypt's prestige in Arab eyes more than a supply of arms from a source independent of the Western Powers. The arms themselves, therefore, were at this stage relatively unimportant; the aircraft, for example, were inferior to the *Mystère* fighters sold to Israel by France. The Soviet Union, while perhaps thinking of a military base in Egypt in the long term, showed no eagerness to establish one as an immediate reply to the Baghdad Pact, as one might have expected if the Russian General Staff had wanted to outflank the new Alliance militarily. It seems likely that the Soviet Government regarded the internal weakening of the Pact as offering the best prospects in the short term, and they aimed to create a situation in which the central link of the Baghdad Pact—Iraq—would falter because it would be a member of the Pact in name only, and thus prevent the organization from effective operation.[1]

The Soviet action in supplying arms to Egypt immediately aroused widespread criticism throughout the non-Communist world, and may have contributed to the decision of Persia to join the Pact on 9 October 1955, in spite of an official Persian Foreign Ministry denial. It also led to Jordan's intended adherence to the Pact on 13 December 1955,[2] a step which the King and Government of Jordan subsequently rejected under the pressure of mob violence, fomented, according to a British Foreign Office statement of 10 January 1956, from outside.

Meanwhile, Soviet political and economic penetration of the Middle East progressed steadily throughout the remaining months of 1955 and early 1956. On 10 July 1955 a Syrian parliamentary

[1] The British Foreign Secretary maintained that the Soviet offer of arms to Egypt was not a result of the Baghdad Pact in a speech in the House of Commons on 12 December 1955, on the grounds that the scope of the offer and many other manoeuvres going on in the area where the fruits of long and careful preparations. But the abruptness of the change of Soviet policy in the Middle East after the accession of Mr. Khrushchev to power makes it unlikely that the arms deal was a policy decision taken by Mr. Malenkov. By the time that Mr. Khrushchev was firmly in the saddle, in February 1955, Iraq had joined the Turkish-Pakistani Pact (the first objection in Soviet eyes), and Britain's adherence (with the underlying American involvement) came in a matter of weeks. All the evidence points to a decision to supply arms having been taken after the signature of the Baghdad Pact.

[2] Central Office of Information Paper R 3889, *The Baghdad Pact*, London 1958, p. 8.

delegation arrived in the Soviet Union, and in August an invitation to Colonel Nasser to visit Moscow was made public. On 10 October the Soviet Ambassador to Egypt, Mr. Solod, offered his country's help for Middle Eastern countries, and agreement was reached on an exchange of Soviet petroleum and industrial equipment for Egyptian cotton and rice. In February 1956 a Soviet-Egyptian agreement on atomic power was announced, under which the U.S.S.R. undertook to establish a nuclear energy laboratory in Cairo, to staff it with Soviet advisers, and to train Egyptian scientists in the Soviet Union.[1]

Syria, Saudi Arabia, and Yemen also attracted the attention of the Soviet Union as possible targets for economic and political penetration. In November the Soviet Legation in Damascus and the Syrian Legation in Moscow were raised to the status of Embassies, and a month later the Soviet Government offered to build an oil refinery in Syria and to supply Soviet technicians and advisers. There were many reports that the Soviet Union had offered arms to Saudi Arabia during her frontier trouble with the British-protected states in the area of the Buraimi Oasis in October 1955. While tension was high in this area the Soviet Union renewed her treaty with Yemen, which was involved a frontier feud with the Aden Protectorate.

These and many other moves were characteristic of Soviet activity in the Middle East in the course of the twelve months which began in April 1955. In every country which was not associated with the West or the Baghdad Pact, Soviet Ambassadors were much in evidence, offering aid, often on flattering, if vague, terms, issuing invitations to visit Moscow, or organizing cultural and tourist exchanges. Technicians, advisers, and economists from the East European countries were also establishing themselves, arranging barter deals for local products which might otherwise have remained unsold on the world market. And all the time a constant barrage of pro-Soviet anti-Western propaganda covered the Middle East from the radio stations of Russia and Eastern Europe.

Nevertheless, the unique development of this period was the Soviet decision to sell arms to Egypt. As we have seen, the timing of the decision followed the creation of a military alliance between states near the Soviet frontier, with the additional support of Britain, a World Power and a signatory of the North Atlantic Alliance.

[1] Royal Institute of International Affairs, op. cit., p. 10. *Tass*, 19 February 1956.

The Baghdad Pact was regarded in Moscow as a potential military threat to the security of the Soviet Union. It may be argued that the Pact was purely defensive, and that the armed forces of its members presented no threat to the vast armed might of the Soviet Union. But this, to the Soviet strategist, would be beside the point. As he sees it, the creation of even the weakest Western military alliance does two things: it makes it legally possible for the strong powers of the West at some stage in the future to find excuses for the establishment of up-to-date offensive bases—perhaps with a nuclear and rocket capability—in the area of the alliance. Secondly, by committing at least one major power to the defence of countries along the Soviet border, so that an attack on one of them might lead to the outbreak of a World War, it restricts and limits the freedom of action of the Soviet Union in dealing with its neighbours.

In the case of the Baghdad Pact, the Soviet Union faced a dilemma in planning its reaction to the new alliance. The best policy might have been to outflank the Pact by supporting a rival military power in the area, but Egypt's military potential was too small to be built up quickly, and in 1955 the Soviet Government sought an immediate riposte to the Pact. An actual Soviet base on Egyptian soil would have been isolated and difficult to maintain. So it appears likely that Mr. Khrushchev decided upon the sale of arms to Egypt. This was a political reaction by limited military means designed to raise Egyptian prestige and build Egypt up as the focal point for Arab loyalties, and consequently to lower Iraq's position in the Arab world. The Soviet decision was, in fact, in the nature of an emergency measure, superimposed on the existing strategy because of Western initiatives in the Middle East, but was not intended to replace the longer-term economic and political campaign to drive Western influence out of the Middle East.

XI

SOVIET POLICY IN ASIA: INDIA, BURMA, AND THE COUNTRIES OF SOUTH-EAST ASIA: 1953–56

THE preceding chapter was devoted to an area of the world—the Middle East—where Soviet strategy aimed at a planned economic and political penetration of the Arab countries of the area. This type of strategy had been tried experimentally even earlier farther east, in the southern and south-eastern parts of Asia, including the Indian subcontinent, Burma, Malaya and Indonesia.

It will be recalled that Stalin's approach to India and south-east Asia was conceived almost exclusively in terms of Marxism-Leninism, and the activities of the local Communist parties. Immediately after the war Stalin apparently believed that the area was ripe for a primitive type of armed uprising, and the Communist parties in India, Burma, Indonesia, Malaya, and Indo-China were set on a path of violence and rebellion. Later, after most of the Communist risings had come to grief in a series of head-on collisions with the forces of growing nationalism in these countries, new tactics of collaboration with centre and moderate left-wing opposition elements were adopted.[1] But in each case the official Communist attitude to the new nationalist Governments was the same: they were portrayed as representatives of the former colonial powers who had been forced or persuaded to act in their stead.

This refusal to recognize the strength of non-Communist nationalism was particularly noticeable in India. Until 1941 no Soviet national had overtly visited the Indian subcontinent,[2] yet Soviet libraries were not lacking in books and journals giving the Marxist view of Indian affairs. The *Large Soviet Encyclopaedia* described Mahatma Gandhi as 'an agent of British Imperialism and the Indian exploiting classes who did not want full independence for

---

[1] The word 'quisling' had been used in the earlier period to describe these leaders. See *Cominform Journal*, 'For a Lasting Peace, For a People's Democracy', 27 January 1950, for a reference to the Indonesian Government.

[2] *Central Asian Review*, Vol. V, No. 1, 1957, p. 55.

India'.[1] The transfer of power to India and Pakistan was interpreted as 'an act which signified that both the Indian landlords and upper bourgeoisie represented by the National Congress, and the Muslim landlords and bourgeoisie whose interests are represented by the Muslim League, had openly gone over to the camp of imperialism and reaction'.[2] That was written in 1949, and as late as 1953 Soviet writers were still following the same line. Professor Varga wrote in *Fundamental Problems of the Economics and Politics of Imperialism*:

> The transformation of India into two Dominions is a compromise between the English imperialistic bourgeoisie and the counter-revolutionary bloc of Indian big bourgeoisie and landowners. It is an attempt of the Indian ruling classes to safeguard and defend the existing social order in India with the help of English imperialism against the growing revolutionary movement of workers and peasants. By concluding that compromise, the Indian bourgeoisie has betrayed the national interests of its country.[3]

The *Large Soviet Encyclopaedia* concluded its article on India as follows:

> At the end of 1948 and 1949 repression against democratic organizations in India intensified. In Bengal, Madras, and other states the Communist party was declared illegal. . . . On 26 January 1950 the Constitution came into force under which India was proclaimed a sovereign republic, but previous decisions about her remaining in the British Empire were not changed.

Curiously enough it was Communist China who first gave practical recognition to the part which could be played by a neutral India. This came as early as 1951–52 during the negotiations to end the Korean War, when the Chinese treated the Indian effort with considerable respect. The Indian Ambassador in Peking was kept in close touch with Chinese policy, and it is now known that the Indian proposals for the resettlement of prisoners of war in Korea were announced after consultations with the Chinese Government.

Shortly after the death of Stalin in 1953 signs of a change in the Soviet attitude towards the 'bourgeois nationalist' Governments of India and her neighbours began to appear. In his speech to the

---

[1] *Large Soviet Encyclopaedia*, 2nd Edition, 1953, Vol. 18. This article was later rewritten in response to an Indian protest.

[2] A. M.D'yakov, *The Crisis of the Colonial System*, Ch. 3, U.S.S.R. Academy of Sciences, 1949.

[3] *Journal of the U.S.S.R. Academy of Sciences' Institute of Economics*, August 1953.

Supreme Soviet on 8 August 1953 Mr. Malenkov praised India's part in the Korean armistice negotiations, and emphasized the importance to Russia of Soviet-Pakistani relations.[1] The contrast in this speech between Mr. Malenkov's severe criticism of the United States and his friendly reference to the new national states of Asia gave a hint that he and his colleagues had recognized the potential value to Soviet policy of a friendly approach to the national governments in former colonial territories. None of these countries wanted to become involved in the struggles of the Great Powers. There was still much emotional anti-colonial feeling among the population, and the general industrial and military weakness of the new Asian countries made their leaders anxious to avoid anything which could divert resources from economic to military purposes.

The new Soviet Government lost no time in putting its theories into practice. In September 1953 the Russians signed a five-year trade agreement with the Indian Government, and helped to arrange exchanges of cultural delegations and film festivals between Moscow and New Delhi. In November 1954 a group of Soviet technicians arrived in India in connexion with offers by the Soviet Government to erect a steel plant worth 100 million dollars in India, aid which was accepted on 2 February 1955, after some months of indecision, by Mr. Nehru's Government.[2] The new Soviet line was confirmed in the same year when Soviet publications reversed the decisions taken at the Third Congress of the Indian Communist party held from 27 December 1953 to 3 January 1954.[3]

The Soviet Foreign Minister, Mr. Molotov, struck a new note on India in his speech to the Supreme Soviet on 8 February 1955 when he rejected previous Soviet opinions on India's status with these words: 'There is great historical significance in the fact that colonial India no longer exists, but the Indian Republic. This is an important turning point in events characterizing Asia's post-war development.'[4]

---

[1] *Pravda*, 9 August 1953.

[2] There were reports in India at this time that the Russians were in such a hurry to provide the plant that they dismantled one already built in a satellite country and reassembled it in India.

[3] This Congress had accused Mr. Nehru's Government of Gandhi-ism, and 'bourgeois nationalism', and was held just after the party's General Secretary, Ajoy Ghosh (who was re-elected), had returned from a prolonged stay in the Soviet Union. Moreover, there was no change in the official Soviet view of India's history and status in the world. The Congress was reported in the *Cominform Journal*, 5 February 1954.

[4] *Pravda*, 9 February 1955.

Then came the spectacular visit of Mr. Nehru to the Soviet Union between 7 and 23 June 1955. On his arrival in Moscow, Mr. Nehru was accorded honours offered to no other foreign visitor to the Soviet Union. He was driven through the streets of the capital in an open car side by side with the Premier, Marshal Bulganin. Reports on his tour indicated that he saw more than was usually shown to foreigners. On one of his public appearances in Moscow he stood in the centre of the entire Soviet Presidium, and on 21 June he addressed a public meeting in the Dynamo Stadium attended by 80,000 people, something which no foreigner had ever done before. Marshal Bulganin introduced Mr. Nehru to the crowds as 'one of the out-standing leaders of the struggle of the Indian people for national independence', and went on: 'The Soviet people are following with great interest and sympathy the efforts which the great Indian people are making to establish in their country a society on Socialist lines, and hail the achievements of the Indian people in advancing their economy and developing their national industry.'[1]

The communiqué issued at the end of the visit included several Soviet concessions to Mr. Nehru's conception of peace as 'not merely the absence of war, but a way of life and of thinking and action', concessions which make strange reading beside Marx-Leninist rulings on 'just wars', and provide a measure of the Soviet Government's eagerness to win the Indian Government's favour. The text referred to the fear of small countries of the tremendous material strength of the Great Powers, and to the universal danger of atomic war, an opinion which Mr. Malenkov had been forced to recant. Before leaving Moscow, Mr. Nehru extended an invitation to the Soviet Premier and to Mr. Khrushchev to pay a return visit to India towards the end of the year. The Soviet leaders arrived in Delhi in November 1955.

In recognition of the splendour of Mr. Nehru's official reception in the Soviet Union in June, the Indian Government spared no effort to impress their Soviet visitors, and wherever they travelled they were met by lavish hospitality and vast crowds. It is possible that the vigour of the Indian welcome led the Soviet leaders, particularly the exuberant Mr. Khrushchev, to misjudge the temper and outlook of informed Indian opinion. The motive behind most of the visitors' speeches was to impress the Indians with Soviet power, to publicize Soviet sympathy for India, to divide India from Britain and the

[1] *Pravda*, 22 June 1955.

Commonwealth, and to convince Soviet and East European opinion that India's 367 million people were already in the Soviet camp. Many of Mr. Khrushchev's attempts to reconcile these three aims misfired, and some were openly exposed by the Indian Press and radio.[1] But this should not obscure the fact that the visit impressed the very large crowds who came to see the Soviet leaders, and the joint communiqué signed on 13 December 1955 contained some Indian concessions to the Soviet point of view on certain international issues. These included Indian approval of the Soviet view that unilateral disarmament by the Soviet Union would be harmful when, in the words of the communiqué, 'her partners in negotiation' intended to increase their armaments.

The visit also produced an economic agreement by which further steps were taken in the Soviet campaign to effect an entry into India's national economy. Marshal Bulganin made renewed offers of technical assistance to India, including help in the building of industrial plants, electric power stations, and the development of the use of atomic energy for peaceful purposes. The Soviet Union also offered to sell rolled ferrous metal equipment, oil drilling and mining machinery, and to supply one million tons of steel to India over a period of three years. She also offered help in organizing prospecting for other mineral resources, and to establish shipping connexions between the two countries. In return, the Soviet Union offered to buy India's raw materials and some manufactured goods.[2] These offers were followed up in March 1956 by a visit to India by Mr. Mikoyan, who said in Delhi: 'We offer India commodities which will

[1] Mr. Khrushchev's boast that the Soviet Union had exploded the most powerful hydrogen bomb did not arouse the expected enthusiasm in India, nor did his statement to the Indian Parliament that the Communist party of the Soviet Union, of eight million members, was the 'ruler and organizer' of 200 million people. It was perhaps an unhappy coincidence for him that the execution of six Georgian officials on 24 November 1955 was announced at a time when he was explaining the happy brotherly relationship of the peoples of the Soviet Union to the Indians. Much of the material in the Soviet leader's crude attacks on Britain was known to be untrue by many Indians, and it was this mistaken approach which led the *Times of India*, for example, to write on 23 November: 'It is only too easy for those who have failed to grasp the spirit of the non-alignment policy to suppose that a manifestation of Asian nationalism such as anti-colonialism is identical with hostility towards the West.'

[2] It is also believed that the East European countries entered the lists to build up India's economy. Czechoslovakia offered to set up a joint Czech-Indian steel plant, Hungary to supply rolling stock, Poland to develop oil and copper deposits, and East Germany assistance in the optical trade.

help to develop India's economy. . . . We are ready to share our experience with India in the creation of her own oil industry.'[1]

There can be no doubt that offers of Soviet economic and technical help made a great impression in Delhi, coming as they did at a crucial point in India's second Five Year Plan, and observers in India at the time emphasized the fortunate timing of the Soviet economic campaign in raising Soviet prestige.[2] Nor was this all, for in 1956 the Soviet Government rewrote modern Indian history in an attempt to attract the Indian intellectuals. A most authoritative and detailed criticism of earlier official writings on India was published in January 1956 in a specialist Soviet journal *Soviet Eastern Studies*. After stating that the study of Eastern affairs in the Soviet Union had been gravely prejudiced by failure to understand the contradictions between imperialism and the native forces of national progress, the article turned specifically to India:

'There is a well-known proposition of Marxism-Leninism', the author declared, 'which states that . . . the proletariat of those colonial and dependent countries where capitalism is comparatively developed may become the leader of a national liberation. . . . But from this unquestionably correct proposition, the incorrect deduction has been made that only the leadership of the proletariat can ensure victory in the struggle for national liberation. Therefore when India, Burma, and some other countries won their sovereignty under the national bourgeoisie, many Eastern experts were unable to appreciate objectively the great importance of this occurrence . . . [it] was treated as the final deal of the bourgeoisie with imperialism.

'In particular, the political line of the bourgeoisie in India and the National Congress headed by M. K. Gandhi has for some years been represented in this way.' [3]

A new Soviet book on India, published in 1957, called *India in the Struggle to Relax Tension in South-East Asia and the Far East* by T. Grigoriev, was even more fulsome in its praise of the Indian Government. India's policy in the Korean War, over the crisis in Indo-China, and her attitude to the South-East Asia Treaty Organization were quoted with approval, and the author concluded: 'From whichever way one looks at it, the key to India's foreign policy is

[1] *Pravda*, 28 March 1956.
[2] See Geoffrey Tyson: *India and the Russian Visitors*, International Affairs, Vol. 32, No. 2, pp. 178–80.
[3] *Sovetskoe Vostokovedenie*, No. 1, 1956, quoted in *Central Asian Review*, Vol. IV, No. 4, 1956, pp. 343–5.

peace . . . a classical example of co-existence between states with different social orders are the relations between the Soviet Union and India.'[1] But perhaps the most striking contrast in all these quotations from Soviet works on India is to be found in the references to Mahatma Gandhi. In 1949 Gandhi was presented as 'always the first traitor to the mass national liberation movement. The struggle against Gandhi-ism . . . is impossible without unmasking his consistent betrayal of the popular movement'.[2] In 1955 Indians were confronted with a 'Mahatma Gandhi, who had such a fine knowledge of his country and its great people, and who played such a big part in your history'.[3]

It is not difficult to see, from the change which came over Soviet policy towards India after 1953, that the Soviet Government had launched a major economic, political, and cultural offensive to drive a wedge between India and the West, to win Indian political favour, and to gain an economic foothold in India. The Soviet Government dealt in the first instance directly with the Indian Government as an equal and as a friendly power, although it would not be true to say that the Indian Communist party was abandoned by the Soviet Union.[4] Initially begun by Mr. Malenkov, the campaign was taken over by Mr. Khrushchev in 1955, and made considerable progress towards creating a more favourable image of the Soviet Union in India, and of Soviet interest in India's economic advance.

India, however, was not the only Asian country to receive friendly attention from Moscow at government level after years of Soviet abuse. Burma's recent history was described in 1951 by a Soviet Orientalist in these terms:

Running up against a mighty popular movement in Burma, the British colonizers, relying on the treacherous national bourgeoisie, split the anti-Fascist League of Resistance and introduced into the so-called Executive Council under the Governor, the leader of the League, Aung San, who represented the bourgeoisie. Having placed at the head of the Executive Council the right-wing Socialist Thakin Nu (later known as

[1] Extracts quoted from *Central Asian Review*, Vol. V, No. 4, 1957, pp. 422–9.
[2] A. M. D'yakov, *The Crisis of the Colonial System*, Moscow, 1949.
[3] Speech by N. S. Khrushchev in India, December 1955, as quoted in *New Time*, No. 52, 1955.
[4] After the defeat of the Indian Communist party by the Congress party in the elections in the State of Andhra in February 1955, the party was set to work on the task of gaining mainly peasant support in Northern India and in the State of Kerala. In 1957 the party won control of Kerala in State elections, and remained in power there until 1959.

U Nu) and having concluded with him a number of treaties enslaving Burma, the British Government on 4 January 1948 declared the so-called independence of Burma. . . . The demagogic manoeuvres of the puppet U Nu Government, which has proclaimed the programme of a 'free socialist Burma' and at the same time has established a terrorist régime for the suppression of the national liberation movement, cannot deceive the people.[1]

That was written in 1951. Two years later, Mr. Malenkov tentatively introduced a new approach with a friendly reference to Burma in his speech on 8 August 1953. But in Burma the Chinese Communists made the first move in December 1954, with an invitation to the Prime Minister, U Nu, to visit Peking. As a result of the visit, the two Governments agreed to co-operate on the main issues of international affairs, and to sign an economic treaty under which China agreed to take Burmese rice in exchange for Chinese machinery and equipment.[2] This agreement was expanded in April 1955, when China offered to supply Burma with textile machinery.

It was not until after the fall of Mr. Malenkov that the Soviet Government extended its Asian drive to include Burma. In July, 1955, a three-year Soviet-Burmese trade agreement was signed, under which the U.S.S.R. agreed to take 200,000 tons of Burmese rice. On 20 October 1955 U Nu arrived in Moscow on an official visit, where he was joined on 31 October by a Burmese economic mission for the discussion of Soviet-Burmese trade and technical help. On 22 November the Soviet Press announced that Russia would supply Burma with industrial plant, road-building machinery, pumps, compressors, cables and cement, 13 million roubles' worth of motorcars, as well as the necessary technical advice and assistance. The Soviet Union also announced that Burma's surplus rice crop would be acceptable in Moscow in payment of technical aid. On 7 December a further announcement was made about Soviet help for Burma's agricultural and irrigation problems, and in April 1956, during a visit by Mr. Mikoyan to Rangoon, the Soviet Government extended their 1955 agreement to five years, and increased the amount of rice which they would take in exchange for machinery and advice from

---

[1] V. A. Maslennikov, *Problems of Philosophy*, Moscow, No. 4, 1951.
[2] Another visitor to Burma early in 1955 was Marshal Tito, and although his stay was largely ceremonial, there were reports that the Burmese Government, still engaged in hunting down Communist and other guerilla bands, was interested in Yugoslav military experience, and considered asking for a Yugoslav Army training mission.

200,000 to 400,000 tons. The Burmese also accepted offers from Czechoslovakia, Poland, Hungary, and East Germany, all of whom agreed to take rice in exchange for cotton, machinery, or technical aid.

Meanwhile, Mr. Khrushchev and Marshal Bulganin paid a brief but memorable visit to Burma as part of their Asian tour. Arriving on 2 November 1955 the Soviet leaders did their utmost to abuse Britain and the West in front of Burmese audiences.[1] The visit also became the occasion for the public reversal of Soviet views on Burmese independence. Speaking at Rangoon on 1 December Marshal Bulganin said: 'The proclamation of the independence of your country, which has embarked on the path of national freedom and economic rehabilitation, is just one item of evidence of the tremendous changes that have lately taken place in Asia.'[2] The contrast with the views expressed by Mr. Maslennikov in 1951 is striking.

India and Burma represented major targets in Asia in which the new Soviet strategy expressed itself as an economic offensive designed to undercut Western economic aid, and in this way to gain Asian political goodwill and later, perhaps, economic control of these uncommitted countries. Neither the Soviet Union nor her East European neighbours required all the rice they accepted from Burma, but the Soviet leaders realized that political capital might be won by helping the Burmese to dispose of it profitably. There can be little doubt that at this stage the Soviet Union's new generosity made a good impression in many circles in India and Burma.

Farther to the south-east, the Soviet Union also reconsidered its attitude towards Indonesia. Since the failure of the Communist rebellion in 1948 the Soviet line on Indonesia had been to describe her as a country possessing 'fictional independence', which 'even now is subordinated to Dutch imperialism, which in its turn is developing more and more into an instrument of American imperialism'.[3] In 1952, however, it became noticeable that the Indonesian Communist party began to show signs of a change of policy, veering away from the violent and uncompromising opposition to

---

[1] On this visit Mr. Khrushchev was widely reported in Rangoon as having said that Burma and other Asian countries had deeply rooted civilizations at a time when England was peopled by savages, but this remark was not reprinted in the Soviet Press.

[2] *New Times* (Moscow) in English, No. 1, January 1956.

[3] *Fundamental Problems of the Economics and Politics of Imperialism*, by E. Varga, Moscow, 1953.

the National Government which came to grief at Madiun in September 1948, towards support for a nationalist coalition and infiltration of the 'bourgeois' political parties.[1] These tactics coincided with a new recruitment policy aimed at making the Indonesian Communist party a mass party. At the party's conference in March 1954, as reported in the Soviet Press, the party had 49,000 full members, and 116,000 candidates; by November 1954 this total had risen to 500,000,[2] and by August 1956 it was reported to have passed the million mark.[3]

It has been suggested that so sudden a rise in the recruitment of party members has generally taken place at a time when there seemed to be a reasonable chance that the party might achieve power, as in Czechoslovakia in 1948. The activities of the Indonesian Communist party and its position in the country in the period 1954-56 did suggest that a government dependent on Communist support could not be ruled out. In June 1955, during the pre-election campaign, the party's Central Committee under D. N. Aidit reversed its election slogans and abandoned the call for a 'dictatorship of the people' in favour of a coalition between the Communists and the Nationalist parties. On 9 September 1955 Aidit contributed an article to the *Cominform Journal* in which he explained the reason for the change of slogan by referring to the prizes available to the party if they could dominate the country's existing parliamentary machinery. At the same time the importance of Indonesian Communism and its prospects achieved recognition by the promotion of Indonesians to posts in international front organizations. And possible signs of Communist penetration into Indonesian Government circles included the signature of the Stockholm 'World Peace Council' Appeal by the Foreign Minister, Mr. Sinarjo, in 1954, and the presence of Indonesian Ministers at Communist-dominated 'Peace' conferences in Budapest and Peking.

Meanwhile, the Soviet Union approached the Indonesian Government with a number of proposals in 1954. Agreements were negotiated on the establishments of Embassies in Moscow and Djakarta, and the Soviet Union contributed the biggest pavilion to the International Economic Fair, which opened in the Indonesian capital on

---

[1] The timing of this change coincided with the Peking Youth Conference, and the emergence in the Indonesian Communist party of a new leader, D. N. Aidit.
[2] *Tass*, 12 November 1954.
[3] *Pravda*, 6 August 1956.

21 August. The Soviet Press had already reported on 14 April that Russia was ready to offer Indonesia economic aid, and East Germany, Rumania, Hungary, and Czechoslovakia all came forward with suggestions on Communist help in the construction of factories in Indonesia. The campaign was temporarily slowed down by the uncertainties of the internal political situation in Indonesia after the elections in September 1955, but Soviet activity was resumed in April 1956 with the return to power of the 'neutralist' Premier, Mr. Sastroamidjodjo. President Soekarno was invited to Moscow in August, where he concluded a Soviet-Indonesian Trade Agreement granting the Russians the right to set up a Mission in Djakarta, and arranging an exchange of Soviet industrial equipment and Indonesian food and raw materials. Czechoslovakia signed a credit agreement with Indonesia on 8 August 1956 for the dispatch of machinery and technicians from Prague.

Perhaps the most interesting point in the Soviet approach to Indonesia is the contrast with Russia's Indian and Burmese policy. Compared with that offered to India and Burma, Soviet economic aid to Indonesia was smaller and less publicized, probably because the relatively advantageous position of the Indonesian Communist party made its adherence to a government coalition a practical possibility in 1955–56. When a non-Communist, uncommitted government was approached by the Soviet Union, the extent and quality of Soviet aid was likely to depend on the relative strengths of the non-Communist government and the local Communist party. The more firmly was the government in power, the more aid was likely to be required from the Soviet Union in order to achieve the desired political and economic influence; the nearer the local Communist party was to a position of power or influence within the government, the smaller was the aid offered to the established non-Communist régime.[1] This appeared to be the case in Soviet-Indonesian relations during this period.

Soviet relations with certain other territories in south-east Asia appeared to follow this general pattern. After the conclusion of the 1954 Geneva Agreement on Indo-China, the Soviet Union made approaches to Laos and Cambodia, the two states whose indepen-

---

[1] This ratio would not, of course, apply to a firmly anti-Communist national government such as those in Pakistan or Thailand. It only operated if the authorities had definite leanings towards neutralism or were uncommitted to any Power *bloc*.

dence was recognized under that treaty. In July 1956 the Crown Prince and Premier of Cambodia paid a visit to Russia, as a result of which the two countries exchanged Ambassadors, and the Cambodian Government accepted an offer of Soviet economic and technical help. The Cambodians also responded to overtures from China in February 1956, and accepted a Chinese grant of equipment to the value of £8 million.

Towards the remaining countries, Malaya, South Vietnam, Singapore, and the Philippines, however, Soviet policy had little room for manoeuvre. The Malayan Communist party was still in the field against growing Malayan nationalism, and steadily losing the struggle: according to an official announcement on 3 July 1955, Communist strength in the jungle had been halved between 1951 and 1955. One attempt to achieve some degree of flexibility was the Malayan Communist party's request, published on 23 June 1955, for a round-table conference to discuss the ending of the emergency.[1] There were also reports in 1956 that in the Philippines, Communist-dominated rebels had put out peace-feelers to the Government. But neither in Malaya, Singapore, South Vietnam, or the Philippines was the Soviet Government in a position to approach the established régimes with offers of economic aid, and the local Communist parties remained the only vehicle for Soviet influence.

This brief examination of Soviet policy in the Indian subcontinent and south-east Asia shows that the post-Stalin leadership in Russia realized the advantages of economic and political penetration of an area where it was hoped in Moscow nationalism could be influenced away from Western ideas, and where offers of economic and technical aid and the frequently uneconomic purchase of agrarian surpluses for political reasons could swing non-Communist governments round to accept at least some elements of the Soviet point of view. The social structures or internal policy of the régime had no bearing on the decision in Moscow: a feudal Prince who would co-operate with Moscow or Peking was more welcome than a government elected on a Socialist programme which would not. For the Soviet Union the years 1955–56 produced no startling recruits for the Communist cause. India and Burma were firmly anti-Communist, and Indonesia remained in non-Communist hands. But no doubt the Soviet leaders

---

[1] A conference was held in December 1955 between the Chief Ministers of Malaya and Singapore and the Communist leader, Chin Peng, but no agreement was reached owing to the latter's refusal to agree to surrender terms.

were content with their policy as the opening phase of a very long-term strategic plan, and were confident of its ultimate success. For, as one authoritative Communist observer, commenting on the outlook in south-east Asia in 1955, put it: 'Developing trade with colonial and semi-colonial countries has a very great political importance.'[1]

[1] *Propagandist*, Budapest, March 1955.

XII

SOVIET POLICY TOWARDS CHINA: 1953-56

EXAMINATION of Soviet policy towards Europe, the Middle East, and south-east Asia after 1953 presents a picture of a strategy involving a stalemate in Europe—geographically the Western bastion of the Soviet position—based on reduced tension, and freedom to conduct a mobile flexible policy of political and economic penetration of the area stretching from Egypt to Indonesia. In Europe, many of the short-sighted restrictions of the Stalin era were removed by Mr. Khrushchev, who understood the value of conceding inessential points while remaining adamant on issues involving the security of the Communist bloc. In Asia, the Soviet aim was to effect an entry into the economic and political life of emerging and uncommitted countries in order to drive out the West, and ultimately bring these states into the orbit of the Soviet Union. These conclusions cover the Soviet Union's western and southern flanks, and it is now time to study her attitude towards her eastern flank; in other words, Soviet relations with Communist China during the same period.

There can be little doubt that to the Soviet Government, normally content to enjoy numerical superiority in its political, economic, and military dealings with other countries, the size of China must have been the unique factor in these relations. China's population was 582.6 million people, according to the official census, taken in June 1953 and announced in 1954.[1] Politically, through Soviet eyes, China probably appeared as a country passing through an extreme revolutionary ferment, not unlike certain stages of the Soviet Union's earlier history. In 1954-55 the Chinese Communist party leadership was in the throes of a bitter campaign against political heresy within its own ranks. On 31 December 1954 new regulations were published increasing the powers of the police, including preventive arrest of those who might commit political offences. The

[1] New China News Agency, 5 November 1954, quoted in Royal Institute of International Affairs, *Survey, 1954*, p. 236. The often-quoted total of 600 million is reached by adding the Chinese population of Formosa and Chinese living in Hong Kong, Malaya, Singapore, and Indonesia.

Government announced a reorganization of the police machinery for controlling city residents in order to give the local authorities tighter control over the activities and opinions of citizens within their areas. Internal tension was forced upwards until on 14 April 1955 the party announced the dismissal (and subsequent suicide) of one of the leading members of the administration, Kao Kang. The charges against him included conspiracy, harming Army-Party relations and carving out a kingdom for himself in Manchuria. On 13 May the purge spread to leaders in the literary field and on 10 June one Hu Feng, a writer who opposed doctrinaire controls of literature, was arrested and handed over to the Public Prosecutor. Meanwhile, the Chinese Press hammered the theme of 'revolutionary vigilance'. On 14 April 1955 one paper wrote: 'Mobilize the whole party to fight evil persons and evil deeds', and continued: 'All who oppose mass accusations are evil persons . . . of course mass accusations may be untrue in some cases, and there may even be false charges, but what is there to fear? When the water falls, the rock will be revealed. What is urgently needed today is to give support and protection to accusers inside and outside the party.' In a speech made public in August 1955 the Chairman of the Supreme People's Court, Tung Pi-wu, complained 'a feeling of peacefulness and relaxation, an extremely injurious state of mind has grown up among the people'.

To counteract this complaint, the whole country was swept by an officially-inspired and organized campaign of spy-mania, which coincided with a number of belligerent references to the international situation. For example, the Chinese Defence Minister, Peng Te-huai, who attended the foundation of the Warsaw Pact in May 1955 as an observer, offered the support of Chinese forces to member-states of the Pact involved in war in Europe. Even during the Geneva Conference in July, Chinese official pronouncements were often at their most threatening. Addressing the National People's Congress, a Vice-Chairman of the National Defence Council, Yeh Chien-ying, declared on 27 July that it was wrong to think that the need to arm the country had passed. 'If we are feeble,' he said, 'we shall invite war. As long as Formosa is not liberated, the task of the People's Liberation Army is not finished.' [1] And indeed China was arming at an alarming rate. According to figures given in 1957, the Chinese Government devoted over 22 per cent of its State budget to defence in 1955 and this represented two-fifths of the amount of funds spent

[1] Peking Radio, 27 July 1955.

on economic development.[1] Militarization, for which the Chinese were probably partly responsible, was also the order of the day in North Korea. There, in spite of Article 13D of the Armistice, which prohibited increases in arms in either North or South Korea, the North Korean Army possessed in 1955 450 more aircraft, 30 more tanks, and 500 more mortars than the authorized strength, according to information at the disposal of the United Nations Command.

These aspects of China's policy certainly impressed the outside world, and underlined the revolutionary fervour of her Communist leadership. To judge from the public pronouncements of Chinese leaders and from the Chinese Press, the world could expect a policy of military expansion and political subversion abroad, and the extremes of terror at home. The latter was unhappily only too true, but there was a contradiction between word and deed in Chinese foreign policy. While maintaining a continuous stream of belligerent propaganda, the Chinese Government found ways of playing a part in the policy of reduction of tension initiated by the Soviet Government in the spring of 1955. Chinese participation in the Afro-Asian meeting at Bandung in Indonesia in April 1955 was characterized by the calm and co-operative bearing of Mr. Chou-En-lai, the Chinese Premier, who led his country's delegation. He even offered to deal directly with the American Government on the Formosa problem or to talk to the 'local authorities' in the island on surrender terms. In March 1955 the Chinese withdrew six divisions from North Korea, and released a number of British and American nationals, both military and civilian, who had been interned or imprisoned in China, some in connexion with the Korean War.

On 1 August 1955 talks opened in Geneva between Chinese and American representatives to try to settle some matters of direct interest between the two States. On 17 August the Chinese made an approach to Japan for the restoration of diplomatic and commercial ties between the two countries; in dealing with India and other Asian countries the Chinese made every effort to appear conciliatory, and to give the impression that their policy was based on the well-known 'five principles of co-existence'.[2] Relations were, in fact, closest with India, whose Prime Minister, Mr. Nehru, had been given a tumultuous public welcome in Peking in October 1954. A local frontier

[1] Peking Radio, 31 July 1957.
[2] These were: (1) Mutual respect for territorial integrity; (2) non-aggression; (3) non-interference in internal affairs for any reason, economic, political or ideological; (4) equality and mutual benefit; (5) peaceful co-existence.

dispute between India and China on the Tibetan border which blew up in November 1955 was settled by a Chinese withdrawal to the accompaniment of much courteous and conciliatory comment; an additional Indian complaint over the publication of a Chinese map which showed parts of India as Chinese territory was answered by an apology from Peking and the disowning of the offending map. China also offered to supply India with steel which she badly needed herself. The Indian Premier's visit was followed in May by that of the Indonesian Prime Minister, and by a delegation from North Vietnam, led by Ho Chi Minh, who secured a promise of valuable economic aid. In June an Egyptian delegation visited Peking and concluded an important trade agreement with China. In short, China allied herself with the Soviet policy of fraternization, with a particular eye on the Asian countries.

It seems clear that during this period China was committed to a foreign policy which by virtue of its timing was probably undertaken on advice from Moscow, and followed the line of co-operation with other countries and a reduction of tension. However, the fervour of China's internal revolution, and many of her utterances which were belligerent and uncompromising, suggested that this policy of *détente* did not come from the Chinese Communists' heart. It is probable that, left to themselves, the Chinese Communist leaders might have preferred a policy of expansion (perhaps even of military conquest) in Formosa, Indo-China or Korea, but agreed to accept direction of part, at least, of their propaganda and political effort from the Soviet leaders. Why were the Chinese ready to follow the Soviet line in international affairs at this stage in their revolution?

Part of the answer to this question undoubtedly lies in the status of the Soviet State and Communist party within the Communist world. The Soviet Union's prestige and experience in international affairs was unrivalled, and the tradition of turning to Moscow for advice was hard to abandon at short notice. Secondly, both the Russians and the Chinese were aware that nothing could be gained for either by divergencies in their policies; this was what the 'external enemy the imperialists' were praying for, and it was in China's interest to accept this kind of advice from her more experienced, if smaller, ally. But this cannot be regarded as a full explanation. It seems very likely that the Soviet Union held some kind of whip-hand over China's ability to carry out an independent foreign policy, and that the Chinese were well aware of their vulnerability in this respect.

The evidence for a strong Soviet position of this kind is convincing. The most obvious field is that of military aid to the Chinese Army. The war in Korea from 1950 to 1953 showed that the Chinese were dependent on the Russians for military equipment and arms beyond the requirements of a largely infantry army. In the summer of 1955 a National People's Congress was held in Peking which was addressed on 27 July by Yeh Chien-ying, a Vice-Chairman of the National Defence Council. In a most revealing speech, he said: 'Our industry must be speeded up in order to remedy China's inability to provide the armed forces with the most modern equipment', a clear admission of China's dependence on the Soviet Union for arms. Details of military aid provided by Russia to China are, of course closely guarded secrets, but we must assume that Moscow was aware of the value of her position of control in this vital sphere.

More data is available about the Soviet Union's trade with China and the economic and industrial aid which Moscow provided. Since the establishment of the Chinese People's Republic in 1949, the Soviet Union negotiated two major economic aid treaties with China, one in February 1950 of the equivalent of 300 million dollars, and one in October 1954 of 130 million dollars. The treaty of February 1950 laid the foundation of a programme of regular Soviet aid to China, and the agreement signed in 1954 was intended to be, on the surface at least, the next stage in this Soviet policy. The terms of the treaty, which was published on 12 October 1954 were generous to China.[1] The Soviet Union undertook to grant her a long-term loan of 520 million roubles (130 million dollars), to provide help in the construction of fifteen new industrial enterprises, and to increase the supplies of equipment already earmarked for 141 projects by an amount estimated at over 400 million roubles. The two countries agreed to complete the sections lying within their territories of two vital railways: that connecting northern China with Russia through Outer Mongolia, and the much longer line from Lanchow westwards

[1] Royal Institute of International Affairs, *Documents, 1954*, p. 322. Royal Institute of International Affairs, *Survey, 1954*, pp. 240–2. The negotiations were also interesting from the internal Soviet point of view, for the U.S.S.R. was represented by N. S. Khrushchev, N. A. Bulganin, A. M. Mikoyan, and N. M. Shvernik. Mr. Molotov was omitted. Because of the timing of the visit, which coincided with the return of the propaganda in favour of heavy industry in Russia and away from Malenkov's economic policies, it is virtually certain that the visitors acquainted the Chinese leaders with their intention to remove Mr. Malenkov at the earliest opportunity.

through Sinkiang to Alma Ata, in Soviet Central Asia.[1] Soviet-Chinese mixed companies, established in 1950 for joint exploitation of the mineral wealth and oil resources of Sinkiang, for civil air transport, and for shipbuilding and repair were to be dissolved and handed over to the Chinese. The Soviet Union presented China with equipment for setting up a model state farm.

In a separate agreement the Soviet Union agreed to return to China the Soviet military and naval base at Port Arthur, and to withdraw its troops from the Liaoning peninsula by the end of May 1955, an undertaking which was punctually fulfilled. The Chinese Army took over all the installations, though there is some evidence that some compensation was paid to the Russians.

At the same time, on 7 April 1956, the Soviet Union undertook to assist China in equipping fifty-five new industrial enterprises in addition to the 156 already under construction, help to the value of 2,500 million roubles.

Every care was taken, in the wording of the treaty and in Press comment upon it, to give the impression that China and the Soviet Union treated each other as equal, joint leaders of world Communism. In his speech to the Supreme Soviet on 12 February 1955, Mr. Molotov said: 'The most important result of the Second World War was the formation . . . of the world camp of Socialism and Democracy, headed by the U.S.S.R., or, more accurately, by the Soviet Union and the People's Republic of China.'[2]

These treaties give the impression that Soviet assistance to China represented an almost unending series of free gifts. Yet this is not so. At sessions of the National People's Congress and in later speeches, broadcast over Peking Radio, Chinese Ministers revealed how Soviet aid to China was carried out in practice. Of the 8,100 million roubles (or 2,025 million dollars) of Soviet aid arranged by April 1956, it appears that only one-fifth was supplied on the credit basis normal for heavy capital equipment. Four-fifths had to be paid for in Chinese counter-deliveries to the Soviet Union or in hard foreign currency. On 20 July 1955, according to Peking Radio, the Chinese Minister for Foreign Trade, Yeh Chi-chuang, told the National People's Congress that 94 per cent of all China's imports of machinery and construction material came from the Soviet Union, and went on to

---

[1] The first half of this line on Chinese soil was completed to Hami by the end of 1959. (*The Times*, 1 January 1960.)

[2] *Pravda*, 13 February 1955.

say that China's import 'shopping list' was compiled to give priority to the industrial projects which the Soviet Union was helping China to set up.

Soviet insistence on payment for its aid to China was underlined in a speech in November 1955 by the Deputy Minister for Foreign Trade, Lu Chi-jen. He revealed that Soviet aid had to be obtained by trade, and that the 1950 and 1954 Soviet loans would finance only part of China's needs. Therefore, he said, the Government had to 'find' meat, tea, wool, silk, tobacco, and minerals to export to the Soviet Union in order to ensure the flow of essential materials for construction projects. Moreover, added the Deputy Minister, 'we must do more to improve the quality of our exports in order to supply the needs of the Soviet Union in a more satisfactory manner'. Since 56 per cent more Soviet equipment would be needed by China in 1955–56, the export quotas of goods required by the Soviet Union would have to be increased.

These Chinese revelations depict—at least on the economic front—a dominant Soviet Union and a suppliant China. But this is not the whole story. China's financial position was additionally complicated by the fact that she was committed to granting more aid to other countries than she was receiving from the Soviet Union. Soviet loans up to 1956 amounted to the equivalent of 430 million dollars; but China had promised loans totalling 760 million dollars to North Korea and Vietnam.[1] China also agreed to pay to North Korea all the goods and expenses incurred as aid from June 1950 to December 1953, that is, during the Korean War.[2]

The strictness of Soviet conditions for supplying aid to China was underlined by the serious food shortages in China in 1955 and the appalling lack of consumer goods. Peking newspapers in April admitted that in 1954 50 million peasants were short of food, and that the production of food would not meet the people's needs 'for a considerable period'. At the National People's Congress in 1955 one Minister called on the population to reduce grain consumption, saying that it would be practicable for each person to eat two-thirds of a pound less each month, thus saving $1\frac{1}{2}$ million tons a year. In November 1956 *People's Daily* was still saying that grain supplies

[1] *United Nations Economic Survey of Asia and Far East*, 1955, New York, 1956, p. 98.
[2] *Izvestia*, 14 August 1955. Interview with North Korean Ambassador in Moscow.

were inadequate.[1] On consumer goods, Peking Radio in November 1956 was still explaining away shortages. After queueing for long periods for meat many citizens had been unable to get any at all, and clothes rationing, particularly for cotton, had had to be reintroduced.[2] But people should understand, said the commentator, that living standards ought not to be raised too quickly.

Examples of this kind were to be found frequently in the Chinese Press and radio in the years 1954 to 1956, and provide additional evidence for the conclusion that the Soviet economic grip on China was severe and far reaching. Aid had to be paid for out of China's own production and was, moreover, directed towards specific projects at this stage probably controlled and certainly designed by the Russians. No Soviet aid was provided to raise the standard of living of the Chinese population as a whole. In fact, the truth behind Soviet economic aid adds realism to Soviet policy towards China in 1954–56 and helps to explain the paradox of the alternating belligerency and conciliation in Chinese politics. The Soviet Union was ready to grant China equality of leadership of the Communist world on the surface, and while the outside world was watching to treat her as a Great Power. For example, the Russians were quick to raise China's prestige in Asia by withdrawing their troops from Port Arthur, although the move was, in fact, in accordance with the new elements in Soviet military doctrine. It is also clear that no Soviet attempt was made to dictate China's internal policy in the handling of her own Communist revolution. Party purges, belligerent propaganda, and even a little sabre-rattling in the Far Eastern situation—this was China's internal affair, so long as it remained in word rather than deed. Soviet policy-planners no doubt realized the value to themselves and to China of intermittent tension in the Formosa Straits, for it served, among other things, to distract American attention from Europe, and to divide Washington from London and Paris. However, when the Soviet Union required a service from China, such as the maintenance of the *status quo* in Korea, Indo-China and Formosa, or Chinese participation in the Soviet campaign to reduce tension in certain areas and to offer economic aid and trade to uncommitted countries, there was little doubt that the Russians possessed the means to ensure Chinese co-operation. The Chinese leaders had neither the desire, nor, in the last analysis, the power to

[1] *People's Daily* (Peking), 24 November 1956.
[2] Peking Radio, 25 and 28 November 1956.

break away from the Soviet Union. They were bound together ideologically, and in 1954–56, at least, the Soviet economic grip was strong enough to handle any signs of indiscipline on the part of Peking.

From the point of view of overall strategy, therefore, it is a safe assumption to make that the Soviet Government was, in fact, interested in maintaining the *status quo* in the Far East and in avoiding a major revolutionary or national war on her eastern borders. Had the Soviet Government been interested in the spread of Communism by force of arms in the Far East, nothing would have been easier than to help China to seize Formosa, to reopen the fighting in Korea, or to pick a quarrel with the small non-Communist states in Indo-China. In fact, neither Russia nor China did any of these things, and all available evidence points to the conclusion that just as the Soviet Union sought to stabilize the situation in Europe so as to have a firm and solid bastion on her western flank, so her policy towards China was aimed at creating a second bastion on her eastern flank. While the western bastion was formed by standing firm on the *status quo* in an improved atmosphere of readiness for negotiations between the Great Powers, the Chinese or eastern bastion was to be established by a close Soviet supervision of the essential components of Chinese power—her military and industrial progress. In each case, the object was to secure the Soviet Union's two main flanks against disturbance or change, while her leaders occupied themselves with the flexible political and economic offensive into the uncommitted areas to the south and east of the Soviet frontier in Asia.

XIII

THE EFFECT OF DE-STALINIZATION ON FOREIGN POLICY: 1956

BY the spring of 1956 Soviet strategy all over the world seemed to have settled down into a recognizable pattern which was consistent both with Communist theory and the practical methods advocated by Mr. Khrushchev. A stable situation existed on the western and eastern flanks of the Soviet Union—in Europe, through a combination of relaxed tension and unshakeable determination to maintain the key positions of Communist rule in Eastern Europe—and in China, through binding Sino-Soviet treaties, based on Soviet strength, which appeared to give the Soviet Union at this stage the ultimate word in Chinese foreign policy. Stability in the East and the West enabled the Soviet Government to pursue an active policy of political and economic penetration into the area between Europe and the Far East, where traditional Western control was being superseded by Arab and Asian nationalism. In other words, the Soviet strategists had created a situation in which they were free to concentrate on one front only. With this classical goal of foreign policy successfully achieved, the Soviet Government seemed to have found a foreign strategy of considerable promise.

The events of 1956, however, severely damaged these hopes, and very nearly cost Mr. Khrushchev a vital part of one of his bastions: Soviet domination of Eastern Europe. The crisis in Eastern Europe which followed the Twentieth Congress of the Soviet Communist party in February 1956, a conference which has become famous for Mr. Khrushchev's 'secret speech' which demolished the Stalin legend, was the Soviet leader's own responsibility, though no one could have predicted the full extent of the upheaval which swept across the Continent as a result.

The drama of Mr. Khrushchev's attack on Stalin, and the undoubted shock which it administered to Communists all over the world, has sometimes overshadowed the earlier and more deliberate change of Soviet tactics at the time of the Congress. It will be remembered that before the Nineteenth Party Congress in October 1952 a preview of a change in tactics was published in the main theoretical journal *Bolshevik* (now renamed *Kommunist*). In February 1956 the same journal appeared with a similar preview, written by a member of the editorial board, A. Sobelev, and called 'The World-Wide Historical Significance of the Socialist Camp'. The article had obviously been prepared well in advance, and it put forward the thesis that in contemporary conditions it is possible to 'utilize parliamentary forms of struggle for power, and for the peaceful development of the Revolution'. It was possible, therefore, to abandon the theory of the inevitability of wars, civil wars, and violent revolutionary upheavals leading to bloodshed, and for the Communists to come to power in capitalist countries by gaining parliamentary majorities.

Mr. Khrushchev himself spoke on this theme in his 'open' speech to the Twentieth Party Congress. He argued that since the prerequisite of every Communist revolution was the disintegration of capitalist society and government by its own contradictions, the main aim of Communist parties should be to increase and deepen these contradictions. Because different capitalist countries are in various stages of development, there must be many ways of increasing the contradictions. Civil war and violence were obviously one way, but there were others, including the peaceful 'capture' of 'bourgeois' parliaments by the Communist party. Capitalist régimes could also be severely undermined by Communist penetration of their overseas markets and sources of raw materials, thus depriving them of outlets for the trade by which they live. As long as the Communist party ultimately emerged as the sole leader of the revolutionary movement, there was, said Mr. Khrushchev, more than one way to Socialism. War against the capitalist world was not inevitable, nor was the armed conflict of the type which took place in Russia in 1917–22 an essential prerequisite for the seizure of power by a Communist party.

It is not possible to estimate at what point Mr. Khrushchev decided to introduce this new element into Communist doctrine, but the events of 1956 were based on his determination to put it into action in the part of Europe under Communist control. In practice this meant adoption of some of the Yugoslav ideas of many roads to Socialism, and their imposition on the East European Communist rulers who had taken part in the Soviet campaign against Marshal Tito.

Mr. Khrushchev was ruthless in pursuit of the new policy, and disregarded the embarrassment and humiliation it brought to many of the most loyal Communist leaders in Eastern Europe. On 2 April 1956 the Central Committee of the Bulgarian Communist party met in Sofia, to discuss the dismissal and demotion of the Prime Minister, Mr. Vulko Chervenkov, a leading Stalinist and loyal supporter of the campaign against Yugoslavia. On 16 April the Bulgarian National Assembly received Mr. Chervenkov's resignation in the presence of a delegation of Yugoslav party leaders, a gesture whose significance was not lost on the Bulgarian public.[1] Some steps were taken at the same time to rehabilitate posthumously the late Traicho Kostov, the former Bulgarian party leader who had been executed in 1949 with 'Titoism' as one of his crimes. A number of his fellow accused, headed by a former Minister, Professor Ivan Stefanov, were released from prison and readmitted to party membership.

In Poland, the First Secretary of the Workers' Party, Mr. Eduard Ochab, announced on 6 April the rehabilitation of a leading Communist associated with 'national' Communism—Wladyslaw Gomulka, who had been under arrest on treason charges since 1951. On the same day General Spychalski, the former Head of the Polish Army's Political Directorate, and twenty-five other leading Communists were also released from jail. On 20 April an amnesty bill was published in Warsaw under which the Government proposed to release 30,000 prisoners, and to reduce the sentences of a further 40,000. The former Chief of Police, General Radkiewicz, and the Minister of Justice, the Public Prosecutor, and the Chief Military Prosecutor were dismissed, and Jakob Berman, the leading Moscow-trained member of the Polish party's Presidium, resigned from all his posts.

In Czechoslovakia two prominent party leaders, Mr. London and Mr. Hajdu, who had been imprisoned for 'Titoism' in 1952, were released, and on 10 April the Czechoslovak Communist party issued a formal apology to Belgrade for the 'unfounded accusations' made against Marshal Tito during political trials in 1952.

The Hungarian Stalinist, Matyas Rakosi, appeared before his party on 18 May 1956 with a confession of his faults, and political

---

[1] There were persistent reports at the time that Mr. Chervenkov's dismissal, ordered by the Soviet Communist party, aroused opposition in the Central Committee of the Bulgarian party, which was composed of Mr. Chervenkov's nominees. This might account for the delay in announcing the news of his resignation.

prisoners accused of 'Titoism' were also released. The Rumanian Government invited Marshal Tito to visit Rumania in June.[1] Even the Albanians, Yugoslavia's most single-minded detractors, managed to utter a word of formal apology to the Yugoslavs during the Albanian party's Third Congress on 25 May.

So far the East European Communist Governments had probably been acting on a central directive from Moscow, based on the new line on different ways to Socialism. There appears to be little doubt that the adaptation of policy in Eastern Europe—what a Bulgarian Communist party newspaper called 'a sharp turn in party policy'[2] —was controlled, and that its effect on Marshal Tito was expected in Moscow to be favourable. There is some evidence that in those countries where the change was most marked the party Press began almost immediately to warn potential dissidents that the new line did not mean the abandonment of Marx-Leninism, thus indicating the presence of the guiding and controlling hand over the new tactics.

However, in June, an entirely new element was introduced into the campaign: the publication in the West of the text of Mr. Khrushchev's 'secret speech' at the Twentieth Party Congress in which Stalin was de-throned, and his reputation was destroyed once and for all. It is true that the damage which can be done to a Communist party by dictatorial tendencies on the part of one leader had been discussed shortly after the Congress, and some East European Communists had included 'the cult of the individual' in their self-criticism in April and May.[3] But the shattering nature of Khrushchev's accusations against Stalin far exceeded any disturbance which local Communist régimes may have felt on this basis. Mr. Khrushchev delved deeply into Stalin's earlier years as First Secretary of the party, and revealed that he had destroyed many of the most loyal Bolshevik leaders in incessant purges, set up concentration camps and filled them with those who aroused suspicion in his mind. Mr. Khrushchev ridiculed Stalin's claim to be a military genius, and described in detail how inept interference on Stalin's part upset the plans of the High Command, and led to defeat in more than one battle. He accused

[1] The visit was to coincide with Marshal Tito's return from the Soviet Union early in June 1956, at Mr. Khrushchev's invitation. Tito was given a flattering welcome in Moscow, emphasized by the dismissal, on the day on which the Marshal arrived, of Mr. Molotov who had been an important figure in the anti-Tito campaign in 1948 from the Foreign Ministry.

[2] *Rabotnichesko Delo*, Sofia, 19 September 1956.

[3] Notably Vulko Chervenkov in Bulgaria and Matyas Rakosi in Hungary.

Stalin of cowardice during the defence of Moscow, and attributed victory to the seizure of the initiative by experienced Generals often acting against Stalin's orders. But above all Stalin was described by his former subordinate as a cruel and vindictive dictator, ignorant and suspicious, whose bouts of megalomania had brought disgrace and ridicule to the World Communist movement. From now on, promised Mr. Khrushchev, this cult of a vain dictator would disappear, legality would be restored, and the excesses of the Stalin régime would never be repeated. The Soviet party and people were called upon to rally round the new collective leadership which alone could ensure that Stalin's rule remained a thing of the past.

From the point of view of Soviet internal politics, it is not difficult to see the advantage which the gradual and controlled publication of part of the evidence on which the demolition of the Stalin legend was founded could bring to Mr. Khrushchev in his rise to supreme power. The full story could, of course, be told to the Central Committee and in the inner councils, where Stalin's cruelties and ignorance were no secret. The wider group of party members could be given an expurgated version, and in this way Mr. Khrushchev could gain a personal reputation which could win him much genuine popularity in the country at large. A break with a criminal past could enable Mr. Khrushchev to carry on the struggle for supreme leadership within the party and Government with a clear advantage over all rivals, for any who kept silent could be identified with Stalin, and those who subsequently spoke out in criticism of the dead dictator would be regarded as merely following in Mr. Khrushchev's footsteps. The plan had the elements of a very clever move for a man who aspired to unchallenged leadership in the Soviet Union.

It must be recognized, however, that the speech was not intended to be a landmark in Soviet foreign policy, and its subsequent impact on Soviet policy abroad was unintentional. With the single exception of the expulsion of Yugoslavia from the Communist camp in 1948, Stalin's foreign policy since 1945 was immune from Mr. Khrushchev's criticism in the 'secret speech'. He did not attack Stalin's policy of post-war expansion, or the decision to launch the Korean War; the blockade of Berlin and the seizure of power by *coup d'état* in Prague in 1948 did not figure in Mr. Khrushchev's catalogue of Stalin's misdeeds. In nearly all the acts by which Stalin had attempted to expand the Communist empire and undermine the position of the West, the 'cruel, megalomaniac and ignorant dictator' of the 'secret speech' had apparently been wise and sane. The tremendous impact which the speech had on foreign policy was largely due to the unplanned method of its release to a wider public than had been intended, thanks to its publication in full by the American State Department on 2 June 1956.

Although the impact was immediate in Communist parties outside the Soviet bloc, for a few weeks the guided 're-direction of effort' in the East European countries continued. The local parties continued their controlled release of political prisoners formerly accused of 'Titoism', and certain relaxations were permitted in Press comment in Poland, Hungary, and Bulgaria. A controlling hand continued to be exercised in restraining those who went too far, and the process appeared to be orderly and planned.[1]

Towards the end of June 1956, however, two events occurred which threw the whole of Mr. Khrushchev's guided policy change out of gear. In Poland an outburst of workers' protests at their standard of living suddenly developed into a violent demonstration against the régime in the city of Poznan. And in Hungary, equally unexpectedly, a meeting of the 'Petöffi Club'—a literary and artistic circle created by the Communists themselves—became a political protest, and aroused the enthusiasm of thousands of Budapest citizens with no direct connexion with the circle.

Of these two events, undoubtedly the riots in Poznan were the more dramatic, partly because they occurred under the eyes of Western businessmen attending the Poznan International Trade Fair. It appears that the workers of a large engineering factory in Poznan, dissatisfied with their wages and working conditions, sent a delegation to Warsaw on 26 June to ask the Government for a revision of wages scales and other financial benefits. On the 27th the delegation returned to Poznan, but the concessions which its leaders had obtained failed to satisfy the workers, and a strike was proclaimed in the factory. On the following day, 28 June, the strikers were joined in the streets by large numbers of citizens of Poznan, who turned a stoppage of work into a mass demonstration against the Communist régime. According to eyewitnesses, the authorities were taken by surprise, and when some shots were fired by members of the Security Police, a running battle developed along the main streets of

---

[1] In Bulgaria, a leading journalist and editor of the daily newspaper *Otechestven Front*, Vladimir Topencharov, was dismissed for critical remarks in a leading article on the leadership of the Bulgarian Communist party.

Mr. Topencharov subsequently recanted.

the city. Demonstrators obtained some arms from sympathizers in the Army, a prison was attacked and opened, and an assault was made on the headquarters of the Security forces, which was repulsed with a number of casualties. Eventually, the Government ordered the regular Army to move in; demonstrators were cleared from public buildings which they had occupied, and by 29 June order had been restored. Official casualty figures placed the numbers at forty-four demonstrators and nine members of the Government forces killed and over 300 injured; 323 people were arrested.[1]

One immediate result of the Poznan riots was the introduction on 6 July of a series of financial concessions to Polish industrial workers. The first political reaction of the Government was to attribute the riots to 'enemy agents and imperialist centres', but it was not long before the Polish leaders came forward with a different and much more accurate explanation. At the Polish Workers' party's Seventh Plenary Session on 18 July, the First Secretary of the party, Mr. Ochab said:

The Seventh Plenum of the Central Committee is holding its debates three weeks after the painful incidents in Poznan. In the appraisal of the reasons for these incidents, it would be wrong to concentrate attention above all on the machinations of provocateurs and imperialist agents. It is necessary to look first of all for the social roots of these incidents, which have become for our party a warning signal testifying to the existence of serious disturbances between the party and various sections of the working class.

Mr. Ochab's statement clearly had the ring of truth for the great majority of his audience and for the Polish people as a whole. But the significance of this speech of 18 July lies in the fact that it was the first major divergence in public between an East European Communist leadership and that of the Soviet Union—at least, that is how the speech was interpreted in Moscow. For three days later Marshals Bulganin and Zhukov arrived unexpectedly in Warsaw, ostensibly as the Soviet representatives at the celebrations in honour of Poland's Communist National Day—21 July. The real purpose of this visit emerged in Marshal Bulganin's speech, delivered at a public meeting in Warsaw on the very day of his arrival: to place on record, with the full authority of the Soviet Government and Communist party, that the Polish explanation of the Poznan riots was unacceptable to the Communist movement. Marshal Bulganin said:

[1] Polish News Agency statement, 17 July 1956.

The recent events in Poznan, provoked by hostile agents, provide fresh evidence that international reaction has not yet discarded its mad plans for the restoration of capitalism in the Socialist countries.[1]

No reference was made to the workers' grievances, whose existence had already been admitted by the Polish leaders, nor to the Poles' own criticism of their party's lack of contact with the working class.

No Polish or Soviet Communist leader could have failed to realize the challenge to Poland contained in Marshal Bulganin's words. No doubt the Soviet visitors expected an automatic recantation by Mr. Ochab in the communiqué which was issued at the end of the Seventh Plenum on 29 July but if so they were disappointed. The communiqué announced a programme of economic concessions to the workers, and although reference was made to the activities of 'hostile elements' in the riots, a considerable part of the responsibility was placed on the unhappy living conditions of the workers and the high cost of living. The Seventh Plenum of the Polish party therefore witnessed a decision by the party's Central Committee to introduce an element of Polish nationalism into party policy, and to uphold it even at the risk of active Soviet displeasure.

A number of moves made in August towards 'democratization' of the political life of the country probably had their origins in the debates at the Seventh Plenum, at which, it is now clear, more than economic concessions and the Poznan riots were discussed. On 4 August Mr. Wladyslaw Gomulka was readmitted to party membership, and all charges against him were withdrawn. The same applied to General Spychalski, General Komar (who was appointed to command the Internal Military Forces), and to Mr. Zenon Kliszko, who was given an under-secretaryship in the Ministry of Justice. These and other measures showed that the Polish leaders felt confident enough in their own strength to act without Soviet approval, and to extend the process of 'democratization' to limits set by themselves, and not by the Russians.

In Hungary there had been similar stirrings of national feeling and calls for liberalization of the régime and for freedom of speech. Reference has already been made to the turbulent meeting of the 'Petöffi Circle' in Budapest on 27 June, and minor disturbances

---

[1] Marshal Bulganin also warned against 'adverse elements in the Polish Press, which, under the flag of national peculiarities, sought to exploit difficulties in building Socialism.'

among industrial workers were also reported. But the essential difference between events in Poland and in Hungary (which was to affect the terrible events of the autumn) was that the Polish liberalization process was firmly in the hands of the official leaders of the Government and the party, who took the initiative deliberately, and carried the population with them; in Hungary, the move for democratization was inspired by unofficial quarters—writers, intellectuals, and students—and the party and Government leaders tried to oppose it. For instance, while the official Polish party Press wrote approvingly of the democratization campaign, the Hungarian paper *Szabad Nep* described the 'Petöffi Circle' demonstration as 'an open stand against the party organized by a group formed round'Imre Nagy'.[1]

Additional confusion was caused in Hungary when the appearance of this intellectual unrest coincided with measures designed to appease the Yugoslav Government similar to those which had been taken in Bulgaria, Czechoslovakia, and Rumania. Early in July the First Secretary of the Hungarian Communist party, Mr. Rakosi, and his Deputy, Mr. Gerö, visited the Soviet Union, and during their absence a number of reforms were announced, particularly in the administration of justice. On the return of Messrs. Rakosi and Gerö from Moscow, accompanied by the Soviet Deputy Premier, Mr. Mikoyan, who, after a brief stop in Budapest, continued his journey to Yugoslavia to visit Marshal Tito, the Hungarian Government announced the resignation of Mr. Rakosi and his replacement by Mr. Gerö. Laszlo Rajk, who had been executed as a 'Titoist', was formally though posthumously rehabilitated. The party also admitted to membership of the Central Committee four new leaders, two of whom, Mr Janos Kadar (later to play a significant part in the autumn revolution) and Mr. Marosan, who, as a left-wing fellow traveller, had suffered under Stalin in 1951 for his views. At a special session of the Hungarian Parliament on 30 July, Mr. Gerö promised strict adherence to legal reforms, and measures to raise the standard of living; another official spokesman announced the release of 11,398 political prisoners.

---

[1] *Szabad Nep*, 1 July 1956. Imre Nagy, a Communist who subsequently became famous during the Hungarian revolution, had suffered under Stalin, but had been appointed Premier in 1953 and ushered in a policy of raising the standard of living. In 1955, when Khrushchev re-established priority for heavy industry, Nagy was dismissed, and had often been criticized for 'liberal' and 'right-wing' views.

One curious feature about this new policy in Hungary was that it seems to have been misinterpreted both by the Soviet Government and by those who were demanding freedom of speech and the Press in the 'Petöffi Circle'. The latter took courage from the fall of Mr. Rakosi, believing it to have been partly due to their protests—and consequently pressed on with their campaign. The Soviet Government, however, seems to have underestimated the 'Petöffi Circle's' influence, and to have considered its protests of no more importance than short-lived strikes among tobacco workers in Bulgaria (which were quickly suppressed) or student demonstrations in Czechoslovakia, which had passed off relatively quietly in May and June. This misunderstanding in Moscow led to a Soviet failure to appreciate the explosive nature of the situation in Hungary, and probably contributed to the passivity of Mr. Gerö's Government in the face of growing unrest. For the moment, however, the Soviet Union believed that Hungary was secure enough to bear the weight of further measures of de-Stalinization to impress Marshal Tito, and Mr. Mikoyan, no doubt, conveyed these views to the Marshal during his visit to Brioni.

However great Mr. Khrushchev's confidence about the security of the régime in Hungary may have been, he certainly seemed anxious enough about the general effect of the liberalization campaign in Poland, and of contacts between Poland and Yugoslavia.[1] Towards the end of July Mr. Mikoyan called at Sofia and Bucharest on his return from Yugoslavia, and shortly afterwards the leaders of the Bulgarian and Czechoslovakia Communist parties took their holidays in the Soviet Union, and almost certainly joined in discussions on the situation in Eastern Europe. On 19 September Mr. Khrushchev paid a sudden visit to Belgrade, and after eight days of discussions with Marshal Tito, returned to the Soviet Union for further talks, accompanied by the Yugoslav President. Marshal Bulganin, Mr. Shepilov, the new Soviet Foreign Minister, and Marshal Grechko, the Commander of Soviet troops in Germany, were also present, and the discussions were later joined by the Hungarian party leaders, Messrs. Gerö and Kadar. The agenda of this lengthy conference has remained a secret, although there was at the time speculation about Yugoslav resentment over a letter signed by Mr. Khrushchev to all the East European Communist parties criticizing Yugoslav policy, and advising against any attempt to copy Marshal

[1] Yugoslavia and Poland had exchanged Parliamentary delegations in July.

Tito's independent methods. It seems equally possible—and the presence of Marshal Grechko makes this explanation plausible— that one purpose of the meetings was discussion of military measures to avert a possible threat to the Soviet position in Eastern Europe arising from the Polish actions. It is possible, too, that Mr. Khrushchev shrewdly estimated that the quickest way to bring the Poles back into line would be a dramatic step towards the re-entry of Yugoslavia into the Soviet bloc, or at least an outright Yugoslav condemnation of recent Polish policy. To achieve this, Mr. Khrushchev might have been prepared for almost any sacrifice, perhaps involving further extensive changes in East European party leaderships, such as a second Premiership for Imre Nagy in Hungary— hence the presence of Mr. Gerö and Mr. Kadar.

Events moved so rapidly in September and October that it is impossible to tell whether any such undertaking was given or accepted. On Mr. Gerö's return to Budapest, the former 'Titoist' Laszlo Rajk was given a State funeral on 6 October. A week later Imre Nagy himself was readmitted to membership of the Hungarian Communist party, and Mr. Gerö and a group of his closest colleagues set off on a pilgrimage to Belgrade, possibly in fulfilment of the Soviet part of some hard bargain driven by Marshal Tito. In view of what happened later, it seems ironic that Mr. Khrushchev was apparently ready to extract his greatest concessions to Tito from the least secure of the East European Communist parties—the Hungarian—and lends weight to the view that Mr. Khrushchev miscalculated the whole temper of Eastern Europe.

If Marshal Tito and Mr. Khrushchev did, in fact, conclude a bargain during their discussions in September 1956, it was quickly rendered obsolete by swift-moving events in Poland. During the summer the Polish Government and party leaders had won a measure of popular support by their campaign to liberalize the régime, and had upheld their explanation of the Poznan riots (which the Polish workers knew to be true) in the face of Soviet insistence on throwing all the blame on 'foreign agents'. On the political front, the régime succeeded in keeping some measure of control of the workers' conception of liberalization; but owing to the catastrophic economic situation, created by years of mismanagement, the Polish Government was unable to carry out all it promises to raise the standard of living and reduce consumer prices for industrial workers. As the autumn approached, the voices demanding a 'new deal' in industry became more strident. According to a Polish journal, workers at the big F.S.O. car factory forcibly expressed their disapproval of the State-controlled trade union movement. When a high party official, Mr. Klosiewicz, visited the factory in October, the workers '. . . manifested their attitude towards the trade unions in Poland, an organization whose role has completely degenerated, and has become something that does not serve for the defence of the workers' vital material interests'.

When offered higher wages, the workers significantly replied, 'We do not want to be better paid workers, we want to rule.'[1]

This is only one of many quotations openly denouncing the régime which were published in the Polish Press at this time, but the workers' dissatisfaction was deep and widespread, and provided a fitting background for the extraordinary trial of those accused of responsibility for the Poznan riots.

Early in September the Polish Prosecutor-General announced that 154 of the 323 people arrested would be brought to trial at the end of the month. The first opened in Poznan, at which three youths were accused of murdering a corporal of the Militia, and nine of stealing arms. At once it became clear that the trial was being conducted along lines very different from previous Communist judicial proceedings. Defence counsel were given freedom to defend their clients, and the prosecution withdrew part of its own evidence on the grounds that it had been obtained under duress. No evidence was presented at all on what the Soviet Government believed to be at the heart of the affair: that the riots were the result of foreign provocation. The Court accepted a defence contention that the prosecution's attempt to prove a distinction between the accused and the mass of the workers was untenable, and in the end a few individuals received minor prison sentences. Many were found not guilty and released, and the trial of others was postponed indefinitely. Later, all those not directly charged with murder or theft were freed unconditionally, and no further trials were, in fact, held.

The result of these judicial proceedings, and the fact that their conduct represented a direct rebuff to the Soviet Union, led to a wave of popular enthusiasm and national feeling throughout Poland. It became common knowledge that, in addition to economic difficulties and the attitude of the working population and the intellectuals to the régime, the Communist party was faced with internal dissensions

[1] *Nowa Kultura* (Warsaw), No. 40, 1956.

inside the Politbureau. Extreme pressure was being exerted by a group of party leaders who believed that the country could only be saved from economic breakdown, perhaps even from a collapse of the régime, civil disturbance, and possible Soviet armed intervention, by a radical reform of the régime, and that the only man with sufficient authority and popularity to do this would be Wladyslaw Gomulka. Against these men, who included Mr. Ochab, the First Secretary, Mr. Cyrankiewicz, the Premier, and General Spychalski, were ranged the so-called 'Natolin Group', so named from the suburb of Warsaw where many of them lived. They believed that firmness in dealing with the population combined with complete reliance on the Soviet Union was the only policy, and their number included Marshal Rokossovski, the Defence Minister, and Messrs. Zawadski, Klosiewicz, the trade union leader, and Hilary Minc, the First Deputy Premier in charge of Economic Affairs.

With public tension mounting the 'Natolin Group' suffered a setback on 9 October when Mr. Minc resigned, ostensibly on grounds of ill health. Attention was centred on the meeting of the Central Committee of the party due to take place on 19 October, especially after an announcement three days earlier that Mr. Gomulka and some of his supporters would attend the session. Rumours reached Warsaw from Western Poland that the Soviet troops stationed there had been alerted: some said that they actually on the move towards the Polish capital.[1]

There can be little doubt that the crisis became acute when it became known that Mr. Gomulka would attend the meeting of the Central Committee arranged for the 19th, for this could only mean that he and his supporters, together with all those opposed to the 'Natolin Group', would dominate the conference. It is not surprising that an attempt was made by the 'Natolin Group' to arrest Mr. Gomulka before the conference opened, but this was frustrated by the Warsaw District Committee of the Communist Party.

On the morning of 19 October the fateful meeting of the Central Committee began. Suddenly, the capital was astonished to learn of the arrival of a powerful Soviet delegation, headed by Mr. Khrushchev himself, and including Mr. Kaganovich, Mr. Mikoyan, and,

[1] The Soviet Union maintained its 'Northern Group of Forces' in Poland, consisting of two armoured divisions and a powerful anti-aircraft formation, all stationed in the 'new territories' in the areas of Stettin and Silesia. Soviet troop movements were confirmed in the Polish Press on 23 October, when Mr. Khrushchev's promise to order their return to base was reported.

surprisingly, Mr. Molotov, who had taken no part in foreign affairs since his dismissal as Foreign Minister in June. According to official Polish sources, the meeting of the Central Committee was suspended, and Mr. Gomulka led a Polish delegation to a conference with the Soviet leaders. The discussions were said to have been stormy, and to have concerned the widespread anti-Soviet feeling in Poland, the composition of the Polish Party leadership, and relations between Poland and the Soviet Union. Polish reports speak of a calm and impressive unity within the Polish delegation, who told the Russians that if the Soviet troops moving on Warsaw from the west entered the capital, they, the Polish party leaders, would give orders to the Polish Army to resist, and the whole country would rise against the Russians. During the night the conference broke up without agreement, and the Soviet leaders returned to Moscow. The Poles resumed their party meeting on the 20th, and on the following day issued the membership of the new Politbureau. Mr. Gomulka headed the list, as First Secretary of the party, and his closest supporters gained places vacated by the defeated 'Natolin Group'. Marshal Rokossovski failed to secure a seat, and shortly afterwards was replaced as Minister of Defence by General Spychalski.

All eyes were now turned towards Moscow for the Soviet reaction to the Polish changes. The newspaper *Pravda*, in its leading article for 20 October bitterly attacked the Polish Press, but this article was clearly written before the Soviet-Polish meeting in Warsaw. On 23 October it was officially announced in Poland that Mr. Khrushchev had telephoned to Mr. Gomulka from Moscow, stating that the Soviet Union 'saw no obstacles to developing relations between the two countries on the basis of the Plenum resolutions', and that Soviet troops would be withdrawn to their bases.[1] When Mr. Gomulka confirmed this in a speech to a mass rally in Warsaw on 24 October his immediate triumph was complete. The Polish Workers' Party had forced the Soviet Communist party to accept tactical defeat.[2]

The significant lessons to be learnt from the Polish revolution of October 1956 were, first, that Mr. Khrushchev retreated before a united stand by a *Communist* leadership which had popular backing,

[1] *Trybuna Ludu*, 23 October 1956.
[2] According to information which became available in 1961, the Chinese Communists advised Mr. Khrushchev against the use of force in handling the Polish crisis. See the *Observer*, 12 February 1961.

and not before an avowed anti-Communist movement. Mr. Khrushchev gave in to Mr. Gomulka not so much because he was afraid of the consequences of a pitched battle in the streets of Warsaw between Russian and Polish troops, but because a tactical retreat before an allied Communist party choosing its own Politbureau would not be regarded as a major defeat for Communism at home in the Soviet Union. After all, on 22 October Soviet troops in Hungary and Rumania were preparing to move against Budapest, precisely because the demonstrations in the streets were not led by the Communist party, but were manifestly *anti-Communist*. Whatever the arguments in favour of, or against, direct Soviet action in Poland, the decisive one in Mr. Khrushchev's mind was probably this: if we retreat tactically in Poland we may save Communism in some form at least, until circumstances permit us to restore a more favourable situation; if we send in the Soviet Army, Poland may be lost to Communism for ever. In Hungary the choice before Mr. Khrushchev, as he saw it, was: if we do not intervene promptly with the Soviet Army, even at the risk of widespread fighting, Hungary will certainly be lost to the Communist camp.

XIV

THE COLLAPSE OF SOVIET RULE IN HUNGARY AND THE RUSSIAN INVASION OCTOBER–NOVEMBER 1956

WHILE the Soviet leaders were occupied with their attempt to control de-Stalinization and to secure the re-entry of Marshal Tito into the Soviet bloc, the gravity of the situation in Hungary seems to have been seriously underestimated in Moscow. Mr. Khrushchev's attitude to Hungary before and during the Polish crisis indicated that he believed in the ability of the Communist party, under the leadership of Mr. Gerö, to nip any really dangerous tendencies in the bud, and considered that whatever the mood of the people might be the Government and the police were in full control of the situation. So confident did Mr. Khrushchev apparently feel that as late as October 1956 he was ready to offer concessions to Marshal Tito at the expense of the Hungarian Communist party. On 14 October Mr. Gerö set off for Belgrade at the head of a special delegation, probably under orders to make a dramatic gesture which would pave the way for Marshal Tito's return to the Eastern bloc. But before Mr. Khrushchev's plans for Marshal Tito could bear fruit Hungary exploded into spontaneous rebellion against her Communist rulers and Soviet domination. Four main factors contributed to the explosion: the deterioration of the economic situation in the country, which was particularly severe in 1956, the irresolution of the Hungarian Communist leaders due to de-Stalinization and the fall of Mr. Rakosi, the underestimation by the Russians of the depth of intellectual ferment, and last, but not least, the Hungarian people's reaction to the events in Poland.

The main economic failures were in agriculture and coal-mining. The harvest of 1956 was catastrophic: wheat and rye production was 20 per cent below the poor figure of 1955, and a coal shortage had led the Government to raise the miners' working norms and cut rail services.[1] Oil wells were waterlogged, and fuel restrictions cut down industrial production, forcing factories to close, and this, of course,

---

[1] *Szabad Nep*, 25 September 1956.

raised unemployment figures. The people knew, however, that in spite of shortages at home, deliveries to the Soviet Union were being maintained, and Soviet economic aid to Hungary was being paid for as the highest priority. All these factors increased the nation-wide dissatisfaction.

The climate produced by the de-Stalinization campaign and the fall of Mr. Rakosi encouraged the Communist writers and students to put forward their own political and economic remedies for the country's dismal situation. At a meeting, 10–11 September 1956, the Hungarian Trade Union Council demanded a radical revision of the wage system, and permission for the workers' representatives to bargain with the State. The Writers' Congress a week later called for intellectual freedom, and elected three outspoken critics of the régime to their governing body. Students in Budapest and elsewhere began to compile resolutions, some of which contained political demands; one meeting on 17 October even called for the resignation of Mr. Gerö, the party's First Secretary. On 19 October these groups sensed victory when the Minister of Education accepted some of their demands, including the abolition of the compulsory study of the Russian language.

The tendency of the Government (in the absence of Mr. Gerö and his colleagues in Belgrade) to waver between concessions and repression encouraged students to hold meetings in support of their resolutions. In the southern town of Szeged an enthusiastic meeting of University students was held on 20 October and elected an entirely new student body to run their affairs. When this became known in Budapest, where the news from Poland had already caused great excitement, tension was raised to fever pitch.[1] Meetings of solidarity with the youth of Poland took place all over Budapest, and it was one of these meetings, called by the official Student Organization, D.I.S.Z., at 3 p.m. on 22 October in the Hall of the Building Institute's Technological University, which turned out to be decisive.

According to eyewitnesses about 4,000 people, mostly students and teaching staff from the Universities, gathered to discuss a formal agenda of students' suggestions for the improvement of University life.[2] A new curriculum, cheaper fares for students on public transport, and better housing were mentioned, but later in the day, voices from the audience began to call for discussion of the political situa-

---

[1] *U.N. Report on Hungary*, Ch. 10, p. 45.
[2] *U.N. Report on Hungary*, paras. 439–40.

tion, the news from Poland, and even the withdrawal of Soviet troops from Hungary. Eventually, these and other demands were put down in a hastily-compiled memorandum. At about 8.30 p.m. a small delegation from the meeting took this list of demands, which later became known as the Sixteen Points, to the Director of the Budapest Radio Station, and asked him to include it in the news broadcast at 9 o'clock.[1] The Director and his censor agreed to some items, but refused to permit the mention of the withdrawal of Soviet troops, free elections, a new economic policy, freedom of the Press, and new elections within the Communist party. The delegation then returned to the meeting and reported their failure; but the audience quickly resolved to print the resolution, and groups of young people set out to find printing presses and to visit offices where work was still going on, to make their resolution public. Before dispersing, the meeting decided to hold a mass demonstration on the following day, 23 October.

It is no exaggeration to say that on that day, 23 October 1956, the Communist hierarchy in Hungary ceased to exist as the Government of the country before a shot had been fired. The people of Budapest, led by the students and factory workers, came out into the streets. The acting leaders of the Government were divided among themselves, and quite unable to make up their minds on what to do. The Minister of the Interior, Laszlo Piros, banned the demonstration at noon; then at 2.30 p.m. the ban was lifted. This decision merely recognized a *fait accompli*, for the streets were full of demonstrators, who had already split into two main groups, and were marching through the streets singing patriotic songs and waving national flags. Shouts went up for Imre Nagy to appear (which he did briefly, asking the crowds to go home quietly), but it was the return of Mr. Gerö from Belgrade and the speech he made on the radio early in the evening which determined the course of events during the next critical hours. Hopes that Mr. Gerö, fresh from his talks with Marshal Tito, might play the part of a Hungarian Gomulka and head a National-Communist front of resistance to Soviet domination were quickly dashed. His speech, more in tone than in content, was understood as a complete refusal to treat with the students or to listen to their programme. Tempers in the crowd rose, and ugly threats were heard, which led to the first acts of violence committed by the demonstrators. One group swept through the streets to the giant

[1] ibid., Vol. II, p. 13.

statue of Stalin, and attacked it with hammers and blow-lamps: at 9.30 p.m. this massive symbol of Soviet domination crashed to the ground. Another group of demonstrators returned to the Radio Building and sent a delegation inside to repeat the demand for the broadcast of their resolution, the full Sixteen Points. The demand was refused, but while the crowd jostled round the entrance of the Radio Station, anxious for news of their spokesmen inside, the Secret Police (A.V.H.) sealed the fate of Mr. Gerö's régime by suddenly opening fire on the people without warning, killing and wounding several demonstrators.

The crowd, infuriated, withdrew from the door, but remained in the Square outside the building. A detachment of Hungarian regular soldiers sent to restore order joined the demonstrators. The A.V.H. opened fire on Army officers who refused to shoot, and about midnight workers on night shift in the factories of the industrial area, hearing of the clashes, downed tools and arrived in lorries, bringing the first supplies of arms to the demonstrators. Shortly afterwards an event occurred which changed the whole nature of the demonstrations: at approximately 2 a.m. on 24 October the first Soviet Army tanks appeared in Budapest.

The armed intervention of the Soviet Union in the Hungarian civil disturbances came allegedly at the request of the Hungarian Government, but the evidence of Soviet military movements in mid-October presented in the U.N. report on Hungary suggests that there is no foundation for this claim.[1] The first reports of Soviet military activity refer to 20–22 October, when officers on leave from the Soviet division stationed at Timisoara, in south-west Rumania, were recalled to duty, and to the 21st, when floating pontoon bridges were assembled on the river at Zahony, on the Soviet-Hungarian frontier.[2] Inside Hungary itself the nearest Soviet troops to Budapest were units of the 2nd Guards Mechanized Division at Cegled to the southeast, and Szekesfehevar to the south-west, both about fifty miles from the capital. Soviet troops of the 17th Guards Mechanized Division were seen moving from their barracks at Szombathely, on the Hungarian-Austrian frontier, towards Szekesfehevar on 22 October. The Hungarian police post at Nyirbator reported to the Ministry of Defence at 1 a.m. on the night of 23–24 October that Soviet troops had entered Hungary from Rumania. It was also reported that on

[1] *U.N. Report*, Vol. I, Ch. 4.
[2] ibid., paras. 157–8.

24 October Soviet troops, having bridged the river at several points near Zahony, crossed into Hungary from the U.S.S.R.

These military moves show that a state of alert must have existed in Soviet military headquarters in Hungary, Rumania, and the neighbouring areas of the Soviet Ukraine at least from 19 October and that the Soviet authorities must have envisaged the possibility not only of using the troops already in Hungary on internal security duties, but of introducing new formations from the U.S.S.R.

The first troops to be seen in Budapest appeared, as has been noted, at about 2 a.m. on 24 October, that is to say, about four or five hours after the first clash between the demonstrators and the Secret Police, and less than three hours after the opening of the meeting of the Central Committee which claimed to have elected Imre Nagy Prime Minister and to have called in Soviet troops.[1] If, therefore, Soviet armoured units stationed about fifty miles away appeared in Budapest at 2 a.m. on 24 October, it can be safely assumed that the actual order to move must have been received by the divisional staff before midnight on the 23rd. Furthermore, Soviet troops were seen passing through Szeged, in southern Hungary, for thirty-six hours, beginning during the night of 23–24 October.[2] The distance between the Soviet garrison town of Timisoara in Rumania and the Hungarian town of Szeged, through which these troops passed during that night is over sixty miles. With tanks and heavy lorries driving through the night on these roads at speeds not more than fifteen to twenty miles per hour, some of the troops brought in from Rumania must have been on the move as early as 8 p.m. on the evening of the 23rd. Now, the Hungarian Communist party's Central Committee was called hurriedly into session between 9 p.m. and 11 p.m. on the 23rd.[3] Indeed, it seems possible that the military order to move had been given to Soviet troops both in Hungary and outside it (thus making it impossible for the instructions to have come from the local Soviet Commander inside the country) *before* the meeting of the Central Committee at which the request for armed

[1] Radio Budapest, 0713 hrs., 24 October 1956. Mr. Nagy subsequently denied having been aware of this statement, and rejected statements that he had called in Soviet troops.

[2] According to the *U.N. Report*, Vol. I, p. 64, some Soviet troops wounded in the Budapest fighting were in possession of Rumanian money, i.e. came from garrisons in Rumania.

[3] At 9 p.m. Radio Budapest announced that the Central Committee would meet 'in the next few days'. At 11 p.m. the Radio stated that, at the request of the Politbureau, the Central Committee was already in session.

help from the Soviet Army was supposed to have been made.[1] It is not without significance that Mr. Mikoyan was known to be in Budapest for a few hours on 23 October; perhaps it was he who received an appeal for military intervention from Mr. Gerö, and relayed the Hungarian leader's request to Mr. Khrushchev in the course of the evening. In this case, the meeting of the Central Committee, which was obviously not regarded as urgent at 9 p.m., but was already in progress two hours later, was called to hear the Soviet decision to intervene.

With the entry of Soviet troops into Budapest a new struggle began. At first the Soviet tanks were content to patrol the streets as a demonstration of strength, but when this failed to impress or cow the Hungarians, individual Soviet tank commanders opened fire on the crowds. The population dispersed into smaller groups, entering and occupying Government buildings and offices, some of which became the centres of armed resistance to the Soviet forces. This was particularly true of the Killian barracks and the large housing block known as the Corvin Cinema building, in which determined groups of students, workmen, and regular officers and men of the Army entrenched themselves. It was here that the first clash occurred between the Soviet tanks patrolling the streets and the man who later became identified as the leader of the armed resistance in Budapest, Colonel Pal Maleter. An early attack on these improvised strongholds by Soviet tanks on 24 October failed, and on the 25th field artillery was brought into action, but without success. Soviet tanks were, in fact, relatively helpless in the streets of the capital: the insurgents put up barricades of tram lines and paving-stones, and assailed their opponents with home-made bombs. There was little that the tank crews could do in retaliation, except fire indiscriminately into the small crowds which still gathered or into houses along the route of their patrols.

After some two days of unsuccessful attempts to restore order in Budapest by military means, the Soviet Government again sent Mr. Mikoyan to Hungary to try to find an interim political solution. At 11.30 a.m. on 25 October Radio Budapest announced the dismissal of

---

[1] The Central Committee's communiqué broadcast by Radio Budapest at 0800 hrs., 24 October, contains the official version of the request for Soviet armed intervention. It was stated to have been made under the terms of the Warsaw Pact of 1955 (which, however, referred only to outside aggression), and declared that Soviet forces stationed in Hungary do not interfere in Hungarian internal affairs.

Mr. Gerö, and his replacement as First Party Secretary by Mr. Janos Kadar, who, it was known, had suffered under the Rakosi régime. Mr. Imre Nagy, in whose name many proclamations had been issued, but who had in fact been held incommunicado at Communist Party H.Q. and forced to give his name to proclamations written by Mr. Gerö,[1] was allowed to address the people in person, and to announce a decision to negotiate with the Soviet Union for the withdrawal of Soviet forces from Hungary.[2]

This broadcast was the beginning of Mr. Nagy's personal identification with the resistance movement, and if it was intended by Mr. Mikoyan as a dramatic concession which could halt the revolution, it came too late. On the following day, 25 October, while fighting was still going on in Budapest, news came that the revolution had swept across the whole country. The Hungarian Secret Police were being disarmed, not without bloodshed, but one feature of the movement in the provinces was that Soviet troops were passive, and in several centres Soviet officers contacted the new Hungarian revolutionary councils, denying all intention of interfering in Hungarian affairs.

On the afternoon of 26 October, Mr. Nagy, presumably still in touch with Mr. Mikoyan, who remained in Budapest from 25 October to the 30th, formed a new Government, and announced that Soviet troops would withdraw to their bases after order had been restored. Since, however, Soviet troops were still unable to restore order in Budapest, this meant either a withdrawal under pressure from the victorious insurgents, or after an agreed truce. In the circumstances—for the rebels were consolidating their position daily—a cease-fire of some sort was clearly unavoidable for the Soviet authorities. Provincial radio stations at Gyor, in western Hungary, and Miskolc in the north-east, had already reported on 27 October that Soviet forces had withdrawn to their barracks in order to prevent bloodshed. The same evening an overnight truce was arranged in Budapest, and a cease-fire was formally proclaimed shortly after midday on the 28th.

A situation unprecedented in the history of the Soviet Union now presented itself to the Soviet leaders in Moscow. First, three (or more) regular armoured divisions of the Soviet Army, dispatched to restore order in an East European capital, had been defeated in four

[1] *U.N. Report*, Vol. II, p. 57.
[2] Radio Budapest, Nagy's speech 1418, 25 October.

days' street-fighting by mixed civilian and military resistance groups, and, in fact, were in many cases occupying military indefensible positions from which they had to be extricated. Secondly, the fury of the national uprising and destroyed all the pillars of the Communist régime in Hungary, including the Secret Police, the Army as a pro-Communist force, and a large part of the Communist party organization; in their place, unofficial elected bodies made inadmissible demands for 'bourgeois' freedoms throughout the length and breadth of Hungary. Thirdly, as a result of a decision taken in Moscow on 25 October to try to save the situation, real power had been placed in the hands of Mr. Nagy, and the pro-Soviet Party leaders like Mr. Gerö had been removed from the scene. But Mr. Nagy showed more signs of heading the revolutionary movement himself than of restoring order along Soviet lines, and by 28 October had identified himself with a much more radical political force than Mr. Gomulka had led in Poland a week earlier.

It is clear that in these circumstances the Soviet Government had no alternative but to play for time. The extrication of the 2nd Guards Mechanized Division from untenable positions inside Budapest was the first priority, and Mr. Nagy announced on the radio at 4 p.m. on the 28th that the withdrawal would begin immediately. At dawn on the next day, the 29th, Soviet troops evacuated the Eighth district of Budapest, and their withdrawal continued slowly during the remaining days of the month. There were widespread complaints that the withdrawal was being deliberately delayed.[1] However, all reports agreed that by the evening of 31 October Budapest was free of Soviet troops, and the regular Hungarian Army and the units of the new 'National Guard' under Major-General Bela Kiraly, into which the armed insurgents were being absorbed, had taken over control of the capital.

Meanwhile, all over Hungary revolutionary changes affecting the government of the country at national and local levels were taking place in an atmosphere of high excitement. New Provincial Councils took control, and obtained pledges of support from the Nagy régime in Budapest. A Revolutionary Military Council was set up in the Army, and Pal Maleter, now a Major-General, was appointed Minister of Defence. The one-party system was abolished, and

---

[1] Notably by an extremist group in the H.Q. of the Hungarian Air Force, which threatened, on 31 October, to bomb Soviet units if their withdrawal was not speeded up.

former political groups such as the Smallholders' party and the Social Democratic party were re-established. Enthusiasm for the new freedom was everywhere apparent, and hopes were raised still further when an official *Tass* statement on 31 October announced that in addition to the military evacuation of Budapest the Soviet Government was 'ready to enter into negotiations with the Government of the Hungarian People's Republic and with other Governments which are party to the Warsaw Pact on the withdrawal of Soviet troops from Hungary as well'.[1]

The Hungarian Government immediately asked the Soviet Government to choose representatives to discuss the evacuation of Soviet troops. It seemed as though the armed revolution in Hungary had been accepted by the Soviet Government, just as it had accepted the political revolution in Poland.

On 31 October, however, within a few hours of the receipt of the *Tass* announcement in Budapest, disquieting news came from the north-eastern provinces of Hungary. At 5.15 p.m. listeners in Budapest picked up a broadcast from the provincial city of Nyiregyhaza containing the following message: 'It has just been reported from Kisvarda (a frontier town) that six days after a flood of thousands of tanks, infantry are now approaching Nyiregyhaza in trucks with light and heavy arms—new Russian combat units.'[2]

At 8.25 p.m. Radio Miskolc, some forty miles farther west, made a similar announcement, ending with the words: 'We have exposed the duplicity of the Soviet evacuation manoeuvre in the Zahony area.'[3]

During the night of 31 October–1 November the city of Debrecen in eastern Hungary reported the arrival of new Soviet columns marching westwards, and by mid-morning of 1 November, all Hungary knew that a new deployment of Soviet troops throughout the country was in progress.

The initial reaction of the Hungarian Government and people was to wait and see. No attacks were made on the Soviet units, but Mr. Nagy delivered a strong protest to the Soviet Embassy, only to receive the answer that the new units were intended to surround and protect airfields during the evacuation of Soviet families from Hungary. Shortly before 7 p.m. the Hungarian Premier announced that Hungary had withdrawn from the Warsaw Pact. Mr. Nagy

---

[1] Radio Budapest, quoting *Tass* at 11 a.m., 31 October 1956.
[2] Radio Nyiregyhaza, 5.15 p.m., 31 October 1956.
[3] Radio Miskolc, 8.25 p.m., 31 October 1956.

proclaimed the country's complete neutrality, and thus placed on a formal footing Hungary's request for the evacuation of all Soviet troops from her territory.

However, the Soviet re-deployment continued uninterrupted during the next night and throughout 2 November. All airfields in eastern and central Hungary were surrounded, and the main railway lines from the Budapest area to the Soviet frontier were occupied by newly-arrived troops. The units already in the Szolnok area crossed the Danube south of Budapest and took up new positions between Lake Balaton and the Yugoslav border, and were replaced by new armoured formations from the East. Road blocks were set up, and the movement of Hungarians in the area was restricted. Other troop moved in to the areas north-east of the capital, and on 3 November Soviet troops appeared for the first time within sight of the Austro-Hungarian frontier.

It was in this situation that Mr. Nagy made a further reorganization of his Government, concentrating power in a small council under his own chairmanship during the immediate emergency, and placing officers known to be loyal to the revolution in charge of the National Guard and the few remaining coherent formations of the regular Army. At the same time the Premier appointed a delegation led by a Minister of State, Mr. Erdei, and including the Minister of Defence, General Maleter, and the Chief of the General Staff, General Kovacs, to meet the Russians to discuss the evacuation of Soviet forces. To add to the prevailing uncertainty, Mr. Kadar, who had presented himself as one of Mr. Nagy's closest supporters, left Budapest, probably late on 1 November, for an unknown destination—which ultimately turned out to be the H.Q. of the Soviet Commander-in-Chief at Szolnok.

Saturday, 3 November, opened with further news of the deployment of Soviet troops, and continued with a meeting between the Hungarian military delegation on the evacuation of Russian forces with a Soviet Army delegation led by Army-General M. S. Malinin.[1] At 2 p.m. Radio Budapest reported that satisfactory progress had been made, and that the delegations would meet again in the evening to discuss the formal military honours to be paid to the Soviet forces when they marched out of their garrisons. The Soviet Generals gave

---

[1] General Malinin has sometimes been described as Soviet C. in C. in Hungary. He was, in fact, the First Deputy Chief of the Soviet General Staff, and came to Hungary specifically for these negotiations.

an undertaking that no more trains carrying Soviet troops would cross the Hungarian frontier.[1]

The last hours of the Hungarian revolution were approaching as the Hungarian and Soviet officers met on the evening of 3 November. No record of this meeting is available, but according to the U.N. report, it was interrupted by the arrival of senior Soviet officials (possibly including General Serov, the Chairman of the Soviet State Security Committee), who ordered the arrest of the Hungarian delegates. At 4.20 a.m. on the morning of 4 November Soviet troops suddenly launched an attack on Hungarian forces in Budapest and other cities, taking the defenders by surprise, and driving them back in the first shock of military assault. Sporadic but bitter fighting broke out all over Budapest and the countryside, but the surprise nature of the attack gave the Soviet Army most of the key positions without serious opposition. However, workers, soldiers, students, and individual army units continued to fight on in the industrial suburbs, in the hills near Lake Balaton, and in the oilfields near Pecs in the south, and opposition was strong enough to require the issue of at least one ultimatum by the Soviet authorities threatening aerial bombardment of resistance areas.[2]

Meanwhile a new pro-Soviet Government made its appearance in Szolnok, the Headquarters of the Soviet Army, led by Janos Kadar. It included Ministers rejected by the revolutionaries, like Mr. Marosan and Mr. Münnich, who now issued appeals to the Hungarian people to rally behind the Soviet forces. Owing to lack of support from any section of the population, the new administration was unable to enter Budapest for some days, and, in fact, its members played no part in the struggle which was fought out between the Hungarian people and the Soviet Army. One of the latter's first tasks on the fateful day 4 November was the arrest of Imre Nagy and his leading supporters. Mr. Nagy was kidnapped by Soviet officers while he was returning from the Yugoslav Embassy under the terms of a Soviet agreement with the Yugoslavs not to molest the fallen Premier if he left their protection. Mr. Nagy was later deported to Rumania.

Scattered resistance to the invaders continued up to 10 November, but by then the campaign in Hungary had succeeded, and the Soviet military hold on the country was complete. Soon afterwards the mass

---

[1] Radio Budapest, 2.18 p.m., 3 November.

[2] Radio Szolnok's (Soviet controlled) report of Soviet ultimatum to the town of Karcag, 1.56 p.m., 4 November 1956.

flight of Hungarians to Austria began. A general strike gripped the country for a few more weeks, but the revolution was over. The Soviet Government re-established its physical control over an area of Eastern Europe which had all but slipped from its grasp, by the use of its armed forces in a conventional war. In contrast to the Soviet-Polish crisis, in which there was no immediate danger that the country might cease to be Communist-controlled, the uprising in Hungary amounted, in Soviet eyes, to a cession of territory and population to the Western 'camp'. This the Russians understood to be so grave a danger to the Communist cause that armed intervention became inescapable.[1]

In this context it is important to try to determine the exact point at which the Soviet leaders finally decided upon armed suppression of the Hungarian revolution. It seems clear that the initial armed intervention during the night of 23–24 October was under way before the Central Committee of the Hungarian Communist party met. This could mean that the Russians moved at the request of Mr. Gerö before he summoned the Central Committee, and it is possible that he consulted Mr. Mikoyan before applying for help to the Soviet Government.[2] It could also mean that the Soviet Government took the decision on its own, without consulting the Hungarians. As in East Berlin in 1953, Soviet troops patrolled the streets of Budapest, opening fire only occasionally on small groups of demonstrators. When the Hungarians replied by garrisoning themselves in strong buildings, and the armoured patrols failed to force them out, the practical dilemma facing the Soviet military and political authorities became simply this: to admit defeat and accept the revolution, or to effect a tactical withdrawal, and resume the military challenge in more favourable circumstances. The Soviet Government decided to follow the second course.

When analysing Soviet strategy and tactics during the Hungarian revolution, we cannot ignore one possibility which is frequently mentioned as having a bearing on the Soviet decision to overthrow Mr. Nagy's régime: that there were two factions inside the Soviet Government, one in favour of accepting the Hungarian revolution, and the

---

[1] This was, apparently, also the view of the Chinese Communists, who offered their advice to the Soviet Government. See the *Observer*, 12 February 1961.

[2] On 25 July 1957, in a speech in Budapest, Mr. Marosan boasted that he called in Soviet troops that night. This, however, is merely intended to preserve the fiction, for Gerö is still officially barred from Hungary, and some figurehead was needed to take his place as the author of the request.

other determined on military repression, which won the day only after the news of the Anglo-French ultimatum to Egypt reached Moscow.[1]

Let us be clear on the timing of the Middle Eastern crisis. The Israeli Army crossed the armistice line with Egypt during the evening of 29 October, and the Anglo-French ultimatum to Israel and Egypt became public at 4.30 p.m. on the following day, 30 October.[2] But news of the mobilization of the Israeli Army, which was announced on 28 October, had been known in London on the 25th,[3] and we can safely assume, since the Soviet Union maintained a Legation in Israel, that it was also known in Moscow at the same time. This means that two days before the Soviet Union agreed to a cease-fire in Budapest, and five days before she announced her readiness to negotiate on the withdrawal of Soviet troops from Hungary the Soviet Government was aware that Israel had mobilized for war. Yet this knowledge, even when taken together with the considerable build-up of Anglo-French forces in Cyprus, and the strong presumption that they were destined for action in the Middle East, did not alter the Soviet tactical decisions to withdraw from Budapest or to agree to discuss the military evacuation of Hungary. In fact, the *Tass* announcement to this effect at 11 a.m. on 31 October came *after* the expiry of the Anglo-French ultimatum at 4 a.m. the same morning. The logical conclusion is that the Soviet will to leave Hungary cannot have been affected by the Israeli resort to war or the Anglo-French ultimatum.

This does not mean, however, that the Soviet Government felt that they could dispense with a precautionary military occupation of Hungary during a critical period. It will be remembered that the radio station at Nyiregyhaza reported at 5.15 p.m. on 31 October that observers in Kisvarda, about twenty miles from the frontier town of Zahony, had seen infantry in trucks passing through their town. These trucks must have been on the move for Hungary at the time when *Tass* promised negotiations on their evacuation. It is also significant that Soviet troops were crossing the Hungarian frontier *before* Mr. Nagy announced Hungary's full neutrality and withdrawal from the Warsaw Pact.[4] This lends weight to the general

---

[1] During his visit to Hungary in 1958 Mr. Khrushchev said that the decision to intervene in 1956 had been taken only after agonizing heart-searching.

[2] Royal Institute of International Affairs, *Documents on the Suez Crisis*, by D. C. Watt, pp. 24–25.

[3] ibid., p. 24.

[4] *U.N. Report*, Vol. II, p. 144, for Mr. Nagy's telegram to the United Nations.

interpretation that the military reoccupation of the country was decided upon in Moscow as soon as it became clear that a military defeat had been suffered in Budapest on 24–27 October.

There is, however, a critical difference between the precautionary occupation of Hungary and the decision to overthrow the Government of Mr. Nagy by force. It is possible that the Soviet Government intended to maintain its prestige by a formidable show of military power, and then to fulfil its promise according to the *Tass* announcement, unaffected by the crisis in Egypt. This attitude may have aroused the suspicions of the Chinese and caused their reported attempt to persuade Mr. Khrushchev to act against the revolutionaries. What did become clear between the *Tass* announcement and the attack on Budapest was the decision of the United States to take a firm stand against the British and French action in Egypt, and it may have been this major split in the Western camp (as seen from Moscow) which turned the scales in the Soviet capital in favour of the forcible seizure of power in Hungary.

This, of course, is speculation, and it may be that the decision to attack Budapest had been taken earlier, in fact as soon as it became clear that Mr. Nagy had identified himself with the revolutionaries who had beaten back the first Soviet assault. All that can be firmly concluded is that the military reoccupation of Hungary which preceded the attack and made it possible could not have owed its origin to the Middle East crisis. The timing of the final decision to use the troops remains a mystery.

XV

SOVIET STRATEGY DURING THE MIDDLE EASTERN CRISIS: OCTOBER 1956

THE year 1956 undoubtedly produced a number of severe tests for the new strategies and tactics adopted by Mr. Khrushchev and his colleagues in the field of foreign affairs. Soviet rule and influence in Eastern Europe were hard hit by the wave of nationalist feeling which swept Poland and Hungary, reaching such proportions in Hungary that the Soviet Army had to be used to keep that country within the Communist bloc. At the same time, the policy of expansion into the Middle East found itself endangered by the military conflict which broke out between Egypt and Israel, and by the subsequent intervention of British and French forces in the area of the Suez Canal. It is of prime importance to find out to what extent Soviet economic and military commitments in the Middle East in the autumn of 1956 were regarded in Moscow as expendable; in other words, what had the Soviet Union achieved in Egypt at the time of the Suez crisis, and was her Government prepared to use force to protect these gains?

The events leading up to the Soviet Union's decision to supply the Arab countries with arms showed that the Soviet campaign to gain influence in the Middle East was planned under three main headings: the identification by means of propaganda of the Soviet Union with the aims of Arab nationalism, the political use of external trade to absorb Arab exports which sometimes remained unsold on the world market, and later, the sale of arms to Arab Governments.

The first of these methods of penetration had appeared well before the Suez crisis. The Soviet leaders, obsessed, as Stalin had been, with numerical preponderance, and possibly with widespread American support for Israel as a State, found no difficulty in siding with the Arabs against Israel, and had added the voice of Moscow radio to the inflammatory propaganda of the Arabs against the new State. Soviet officials and delegations frequently visited Egypt and Syria, and Arab Governments were encouraged to send students, technicians, and scientists to visit or study in the Soviet Union. This policy was initially effective, and from 1954 onwards gave the Soviet Union an increasingly favourable Press in Cairo and Damascus.

Soviet popularity in Egypt and Syria was increased by the series of barter trade agreements effected during 1955 and 1956. Egypt's trade problem was to find profitable markets for her cotton yarn and rice. Her prices in the post-war market had generally been rising, forcing some potential buyers to look elsewhere, and therefore when the Soviet Union agreed to take Egyptian cotton and rice at artificially high prices or through favourable barter arrangements, she went a long way towards earning Egyptian gratitude. Beginning in April 1955 with a trade agreement which gave Egypt £E.2 millions' worth of Soviet paraffin and crude oil and £E.1 million's worth from Rumania, in exchange for cotton yarn, the Soviet bloc gradually diverted Egypt's external trade in this and other commodities towards itself. In August 1955 the Soviet Union and Rumania took a further £E.1,800,000 worth of cotton yarn and 60,000 tons of rice, and Communist China agreed to buy a substantial amount of Egyptian cotton, too.[1] On 7 September 1955 yet another barter deal was made between Egypt and Russia: half a million tons of Soviet oil was exchanged for 60,000 tons of Egyptian rice. One year after the first agreement, on 17 April 1956, the two countries once again exchanged cotton for oil.

Figures published in 1956 give a clear idea of the growth in the Soviet bloc's trade with Egypt: in 1954 the total value of all trade between the Soviet bloc and Egypt was just over £30 million; in 1955 it was well over £49 million; a rise of 60 per cent.[2] By 1954 the Communist bloc had acquired a share of between 14 per cent and 15 per cent of all Egypt's external trade; a year later this figure had doubled,[3] and by July 1956 the percentage was 34.3 per cent.[4] Of Egypt's cotton exports, 36 per cent went to the Soviet bloc (mostly to Czechoslovakia and Rumania) in 1956, compared with 25 per cent in 1955.[5] It should also be noted that on 12 February 1956 the Soviet Union offered to equip a laboratory for nuclear research in Egypt,

---

[1] Details of these agreements can be found in *The Times* of 29 April and 11 August 1955.
[2] *The Times*, 27 February 1956. The figures of Egyptian exports to the Soviet bloc are: 1954: £37,025,325, and in 1955 £49,750,000. Both figures exclude the value of the arms deal which, if included, would raise the percentage of increase to 250 per cent.
[3] *The Times*, 15 September 1956.
[4] Board of Trade, *Information on Egypt*, 5 September 1956.
[5] ibid.

an offer which was followed by the arrival in Cairo of a Soviet delegation whose leader stated that Russia was ready to supply Egypt with
uranium, and to assist in prospecting the desert for this and other
minerals. This was an example of another aspect of Soviet penetration: to secure contracts to build or prospect on Egyptian territory—
valuable concessions which could lead to an important strategic foothold for the Soviet Union in the Middle East. Hungary, for example,
secured a contract to build swing bridges over the Nile, and Czechoslovak technicians were commissioned to build a cement factory.[1]

At first sight it appeared that the Soviet Union and her allies
represented a genuinely profitable market for the produce by which
Egypt made her living. But there was more to it than that. By selling
her crops to the Soviet bloc at higher prices than the world market
could offer, Egypt compelled her former customers to seek cotton
and rice elsewhere. Few external buyers dealing on normal commercial terms could match the Russian prices, and this placed the
Egyptians in a position of partial economic dependence on the
Soviet Government. The Soviet Union was in a strong position, and
was quite prepared to use her advantages whenever it suited her
interests. By 1956, according to some reports, the Soviet Government already owed a sum of £10 million to Egypt, whose payment
the Egyptians could not enforce.[2] Moreover, if the Russians decided
to raise their prices for Egyptian imports, there was little that Cairo
could do to redress the balance. On the purely commerical side, the
Soviet Union was by 1956 certainly beginning to reap the benefits of
a favourable economic relationship with Egypt, and had won
valuable positions for the exercise of Soviet political pressure on the
Egyptian Government.[3]

Thirdly, Soviet policy was expressed in the decision to supply
arms to Egypt, and in the agreement between Egypt and Czechoslovakia for this purpose which was signed on 27 September 1955.
The prestige gained by Colonel Nasser and by the Soviet Government throughout the Arab world made the deal worth while to the
Soviet Union, quite apart from the military value of the arms to

[1] *The Times*, 11 October 1955, and *Financial Times*, 29 March 1956.
[2] See the *Neuer Züricher Zeitung*, 12 September 1956.
[3] Characteristic of the Soviet policy of extracting the greatest benefit from
Egypt with the least firm commitments was her skilful use of the Aswan Dam
proposal. Throughout this critical period, Soviet spokesmen managed to give
the Arabs the impression that Russia would finance the Dam, without giving a
formal promise, even when the United States withdrew her offer of financial
assistance in the summer of 1956.

Egypt. But the agreement had economic value also, for the supply of arms represented a quick and relatively easy way of covering a trade gap with a country with whom economic relations had become unbalanced for reasons of political strategy. If the Soviet Union bought large quantities of Egyptian cotton for political reasons, and Soviet exports of equivalent value were not available or were subsequently offered at prices which Egypt could not afford, then the sale of arms could be a satisfactory means of restoring the balance, if both sides agreed to it.[1] In the case of Egypt in 1955, arms were what her Government wanted, and the Soviet leaders were only too glad to kill two birds with one stone.

The supply of arms and military technicians by a country like the Soviet Union raises once again the question of prestige. What would be the attitude of the Soviet Government if the country to which her arms had been supplied came under armed attack? Or to put the question in practical terms, did the Soviet Union consider going to the help of Egypt militarily during the Suez crisis of 1956 because of the military aid supplied to the Egyptians by the Soviet Government and her allies?

The first relevant point here is the undeniable fact that while Colonel Nasser was always anxious to publicize the fact that it was the Soviet Union which had supplied the arms in 1955—the Egyptian President included this claim in his speech on 26 July 1956, announcing the nationalization of the Suez Canal—the Soviet Government tried to attribute the deal to Czechoslovakia. Thus, on 21 September 1955, six days before the announcement of the deal, the Soviet Government assured the Israeli Government that no arms were to be supplied to Egypt by the Soviet Union.[2] And at the Press Conference given by Mr. Khrushchev and Marshal Bulganin at the end of their visit to Britain in April 1956, Mr. Khrushchev said: 'Actually we are not supplying arms to anyone, and we would like other countries to act similarly. But arms are being supplied.' In case of difficulty, therefore, the Soviet Government could always deny responsibility for the deal, and thus avoid a serious fall in Soviet prestige. This cautious approach was partially due to lack of pre-

---

[1] It may be asked why, if Russia could satisfy Egypt's need to export cotton and rice in this way, she needed to cover the gap at all, since Egypt would be at Russia's mercy. But if Russia consistently defaulted, Egypt's economy might suffer so severely that the pro-Soviet Government might fall, and be replaced by leaders who preferred to look to the West.

[2] *Daily Telegraph*, 22 September 1955.

cedents, for never before had Soviet arms on any scale been supplied
to a foreign country not bordering on the Soviet Union, and in time
of peace.[1] Elementary prudence demanded that the deal should include an escape route for Soviet military and political prestige.

It was natural, too, that the arrival of the arms shipments and
their destination should be kept secret, although from time to time
during 1955 and 1956 correspondents in Cairo and London wrote of
Soviet ships unloading arms at Alexandria or Port Said. One London
journal described the unloading of '133 huge cases of Czech arms'
from the *Stalingrad* only ten days after the announcement of the
Egyptian-Czech arms deal.[2] Another paper gave the news that forty
Soviet jet bombers and thirty Mig 17s had arrived in Egypt by
March 1956, and that a team of Czechoslovak technicians was
engaged in training Egyptian pilots on airfields near Alexandria.[3]
Between 200 and 300 Egyptian officers and N.C.O.s were reported
to be under training at Soviet bases in Poland, and officers were said
to pass through Yugoslavia on their way to East European training
centres.[4] In May and June 1956 Soviet warships were handed over
to the Egyptian Navy. We do know, however, exactly what the
Egyptians had in the way of Soviet arms at the time of the Suez crisis
from the dispatch of the Allied Commander-in-Chief, General Sir
Charles Keightley, on the operations themselves.[5] The General listed
the Soviet arms opposed to him as eighty Mig 15s, forty-five Il-
yushin-28 jet bombers, 150 Soviet tanks (JS 3s, T-34s, and T-34-
85s), an unknown number of Soviet self-propelled guns SU 100s,
anti-aircraft guns, armoured troop carriers, and other equipment.
This figure specifically excluded Soviet arms deployed against the
Israelis in the Sinai peninsula; these would probably bring the
figures of tanks up to 300, the jet fighters up to 100, but would not
alter the size of the bomber force.[6]

These were the Soviet political, economic, and military commitments in Egypt when Colonel Nasser nationalized the Suez Canal

---

[1] The obvious parallels are Spain during the Civil War and China during the
struggle against Japan. In both cases Soviet arms shipments came after fighting
had been under way for some time.

[2] *The Economist*, 5 November 1955.

[3] *Daily Telegraph*, 23 March 1956.

[4] *The Times*, 24 March 1956.

[5] Supplement to the *London Gazette*, 10 September 1957.

[6] The IL-28s, among the aircraft, the JS 3s and T-34-85s among the tanks,
and the SU 100s were up-to-date weapons in use in the Soviet Army. The
Mig 15 is less modern—many were used in Korea.

on 26 July 1956. As soon as the crisis broke the Soviet Government expressed its full support for Egypt's action, and circulated its views that under international law the Egyptian position was legal and justified. Throughout the months of negotiation which followed the Soviet Union used her influence on the side of Egypt, and helped the Egyptian Government to overcome the effects of the blocking of her sterling balances in Britain and France by supplying wheat to be paid for in Egyptian currency, and by releasing trained Soviet navigational pilots for work on the Suez Canal.

The Soviet Government sent Mr. Shepilov, the Foreign Minister, to the first London Conference on the Canal problem, which met at Lancaster House on 16 August. In her acceptance of the invitation, Russia suggested that several of her European associates should be invited to attend the Conference on the grounds that they—Czechoslovakia, Hungary, and Poland—were successors of the Austro-Hungarian Empire, one of the signatories of the 1888 Convention on the Canal. She also proposed that invitations should be extended to Rumania, Bulgaria, and Yugoslavia, and to Communist China, though without explaining Peking's relationship to the Convention. At the Conference itself the Soviet delegation concentrated on presenting the whole dispute over the Suez Canal as a simple and clear-cut struggle between Western 'colonialism' and Afro-Asian nationalism. The Moscow newspaper *Pravda* summed up Soviet support for Egypt in this way:

> The Soviet Union cannot agree that the part of Egypt's territory through which the Suez Canal passes should be regarded as a territory over which Egypt has no sovereign rights. The plans for international operation of the Suez Canal, in effect, mean an attempt to create a stronghold of colonialism with the object of restoring the obsolete, old system in the Arab East. The proposals of the Western Powers run counter to the aspirations of the Egyptian people, and arouse the strong opposition of other Asian and African nations.[1]

It was, perhaps, with a view to emphasizing the concept of 'colonialism' versus 'national liberation' in the Suez crisis that the Soviet Government withdrew its own proposals, and instead backed an Indian plan, based on Egypt's unconditional right to nationalize the Canal. But as the negotiations dragged on through the summer and autumn of 1956 an interesting note of caution began to appear in the Soviet approach. Writing in a pamphlet on the Suez Canal in

[1] *Pravda*, 19 August 1956.

1956, a Soviet observer stated that the completion of the Volga-Don Canal in Russia increased the importance of Suez to the Soviet Union and that the affairs of the Canal should not be settled by Egypt and Britain alone.[1] Nationalization by Egypt was obviously a useful stick with which to beat Britain and France in the short term, but in Soviet eyes there existed the danger that a future Egypt, governing the Canal unfettered by any international agreements or associations, might be anti-Soviet on its own account, or even aligned with the West. Soviet proposals and policy, therefore, while supporting Egypt's right to nationalize the Canal, showed signs of insisting on Soviet participation in one form or another in its future régime.

Thus, after the London Conference, the Soviet Union suggested the setting up of a preparatory commission, composed of Egypt, India, America, Russia, France, and Britain, to draft a new Convention agreeable to Egypt and the Canal users. When Egypt proposed a conference on this subject in Cairo, the Soviet Union accepted on 14 September, and five days later Marshal Bulganin recommended a meeting of the Heads of Governments of the Powers involved in the Suez issue. No doubt part of the Soviet Government's vigorous hostility to the proposals for a Suez Canal Users' Association was due to fears that the organization might become the basis for an accommodation with Egypt from which Russia would be excluded. It was in this spirit, too, that the Soviet Union vetoed the second part of the Anglo-French Resolution for a settlement over Suez in the United Nations Security Council on 13 October, for this also promised to produce a settlement without direct Soviet participation.

By the middle of October 1956 the crisis produced by the Egyptian nationalization of the Suez Canal had become less urgent. The Canal was on the whole functioning satisfactorily, and its users were accustomed to Egyptian ownership. The crisis which followed in October and November arising from the outbreak of fighting between Israel and Egypt presented the Soviet leaders with entirely different problems, connected with the military equipment handed over to the Egyptian Army, and the Soviet advisers working in Egypt. All reports agree that the jet bomber force of IL-28s was not used by the Egyptians either against the Israelis operating in the Sinai peninsula or the Anglo-French air force which attacked objectives

[1] G. S. Nikitin in *Suetski Kanal* (The Suez Canal), Moscow, 1956.

in Egypt on 31 October. Most of the Soviet aircraft were flown from airfields near Alexandria first to Luxor in Upper Egypt [1] and later to Syria, via, it is believed, Saudi Arabia. It is clear that the Soviet authorities took a decision not to allow the Egyptians to use this force of forty-five modern aircraft, and at the same time not to risk its capture by Egypt's opponents. The advisers and technicians employed in Egypt received instructions to avoid taking part in the fighting, and immediately after the first air attacks, some 380 of them, Russians and Czechs, presented themselves at the Sudanese frontier, and were ultimately flown back to Prague and Moscow via Brussels.[2] Most of the fighter aircraft were destroyed on the ground, but Soviet-made tanks and self-propelled guns were used by Egyptian crews in the fighting in Port Said.

Failure to agree to the use by Egypt of the most effective Soviet-made weapons such as the IL-28 aircraft already in Egypt cast doubt on the Soviet and Chinese threats to send 'volunteers' to Egypt to fight against the British and the French. The first suggestion of the possible dispatch of 'volunteers' was made by Mr. Khrushchev at a reception at the Rumanian Embassy in Moscow on 23 August. 'If Egypt is attacked,' he said, 'it will be a just war for the Arabs, and there will be volunteers.' This remark was not reported in the Soviet Press, but it was widely repeated in Cairo, where, three days later, the newspapers were referring to '100,000 Soviet Muslims, seeking permission to leave for Egypt'. Communist China also reported the readiness of her people to 'volunteer' for service in Egypt, but it is a fact that the Soviet Union only returned to this threat on the day of the cease-fire in Egypt, 6 November. And it was not until 10 November, four days after the cease-fire, that *Tass*, the Soviet News Agency, put out its solemn announcement that the 'Soviet authorities will not hinder the departure for Egypt of Soviet citizen volunteers'— whom it described as 'great numbers of pilots, tank men, gunners and officers who took part in the Great Fatherland War, and are now on the reserve'. The threat was repeated two days later, on the 12th, but in view of the fact that fighting had ceased in Egypt, it seems unlikely that the threat was ever meant to be carried out.[3] Moreover, the material conditions for the activization of several thousand Soviet

[1] Supplement to the *London Gazette*, 10 September 1957, p. 5332.
[2] *The Times*, 13 November 1956.
[3] Chronology taken from *Documents on the Suez Crisis*, selected by D. C. Watt, Royal Institute of International Affairs, February 1957, pp. 24–30.

'volunteers' in Egypt did not exist in November 1956, and Moscow quietly withdrew the offer on 8 December.[1]

Of greater potential importance was the direct Soviet military threat to Britain and France in November 1956. Here again, detailed chronology is of the utmost importance. Air operations against Egypt by the British and French began on 31 October, and immediate Soviet reaction was confined to a Government statement calling on the United Nations to take strong measures against the 'colonial powers'. On the following day, 1 November the Soviet President, Marshal Voroshilov, sent letters to Mr. Nehru and the President of Indonesia suggesting a Conference on Egypt by the Bandung Powers. On 3 November Britain and France indicated their willingness to hand over their responsibilities in Egypt to a United Nations' force, and as soon as this was accepted, to cease military operations. On the 4th a Canadian resolution was passed by the General Assembly of the United Nations requesting the Secretary-General to set up an Emergency Force to secure and supervise the cessation of hostilities. The resolution was accepted by Egypt on the same day, and the Egyptian Government offered to order a cease-fire at once. Fighting between Israel and Egypt had died down after the surrender of the last Egyptian force east of the Suez Canal on 2 November. British and French forces which had landed at Port Said on 5 November agreed to a cease-fire at midnight on the 6th.

The Soviet Union failed to play any part in these negotiations, presumably because at this precise time, 3–4 November, her own troops were engaged in the attack on Budapest. On 5 November, however, when the Soviet attack on Hungary had achieved its initial objectives, the Soviet Government intervened in the Egyptian crisis. In a Note handed to the British Ambassador in Moscow, on the evening of the 5th, and broadcast the same evening, the Russians declared:

> The Soviet Government considers it necessary to draw your attention to the aggressive war being waged by Britain and France against Egypt, which has the most dangerous consequences for the cause of peace. . . .

---

[1] It is true, as has been pointed out, that some items of equipment and stores found in Egypt, e.g. 1 million blankets for an Egyptian Army of 100,000 men, and ammunition for weapons not yet delivered, might have indicated a Soviet intention to send troops of one kind or another to Egypt ultimately, but the fact remains that at the time the threat was made no Soviet force of any size could have maintained itself on Egyptian soil. (See *Middle East Crisis*, by G. Wint and P. Calvocoressi, a Penguin Special, p. 85).

In what position would Britain have found herself if she had been attacked by more powerful states possessing every kind of modern destructive weapon? And there are countries now which need not have sent a navy or air force to the coasts of Britain, but could have used other means, such as rockets. . . . We are fully determined to crush the aggressors and restore peace in the Middle East through the use of force.

This was, of course, a serious threat which altered the nature of the crisis. At the same time Marshal Bulganin wrote to President Eisenhower stating that the situation in Egypt called for immediate action by the United Nations, and proposed that the United States and the Soviet Union, as states possessing 'nuclear weapons as well as powerful armies and navies should use these means under United Nations auspices to 'curb aggression' in the Middle East. Co-operation with the United States Sixth Fleet in the Mediterranean was specifically mentioned. The Soviet representative at the United Nations called on the Security Council at 1 a.m. on 6 November to endorse joint Soviet-American intervention if the British and French did not halt within twelve hours. The American Government immediately rejected the Soviet proposal, and instantly warned Russia on the same day that rocket attacks on Britain or France would be followed by American retaliation. The Soviet Government must have known of the American counter-threat well before its own twelve-hour ultimatum expired at 1 p.m. (New York time) or 6 p.m. (G.M.T.), and the American action was also known in London before the British Prime Minister announced the final cease-fire in the House of Commons at 6 p.m. on 6 November. This implies that the Soviet threat to intervene cannot have been the only factor in the cease-fire decision, since the Soviet threat of war had been challenged by the United States before the Soviet time-limit expired, and had, in effect, by-passed the whole Suez operation.

But one vital question still remained: Was the Soviet threat pure bluff, or was Russia prepared to use her strength in certain circumstances?

Certainly the need to distract world opinion from the Russian invasion of Hungary provided one motive for these Soviet moves in the Middle East. Intervention was also valuable in maintaining the level of Soviet prestige in the Arab world. At the same time it is possible that the Russians might have carried out their threat if the United States had agreed to join them in the venture. The Soviet military machine had obviously been alerted during the Hungarian and Polish crises, and it is likely that a considerable number of transport aircraft and airborne troops were already operational at the same time that the threat was made. The Soviet Union's leaders very probably saw in the hostile American attitude to the Anglo-French attack on Egypt a remote possibility of entering the Middle East physically and legally. If Soviet forces could move in under United Nations auspices and as allies of the United States, they could achieve in a few days what might normally take months or years: the right to be a regular military and political power in the Middle East with legal participation in all future settlements in the area. The British and French attack on Egypt provided, it seemed to the Russians, a unique combination of factors: psychological readiness among the Arabs for Soviet military help,[1] a strong majority in the United Nations against the attack on Egypt, and a wave of anger in the United States against Britain and France which might lead to some form of Soviet-United States co-operation. Clearly the chance was worth taking, for the prize—a Soviet armed contingent or air base in the Middle East, operating under the auspices of the United Nations—was certainly glittering. Only when the Soviet offer was rejected on 6 November, and America refused to collaborate, the Soviet Government was forced to fall back on propaganda, and on proposals for the dispatch of 'volunteers'.

Soviet policy throughout the Middle Eastern crisis can, therefore, be conveniently divided into three phases. Each of them was to a certain extent an improvisation, for the Soviet Government had not planned with Colonel Nasser the nationalization of the Suez Canal, and the whole incident appears to have come as a surprise to the Soviet leaders. During the actual dispute over the future of the Suez Canal, from August to mid-October, the Soviet Union strove to co-ordinate direct propaganda support for the Egyptian case with a cautious policy towards the West in order to prevent an exclusive Anglo-French-Egyptian deal on the Canal. In the second crisis, caused by the Israeli invasion of Egypt and the Anglo-French attack on Egyptian airfields, the Soviet Union refused to allow the Egyptians to use their best piece of Soviet military equipment—the Ilyushin jet

[1] According to General Keightley's despatch, Egyptian resistance in Port Said was encouraged by loudspeaker vans which toured the town saying that Russian help was on the way, that London and Paris had been bombed, and that the Third World War had begun (p. 5333). Many Arabs believed that the Soviet threat to attack London and Paris had, in fact, brought about the cease-fire in Egypt on 6 November, and this belief is still widespread.

bomber force—in the fighting against Britain, France, or Israel, and themselves remained inactive until the more urgent crisis in Hungary had been solved. After that the Soviet leaders saw one brief chance of bringing a force of Soviet troops into the Middle East, attempted to seize it, and were rebuffed by the Americans. They therefore covered up their failure with a belated offer of 'volunteers', intended, apparently, to arrive in Egypt some weeks after the fighting was over. The Soviet Union's behaviour during the Middle Eastern crisis of 1956 provided no evidence that she would go to the help of a non-Communist ally with no common frontier with the Soviet Union, even if that ally was attacked while in receipt of Soviet arms. The Soviet Union did, however, retain a considerable amount of goodwill among the Arabs for her apparent readiness to intervene and to challenge Britain and France to military action. It is very likely that the lesson which the Russians themselves learnt from this crisis was that planning for the Middle East succeeds when the area is at peace, but when it is disturbed by all too frequent political explosions a foreign policy of economic penetration can suffer when the political initiative is lost. This was a sharp lesson for a Government which probably believed that its Middle Eastern policy would effect a smooth and uninterrupted transfer of influence in the area from the West to the Communist powers.

XVI

THE TACTICS OF RECOVERY
JANUARY–JUNE 1957

IN the winter of 1956–57 the Soviet leaders faced the consequences of serious reverses in their foreign policy which were barely concealed by the controversy in the Western World over the Anglo-French intervention in Egypt and the rift between those two countries and the United States. Seen from Moscow, the bitter feelings, the mutual recriminations and the economic difficulties of the Western Powers were valuable propaganda material and useful camouflage. But they could not make up for the defeats suffered by the Soviet Union in the last six months of 1956.

These were serious indeed. In Warsaw, the Soviet leaders, headed by Mr. Khrushchev, had been outmanoeuvred by Polish fellow Communists, and had given way under thinly-disguised duress. In Hungary, a popular uprising had overthrown the Communist régime, and the Soviet Union had resorted to limited warfare to put down the national revolution and impose a puppet administration by force of arms. Hungary was still in ferment at the end of 1956: strikes and lock-outs had brought the economic life of the country almost to a standstill; the people were sullen, uncooperative and unforgiving, implacably hostile both to the Kadar régime and to the Soviet Army of Occupation. Western Communist parties were losing members—many of them leading figures—or were in danger of falling apart in splinter groups. Virtually all cultural and technical contacts between Russia and the West had ceased, and several Western capitals had witnessed mob attacks on Soviet Embassies or Legations in protest against the invasion of Hungary. Even in the Soviet Union itself there was some evidence of official nervousness at potential popular dissatisfaction. A prominent journal, discussing Soviet local elections to be held in March 1957, wrote: 'It is not excluded that individual, hostile, anti-Soviet elements will try to utilize the election campaign for the aims of slandering the Soviet régime'.[1]

Only in the Arab countries of the Middle East was Soviet prestige

[1] *Partiynaya Zhizn* (Party Life), No. 2, 1957.

unaffected by the Hungarian and Polish events, thanks partly to the Egyptian censorship which suppressed news of the events in Budapest, and partly to Soviet support for Egypt during the Suez crisis.[1] But from the Soviet point of view, Suez contained elements of a tactical reverse as well as providing a stick with which to beat Britain and France. The United States proclaimed a new interest in the Middle East with the introduction of the Eisenhower Doctrine of aid to Middle East countries, which could lead to definite America military and political commitments in an area from which the Soviet Union had hoped to exclude all Western influence. At the same time, the Soviet Union had lost a considerable amount of military equipment during the fighting in Egypt, and her recently-supplied jet bombers had been forced to make an undignified exit—together with their technical staffs—in the face of the enemy. The Western world had probably acquired many of the closely-guarded details of the scope, timing, and nature of Soviet military aid to Egypt from September 1955 to November 1956, and could, the Soviet leaders would assume, reconstruct much of the Soviet arms programme intended for the future. But even more unwelcome was the fact that the Egyptian Army had been surprised and completely defeated in the field by the Israelis. Few principles have remained so firmly fixed in the Soviet military mind as 'safety in numbers', yet in the Sinai desert the small, high-trained and mobile army maintained by Israel had scattered an Egyptian Army which had already received Soviet weapons and training. And there is nothing more cordially disliked by the Soviet leaders than an alliance with a nation whose troops have suffered defeat on the battlefield.

Mr. Khrushchev's tactics aimed at restoring the Soviet position were characteristic of his realism, and his recognition of the real danger points in the situation. The most urgent threat from the crisis in Poland, Hungary, and the Middle East was to the doctrine which provided the binding link of the Soviet Empire, so his first step was to protect and restore confidence in Communism in the shaken capitals of Eastern Europe. First he called a meeting of the East European Communist leaders in Budapest on 1 January 1957, though, understandably enough, without Polish representation. After

[1] When relations between Egypt and Russia deteriorated after 1958 the Government of the United Arab Republic printed a special issue of an illustrated magazine on the Hungarian Rising, containing most of the action photographs published in the European and American Press at the time, but suppressed in Cairo and Damascus.

four days of discussion between the party leaders of Hungary, Rumania, Czechoslovakia, Bulgaria, and Albania and a Soviet delegation under Mr. Khrushchev and Mr. Malenkov, a communiqué was issued proclaiming the unshakeable unity of the Soviet bloc, and laying down the official Soviet version of the Hungarian rising.[1]

The Budapest meeting was preceded and followed by a series of visits to Moscow by the leaders of the individual Communist parties of the Soviet bloc. During these visits the European Communist Governments re-affirmed their loyalty to Moscow, while the Russians adjusted those aspects of Soviet-East European relations—particularly economic and military—which gave rise to the type of resentment underlying the events in Poland and Hungary. First to be invited to Moscow were the Rumanians, who arrived in the Soviet Union in November 1956, and expressed solidarity with their hosts on all ideological problems and on the Hungarian rising. In exchange, they received economic concessions, including a postponement of interest payments on existing Soviet credits, and additional supplies of grain and foodstuffs. Immediately after the Budapest conference it was the turn of the East Germans, the only other East European leadership which had stood by while the Soviet Army put down a rising by their own workers. On 3 January 1957 Herr Grotewohl, the Prime Minister, and Herr Ulbricht, the party Secretary, arrived in Moscow, and held discussions with the Soviet leaders for four days. The East Germans expressed full confidence in the Soviet Union in spite of the collapse of Communism in Hungary, and in return the Russians offered them substantial concessions. Soviet troops, under Sections 3 and 5 of a new Agreement, would remain in East Germany as allies under the Warsaw Pact, and the East German Government was given certain rights in matters of transport, communications, and accommodation of the Soviet forces.[2] On the economic side, the Soviet Union agreed to increase the volume of trade with East Germany in 1957, and to ensure that Soviet deliveries of machinery, foodstuffs, and raw materials would be 30 per cent higher than in 1956. The Russians also offered a credit of 340 million roubles in

[1] The inclusion of Mr. Malenkov, the former Premier and Mr. Khrushchev's rival in the Soviet delegation, was intended to show the desired solidarity within the Soviet Communist party.

[2] A more comprehensive military agreement embodying further concessions to the East Germans was concluded in 12 March. This placed Soviet soldiers under German law, and required 'consultations' with the East German authorities before troop movements could be carried out.

freely convertible currency—a welcome gesture at a time when the East German economy was in difficulties partly because of reduced Polish coal deliveries since the October revolution in Warsaw.

The next East European delegation to go to Moscow came from Czechoslovakia, and stayed in the Soviet capital from 25 January to 3 February. Once again political and ideological solidarity with the Soviet leadership was loudly proclaimed, but the main part of this particular communiqué was devoted to proving that any 'irregularities' in the terms on which Czechoslovakia's uranium had been supplied to the Soviet Union were now a thing of the past. The exploitation of Czechoslovak uranium deposits under a complete monopoly by the Soviet Union had long been a source of resentment in Prague, and the references to 'fair, mutually beneficial prices' in the communiqué were probably intended to be a welcome concession to the Czechs. Additional supplies of Soviet grain and iron ores were promised to Czechoslovakia.

The Czechoslovak delegation was followed by a Bulgarian one, which arrived in Moscow in 10 February. Here, too, economic concessions were made by the Russians, including new industrial credits of 200 million roubles and further supplies of machinery and fertilizers to help to overcome unemployment in Bulgaria.[1] Both the Czechoslovak and Bulgarian party communiqués, besides expressing solidarity with the Soviet Union, launched new attacks on 'revisionism' in the Communist world, and it was noted with particular interest that the Bulgarian Prime Minister, Mr. Yugov, renewed the offensive against Yugoslavia in a bitter speech he made at a reception in the Kremlin on 18 February. No doubt Soviet tacticians remembered that when conducting a defensive operation from weak positions a diversionary counter-attack on another sector often brings useful results.

The remaining European Communist countries, Hungary and Albania sent delegations to Moscow in March and April 1957. To the Hungarian leaders the Soviet Government promised a long-term loan of 750 million roubles (200 million of it in convertible currency) and also wrote off debts incurred in Hungary's 'purchase' of the joint Hungarian-Soviet companies. A month later, on 27 May, a new

---

[1] This had been openly admitted by the Bulgarian Communist paper *Rabotnichesko Delo* on 11 June 1956, which described it as 'the temporary phenomenon of the notorious unemployment existing in the towns'. It was later partially solved by the dispatch of 10,000 Bulgarian youths to Soviet Central Asia for work in mines and on the land.

agreement on the conditions under which the Soviet Army would remain in Hungary was signed in Budapest, incorporating certain formal concessions on the legal status of Soviet servicemen stationed abroad.[1] Finally, an Albanian delegation which visited the Soviet Union from 11–17 April was granted a remission of all debts to the Soviet Union, and a promise of deliveries of large quantities of wheat and other foodstuffs on credit terms.

It is clear that the Soviet Union recognized at least two of the underlying causes of the Hungarian and Polish outbreaks: economic exploitation, and the presence of Soviet troops in East Germany, Poland, Hungary, and Rumania with extra-territorial status, and was prepared to do something to remove them. However, far more important in Soviet eyes was the support received at this critical juncture from Communist China, whose Government and party leaders now came forward with two practical expressions of Sino-Soviet solidarity.

First, on 29 December 1956, the official Chinese Communist newspaper, the Peking *People's Daily*, printed an article entitled 'More on the Historic Experience of the Dictatorship of the Proletariat', based, the author claimed, on discussions held at a recent meeting of the Chinese Politbureau. The article analysed the state of the Communist world at the end of 1956, and dwelt on problems such as the Hungarian rising, the Polish 'deviation', and the role of de-Stalinization. The Chinese leaders then put forward their first major original contribution to Communist doctrine: the theory of 'fundamental and non-fundamental contradictions', the former appearing between 'capitalism' and 'communism', and within the 'capitalist' world, the latter existing within the Communist world. It was possible, according to the Chinese analysis, to follow wrong as well as right paths within the framework of Communist policy, and this is what Stalin did, although it was always to be remembered that his positive contributions to Communism outweighed his errors. The Soviet Union also made mistakes, among them 'Great Power chauvinism', in its relationship with the smaller East European countries, and the latter erred in the direction of excessive nationalism. But these were non-fundamental contradictions and had nothing to do with the

---

[1] It is interesting to note that Poland received better treatment than Hungary or East Germany. Soviet troops needed Polish 'permission' to re-deploy or to carry out large-scale exercises, but only 'consultations' were promised with the Hungarian and East German authorities.

Hungarian rising, which quickly developed the characteristics of fundamental contradictions, since the issue was between a Communist and a non-Communist future for Hungary. Therefore—and this was the valuable point from the Soviet angle—the Soviet intervention in Hungary was justified. In any case, continued the Chinese, the Soviet Union had now learnt its lesson, had corrected its errors, and remained the 'centre and core of our movement'. Turning to the Yugoslavs, the Chinese stated that their attitude was wrong because they were turning non-fundamental contradictions into fundamental ones, and thus doing a disservice to the Communist cause as a whole. Finally, and significantly, the Chinese declared that although the non-fundamental contradictions were not basic, they ought to be resolved, because they could 'help the enemy, the imperialists, who are bent on destroying us'.[1]

This article was reprinted in full in the Moscow *Pravda*, including the critical remarks against the Soviet Union. This was one indication of the anxiety of the Soviet leaders at that time to obtain Chinese support—they were ready to allow the Soviet public to hear the Chinese describing Russia the 'core' of the Communist world, instead of its 'leader'. It also showed how great a value the Russians placed on Chinese support for Soviet policy, especially within the Communist hierarchies in a doubting Eastern Europe.

But the Chinese went still further in declaring their solidarity with the Russians. A Chinese Government and party delegation, led by Mr. Chou En-lai, the Premier, arrived in Moscow on 7 January 1957 on the first stage of a tour of the Communist states of Europe. While in Moscow, the Chinese, whose visit coincided with that of the East German delegation, put their signatures to a Sino-Soviet-East German communiqué endorsing Soviet policy in Hungary and the Middle East, and calling especially for unity and solidarity among Communist countries.

Mr. Chou En-lai then visited Warsaw, from 11 to 16 January, where, significantly, he modified his unqualified deference to Soviet leadership and gave public approval to Mr. Gomulka's policy for Poland. After a flying (and unpublicized) visit to Budapest, the Chinese leader returned to Moscow on 17 January. In the Soviet capital a mass meeting at which Mr. Khrushchev, Marshal Bulganin, and Mr. Chou En-lai spoke provided the climax to the Chinese tour.

[1] From *People's Daily*, Peking, 29 December 1956, reprinted in *Pravda*, Moscow, 30 December 1956.

Mr. Chou attacked the Hungarian revolution with such bitter intensity that one wonders whether an additional Russian motive for the tour—besides the demonstration of support for Soviet policy—may not have been a desire to show the Chinese just how difficult was the Soviet Union's problem in dealing with the East European countries.[1] When Mr. Chou left for Afghanistan on 19 January the Soviet leaders may well have congratulated themselves that they had shocked their powerful and restless allies into realizing that the 'centre and core' of the Communist world needed more active and sympathetic support than had originally been forthcoming from Peking.

Vehement expression of his confidence in the future of Communism, of the need for the unshakeable unity of the Communist states of Europe, aided by timely economic and legal concessions, and unconditional Chinese support for Soviet policy were the main tactical measures taken by Mr. Khrushchev within his own camp to repair the ravages of 1956. But characteristically, he went over to the attack by launching a new tactical counter-offensive in the direction of the Western Powers in the hope of driving a wedge between non-Communist Europe and the United States.

The campaign opened with a speech by Mr. Shepilov, the Soviet Foreign Minister, to the Supreme Soviet on 12 February 1957. Mr. Shepilov began with a review of the world situation designed to distract attention from the seriousness of the crisis through which the Soviet bloc had just passed. He suggested that the 'danger' to the peace of the world from the United States was greater in 1957 because Britain and France had emerged from the Suez crisis considerably weakened, and cited the introduction of the 'Eisenhower Doctrine' for the Middle East as 'proof' that America was about to move into that area to take over British and French commitments and interests.

Basing himself on this theory, Mr. Shepilov proceeded to make a series of proposals aimed at dividing Europe from America.[2] For the Middle East, Mr. Shepilov suggested a joint undertaking by the Soviet Union, Britain, France, and the United States not to interfere by political or military means in the countries of that area or to offer economic aid for political ends. He proposed an agreement to abstain

---

[1] Mr. Chou, for example, did not visit the more 'stable' East European Communist states, Bulgaria, Rumania, or Czechoslovakia.

[2] These proposals were first sent as Notes to the three Western Powers on 11 February, but publicized by the Soviet Government before the Governments concerned had had time to study them.

from including Middle Eastern countries in military alliances with a Great Power, to abolish all military bases, and to halt deliveries of arms. These provisions were aimed at the Eisenhower Doctrine and the Baghdad Pact, which, the Soviet Union probably believed, would now secure American participation as part of the United States 'succession' policy in that area of the world. Mr. Shepilov went on to offer Soviet friendship to individual countries, not only of the traditionally uncommitted areas, such as India, Burma, Indonesia, and Ceylon, but to countries already associated with the West, and even to members of N.A.T.O. Friendly references were also made to Pakistan, Japan, Persia, and Afghanistan, each containing an offer of Soviet aid or support if it altered its relationship with the United States.[1]

The main countries of Western Europe were approached with suggestions of Soviet co-operation in the field of disarmament, collective security, and trade. On 18 January 1957 *Pravda* committed itself to the remarkable statement that 'to say that Britain has ceased to be a Great Power would be premature'—a pronouncement apparently calculated in Moscow to attract Britain and draw her away from the American alliance. Britain was referred to in Moscow Radio broadcasts in English as 'the most important country of Western Europe'.[2] The invitation to Sir Anthony Eden to visit Russia was extended to Mr. Macmillan on 2 February 1957 and attempts were made from mid-January onwards to renew cultural contacts broken at the time of the Hungarian rising. On 21 May a new committee was set up in Moscow for expanding cultural links with countries abroad.

As far as France was concerned, a Soviet Note of 18 May offered direct Soviet-French negotiations on European security, and told the French that the N.A.T.O. Alliance was becoming increasingly dominated by Germany. The Russians also suggested the establishment of Chambers of Commerce in Paris and Moscow, and talks on atomic energy for peaceful purposes between the two countries. At

---

[1] The anti-American bias of Mr. Shepilov's speech was underlined by a 'security' campaign in the Soviet Press against alleged espionage by the United States, which included reports of a Press conference given in Moscow on 6 February by four men stated to have been American spies caught red-handed on Soviet soil. (*Pravda*, 7 February 1957.)

[2] Broadcasts in German paid the same compliment to Germany, and were reminiscent of Stalin's famous gambit that the Russian and German people had suffered most during the Second World War.

the same time the Scandinavian countries also received special mention, and West Germany was called upon to play her part in a 'decisive turn' for the better in relations with the Soviet Union.[1]

Overlapping the two campaigns in Western and Eastern Europe came renewed Soviet emphasis on the military might of the Soviet armed forces. A series of nuclear tests was carried out in the first part of 1957, with explosions on 19 January, 8 March, and on 3, 6, 10 and 12 April. A Conference of Outstanding Servicemen opened in Moscow on 16 March in a blaze of publicity, and hundreds of Soviet officers and men heard Marshal Zhukov, then the Minister of Defence, prophesy that in any future war atomic weapons would inevitably be used as the main striking weapon.[2] And the Soviet Union sent Notes to many countries of N.A.T.O.—Norway, Denmark, and Western Germany among them, expressing Russia's concern at their 'lack of independence under United States' domination'; these messages also drew their recipients' attention to the danger of underestimating the military power of the Soviet Union.

The campaign to drive a wedge between Britain and the European members of N.A.T.O. and America was, however, broken off before it could register any visible progress. The interruption was due to the Bermuda Conference between Mr. Macmillan and President Eisenhower, which was held from 20 to 23 March 1957 and to the meeting of the N.A.T.O. Council in Bonn in May 1957. The Bermuda Conference, at which Anglo-American relations were restored to a workable degree of harmony, confirmed the British and American view that the security of the free world must continue, in the absence of a disarmament agreement, to depend on the nuclear deterrent, and that limited numbers of weapon tests would still be necessary. Mr. Khrushchev concluded from the results of the Conference that Britain and America had joined forces again, and he immediately adopted a new tactical approach. On 31 March the Soviet Foreign Office accused the British and American Governments of making 'immediate preparations for an atomic war, as shown by the decision to step up the activities of the aggressive North Atlantic and Baghdad blocs'.[3] This was followed by a new Soviet suggestion on the suspension of nuclear tests to the United Nations' Disarmament sub-

---

[1] This approach had already been made in a Soviet Note to Bonn delivered on 8 February, and broadcast by Moscow Radio on 11 February 1957.

[2] *Red Star*, Moscow, 17 March 1957.

[3] *The Times*, 1 April 1957.

committee, which was re-convened on 18 March. On 30 April, no doubt as an attempt to win a propaganda advantage in the light of the Anglo-American decision on the continuing need for tests, the Soviet delegate, Mr. Zorin, who had already tabled his Government's proposals on reductions in conventional forces, and on inspection and control, suddenly urged the immediate cessation of tests, independent of disarmament, and without control. The suggestion was accompanied by the inauguration of a new and vigorous propaganda campaign against nuclear tests, which included appeals by the Communist-dominated World Peace Council to the peoples of the world over the heads of their Governments. Yet the Soviet Union continued to test its own nuclear weapons throughout the campaign, for, as Mr. Gromyko, the new Soviet Foreign Minister, said on 10 May: 'We in this country are being forced to continue the manufacture of atomic and hydrogen weapons, and more than that, to manufacture ever newer types of atomic and hydrogen bombs, new types of rockets, and to strengthen our defence potential in every possible way in the interests of our security. The Soviet Union is also continuing to test atomic and hydrogen weapons.' He then went on to describe what he called 'the growing wave of protests against tests carried out by Britain'.[1]

The second event which probably caused Mr. Khrushchev to change his tactics was the decision of the N.A.T.O. Ministerial Council in May 1957 to equip N.A.T.O. forces with nuclear weapons.[2] This move was interpeted in Moscow as further evidence that the Western Alliance had recovered its unity, and that wedge-driving tactics between the European and North American members had little hope of success. Certainly, no appreciable notice of Soviet tactics had been taken in Scandinavia, or in Bonn of a stern Soviet Note delivered on 27 April which, *inter alia*, threatened that in the event of war West Germany would be destroyed before outside assistance could reach her.

Mr. Khrushchev's conviction that Western unity has been restored, coupled with a feeling that his country's recovery from the effects of the Hungarian rising was sufficiently advanced, led him, in mid-May, to mention a new Summit meeting between the four Great Powers. At the same time, in an interview with an American correspondent, Mr. Khrushchev suggested bi-lateral negotiations

---

[1] *Pravda*, reporting a speech to the Supreme Soviet, 11 May 1957.
[2] See *Handbook of NATO*, 6th edition, p. 34, Paris, 1958.

between the Soviet Union and the United States.[1] He stated that a direct agreement between the Soviet Union and the U.S.A., as the two most powerful military and industrial states in the world, would mark the beginning of the solution of all world problems. And in a television interview given to American Press correspondents on 2 June, Mr. Khrushchev emphasized that the most important aim of Soviet policy was the establishment of normal relations between the United States and Russia.

Mr. Khrushchev's approach to the United States, which he addressed once more as the leader of a unified Western Alliance, marked the end of the phase in Soviet foreign policy aiming at recovery from the failures of 1956. Since the restoration of Communist rule in Hungary and the interruption of the Soviet move into the Middle East resulting from the Suez crisis, Mr. Khrushchev had conducted a determined struggle against wavering elements inside the Communist parties in Eastern Europe, many of whose leaders may have found their faith in Communism weakened by Soviet suppression of the Hungarian rising. This Mr. Khrushchev countered by economic and national concessions to the East European countries and by calling in the Chinese Communists to express in public their faith in Soviet policy and the future of Communism. Another obstacle to the Soviet recovery was the condemnation of Soviet policy in Hungary prevalent in Western countries. Mr. Khrushchev attempted to dispel this mistrust by exploiting the differences between Britain and France and the U.S.A. and by trying to drive a wedge between the United States and the rest of the Western World. When, however, he came to the conclusion after the Bermuda and Bonn meetings that Western unity had been restored under American leadership, Mr. Khrushchev turned his attention to a new Summit meeting, and to bi-lateral talks between Russia and the United States.

Mr. Khrushchev clearly worked on the principle that in foreign policy no defeat is total, and that there is always something to be salvaged, even from the most discouraging failure. Moreover, there comes a time when, in view of the generally relaxed attitude of the Western world, and the passivity of many of the uncommitted nations, the memory of defeats and failures becomes blurred, and a positive foreign policy, an active strategy with flexible tactics can be resumed. This point, in relation to Soviet foreign policy, after the

[1] Interview with Mr. Catledge, of the *New York Times*, 11 May 1957.

failures of 1956, was probably reached in the course of the summer of 1957, particularly after Mr. Khrushchev had eliminated the Malenkov-Molotov-Kaganovich-Shepilov group in the leadership of his own Soviet Communist party. It was again characteristic of Mr. Khrushchev that he went straight for the biggest prize of all—a meeting with the leaders of Britain, France, and the United States, at which he could discuss and decide the future of the world on equal terms with those who had so recently witnessed his discomfiture in Poland and Hungary. For this more than anything would prove to his own countrymen and to the world at large that policies based on disapproval, even on bitter hatred of Soviet policy, are no match for the realities of Soviet military, political, and economic power. If Mr. Khrushchev could show the doubters in his own camp that sooner or later the rest of the world would have to disregard the issues raised by the invasion of Hungary and discuss world problems with the Soviet Union in something like the spirit of 1955, then the tactics of recovery of 1957 would have been a success.

XVII

THE PRESSURE ON WESTERN EUROPE
1957–60

AFTER the Soviet recovery from the immediate crisis arising from the Hungarian revolution, the Russian leaders resumed an active foreign strategy in three main directions. The first was towards the Western Powers and had the dual aim of weakening the military and political position of the United States and her chief allies on the European Continent, and of returning to equality in the Councils of the Big Four through a high-level conference or a meeting between the Heads of the Soviet and American Governments. The second direction of Soviet foreign policy was the Middle East and Africa, where the Russians aimed at maintaining a balance between the stability necessary for the Soviet economic offensive in these countries and the degree of tension required to prevent a return of Western influence to the area. The third main direction was China, where Soviet policy sought a reliable and obedient ally to form the eastern bastion of the Soviet global strategic position. In the chapters which follow each of these operational sectors will be examined in turn, beginning with what must have been regarded in Moscow as the most important of all—the Western Alliance.

Suggestions for summit talks and meetings between the leaders of the great powers which made their appearance during the recovery campaign remained a constant theme of Soviet speeches, diplomatic Notes, and interviews with foreign newspapers throughout the period from 1957 to 1959. But at the same time, the Soviet Government pressed home a campaign against the strengthening of the N.A.T.O. Alliance. In order to understand the tactics of this campaign, it is necessary to look briefly at one important aspect of Soviet global strategic thought. Russian strategic concepts have always been dominated by the division of the world into three major land masses, and a number of smaller areas which can be dominated by the land, with assistance from sea, and later air, power. Thus, as the Russians saw it, the major land mass of the world was that of Eurasia and the islands attached to it, including the British Isles, the islands of the Mediterranean, Ceylon, Japan, and the archipelagos along its south-eastern coasts. Secondly, there were the Americas and their continental island groups in the Carribean. Thirdly came Africa, and finally, the area of Australasia, Antarctica, and Indonesia, probably regarded as a kind of dissected continent, which, nevertheless, could be controlled by a land power established at some suitable point within the area.

Many Russian strategic thinkers, both before and after the revolution found some degree of balance of power in the fact that some of these major continents contained one supreme land power, for example, Russia in Eurasia, and the United States in the Americas. If, therefore, one of these great land states extended its physical presence into one of the other land masses, this constituted an extension of power tantamount to an 'invasion', and created a 'bridgehead' situation, of the kind which has dominated so much of Soviet stratetic thought.

Looking back for a moment to the end of the Second World War, the Soviet leaders from Stalin onwards probably interpreted the global policy of the United States as expansionist, partly because of the creation of six of these bridgeheads in the Eurasian land mass by means of American land, sea, and air power. They were: Western Europe, militarily united under N.A.T.O.; Japan; Korea; Formosa; the Philippines, and Okinawa. The United States was probably also regarded as having moved into south-east Asia, through its membership of the South-East Asia Treaty Organization.

The Soviet version of the creation and development of the West European bridgehead runs like this: in 1944, the bridgehead was set up as a result of the landing in Normandy; after 1945, there were signs that the United States would withdraw from the bridgehead: the bulk of her troops returned to the U.S.A. and those which remained were so few in number that not even one Army Headquarters was required to control them. Then, beginning with the Truman Doctrine and the Marshall Plan, this trend was reversed, and since the creation of N.A.T.O., in 1949, the U.S.A. followed a policy of strengthening the West European bridgehead, by setting up a powerful land, sea, and air base, and extending it territorially to Greece and Turkey. Soviet propaganda frequently explained the East German workers' rising in 1953 as an American attempt to extend their 'bridgehead' farther inland. Soviet moves designed to liquidate or weaken N.A.T.O. coincided exactly with moves to strengthen the Organization's military strength in Western Europe. N.A.T.O., in fact, was regarded in Moscow not only as a military base of considerable power, but as a bridgehead which had no right to exist. Therefore, in addition to ideological considerations, on the basis of which Stalin divided the post-war world into two 'camps', the Soviets always regarded United States' membership of N.A.T.O. as a penetration of the Eurasian land mass by the strongest power of the American land mass.

In 1957, eight years after its foundation, N.A.T.O. took a step which, in Soviet eyes, marked a new watershed in the history of this American bridgehead in Eurasia. For in that year the United States, having welded the armed forces of the N.A.T.O. powers into a defence force with unified command, proposed to make the power of the Alliance effective by introducing atomic and nuclear warheads to the N.A.T.O. armouries in the event of war, and by setting up bases for Intermediate Range Ballistic Missiles (I.R.B.M.s) sited on N.A.T.O. territory. The first decision was taken in principle at the N.A.T.O. Council's meeting in Bonn in May, and the second at the meeting in Paris in December, which was attended by the Heads of Governments. At the Bonn meeting the United States Government offered to place at the disposal of the Supreme Allied Commander, Europe, General Norstad, atomic and nuclear warheads for use by existing or future artillery weapons. The warheads were to remain United States property, and could only be used as part of the N.A.T.O. defensive counter-stroke with the agreement of the N.A.T.O. Council and the United States Government. Ownership by other countries was specifically excluded, especially Western Germany, which had undertaken not to possess these weapons.

In December 1957, therefore, the Soviet Government had to take into account a N.A.T.O. Alliance which was about to increase its military strength and efficiency inside the 'bridgehead' of Western Europe. This, of course, might be militarily dangerous to the Soviet Union, and it would certainly increase the obstacles in the way of a seizure of power by the Communists in West European countries. Remote though such Communist successes might have seemed at that time, hope was never abandoned in Moscow that conditions could develop which would play into the hands of the local Communist parties. Immediately Soviet diplomacy went into action to secure the withdrawal of Western Germany from the Alliance, and to prevent her territory being used for the deployment of N.A.T.O. forces; and to deter as many members of the Alliance as possible from accepting the new weapons and bases offered by the United States.[1]

The campaign opened just before the December meeting of N.A.T.O. with a series of letters from the Soviet Prime Minister, Marshal Bulganin, to President Eisenhower, Mr. Macmillan, Dr. Adenauer, and M. Gaillard, the French Prime Minister, followed by further letters to the Heads of all the N.A.T.O. Governments.[2] The tone and approach of each letter varied according to the recipient: M. Gaillard, for example, was reminded of the German threat and of the danger that France might succumb to an alliance dominated by the Anglo-Americans. Dr. Adenauer was warned that acceptance of atomic weapons by his Government would rule out reunification of the two parts of Germany. Mr. Macmillan received a warning about the dangers of allowing American air bases, from which aircraft carrying nuclear bombs were able to patrol over British cities. President Eisenhower, however, was addressed as the leader of one of the two powers with direct responsibility for the maintenance of world peace, and in this capacity was invited to discuss it in bi-lateral talks between the United States and the Soviet Union.

On 21 December 1957 the Supreme Soviet met in Moscow to pass a resolution on East-West relations.[3] Its main items were: an undertaking by the U.S.S.R., Britain, and the U.S.A. to suspend nuclear tests from 1 January 1958, and to refrain from using nuclear weapons in any circumstances; to give up plans for the deployment of nuclear weapons in Germany, Poland, and Czechoslovakia; to carry out reductions in armed forces, to adopt a policy of non-interference in the Middle East, and to maintain the *status quo* in Germany and Central Europe. The Soviet view on Central Europe was reaffirmed in an interview which Mr. Khrushchev gave to a

---

[1] These Soviet aims were not, of course, new, and many items were characteristic of earlier Soviet approaches to the West. But the development of the campaign in all its phrases from December 1957 onwards represents a striking example of Soviet tactics in East-West relations, and requires independent study in this context.

[2] See *The Times*, 12 and 13 December 1957.

[3] *Observer*, 22 December 1957.

British newspaper.[1] The Soviet leader stated that no negotiations between East and West could be successful if the Western Powers tried to change the economic and social structure of the East European countries; and a neutralized and atom-free Germany would, he said, be one solution of the German problem favoured by the Soviet Union. The Soviet Government followed up these moves by circulating a Memorandum in January 1958 to all members of the United Nations and to Switzerland, suggesting high-level talks on the reduction of troop strengths, the creation of an atom-free zone in Central Europe, and measures to prevent a surprise attack in Europe. In addition, the proposal to set up 'zones of peace' on Europe, free of nuclear weapons and ballistic missiles was extended to cover Scandinavia and the Baltic, and, less directly, Italy and the Adriatic.[2] In letters from the Soviet Government published on 8 January the Greek and Turkish Governments were also encouraged to support a 'zone of peace' in the Balkans. Each of the smaller powers addressed by Marshal Bulganin was also warned of the destruction which nuclear weapons could cause in their cities and to their peoples in the event of war.[3] At the same time the Soviet Union announced a further reduction in its armed forces. The Soviet Army, Navy, and Air Force, according to *Tass*, would be cut by 300,000 men; 41,000 men would be withdrawn from Germany and 17,000 from Hungary.[4] One significant element in the Soviet campaign against the strengthening of N.A.T.O. was the suggestion in some of the Soviet Notes that a 'time limit' should be introduced, so that the talks on European security could be held within two or three months.[5] The motive behind this suggestion was clearly to get the projected negotiations under way before N.A.T.O.'s increase in fire power in the European bridgehead became effective.

[1] *Daily Express*, 23 December 1957.

[2] In his Note to Italy, Marshal Bulganin put forward the ideas of a referendum of public opinion in Italy on the siting of missile bases, which had been accepted in principle by the Italian Government.

[3] Marshal Bulganin's covering letter to Turkey stated that I.C.B.M.s would not be needed for use against that country, since Turkey was within range of what the letter called 'simpler rockets'.

[4] Allied officers attended departure ceremonies of Soviet troops in Juterbog, H.Q. of 3rd Guards Mechanized Army. There is, however, no information as to whether the units withdrawn from Germany and Hungary were disbanded or re-formed inside the U.S.S.R. as new, more up-to-date formations.

[5] Marshal Bulganin's Memorandum, as reported in *Soviet News*, 10 January 1958, p. 29.

The Soviet campaign to keep nuclear and ballistic weapons as far away as possible from the borders of East and Central Europe merged naturally with the Polish plan for a nuclear-free zone in Central Europe, first presented to the United Nations on 2 October 1957 by the Polish Foreign Minister, Mr. Rapacki. Early in February 1958 it was announced that the Polish and Soviet Foreign Ministers had met to discuss the Plan in detail, and on the 14th the Polish Government sent an amended version to the four Great Powers and the countries which it was intended to cover. The Polish Plan suggested the establishment of a zone in Central Europe in which no nuclear, atomic, or ballistic weapons or bases would be installed by any power; an effective control system would come into being, supervised by representatives of N.A.T.O. and the Warsaw Pact, or by neutral officials; later, in the favourable atmosphere created by the absence of weapons of mass destruction, conventional arms and troops could be completely withdrawn from the zone.

The Rapacki Plan, as it came to be known, was discussed all the more sympathetically by the N.A.T.O. powers because it was generally felt to be a genuine Polish initiative, originating in understandable Polish fears.[1] However, the basic disadvantages of the Plan from the point of view of Western defence was, first, that it asked N.A.T.O. to surrender the only weapons in which the Soviet armed forces did not have outright superiority, and second, that the proposed nuclear-free zone would be entirely at the mercy of a large mass army, armed with conventional weapons. In practical terms, if the Rapacki zone covered Poland, Czechoslovakia, and the two parts of Germany, Western Germany would be quite indefensible against a conventional attack by the Soviet Army, or against subversion involving para-military forces. The Soviet armed forces, in the event of war in Europe, could plan on the basis that they would not have to fight an enemy on West German soil with nuclear, atomic, or ballistic armaments. There were, of course, other doubts about the value of the Plan—such as the details of the control system, and its effect on German reunification—but the separation of nuclear and conventional armaments was the point which most clearly favoured Soviet military requirements to the detriment of those of N.A.T.O.

[1] One argument in favour of the belief in a Polish origin for the Plan was that of timing. The Plan appeared first in October 1957, at a time when the Soviet Union was still engrossed in military threats in the Middle East. The Soviet Government's campaign of which the Polish Plan later became a part was more clearly linked with the decisions of the N.A.T.O. meeting of December 1957.

The month of March 1958 was spent by the Soviet Government in urging the powers forward towards a Summit conference, and in extending its proposals designed to weaken Western military power.[1] At the same time, the Soviet Government carried out a highly concentrated series of nuclear test explosions, four of which were in the megaton range.[2] While this series of explosions was taking place the Soviet Union notified the United States that it was opposed to any substantive debate on disarmament at that time in the Security Council.[3] But at the end of the test series, on 31 March 1958 the Soviet Government announced the unilateral suspension of all nuclear weapon tests. This decision marked the beginning of a renewed campaign to present the Soviet Union as the only nuclear power opposed to nuclear tests. It included messages from the Supreme Soviet to the American Congress and the British Parliament urging the United States and Britain to suspend all nuclear tests, and letters to West Germany and other countries seeking support for the Soviet decision. In the middle of April, Soviet Government spokesmen drew attention to flights over the Arctic Circle by American aircraft carrying atomic or hydrogen weapons.[4] On 21 April the Soviet Union summoned the Security Council to meet and adopt a Soviet resolution calling on the United States to end these flights, but the motion was rejected after Western spokesmen had recalled that it was the Soviet Government which had refused a Western offer of an inspection system for the Arctic in May 1957.

The Security Council meeting coincided with the opening on 17 April of preparatory Ambassadorial talks in Moscow intended to work out details of a future high-level meeting. While these talks were going on, a big gathering of political, military, and economic leaders of the Soviet bloc countries, involving the convocation of both the Warsaw Treaty and the Council of Mutual Economic Aid, took place in the Soviet capital. It was at this meeting in Moscow in May 1958 that the Council for Mutual Economic Assistance, which

[1] On 15 March Mr. Khrushchev offered to ban arms in outer space in return for the liquidation of foreign bases in Europe, the Middle East, and North Africa. (*Observer*. 16 March 1958.)

[2] *Manchester Guardian*, 2 October 1958. An announcement by the Japanese Meterological Board on 20 March 1958 attributed a sudden increase in radio-activity over Japan to Soviet tests believed to have been held in the Arctic Circle on 14 and 15 March.

[3] *Tass* statement, 23 March 1958.

[4] At a Press conference on 18 April 1958 addressed by Mr. Gromyko.

had been relatively inactive between 1949 and 1956, came to life as an effective instrument for the promotion of the economic integration of the bloc. Some specialization had been introduced in 1956 and 1957, and twelve special commissions dealing with coal, oil, agriculture, and other resources were in existence. But after 1958 the Council met in plenary session every six months, and planned the expansion of the chemical industry, agriculture, metallurgy, transport, and electric power. This use of the Council for Mutual Economic Assistance bound the East European countries closer to the Soviet Union, and made them more dependent economically on each other. The communiqué issued after the meeting of the Warsaw Treaty powers dovetailed into the current campaign: on the one hand its signatories threatened to establish rocket bases in East Germany, Poland, and Czechoslovakia if I.R.B.M.s were set up in Europe; and on the other, they announced reductions in the strengths of the East European armed forces.[1] The communiqué emphasized that no discussion of East European affairs at an East-West meeting would be countenanced by any of the member-states of the Warsaw Pact.

Shortly after the meeting of the Warsaw Treaty powers Mr. Khrushchev, who, in March had replaced Marshal Bulganin as Soviet Premier, kept up the pressure on the West by every means in his power. For example, he released prematurely to the Press confidential exchanges between the Soviet Union and the Western Powers in the hope of showing the world that the West, in stressing the need for careful preparation for talks at the Summit, were trying to delay East-West negotiations.

On the other hand, there was some progress on disarmament. The Soviet Government agreed to consider a new approach to the control of the suspension of nuclear tests. On 9 May 1958 the Russians accepted an invitation to take part in a technical conference on this subject, and named a Soviet delegation to go to Geneva for the talks, which opened on 1 July. The conference reported on 21 August that it was technically feasible to set up an organization which could detect violations of an agreement on the suspension of nuclear tests; on the next day the United States and Britain proposed the opening

---

[1] The agreed reduction of the Rumanian Army was by 55,000 men; by Bulgaria, 23,000; by Poland, 20,000; by Czechoslovakia, 20,000; by Albania, 1,000. All Soviet troops would be withdrawn from Rumania, and one further division from Hungary would return to the U.S.S.R.

of negotiations on this subject in Geneva on 31 October. The two countries also offered to suspend their nuclear tests for one year from that date. The Soviet Government reacted by accepting the Geneva meeting, but described the British and American suspension offer as a 'new manoeuvre' to hold up the suspension of nuclear tests.[1] This incident is significant because it illustrated an important aspect of Soviet tactics in the disarmament field. The Soviet Government is often more ready to take part in technical and scientific talks than in negotiations to put the findings of the scientists into effect, since its representatives may acquire new information on technical matters in the course of the discussions. This explains Mr. Khrushchev's readiness to send representatives to technical conferences at a time when he opposed suggestions for East-West meetings on any but Soviet terms. As soon as the Western Powers attempted to use the conclusions of the technical conference on the control of test suspension as a basis for wider negotiations the Soviet Government reacted adversely.[2]

Meanwhile, on 22 August, the Western Powers suggested to the Soviet Government a resumption of the Moscow meeting of Ambassadors which had begun on 17 April, and had lapsed at the end of May. At this time, however, both the Soviet Government and the Western Powers were closely engaged in the Middle Eastern crisis of July–August 1958, and East-West exchanges on a Summit conference to discuss Europe were overshadowed by Mr. Khrushchev's offer to fly to New York for talks on the Middle East on 23 July.[3] This meeting, however, did not take place, and was, in fact, one of a series of setbacks suffered by the Soviet Government in foreign policy since the N.A.T.O. meetings of May and December 1957. Soviet policy had failed to make any N.A.T.O. Government change its mind on the Bonn and Paris decisions, or to influence the debates in the Parliaments of the N.A.T.O. countries on the American offer to set up missile bases on their territory. Several countries, including

---

[1] *Tass* statement, 23 August 1957.

[2] Mr. Zorin rejected the West's offer of one year's suspension in a speech on 27 October to the Political Committee of the United Nations General Assembly, but the Soviet Union was ready to enter another purely technical conference on 10 November, on inspection measures to detect a surprise attack. On 6 October the Soviet Union again made an effort to regain the initiative by introducing a draft resolution in the United Nations for an unconditional ban on nuclear weapon tests.

[3] *The Times*, 26 July 1958. For a study of the crisis in the Middle East in the summer of 1958, see Ch. XVIII.

Britain, and later Turkey and Italy, agreed to the establishment of rocket bases, and others to the equipment of their forces with short-range missiles.[1] Soviet policy failed to attract any N.A.T.O. Government to disengagement or to 'zones of peace' in Central Europe. But from the Soviet point of view some practical steps towards high-level talks had to be taken to keep the prospect alive, and the evidence strongly suggests that the Soviet Government sensed the need for a change of tactics when the talks they wanted failed to materialize quickly enough to prevent the strengthening of N.A.T.O. In the light of this unsatisfactory hold-up in the Soviet campaign, Mr. Khrushchev's tactical assault on the Western position in Berlin in November 1958 appears less sudden and less surprising. A new tactical shock was clearly necessary to get the campaign moving again.

At a Polish-Soviet rally in Moscow on 10 November 1958 Mr. Khrushchev declared that the time had come 'for the signatories of the Potsdam Agreement to renounce the remnants of the occupation régime in Berlin'. To emphasize his point, the Soviet leader stated that his Government would hand over its powers in Berlin to the East German régime, and called on the Western Powers to come to terms with this administration. On 27 November *Tass* released a list of Soviet proposals on Berlin suggesting that West Berlin should become a free demilitarized city within the territory of a sovereign East German Republic, to which the U.S.S.R. proposed to hand over its rights and functions in Berlin. Contacts between Soviet and Western representatives would cease, and the East German régime would be responsible for access to the city. The Western Powers were offered six months in which to come to an agreement with the Soviet Government on these lines. But if these proposals were rejected, according to the Soviet statement, there could be no further discussions on Berlin; on 27 May 1959 the Soviet Union would carry out its plans regardless of Western opposition.

These proposals were received with great alarm in the Western capitals because, in effect, they delivered an ultimatum to Britain, France, and the United States to evacuate West Berlin and to recognize the East German régime (and consequently the existence of two sovereign German states) under duress. The three Governments answered in unison that there could be no question of agreeing to these conditions, although each Government's Note to Moscow

[1] After prolonged debate, Greece accepted the American offer in part in 1960.

contained an offer to discuss the future of Berlin in the wider framework of Germany and European Security.[1]

It was not difficult for observers in the West to guess why the Soviet Government was generally anxious for an end to the existence of a non-Communist West Berlin. The Western sectors represented a permanent exhibition of a freer way of life in an island of territory within Communist-controlled East Germany, and provided a channel of escape for the many thousands of East Germans who year after year fled to the West as political refugees from Communism. The population of West Berlin was solidly anti-Communist, and had first-hand experience of Soviet methods during the blockade of the city in 1948-49. West Berlin, in short, was an unwanted Western intrusion into the Communist empire, and any action to remove it would be a resounding victory for Soviet policy. But West Berlin was a hard nut to crack. The issue for the Western Governments and peoples was a clear one, for America, Britain, and France were committed to go to war in the event of an armed attack on their sectors of the city.[2] No sympathy existed in the West for the proposed recognition of East Germany, a régime which had been forced to call in Soviet troops to put down demonstrations by their own workers.

The months which followed this Soviet ultimatum were full of diplomatic activity which included a hurriedly-arranged visit to Moscow by the British Prime Minister, an unofficial journey to the Soviet capital by the former deputy Commander-in-Chief of N.A.T.O., Field-Marshal Montgomery,[3] a full-scale Foreign Ministers' conference in Geneva, an agreement to exchange personal visits by President Eisenhower and Mr. Khrushchev, and finally, the proposal that the four Heads of Governments should meet in Paris in May 1960. These diplomatic moves were linked by an exchange of four Western and four Soviet Notes on Berlin and Germany, three major speeches by Mr. Khrushchev and one by the East

[1] The British Note was delivered in Moscow on 31 December 1958. See *The Times* for the full text.

[2] Under the declaration at the end of the London Conference on Germany in October 1954, Britain, France, and the U.S.A. undertook to regard any attack on West Berlin as an attack on their armed forces.

[3] It would be quite wrong to believe that the Soviet Government attached little or no importance to Lord Montgomery's visit. In view of the Field-Marshal's standing and recent commands, the Soviet Government probably discounted the unofficial nature of his visit, and regarded it as a further British 'reconnaissance', perhaps as a follow-up to Mr. Macmillan's, to clarify certain aspects of the Soviet Union's intentions.

German Prime Minister, Herr Grotewohl, against the background of a sustained campaign in the Soviet and East European Press.

Soviet foreign policy planners certainly worked at high pressure in the months which followed November 1958. The Soviet Government quickly tried to correct the impression that it had issued a formal ultimatum to the West.[1] Step by step Mr. Khrushchev and his spokesmen retreated from their time limit, extending it first to one year, then eighteen months, and finally, all references to it were dropped when Mr. Khrushchev spoke in Moscow on his return from the United States in September 1959.

Indeed, although Mr. Khrushchev's tactics carried a certain risk of conflict at the outset, they achieved at least some of the objectives of the Soviet Government. Discussions between East and West on a fundamental issue—Germany and European security—were reopened at a time and in circumstances chosen by the Soviet Government, and gave the Russians a chance of bringing up the recognition of East Germany, a de-militarized or atom-free zone in Central Europe, and the future of N.A.T.O.'s military bases against the background of the West Berlin crisis. Continued discussions on recognition of East Germany, for example, might, in the Soviet view, be suggested as the only alternative to a complete break-down in negotiations and the consequent increase in the danger of war.

Viewed in this light, the Soviet approach to the West on Berlin, Germany, and European security appeared logical. The first Soviet tactical move after the Western stand on its rights in Berlin [2] was to send the West a draft 'peace treaty' with the two parts of Germany, and a suggestion of a multi-national 'Peace Conference' to put it into legal shape. According to the Soviet draft, such a conference should deal either with two separate German States, or a confederation of the Eastern and Western parts of the country; but in either case reunification should be considered as a matter for negotiation between them alone. The future Germany or Germanies should be neutral, deprived of the right to possess nuclear weapons, guided missiles, bombers or submarines, and West Berlin should be a 'free city'. All foreign troops would be withdrawn within an agreed time limit.[3]

[1] *Pravda*, 26 January 1959, Mr. Mikoyan's Press Conference.
[2] It should be remembered that in the interval the people of West Berlin had voted decisively against the Soviet plan in the city's elections on 7 December 1958.
[3] *The Times*, 12 January 1959.

Speeches by Mr. Khrushchev and other Soviet leaders maintained the impression of urgency by frequent reminders that failure to meet the Soviet requirements would lead to a separate peace treaty between Russia and East Germany. The latter would then be free to invoke the Warsaw Treaty if a Western air-lift was organized to maintain contact with West Germany.[1] For their part, the Western powers decided that the Berlin situation should be dealt with at a meeting of Foreign Ministers, which could prepare the ground for a conference of Heads of Governments, and this was proposed to the Soviet Government in a series of Notes on 16 February 1959. A week later the British Prime Minister, Mr. Macmillan, paid a visit to Moscow and impressed on the Soviet leaders the determination of the Western Powers not to yield on the major issues on Berlin, including Allied rights to be in the city, and to have full and unrestricted access to it. Clearly Mr. Macmillan succeeded in impressing this on Mr. Khrushchev, because the next Soviet Note to the West shifted its ground slightly. On 2 March the Soviet Government accepted the idea of a Foreign Ministers' Conference, in spite of the fact that Mr. Khrushchev had on many occasions expressed doubts about the value of meetings at this level. A suggestion in the Soviet Note that the Conference might last several months was understood in the West to imply a relaxation of the rigid time limit ending on 27 May, obviously an encouraging sign.

Details of the Conference were quickly settled, and on 11 May 1959 the four Foreign Ministers met in Geneva. Mr. Khrushchev, meanwhile, had paid a much-publicized visit to East Germany between 4 and 12 March, probably to give the impression that the Soviet Union was genuinely consulting the East German leaders in these negotiations and to allay fears in Pankow that Russia would compromise with the West at East Germany's expense. A further Soviet Note on the eve of the Conference reminded the West of the basic Soviet aim in Europe—the weakening of American power on the Continent—by recording once again Soviet complaints about American bases and the establishment of rocket sites in West Germany. The Consultative Committee of the Warsaw Pact also met to give its support to Soviet views.

The Geneva Conference of Foreign Ministers was held in two stages, separated by an agreed adjournment. An early Soviet attempt was made to raise the status of the two advisory delegations from

[1] e.g. Mr. Khrushchev's speech at Tula, 17 February 1959.

East and West Germany to that of full members of the Conference, and to insist on Polish and Czechoslovak participation. But the main Soviet tactics required Mr. Gromyko to persuade the West to negotiate on the basis of the Soviet draft treaty of 10 January. The Soviet Foreign Minister therefore made persistent attempts to represent all Western statements as 'comments' on the Soviet plan as a working document for the Conference.

After both attempts had failed, the Soviet delegation put forward its plan for the solution of the German problem. The aim was to keep Germany divided into two states, to maintain the Communist grip on the East, while leaving Western Germany open to Communist subversion and penetration. Thus, Articles 16 and 17 of the Soviet draft treaty stated that the Communist party and allied groups should have 'unhampered activity' rights in West Germany, but all 'revanchist and revisionist' activities should be banned. Since the activities of all German political parties except the Communist could automatically be labelled 'revanchist' or 'revisionist' by the Russians, the Soviet draft represented little more than an attempt to legalize Communist political expansion into Western Germany. Another article of the Soviet draft treaty relegated German reunification to be decided at some future date by the two separate German Governments. Under this plan, of course, the East German representatives could obstruct and delay negotiations to this end until or unless a future all-German régime could be found which would give the Communist party a dominating position in a new united Germany. No provision was made in the Soviet draft for free elections on this issue, nor was Germany to be permitted to control her own foreign policy. Finally, in the articles advocating an initial confederation between East and West Germany, the Soviet draft demanded equality of representation between the 17 million East Germans and the 52 million Germans who live in the West.

It was small wonder that Western spokesmen described their opposition to this draft as 'fundamental'. On 9 June, therefore, Mr. Gromyko put forward a new version of his proposals which, however, differed very little from the previous draft except for an offer to the West of one year's guaranteed tenancy in West Berlin while negotiations on a new status were in progress. The new Soviet plan made the one-year extension dependent on four conditions: the reduction of Western forces in the city to 'symbolic levels'; the cessation of 'hostile propaganda' from West Berlin (the Russians certainly had the American radio station R.I.A.S. in mind); the cessation of 'subversive activities'; and the non-deployment of nuclear weapons and bases in the city.

The Western negotiators immediately pointed out that these proposals in no way relaxed the threat to act unilaterally over West Berlin, but they did offer some concessions to the Soviet viewpoint on the strength of their garrisons in West Berlin, on their readiness to entrust certain procedural duties to East German officials, and on what they termed 'interference in internal affairs' of the authorities in other parts of the city. They also denied any intention of stationing nuclear weapons in Berlin. No Soviet reply on these points was forthcoming, except for an offer to extend the time-limit to eighteen months, and by general agreement the Conference adjourned on 19 June.

When the Foreign Ministers reassembled on 13 July little more was achieved beyond further affirmation of the impossibility of either side accepting the other's plan, even as a basis for discussion. However, as a contact point between East and West the Conference was overshadowed by the visit of the Vice-President of the United States, Mr. Nixon, to the U.S.S.R., where he opened an American Exhibition in Moscow. It was widely felt that Mr. Nixon's journey was a prelude to an exchange of visits between Mr. Khrushchev and President Eisenhower. News of an agreement between the two leaders to visit each other's countries was confirmed on 3 August, and with it, the Foreign Ministers' Conference at Geneva unobtrusively concluded its work.

As an object lesson in Soviet tactics over Europe, the Conference of 1959 has a place in this study. The Soviet Government, by suddenly raising in an alarming context an issue which had been quiescent for years, and by the maintenance of tension, while discreetly withdrawing from exposed positions at the first sign of danger, succeeded in persuading the Western Powers at some urgency to negotiate on issues raised by the Soviet Government at a time and place of their own choice. It would be an exaggeration to say that the Soviet Government deliberately raised the Berlin issue in November 1958 to compel the Western Powers to agree to a Summit Conference. But it is probably true to say that the Berlin issue was raised in order to recapture the initiative in the diplomatic field, to reactivate the pressure on the Western bridgehead suspended during the Middle East crisis, and to try to force the West once again on to the political and diplomatic defensive.[1] The grave threat of unilateral action over Berlin was probably designed to call attention to the seriousness of Soviet intentions by means of an injection of the threat of war into the problem. Once negotiations on Berlin and Germany had begun, the Soviet Government discreetly played down, and ultimately abandoned its ultimatum, and returned to the task of weakening or paralysing American power through a reduction in N.A.T.O.'s strength and the exclusion of the German contingent from its ranks.

The Berlin crisis represented, therefore, the second stage of the Soviet counter-offensive in reply to N.A.T.O.'s decision to increase its military, political, and economic effectiveness on the Continent of Europe. The first stage, which began in December 1957, failed partly because the Soviet planners were unable to present an attractive alternative policy for those who relied upon N.A.T.O. for their security, since all Soviet proposals were so transparently related to the need of Communist expansion. Failure was also due to the interruption of the Middle Eastern crisis in July 1958. The resumption of the counter-offensive with the assault on West Berlin led ultimately on an exchange of visits between Soviet, American, and West European leaders and to agreement to a Conference at the Summit in May 1960. But at the time, these Soviet moves failed to affect the progress of N.A.T.O.'s defence plans and many N.A.T.O. countries, including Britain, Italy and Turkey, accepted rocket bases and nuclear stockpiles in their territory. Whatever goal Mr. Khrushchev set for himself when he launched the crisis over Berlin, he did not succeed in breaking up the Western Alliance. Indeed, with a new N.A.T.O. armoury in the European bridgehead and Western Germany still a member of N.A.T.O. it was probably true to say that the shrewd Soviet leader had already concluded that N.A.T.O. would not in the foreseeable future be dismantled by any Soviet act. However, the news that an exchange of visits between Mr. Khrushchev and President Eisenhower had been agreed upon made it clear that the Soviet leader had achieved one of his post-1956 aims: acceptance at the highest level with the chance of bi-lateral negotiations with the American Government. There can be little doubt that Mr. Khrush-

[1] Among Soviet aims may also have been the idea that if the Western Powers were closely engaged in a major negotiation on a European problem, they would have less time and energy available for challenging Soviet economic progress at home and abroad.

chev was impressed by what he saw in America in September 1959, for he returned from Washington and Camp David with a new appreciation of the factors working against all-out war in the United States. He declared on his return to Moscow that the 'responsible' leaders of the United States (including President Eisenhower) were opposed to war, and suggested that miscalculation or human error was the greatest danger to the peace of the world. It is also probable that he confided to his colleagues in Moscow that he had taken the measure of President Eisenhower, and that it would not be difficult to extract concessions from him at a Summit meeting before the next American Presidential election in November 1960.

Mr. Khrushchev's attitude to President Eisenhower after his talks at Camp David helps to explain his violent reaction to the U-2 incident in May 1960, and his refusal to take part in the Summit Conference in Paris later that month. The admission by the American Government that U-2 flights had been undertaken for a number of years and were an integral part of United States' policy towards the Soviet Union exposed Mr. Khrushchev in the eyes of his colleagues and the Communist movement at large to the charge of having misjudged President Eisenhower, and of adopting a policy of *détente* towards a Government which had no intention of reciprocating.[1] Mr. Khrushchev therefore found it necessary to take up a violently anti-American position, to abuse the President personally, and to obliterate at all costs the impression that he, Khrushchev, had been 'taken in' by a more shrewd and cunning American statecraft.

This, indeed, was Mr. Khrushchev's attitude throughout the summer of 1960, but it could not entirely conceal his underlying conviction that the correct Soviet strategic approach to the West should continue to be one of general *détente* in order to press on with a policy of undermining the West's authority and influence in the uncommitted areas of the world. For this he still required a degree of guaranteed stability in Europe, and his decision not to sign a separate peace treaty with East Germany on his return from Paris was certainly consistent with his aim. In fact, the evidence provided by

---

[1] This exposure of Mr. Khrushchev came at a time when he had found it necessary to remove some of his closest colleagues from the party Secretariat, and place two Marshals, Konev and Sokolovski, on the retired list. The implication is that he was already under fire in the party heirarchy on other matters and that he may have feared that his internal rivals might use the U-2 incident against him.

Soviet policy in Europe during 1959 and 1960 leads to the conclusion that while the Soviet planners wanted to secure as a first priority the elimination of American military power from the European bridgehead they still required a generally stable situation on their Western flank. If they could not achieve this by extracting concessions from the West, they would reach it through deadlock. This would enable them to concentrate their attention on the Middle East and Africa, and it is to current Soviet strategy and tactics in this area that we must now turn.

XVIII

THE CHALLENGE OF THE MIDDLE EAST
AND AFRICA: 1957–60

THE evidence presented in the preceding chapter led to the conclusion that beginning in 1957 the Soviet Government undertook a dual campaign to weaken the N.A.T.O. Alliance and to resume Russia's association with the United States, Britain, and France at the highest level as one of the arbiters of world politics. This was, perhaps, the most active Soviet interest, but during the period—1957 to 1960— Mr. Khrushchev and his colleagues were also faced with a series of new crises in the Middle East, with the problems of Africa never very far in the background. Soviet policy in the Middle East—the only non-Communist area in which Soviet prestige remained unaffected by the Hungarian tragedy—was mainly directed towards increasing economic influence, which required political stability. Yet during these three years the tune was more often called by the local Arab Governments than by the Soviet leaders in Moscow.

Consider, for example, the internal crisis which developed in Jordan in the spring of 1957, in which the radio stations of Egypt and Syria played an active part. The crisis followed Britain's decision on 21 January 1957 to discuss the ending of her Treaty with Jordan. Negotiations came to a swift conclusion, and on 16 March a joint announcement proclaimed the termination of the Treaty, and with it Britain's subsidy to the Jordanian Army and her right to maintain troops on Jordan's territory. However, between the Jordan Government of Mr. Nabulsi, which conducted the talks, and the King of Jordan a difference of opinion arose on the significance of the formal break with Britain. To the King, the agreement gave a position of new strength, from which he could consolidate his own hold on Jordan, and an opportunity to lead the struggle against the war of subversion waged by Egypt and Syria against Jordan, a war on which the Soviet Union looked with increasing favour. Mr. Nabulsi, on the other hand, and some of his civil and military colleagues, regarded the agreement as a chance to adjust Jordan's foreign policy in alignment with that of Egypt and Syria. The King repeatedly warned his people of the danger of Communism; at the same time, Mr. Nabulsi declared his intention to establish diplomatic relations with the Soviet Union.[1]

On 10 April 1957 Mr. Nabulsi resigned, confident that the King could find no one to appoint in his place, since the mob appeared to be enthusiastic in the Premier's support. Jordan was on the verge of widespread disorders: the Chief of Staff of the Army, General Nuwar, fled to Syria on 14 April and an attempt at mutiny occurred among troops stationed at the Jordan Army base of Zerqa, apparently with the connivance of the Syrian troops deployed in the area. Cairo and Damascus Radios called incessantly for riots and demonstrations in Jordan, and agitators moved in among the crowds whipping up anti-Western and pro-Egyptian feeling. On 20 April General Nuwar's successor, General Hayyari, also fled to Syria, the mobs came out into the streets, and the Egyptians and Syrians openly proclaimed the success of their supporters' cause in Amman.

However, determined action by King Hussein restored law and order almost as suddenly as it had broken down. A personal appearance by the King at the military camp at Zerqa swung the loyalty of these troops back again to the monarchy, and 24 April, attributing the disorders to international Communism, the King declared martial law and dissolved all political parties. A Cabinet of older politicians was formed, which set about stamping out the riots and arresting troublemakers. The Government ordered the immediate withdrawal of Syrian troops from the northern part of Jordan, and began to 'jam' Cairo Radio. Loyal troops took over key points, and by the middle of May the situation was completely under control. Moreover, at a critical point in this crisis the American Sixth Fleet, which was cruising in the Eastern Mediterranean, approached the Lebanese coast and actually landed small parties of marines and sailors on shore leave in Beirut. The American Government also came to Jordan's financial aid by an immediate grant of up to 10 million dollars. In addition, the King of Saudi Arabia gave his support to King Hussein, first with financial help, and later, in June, by paying an official visit to Amman. During King Saud's stay in Jordan the Government pointedly demanded the recall of the Egyptian military attaché and consul in Jerusalem.

It seems likely that the April crisis in Jordan was inspired by

[1] See *The Contemporary East* (Moscow), No. 3, September 1957, 'Jordan During the Crisis', by P. Demchenko,

Egypt and Syria, who, utilizing dissatisfaction among the Palestinian refugees in Jordan, tried to overthrow the Royal régime. President Nasser probably thought that the end of the Anglo-Jordan agreement in March was a signal for the collapse of King Hussein's Government, with its anti-Egyptian convictions. Indeed, the speed with which the negotiations between Britain and Jordan were completed may have convinced the Egyptian Government that Britain had given notice of her lack of interest in the fate of Jordan after the withdrawal of Anglo-French forces from Port Said. President Nasser may also have wanted to test the seriousness of the Eisenhower Doctrine before it had had a chance to estabish itself firmly in people's minds. The flight of two Jordanian Generals to Syria, and the probable involvement of the Syrian forces in Jordan in the Zerqa mutiny, as well as the incessant calls for riot made by the Cairo and Damascus Radios, are evidence of an Egyptian-Syrian plot to seize power in Jordan. But they do not of themselves indicate Soviet involvement in this intrigue. The plot in Jordan failed partly owing to the steadiness and courage of the King, and partly to the widely-known presence of American power in the vicinity. But its collapse was also due to the inept revolutionary tactics used by the supporters of the Egyptian point of view. There appears to have been little co-ordination between the mutineers at Zerqa and the senior officers in Amman, and the latters' flight to Syria may, from the point of view of an insurrection, have been premature.[1]

The Soviet Union, while supporting the Egyptians and the opposition elements in Jordan and Lebanon in their Press and radio coverage, and producing lurid accounts of the events in Amman and Beirut for home consumption, was not overanxious to associate itself with these two revolutionary failures.[2] A Soviet appreciation of Egypt's lack of success in Jordan and Lebanon in April and May

---

[1] A subsequent Egyptian-sponsored move in Lebanon at the end of May also came to grief. Riots broke out in Beirut and other towns, during which political agitators led the crowds in chanting pro-Egyptian slogans, and attacked public buildings; but troops restored order and when a general election was held on 9 June the Government, which had accepted the Eisenhower Doctrine, won a comfortable majority.

[2] The Soviet journal *The Contemporary East* (Sovremenny Vostok) attributed the suppression of the Zerqa mutiny to irregular bands belonging to the Muslim Brotherhood. It also tried to prove that the Chief of Staff, General Nuwar, fled to Syria *after* the suppression of the mutiny, whereas he left Jordan on 14 April before the mutiny occurred, possibly intending to return with victorious mutineers.

1957, in fact, played a part in framing Mr. Khrushchev's policy towards the Syrian crisis which broke out two months later.

Soviet interest in Syria had certainly reached a high peak in July 1957, when a Syrian delegation led by the Minister of Defence, Khalid el-Azm, and including the Chief of the General Staff, General Nizam al-Din, and other Staff officers, paid a much-publicized visit to Moscow and Prague.[1] The Syrians were the guests of the Soviet Government from 24 July to 7 August, and returned to Damascus from Czechoslovakia on 16 August. A communiqué published in Moscow announced that agreement in principle had been reached between Syria and the Soviet Union on Soviet help in the construction of roads, railways, and hydro-electric schemes, on the terms of a Soviet loan, and on a further expansion of Soviet-Syrian trade. Among projects considered at the discussions were the enlargement of the port of Latakia and a railway link with the main line to Baghdad. No details were announced of the military agreement, but the Syrian Ambassador in Moscow was quoted in the Damascus Press as saying on 5 August: 'I am now in a position to state that Syria's military requirements will be fulfilled.'[2] Syria's Minister of Public Works, Fakher Kayyali, another member of the delegation, admitted that over half of the Syrian Budget was reserved for arms purchases from the Communist bloc.[3] And when the delegation returned from Eastern Europe, its leader, Khalid el-Azm, praised the Soviet Union in extravagant terms: 'The U.S.S.R. has given us political support and supplied us with arms. Its stand during the Suez aggression was honourable, and you well remember . . . how we received reports of Soviet intervention, and how this intervention delivered the Arabs from the major catastrophe which imperialism wanted to inflict upon them. The U.S.S.R., we believe, will continue along this line.'[4]

It is significant to note that this new Soviet agreement with Syria

---

[1] Syria and Czechoslovakia had concluded a three-year trade agreement in May 1957, described by a Damascus paper (Al Nasr) as 'above all a political move'. On 10 July, Moscow Radio declared that Soviet-Syrian trade had increased sixfold in 1956–57, and that Bulgaria had doubled her exports to Syria in 1956.

[2] *Rai Al-Aam*, Damascus, 5 August 1957. Syria had received from the Soviet Union by mid-1957 arms to the value of £50 million according to *The Times* of 3 October 1957. These inclued 200 T.34 tanks, 50 SU-100s (self-propelled guns), 140 large-calibre field guns, 185 A.A. guns, and 70 fighters (Mig 17s). Over 200 Soviet military advisers were said to be attached to the Syrian Army.

[3] *Commonwealth Survey*, 3 September 1957.

[4] Damascus Radio, 16 August 1957.

coincided with an approach to Turkey. The Soviet Government had undoubtedly noted signs of Turkish dissatisfaction with her N.A.T.O. partners, partly over the Cyprus problem and partly due to the reported rejection by the United States of a Turkish request for a loan to ease the country's economic difficulties.[1] A new Soviet Ambassador, who arrived in Ankara in April 1957, recalled his association with Turkey during the 1920s, at a time when Soviet-Turkish relations had been close, and suggested a visit by a Turkish economic delegation to Moscow during the summer. A group of Turkish bankers did travel to the Soviet Union in July 1957, and the Turkish Press began to write in unusually friendly terms of Soviet willingness to build a number of factories in their country. In August a Soviet economic delegation arrived in Turkey in connexion with this project, and its visit was followed up by a group of Soviet technical advisers early in September. Negotiations for a Soviet loan to Turkey were not in the end successful, but the fact that the approach was made and delegations were exchanged indicated the considerable importance attached in Moscow to friendly relations with Turkey at a time when an important step forward in the campaign to increase Soviet influence in Syria appeared imminent. In this case a closer relationship with the intervening country, Turkey, would certainly reduce the dangers during the delicate transitional period.

The next event was a sudden rise of political tension within Syria itself. The decision of the Syrian Government to enter into a commitment of such magnitude with the Soviet Union was not without its critics at home in Damascus. In particular, the People's party, which had thirty-four members in Parliament, together with some thirty Independent deputies, accused the Government of maintaining the state of martial law in Syria long after it was needed solely for the purpose of keeping themselves in power and of hampering the political activities of the Opposition.[2] Pressure by the Parliamentary Opposition was strong enough to force the Government to lift martial law when Parliament reassembled in mid-July.

While one element in the Syrian Government held the limelight with its far-reaching deal with the Soviet Union, another appeared

---

[1] See the *Financial Times*, 16 May 1957.

[2] Both the Ba'ath Socialist party and the Syrian Communist party supported the retention of martial law, the latter at the meeting of its Central Committee held on 11–13 May, 1957.

to be more interested in strengthening the Egyptian connexion. Talk of federation between Egypt and Syria was revived in July 1957, and the Syrian President, Shukri el-Kuwatli, paid two visits to Cairo in August for discussions with Colonel Nasser. On 13 August, while the President was out of the country, and shortly after the return of the Minister of Defence and his Chief of Staff from Moscow, the Syrian Government suddenly declared three members of the American Legation *personae non gratae*. The United States Government reacted vigorously, and denied Syrian allegations that the American diplomats had been detected in a plot to overthrow the Syrian régime by a *coup d'état*. On 17 August it was announced that General Nizam al-Din, who had been in Moscow a few days before with the Syrian delegation, had been replaced as Chief of Staff by a leading supporter of Communism among Syrian officers, Colonel Bizri. The change was followed by dismissals and arrests in the Army and Police, and in September by a wholesale transfer of officials in the Syrian Foreign Ministry.[1] Coming so soon after the Syrian-Soviet talks in Moscow, and in the absence of the pro-Egyptian President, these changes indicated an imminent shift of emphasis from a nationalist Government to an administration determined to place its foreign policy, at least, largely in the hands of the Soviet Union. By the last week in August 1957, Syria appeared to be governed by men who, while paying lip-service to the project of federation with Egypt, were prepared to go a great deal farther than Colonel Nasser in committing the country to Soviet economic and political policies.

This, at least, was the view taken in the United States, and probably also in Turkey, Syria's northern neighbour. On 22 August the State Department sent one of its most experienced observers, Mr. Loy Henderson, to the Middle East to try to assess the effect of the new political situation in Syria. Mr. Henderson's report prompted the American Government to send arms to Jordan, the Lebanon, and Iraq as a gesture of support, and to strengthen the hand of these Governments in the struggle against subversion. On 7 September President Eisenhower specifically warned Syria that she was approaching the state of domination by pro-Communist elements foreshadowed in the Eisenhower Doctrine.

It was at this point that the Soviet Union made a dramatic intervention in the Syrian crisis. Three days after President Eisenhower's warning, on 10 September, Mr. Gromyko, the Soviet Foreign

---

[1] *The Times*, 4 September 1957.

Minister, held a special Press Conference in Moscow at which, among other accusations, he claimed that the United States, Britain, and Turkey had launched a 'provocative campaign' against Syria. This theme was immediately taken up by the Press in Moscow, Damascus, and the capitals of Eastern Europe. Communist propaganda spoke of massive concentrations of Turkish troops along Syria's northern frontier, poised ready to invade as soon as N.A.T.O. manoeuvres had reached their climax in the Eastern Mediterranean area. On 13 September the Soviet Premier, Marshal Bulganin, addressed a letter to the Turkish Prime Minister, Mr. Menderes, warning him of the consequences of aggression against Syria and threatening Soviet retaliation. On 17 September an anti-Soviet bomb incident was reported in Damascus, and the possibility that it was engineered by the authorities cannot be ruled out. Two days later, a Soviet Naval Squadron which had been invited to call at a Syrian port, arrived off Latakia and, encouraged by the Government, the population gave the visitors a tumultuous welcome. On the next day, 20 September, all Syrian Army leave was cancelled; roads between Latakia, Homs, and Aleppo were closed by the Army, and an emergency meeting of the Syrian Defence Committee was held on the 21st. The stage seemed set in Syria for an act of major military and political importance.

Nothing, however, immediately occurred. The propaganda campaign against Turkish military moves continued but the actual crisis remained suspended in mid-air. On 25 September King Saud of Saudi Arabia arrived in Damascus on his return from a visit to Europe, and in spite of earlier criticism of his acceptance of the Eisenhower Doctrine, he was received courteously by the Syrian President. The King was joined by the Prime Minister of Iraq, Nuri es-Said, in talks which appeared to reassure the visitors on the score of Syria's commitments to the Soviet Union. On 30 September Mr. Menderes replied to Marshal Bulganin's message and stated categorically that Turkey had no aggressive intentions against Syria. In fact, by the end of September the crisis appeared to have subsided; as if to give evidence of this, the Soviet Naval Squadron which had been visiting Syrian ports sailed for home on 2 October.

Suddenly, the scene changed again. On 7 October Mr. Khrushchev unexpectedly returned to Middle Eastern affairs in an interview with the *New York Times*. After boasting of Soviet military might (and of the launching of the first Sputnik three days previously), Mr. Khrushchev accused the United States of inciting Turkey to go to war against Syria, and declared that if war broke out in the Middle East the U.S.S.R. would not remain passive. On the following day, 8 October, the Syrian Government decided to bring its accusations against Turkey before the General Assembly of the United Nations, and also made a formal protest to the Turkish Government about military activity along Syria's northern frontier.[1]

On 11 October Mr. Khrushchev again intervened with a move designed to give the impression that a major international crisis had broken out. Ignoring the Western Governments, he sent letters to the British Labour party and to the Socialist parties of France, Belgium, Holland, Norway, Denmark, and Italy, asking each to use its influence to prevent aggression in the Middle East, and proposing inter-party talks with the Soviet Communist party.[2] On 13 October the Moscow paper *Soviet Russia* claimed to have evidence that American troops were among the Turkish forces drawn up on the Syrian border, and the Soviet Army paper *Red Star* published what purported to be an Order of Battle of the Turkish Army along the Syrian frontier, showing the movement of divisions and armoured brigades towards Syria from their normal stations within Asia Minor;[3] 13 October also witnessed the landing of an Egyptian battalion at Latakia, and a reminder from Cairo that Egypt's and Syria's forces were under one command. On 15 October the Egyptians reported the proclamation of a state of emergency in Syria.[4] Mr. Gromyko sent a letter to the United Nations stating that the U.S.S.R. was ready to help to 'crush aggression with its military forces'. That was published on 16 October and was followed by a *Tass* statement that Mr. Loy Henderson had presented an American plan for a joint attack on Syria to the Governments of Turkey, Iraq, Jordan, and Lebanon. On 21 October *Pravda* printed an interview with the pro-Communist Syrian Chief of Staff, General Bizri, on American and Turkish violations of Syrian air space. On the 23rd Moscow announced that one of Russia's senior Deputy Ministers of Defence, Marshal Rokossovski, had been appointed to command the troops of the Trans-Caucasus Military District, which borders on Turkey and Persia. On 24 October the Soviet Ministry of Defence reported com-

[1] The Syrian request for a debate was accepted by the Assembly on 18 October, and a session devoted to the Syrian case was opened on 22 October.

[2] *Manchester Guardian*, 16 October 1957.

[3] *Red Star*, September 1957.

[4] The interesting implication being that regulations had been relaxed since the previous defence measures of 20–21 September.

bined military and naval exercises by the armies in the Trans-Caucasus and the Black Sea Fleet, and a bellicose statement was made by the Fleet's Commander, Admiral Kasatonov. The same day the Soviet Minister of Defence, Marshal Zhukov, added his threats during a visit to Albania. According to Tirana Radio, he said: 'The Soviet Government has made authoritative and appropriate pronouncements that if war is declared, the Soviet Union will not remain with its arms folded. We are all ready to strike at any military adventure organized by the United States near our southern borders. We resolutely informed the Turkish Government of this also.' And the Egyptian Government took this opportunity to announce a forthcoming visit of their Commander-in-Chief, General Amer, to Moscow.

This moment, 24 October, appears to have been the summit of the crisis. Two days later, on the 26th, it was already clear that the debate in the United Nations was not gaining widespread sympathy for the Syrian and Soviet campaign. Arab opinion was divided over the Syrian refusal (after an initial acceptance) of an offer of mediation by the King of Saudi Arabia, and the Afro-Asian group of states did not line up behind those who talked so much of war. A communiqué expressing Anglo-American solidarity with Turkey was issued by Mr. Macmillan and Mr. Dulles on 27 October, and Mr. Khrushchev received a series of rebuffs from the West European Socialist parties in reply to his letter of 11 October. Unexpectedly, he appeared in affable mood at a Turkish Embassy reception in Moscow and, indeed, this simple act marked the end of the crisis. The debate in the General Assembly petered out on 1 November without even a formal vote on Syria's complaint. And although sporadic Soviet accusations against Turkey continued to appear,[1] by the first week of November the Syrian crisis of 1957 had passed into history.

In assessing Soviet motives during this crisis, it must be remembered that the political changes in Damascus in August definitely moved Syria nearer to Communist domination than any other Middle Eastern country, and that they followed closely on a significant success for the Soviet Union in the economic penetration of Syria. United States reaction, which was shared by Turkey, was one of alarm at the possible emergence of a Soviet satellite state in an entirely new area of the world. The United States Government, in

[1] For example on 5 and 26 November; on the latter date, Marshal Bulganin wrote another letter to Mr. Menderes maintaining the Soviet charges.

view of the seriousness of the situation, offered arms to Syria's neighbours and raised the subject of applying the Eisenhower Doctrine to the Syrian situation. At the same time, and quite by chance, N.A.T.O.'s naval forces in the Eastern Mediterranean, and the Turkish Army, were on exercises in September 1957, the normal time for this part of the world. It is against this background that the Soviet moves during the crisis have to be considered. There can be no doubt both in the first phase (10–25 September) and in the second (beginning on 7 October) the Soviet Government deliberately set out to create the impression that Russia was ready to go to war over the Middle East. Only in this way can the unusual publicity given to military and naval exercises and to the appointment of Marshal Rokossovski be explained.[1]

As a result of the visit to Moscow by pro-Communist elements in the Syrian Government, a promising move towards the expansion of Soviet political, as well as economic, influence took place in Damascus at the end of July 1957. This was followed by a firm American reaction which assumed that the transfer of power in Syria to a thoroughly pro-Communist régime was a practical possibility. The Soviet reaction of 10 September—which came in any case during the spate of extremely belligerent propaganda which followed the firing of Russia's first I.C.B.M.—was probably designed to counter the effect of American firmness, to prove Russia's ability to play the part of a Great Power in the Middle East as well as in Europe, and in this case to afford some degree of protection to the new régime in Syria.[2]

Much more vigorous and threatening, however, were the Soviet tactics during the second phase of the crisis, which began with Mr. Khrushchev's interview on 7 October. In this case it is logical to attribute the new crisis to an accumulation of Soviet intelligence reports amplifying the apparent build-up of American and Turkish military power. The Soviet Government undoubtedly received reports of military exercises by the Turkish Army in the south-eastern provinces of the country—which the Turks never attempted to conceal. To these reports the Russians added N.A.T.O. manoeuvres in

[1] Transfers of military district commanders are never announced in the Soviet Press, nor are the dates of military or naval exercises.

[2] Significant in this connexion was Mr. Khrushchev's statement to Mr. Aneurin Bevan, contained in *Tribune*, in which he showed anxiety at the presence of Syrian exiles in Turkey. Mr. Khrushchev may have based some of his actions on fears that the Syrian régime could be overthrown by a *coup d'état*—so frequent an occurrence in the Middle East.

the Mediterranean, the special mission of Mr. Loy Henderson to the Middle East, President Eisenhower's references to the application of his Doctrine for the Middle East, and the supply of arms to Jordan and Lebanon, and came to the conclusion in their own minds that the United States had decided upon intervention in the Middle East through the use, or at least the display, of force. In the Soviet view, such United States' 'intervention' had succeeded in deciding the internal situation in Jordan during the April crisis, and success breeds success. Probably the Soviet authorities communicated their interpretation of the situation to the Syrians only after Mr. Khrushchev had made his statement on 7 October, for this would explain the relatively late proclamation of a state of emergency—15 October in Syria, allegedly the threatened area. Syrian emergency measures, in other words, seem to have depended on the way the Soviet Union understood the situation, rather than on an on-the-spot appreciation by the Syrian authorities themselves.

If this reconstruction of events is correct, the crisis falls into perspective. Mr. Khrushchev was, of course, particularly sensitive about a worsening of the international situation on the eve of the fortieth anniversary of the Bolshevik Revolution, and of the launching of the world's first artificial satellite. He was also about to try his strength against Russia's most successful soldier, Marshal Zhukov.[1] It was in Mr. Khrushchev's interest to frighten the powers of Western Europe, and to rally them and the Arab nations against American intervention in Syria. He therefore characteristically took measures which would have convinced him of his opponents' seriousness and readiness to act, had the roles been reversed. These were, of course, unnecessary, because neither the United States nor Turkey had any intention of intervening in Syria with military force, and when no intervention took place, and the Syrian case failed to arouse Afro-Asian sympathy in the United Nations, the Soviet Union realized that the danger of war did not exist. She therefore quickly lost interest and allowed the charges against the West to go by default.

One of the lessons suggested by Soviet tactics in the Middle Eastern crisis of 1957 is a certain lack of confidence on the part of the Soviet Government in dealing with crises in Arab countries. Although the Soviet Union was always ready to exploit Arab

[1] The first Sputnik was launched on 4 October, Marshal Zhukov was dismissed on 26 October, and the fortieth anniversary of the Revolution was celebrated on 6–7 November 1957.

grievances and use them in propaganda against the Western Powers, the evidence of tactics seems to show that while pursuing her general aim of economic and political penetration of the Middle East, the Soviet Union was constantly taken by surprise by local Arab policies, plots, and crises. For reasons of prestige or fear, the Soviet Government felt obliged to intervene as each crises occurred, but her part was always that of an alarmed, puzzled or even exasperated protector, who would have preferred a period of political stability in which her long-term plans could gradually mature. And it is a fact that shortly after the Syrian crisis the Soviet Union allowed the promising, pro-Communist régime in Syria to be absorbed into the United Arab Republic without a struggle. Syria had, in fact, only a few months more of independence before she submitted herself to the political system established in Cairo by President Nasser. On 18 November 1957 both the Syrian and Egyptian Parliaments voted for federation between the two countries, and the actual union was proclaimed on 1 February 1958. President Nasser became the first President of the United Arab Republic, and President Kuwatli of Syria its Vice-President. Up to the last moment the Soviet Union continued to spread her influence in Syria. On 10 December 1957 a high-powered Syrian delegation, including the Deputy Commander-in-Chief of the Army, visited Moscow and held discussions with Soviet Government and military leaders. A new round of talks with Czechoslovakia produced, on 29 December, a Czech loan of £60 million for economic development in Syria.

Whatever may have been the real feelings of the Soviet leaders on the union of Syria and Egypt, the Government hastened to congratulate President Nasser, and to invite him, on 29 March 1958, to pay a state visit to Moscow. Yet as soon as the union was an accomplished fact the new state's leaders took steps to alter the political situation in Syria in a way which could hardly have aroused enthusiasm in the Soviet capital. All political parties, including the Communist party, were suppressed, and several leading figures of the régime which had relied so heavily on the Soviet Union, such as Khalid el-Azm and General Bizri, the Army's Chief of Staff, were excluded from office or demoted.[1] Moreover, the most prominent Syrian Communist, Khalid Bikdash, left for Eastern Europe on 6 February.[2] On the Egyptian side, there were reports that President

---

[1] In 1959 General Bizri was reported to be in exile in Eastern Europe.
[2] *New York Herald Tribune*, 8 February 1958.

Nasser was concerned about the size of the arms purchases made by the former Syrian régime, and Soviet officials were reticent about the future of their economic aid promised to Syria before its union with Egypt.[1] Nevertheless, President Nasser received a reception of great splendour in Moscow on 29 April, in spite of the fact that the extension of his régime to Syria appeared to put an end to the existence of a valuable and thriving Communist party in the Middle East.

Before long the Soviet Government was faced with further disturbances in the Arab countries, and with new tactical problems arising from these unplanned and unexpected crisies. In May 1958 the political situation in the Lebanon, where a pro-Western Government in favour of the Eisenhower Doctrine was faced by strong pro-Egyptian opposition in Parliament and in the country, began to deteriorate rapidly. This opposition, possibly at the suggestion of the United Arab Republic, resorted to armed attacks on Government supporters and institutions, and serious street fighting broke out in Tripoli and Beirut. Opposition elements among tribesmen from the Jebel Druze moved into the suburbs of Beirut, and although Government forces succeeded in maintaining their hold on the main centres, their opponents seemed to have sufficient men and arms to disrupt the life of the country indefinitely. The main target of the opposition was officially the removal of President Chamoun; he, in his turn, appealed to the United Nations against what he called 'massive interference' by the United Arab Republic in Lebanon's internal affairs, and requested the dispatch of a corps of United Nations' observers to keep a watch on the Lebanese frontiers. A small force did arrive, but had no effect on the internal disturbances which plagued Beirut and other towns. In addition, the Secretary-General of the United Nations, Mr. Hammarskjöld, in his report on the Lebanese situation, cast some doubts on President Chamoun's charge of interference by the United Arab Republic in terms of arms and men, though he did confirm the existence of a sustained propaganda offensive against the Lebanese Government from this quarter.

At the beginning of July reports were current of a new series of plots against the Jordan Government, and of arrests of Army officers in Amman, where tension was said to be mounting daily. It was in these circumstances that the outstanding event of 1958 in the Middle East occurred: the military *coup d'état* in Iraq which led to the death of King Feisal II, his Premier, General Nuri es-Said, the

[1] *Daily Telegraph*, 19 May 1958.

Crown Prince Abdul Illah, and the destruction of the Royal Family. Mobs searching for General Nuri es-Said burned the British Embassy, and the pillars of the old régime were brought down all over the country by a combination of mob violence and planned insurrection. A new administration was set up under an Army officer, Brigadier Abd el-Kassem, and on 27 July a Provisional Constitution declared Iraq to be 'part of the Arab nation', but an 'independent sovereign Republic'. One of its first acts was to establish friendly contacts with the United Arab Republic, and to restore diplomatic relations with the Soviet Union, which had been severed in 1954 by a previous Government.

As the news of the collapse of the régime in Iraq flashed round the world, the two small countries which appeared to be in the path of the new Middle Eastern hurricane—Lebanon and Jordan—appealed to the United States and Britain for armed help. On the next day, 15 July, American marines landed at Beirut, and British airborne troops were flown in to Jordan, where they received a warm welcome from Governments and peoples alike. This move was the first in a considerable and smoothly-executed American military build-up in the Middle East. Troops were flown to Adana in southern Turkey from Germany, and air reinforcements crossed the Atlantic with impressive strength and precision. Whatever the dangers of the Iraqi crisis, there was no doubt that the American Government intended to be able to take its decisions on the basis of a military presence in the threatened area.

The Soviet Union was clearly taken aback by the vigour and speed of the Western action, but at once launched a full-scale campaign to exploit the dispatch of American troops to Lebanon and British troops to Jordan. Almost as an unconscious reflex came a repetition of the technique used in dealing with the 1957 crisis in the Middle East: on 18 July the Ministry of Defence announced that military manoeuvres were to be held first in the Trans-Caucasus and Turkestan Military Districts, and then in Bulgaria, with the participation of Soviet Air and Airborne forces under Marshal Skripko. There followed a period of bewildering Soviet diplomatic, political, and propaganda activity with little evidence of consistency or confidence on the part of Mr. Khrushchev. At a time when Anglo-American action in Lebanon and Jordan had stabilized a dangerous situation, and no invasion of Iraq by supporters of the old régime had been carried out, Mr. Khrushchev dramatically called for a Summit meeting 'to take measures to terminate the military conflict which has begun'. While Muscovites took part in demonstrations outside Western Embassies, Mr. Khrushchev's representative at the United Nations, Mr. Sobolev, vetoed a Japanese compromise resolution on the Middle East. The Soviet leader, however, accepted on 23 July Mr. Macmillan's proposal for a heads-of-state meeting within the framework of the Security Council, and then abandoned his acceptance in favour of an enlarged conference within the United Nations, in which Mr. Nehru and the leaders of the Arab states could take part. On 28 July Mr. Khrushchev reverted to the suggestion of a five-power meeting in the presence of the Secretary-General of the United Nations. But on the 31st the Soviet Premier, accompanied by his Minister of Defence, Marshal Malinovski, flew to China for a conference with Chairman Mao Tse-tung. On his return to Moscow, Mr. Khrushchev once again revised his position on the Middle East, and suggested an Extraordinary Session of the General Assembly of the United Nations. This Session opened on 13 August, but failed to develop along the lines suggested by the Soviet Union. Instead of outright condemnation of the Anglo-American action in Lebanon and Jordan, a joint resolution was put forward by the Arab powers, calling for a settlement of the Middle Eastern situation by the Arabs themselves. The resolution did not insist upon the immediate withdrawal of American and British troops, as Soviet spokesmen had demanded. With the acceptance of this resolution on 21 August— somewhat reluctantly by the Soviet Union [1]—the immediate crisis in the Middle East drew to a close.

What, then, was the underlying motive of Soviet tactics during this crisis which was sparked off by the revolution in Iraq? First, let us consider the responsibility for the *coup d'état* itself. Here all the signs indicated that the Iraqi revolution of 14 July 1958 was a surprise, not only to the Western Powers, but to the United Arab Republic and to the Soviet Union. President Nasser was, in fact, on a visit to Yugoslavia when the news came, but he cut short his stay, returned to Cairo, and thence, on 17 July, flew to Moscow for talks with the Soviet leaders. After a hurried conference during which, it was reported, Russia declined to commit herself to military aid to the United Arab Republic in the event of war over Iraq, President Nasser left for Cairo, where he made a number of inflammatory prophecies

[1] On 22 August *Tass* complained of 'certain inadequacy in phrasing' in the joint Arab resolution.

S.F.P.—Q

on the imminence of similar risings in Beirut and Amman. He then visited Damascus, to receive emissaries of the new Iraqi régime, and also the Sheikh of Kuweit. President Nasser's movements did not appear to be those of a man who was executing a carefully-laid master plan prepared in advance. He acted rather as an astute tactician who, after an initial surprise, was determined to take full advantage of, and credit for, events which had occurred without his prior knowledge. Thus, Cairo and Damascus Radios broadcast ceaselessly to Jordan calling for the overthrow of King Hussein, and to Lebanon with the message that victory was at hand. Israeli listeners were told that Egypt, Syria, and *Iraq* were already one country, ready to march on Tel Aviv.[1]

Likewise, there is no evidence that the Soviet Union had foreknowledge, or was the author, of the rising in Iraq. The Soviet Union had no diplomatic relations with General Nuri es-Said's Government, and in the absence of a privileged diplomatic refuge from which a military attaché, or political intelligence network could operate, the Soviet Union would probably have found it difficult to organize such a sudden *coup d'état*. Moreover, the Communist party in Iraq was illegal, and this restricted the ability of its members to act as intelligence agents for the Soviet Union. It would have been strange if the Soviet Union had been able to operate so successfully in Iraq, where two of its networks—the diplomatic mission and the Communist party—were non-existent or banned, and yet had been unable to ensure the continuation of a pro-Soviet régime in Syria, where it possessed both.

In all probability, the *coup d'état* in Baghdad was the work of a purely Iraqi underground movement in the Army, in alliance with certain banned political elements, and that some unexpected political-military move enabled the conspirators to execute a hastily prepared plan. In this connexion it was reported that the troops whose leaders carried out the *coup d'état* had been ordered by the previous Government to move to Iraq's western frontiers in view of the disturbances in Lebanon and the reported renewal of threats against the independence of Jordan, and were passing through Baghdad on the night of 14–15 July. It is probable that General Nuri es-Said wanted to be able to march into Jordan with all speed if a pro-Nasser régime seized power by force. The tragic irony was that he was apparently quite

[1] Damascus Radio, 29 July 1958, and Jordan's People's Radio (a Cairo station), 2 August 1958.

unaware of the fatal threat to his own position in Iraq which his move to protect Jordan entailed.

Against this background, Soviet tactics once again revealed an understandable lack of confidence in a very delicate situation. The Soviet Government was anxious to extract the maximum propaganda value out of the Western troop movements into Lebanon and Jordan without, however, drawing attention to the efficiency, success and speed of the operation. Mr. Khrushchev was also intent on using the crisis to arrange the high-level meeting with the leaders of Britain, France, and the United States which he had sought so persistently since Russia's isolation after the Hungarian rising, but for several critical days he appeared to be unable to make up his mind on the best way to achieve it. At the end of July he flew to Peking to consult the Chinese Government. This move could be interpreted as evidence of Chinese pressure on the Soviet leaders not to go to the Summit against a background of Western success in the Middle East; on the other hand, Mr. Khrushchev may merely have wished to consult the Chinese and to prove, to the Communist world at least, that Moscow and Peking were acting in concert.[1]

When the crisis finally died down in August 1958 it was clear that the Soviet Union had both gained and lost from the events in the Middle East. She had failed to prevent an Anglo-American military move into the Middle East, and her military advisers were probably taken aback by its efficiency and speed. She had also failed to secure a universal condemnation of the Western action in the United Nations. But the Soviet Union acquired two important advantages from the crisis. The first was the secession of Iraq from the Baghdad Pact, which reduced the effectiveness of the military alliance along the southern frontier of the Soviet Union. In spite of the fact that the forces of the Baghdad Pact were quite incapable of taking the offensive against the Soviet Union, it was hoped in Moscow that the blow to Western prestige would dissuade other countries from joining it or forming similar regional defence organizations.

The second advantage of the *coup d'état* was the reappearance of a new and legal Communist party in Iraq. And this advantage led the Soviet Government to consider a change of tactics in the Middle East. When the United Arab Republic absorbed Syria, the active Syrian Communist party was forced to go underground, but the new Iraqi Republic allowed the local Communist party to

[1] See Ch. XIX for further discussion of this point.

function legally and to spread its influence among the Baghdad and Mosul mobs. Very soon after the revolution there were signs that the Soviet leaders found compensation for the anti-Communist stand of the United Arab Republic[1] in the appearance of a strong and loyal Communist party in Iraq. This party could help to solve one of the Soviet Government's basic problems in the Middle East: how to control the wild and often badly-timed crises sparked off by the Arab leaders themselves. With the latest of these crises only just over, it was essential, in Soviet eyes, to find a political group in the Arab states which would place itself unreservedly under the orders of the Soviet Union, and the most promising candidate for this position was the Communist party of Iraq.

The Communist parties in the United Arab Republic, although illegal and without leaders, had at least been able to publish a newspaper,[2] and had expressed dissatisfaction with President Nasser's internal policy. Shortly after the *coup d'état* in Iraq this paper, which was particularly resentful of the suppression of the Communist party in Syria, printed a statement by the Syrian Communist leader, Khalid Bikdash, who had been allowed to return to Damascus, describing the constitution of the United Arab Republic as 'far from democratic'. But a real ideological cleavage between the Communists and President Nasser appeared in late October 1958, in an article in *L'Unita*, the paper of the Italian Communist party. The paper wrote: 'To continue to maintain, as some leaders of the Syrian, Jordan, and Iraqi Ba'athist movement do, that at the present stage of the Arab peoples' struggle . . . one can dispense with not only the active collaboration of the Communists, but with the very existence of the Communist parties, means ignoring reality, with all the consequences which could follow from this.'[3]

This article in the Italian Communist Press was followed by mounting criticism in other Communist journals, which roused President Nasser to reply in violent terms against the Communists in a speech to a mass meeting in Port Said in December 1958. After this speech, widespread arrests of Communists took place in Syria,

---

[1] Even before the Iraqi *coup d'état* doubts had been reported about the Soviet Union in the United Arab Republic. On 13 June 1958 the *Manchester Guardian* reported the publication of a series of articles in Cairo papers criticizing the Soviet Union.

[2] On 9 August 1958 the British Communist party weekly *World News* referred to the 'newly-founded central organ of the Egyptian Communist party *Unity of the People*'.

[3] *L'Unita*, 26 October 1958.

and Khalid Bikdash fled from Damascus for the second time.[1] On 17 January 1959 *L'Humanité* in Paris took up the anti-Nasser theme in an article which threatened: 'Experience shows that the existence of the Communist parties does not depend on the wishes of nationalist leaders, not even the most influential, nor of anyone else . . . it is not within anyone's capabilities to exclude the Communists. . . .' The illegal Egyptian Communist party issued a violent personal denunciation of President Nasser: 'Nasser saw the rise of liberty in Iraq as an unnatural phenomen which to him must be the result of Communist plotting. Nasser praises the 'patriotism' of the rulers of Sudan, who have suppressed all democracy; but the Iraqi Government, which enjoys the love and support of the people, is subjected to daily attacks in United Arab Republic broadcasts and the Press.'[2] And the statement, enlarged in a later issue of *World News*, went on: 'The popular classes in Egypt can no longer stand the existence of such conditions. They are angry, they are moving!'[3]

Tension between the United Arab Republic and Iraq rose rapidly to a climax during the trouble which broke out in Mosul in March 1959. Under the direction of certain Iraqi Communists, about 2,000 so-called 'Peace Partisans' converged on this city, which is partly inhabited by the Kurdish minority in Iraq, ostensibly to demonstrate against the signature of a Treaty of Mutual Aid between the United States, Persia, Turkey, and Pakistan. Soon a crowd estimated at over 100,000 had gathered and, provoked by pro-Communist agitators, attacked public buildings and people known to be opposed to a further spread of Communism in Iraq. The disorders which followed were put down by the local military commander, and his action developed into a rising against the Government, largely on the Communist issue. After a few days of fighting, the troops of General Kassem disarmed the rebels and brought their leaders to Baghdad under arrest. Immediately a crisis flared up between Iraq and the United Arab Republic. On 10 March the Iraqi Government expelled nine members of the United Arab Republic's Embassy in Baghdad, charging them with complicity in the Mosul revolt. President Nasser retaliated, and in a speech in Damascus he described the Iraqi and Syrian Communist parties as 'agents of foreigners', who acted on

[1] Khalid Bikdash appeared at the twenty-first Congress of the C.P.S.U. in January 1959.

[2] *Daily Worker*, London, 12 March 1959: the statement was believed to have been issued on 9 January 1959.

[3] *World News*, 21 March 1959.

instructions from foreign Communist centres. In spite of Mr. Khrushchev's attempt in March to 'mediate' between the two Arab republics, relations continued to be strained, and propaganda exchanges were often heated. At the celebrations in Peking on the tenth anniversary of the Chinese People's Republic in October 1959, the Chinese joined in the campaign against the United Arab Republic, which Peking Radio described as 'a terroristic dictatorial régime'. And at the same time the Soviet Government complained that the Egyptians were obstructing the import of Soviet books and films. The Soviet Press also complained that in 'certain Arab countries' the 'evil theory' was widespread that the Arabs now faced a new struggle against Communist imperialism, and called on all Arabs to reject this concept, and to continue to work against Western influence.[1]

The dispute over Communism between the Soviet Union, Iraq, and the United Arab Republic did not mean, however, a breakdown in diplomatic relations between Cairo and Moscow. On the contrary, the Soviet Government continued its economic aid to the United Arab Republic, and on 23 October 1958 offered a credit of 400 million roubles in local commodities in twelve annual instalments from 1964 to 1976.[2]

On 11 March 1959 a group of Soviet engineers arrived in Cairo to work on the first stages of the Aswan Dam project, and in May the Egyptian Minister of Public Works visited Moscow at the invitation of the Soviet Government. On this occasion the Minister stated that 'technical and economic co-operation will restore full understanding between the Soviet Union and the United Arab Republic.'[3] *Tass* published a statement by Mr. Khrushchev on 22 May in which the Soviet Premier said: 'The Soviet Union has no conflict with the United Arab Republic, and the people of the United Arab Republic have no more sincere and loyal friend than the Soviet Union.'[4]

At the same time the Soviet Government offered economic aid equally readily to Iraq. On 12 October 1958 Iraq and the Soviet Union signed an important economic agreement on the exchange

---

[1] *New Times*, 14 October 1959.

[2] Other projects included an agreement by which the Soviet Union undertook to build five new aerodromes in Egypt and a number of factories. (Cairo Radio, 22 December 1958.)

[3] Moscow Radio in Arabic, 19 May 1959.

[4] In January 1960 it was announced that the Soviet Union would take part in the second phase of the construction of the Aswan Dam, and had granted a further credit, repayable in twelve years, at $2\frac{1}{2}$ per cent interest.

of Soviet machinery, cars, tractors, and medical supplies for Iraqi food, hides, and cotton. A permanent Soviet trade mission arrived in Baghdad to develop further economic contacts. Later in the month East Germany and Czechoslovakia opened negotiations for trade agreements with Iraq, and in April 1959 there were reports that Soviet arms shipments were arriving in the country. Certainly Soviet tanks and aircraft, which must have been supplied under an aid agreement in the course of the year, appeared at the parade in Baghdad on the first anniversary of the revolution—14 July 1959.[1] Soviet policy aimed at avoiding entanglement in the dispute between the United Arab Republic and Iraq. The Soviet leaders tried to prevent their ideological support for Arab Communists from interfering with their campaign to influence and ultimately dominate the economics of the United Arab Republic and Iraq. They hoped that support for the Communist party in Iraq and elsewhere could go hand in hand with continued efforts to secure a trading foothold in as many Middle Eastern countries as possible.

The Soviet Union, however, was also looking farther afield, beyond the Middle East to the continent of Africa. African study centres were set up in Moscow and elsewhere, and began to probe the newly-independent African states in search of diplomatic, political, and economic footholds south of the Sahara Desert. In the autumn of 1957 an article in the Central Asian paper *Kommunist Tadjikistana* revealed that responsibility for the study of Africa had been assumed by the Oriental Institute of the Soviet Academy of Sciences. The article continued: 'The significance of Africa has grown immeasurably from the point of view of world politics and economics. . . . Africa has been transformed into the last reserve of contemporary imperialism. The endeavour of the Institute is that its work should have significance both for scientific establishments and for state organizations who are engaged in practical activity in the countries of the East.'[2]

Before the establishment of Ghana as an independent state in March 1957 the Soviet Union had maintained diplomatic relations only with Ethiopia in Africa south of Egypt and Libya. Addis Ababa had a Czechoslovak Minister and a permanent Bulgarian trade delegation, which also showed some interest in the areas of Somalia

[1] *Daily Telegraph*, 16 July 1959.
[2] *Kommunist Tadjikistana*, 28 November 1957. Interview with the Head of the Institute, B. Gafurov.

preparing for independence under United Nations auspices. The Soviet Embassy in Addis Ababa contained two military attachés, and attempts were made to infuse some vigour into cultural and diplomatic exchanges between the Soviet Union and Ethiopia.[1] But the creation of Ghana transferred Soviet attention to West Africa. Although the Ghana Government delayed acceptance of a Soviet offer to establish full diplomatic relations until January 1958 the independence celebrations in Accra were given the widest possible publicity in the Soviet Union and a large Soviet delegation, headed by Mr. Benediktov, attended the foundation of this new member of the British Commonwealth. The Soviet Orientalist, Professor Potekhin, who undertook the leadership of the campaign to spread Soviet influence in Ghana, spent some time at Accra University, in 1957–58, ostensibly to write a book on Ghana's cultural heritage. The Professor had already contributed an article on Soviet policy in West Africa to *Kommunist*—No. 6 of 1957—in which he recommended that pro-Soviet elements in Ghana should be sought among the workers and trade unions rather than the bourgeoisie, and that every effort should be made to commit Ghana's foreign policy to that of the Bandung powers in Asia.

Even more favourable prospects for Soviet penetration appeared with the creation of the independent State of Guinea, which voted to leave the French Union in October 1958 and which was immediately recognized by the Soviet Union, China, and the East European countries. On 18 November 1958 a trade and cultural agreement was concluded between Guinea and East Germany, which provided for an exchange of East German textiles and chemical products for Guinean foods. An East German trade mission was set up in Conakry and the Government undertook to place Guinean students in East German universities. On 1 December Czechoslovakia and Guinea signed an agreement on the training of Guinean workers in Czechoslovak institutes. In August 1959 the Soviet Government entertained a delegation from the Government of Guinea, and early in 1960 there were reports that over 40 per cent of the cost of Guinea's three-year development plan had been underwritten by countries of Eastern Europe.[2]

[1] The Emperor of Ethiopia paid a state visit to the Soviet Union in 1959, and two Soviet Army delegations visited Addis Ababa in 1960.

[2] On the other hand, in spite of these extensive economic and financial commitments, in April 1960 Mr. Touré, the President of Guinea, said emphatically: 'Communism is not the path for Africa.'

Meanwhile the Soviet propaganda campaign directed towards Africa widened its scope. Soviet broadcasts were increased in October, and again in December 1958, and for the first time an African language—Swahili—was used. It is believed that an African department was set up in the Soviet Ministry of Foreign Affairs in 1958; and in the sphere of 'International Front' organizations the Soviet Union created an African Commission as part of the Soviet Committee for Afro-Asian Solidarity. Its chairman was the ubiquitous Professor Potekhin.[1] The 1st December each year was set aside in the Soviet Union and Eastern Europe as 'Quit Africa Day'. and a Friendship University was established in Moscow. The Soviet Government sent a delegation to the All-African People's Conference, held in Accra from 8–13 December 1958. The Conference received a message from Mr. Khrushchev himself on 5 December—an indication of the importance given to Africa in Moscow—in which the Soviet leader emphasized Soviet support for what he called the righteous struggle of the African peoples against colonialism. The Soviet Union and China were represented at the conference of the Afro-Asian Solidarity Committee in Conakry in April 1960, although many reports of the meeting underlined that inept Soviet and Chinese tactics and behaviour reduced the effectiveness of their presence. It is particularly interesting to note that one of the anxieties of the Soviet Union is the attraction for many African nationalist leaders—some of them Christians—of non-violent methods of opposition. Africans were reminded by Soviet propaganda of the need to 'seize' their independence from the colonial powers. The Soviet paper *Izvestia*, for example, went so far as to describe non-violence as 'a trick of the imperialists'.[2]

There can be no doubt that Soviet attempts to influence and dominate Africa south of the Sahara are only in their infancy, handicapped as they are by lack of experience of African conditions, of African linguists, and of well-known African revolutionaries with pro-Communist leanings. But the effort to displace the West in Africa will go on, and certainly no opportunity of political, economic, or diplomatic penetration will be discarded by the Soviet authorities. But the dilemma which faces the Soviet Union and China in Africa and the Middle East arises from the ever-widening gap between Communism and nationalism in the area. If the Soviet Government

[1] *Tass* statement, 29 December 1958.
[2] *Izvestia*, 16 December 1958.

commits itself to support volatile Arab or African leaders, the Soviet Union may gain much goodwill; but it may also find itself face to face with a threat of war, for each nationalist leader will expect the Soviet Union to come to his aid in any serious clash with the powers of the Western world or with his local rivals. If, on the other hand, the Soviet Government supports a local Communist group, then Soviet prestige and popularity among the nationalists may suffer, as happened in the United Arab Republic. What the Soviet Union requires in these countries is a series of Communist governments able to provide a really reliable political instrument, ready to obey orders. Until that time comes the Soviet Union would probably prefer a degree of stability in the Middle East to enable economic offers to win maximum prestige and spread Soviet influence as widely as possible. As far as Africa is concerned, however, since the main task of removing Western political régimes has not been achieved, the Soviet Union might prefer some element of violence to hasten the departure of the Western Powers as in the early days of the Congo Republic. For the next few years the Soviet Union will certainly struggle for a Communist presence in equatorial Africa without, however, undertaking commitments of a military or political nature which could lead to war with the United States. The actual strategy and tactics employed in the penetration of Africa may depend on the outcome of the dispute on Communist policy between Moscow and Peking, both of whom have their own views on the conduct of the struggle in colonial and underdeveloped areas of the world. It is, therefore, appropriate to return at this point to Sino-Soviet relations, one of the most delicate and important problems which the Soviet leadership will have to face in the next decade.

XIX

THE PROBLEM OF CHINA: 1957–61

IT has been noted in earlier chapters that the alliance between the Soviet Union and China had every reason to be a solid and lasting one, since each country had much to gain from the association and everything to lose by its dissolution. The Soviet Union had supplied China with a considerable amount of financial and economic aid: from 1950 to 1955 Soviet loans to China totalled $1,325 million, and Chinese exchanges with the Soviet Union accounted for nearly 50 per cent of Peking's total trade. The Soviet Union had backed Chinese foreign policy during the Korean War, her claim to Formosa and the offshore islands Quemoy and Matsu and the Chinese demand for a seat on the Security Council. The Soviet Union had also initiated a programme of close scientific collaboration with China, providing her with, among other things, research nuclear reactors, and training hundreds of Chinese students at Soviet universities.[1] Although details are not available, there can be no doubt that the programme of military aid from the Soviet Union to the Chinese armed forces was very considerable.

In return for this practical and moral help, the Chinese were prepared to acknowledge Soviet leadership of the Communist bloc—a very necessary admission for Soviet prestige in Eastern Europe and Asia—and to support Soviet policy at home and abroad, for example, on the suppression of the Hungarian revolution and on the German question. On problems of Communist ideology the Chinese generally gave way to Soviet pronouncements, though sometimes after a brief experiment in producing a Chinese interpretation of the point at issue. It was, therefore, logical for both sides to do everything in their power to maintain the alliance, and present to the Communist and non-Communist worlds a picture of a united alliance in which the two greatest partners contributed according to their development and capabilities.

[1] There were many reports that Russian students were horrified at the extraordinary diligence of their Chinese colleagues, some of whom worked up to eighteen hours a day, giving the impression that China intended to overtake not only Britain but also the U.S.S.R.

This general agreement on principles did not rule out, however (according to Peking), forward moves by one partner or another where local conditions seemed favourable. The Chinese Communist leaders probably felt that thanks to the size of their country and their long-standing contribution to the cause of world Communism, they were entitled to experiment on their own, both in home and foreign affairs, and saw no reason for the Soviet Union to object. Nor did the Soviets want to do so, in principle. But in practice some of the Chinese innovations affected claims to authority in the Communist world which the Soviet Union could not abandon without weakening her position of pre-eminence throughout the bloc.

To understand this point it is necessary to look back to 1957, when the Chinese Communist party publicly supported the Soviet suppression of the Hungarian rising. The declaration of the Chinese party made during Mr. Chou En-lai's tour of Eastern Europe in support of the Soviet action contained a sting in its tail for Soviet ideological supremacy: the addition to Marxist doctrine of the discovery that there are two kinds of contradictions—basic ones, between capitalist and Communist countries, and non-antagonistic ones between Communist countries, or between groups within a Communist country.[1] The Soviet leaders, while grateful for public Chinese support over Hungary, were probably less happy about their claim to be the Communist party which was able to produce an ideological explanation to cover the Soviet action in Hungary, outbreaks of strikes in Communist countries, and internal party criticism.[2] In May 1957 the Soviet ideological journal *Kommunist* took *Literaturnaya Gazeta* to task for summarizing Chinese articles on the liberalization campaign in China, launched by Mao Tse-tung under the title of 'Let a hundred flowers bloom, let a hundred schools of thought content'. *Kommunist* declared that Chinese views on this subject were not applicable to the Soviet Union.

This was, of course, only one example of Soviet anxiety at Chinese interest in ideological parity. Further developments in this direction became obscured when the Chinese launched a 'rectification campaign, in which Mao Tse-tung arrested the drift towards

[1] *N.C.N.A.*, 18 June 1957, published version of Mao Tse-tung's speech of 27 February, and *People's Daily*, 29 December 1956, editorial on the proceedings of the Politburo of the Chinese Communist party.

[2] In his speech on 27 February Mao admitted that there had been strikes in China in 1956.

freedom of criticism and re-imposed strict party control over thought and writing.[1] An attack on 'right-wing' elements in the Chinese Communist party was made at the meeting of the National People's Congress in June and July 1957: three Ministers (those of Communications, Timber Production, and Food) were dismissed, and a new slogan was announced: 'Only by letting the weeds show themselves can they be uprooted'. Widespread arrests of 'plotters' were reported, particularly in rural areas, and a Government decree restricted graduation in universities to students who had passed political examinations. Among the most significant points to emerge from this meeting was the Chinese admission of the extent of criticism of the Soviet Union inside the Chinese Communist party. Mr. Chou En-lai, in his report to the meeting, described how 'rightists' attributed errors in the Five-Year Plan and in construction projects to planning on the basis of 'Soviet experience'.[1] Furthermore, another speaker, Chien Chu-jui, revealed that widespread anti-Soviet feelings had been aroused by the plunder of Manchuria by Soviet forces in 1945–46.[2] These admissions of hostility to the U.S.S.R. in the Chinese Communist party, and the action of the Chinese censorship in permitting their publication, certainly did not go unnoticed in Moscow.

The Soviet Government, however, no doubt took comfort from the hurried retreat of the Chinese leaders from their campaign of liberalization—the so-called 'Hundred Flowers' movement—and regarded it as evidence that the Chinese were aware of the dangers of drifting away from the Soviet Union. The retreat also ended, temporarily at least, the mood of almost patronizing righteousness which had developed in Peking after Mr. Khrushchev's East European troubles in 1956. Chinese declarations of loyalty to the Soviet leadership made during the great gathering of Communist parties in Moscow in November 1957 to mark the fortieth anniversary of the Bolshevik Revolution were fluent and specific.[3] And Mao Tse-tung disclaimed any desire to impose his theory of antagonistic and non-antagonistic contradictions on other Communist countries.

[1] The party directive on 'rectification' was published by *N.C.N.A.* on 30 April 1957.

[2] *N.C.N.A.*, 15 July 1957.

[3] Mao Tse-tung's tribute, for example, included this acknowledgement: 'Every organization must have a head, and the C.P.S.U. is best fitted to be head of the international Communist movement.'

During the months which followed the fortieth anniversary celebrations, the Chinese remained closely in touch with Soviet internal
and foreign policy. In February 1958 the Chinese Government gave
public support to the Soviet request for a meeting of the four Great
Powers at the Summit, and played their part in the moves for the
creation of 'zones of peace' by agreeing, on 19 February, to withdraw
all Chinese troops from North Korea by the end of 1958. Both China
and the Soviet Union supported a North Korean proposal for an
atom-free zone to cover both parts of that divided country. Indeed,
there is some evidence that the Chinese leaders overestimated the
effect of Soviet military-scientific achievements, such as the firing of
the I.C.B.M. and the Sputniks in the autumn of 1957. The Chinese
People's Daily of 25 November 1957 wrote that as a result of Soviet
weapons development the superiority of the anti-imperialist forces
had reached 'unprecedented heights . . . and that is why we say that
this is a new turning-point in the international situation'. This
Chinese exaggeration of Soviet strength was to have an important
effect on Sino-Soviet relations in the years ahead.

The next test of Sino-Soviet inter-party relations came from
Belgrade, in the shape of the programme of the Yugoslav Communist party. After a preliminary circulation among interested
parties, this was published on 14 March 1958 in preparation for the
party's Congress in Ljubljana on 22 April. The Yugoslav programme
both irritated and embarrassed Moscow and Peking, for it explained
in closely argued dialectic why the Yugoslav Communist party
carried its belief in separate roads to Socialism to the length of
denying the primacy of the Soviet Union in the international Communist movement. On 18 April 1958 the Soviet journal *Kommunist*
published a severe attack on the Yugoslav programme, and restated
the Soviet claim to supremacy in forcible language:

The participants of the meeting of the representatives of the Communist and Workers parties of Socialist countries which was held in
November 1957 noted in the declaration adopted that the invincible camp
of Socialist states is headed by the Soviet Union. The leading role of the
Soviet Union in the struggle for social progress, for the freedom of the
peoples, and for peace is reflected in these words.[1]

On the following day the Soviet Union's displeasure was con-

---

[1] *Kommunist*, April 1958. The declaration referred to was that signed by the
Communist parties at the fortieth anniversary meeting of the Chinese, but not the
Yugoslav leaders.

firmed by the decision not to send a delegation to the Yugoslav Congress. Only the Soviet Ambassador in Belgrade attended as an observer; China and the East European countries followed suit, and even they (with the single exception of the Polish Ambassador) walked out of the meeting before a speech by Mr. Ranković.

The Yugoslav Congress enthusiastically upheld Marshal Tito's policy towards the Soviet bloc and his determination to remain ideologically and politically independent, regardless of Soviet or Chinese criticism. This burst over Yugoslavia in full force in the days which followed the Congress, beginning with a bitter attack on the Yugoslav party in the Albanian paper *Zeri i Popullit* on 4 May. On the 5th, the opening day of the second session of the Eighth Congress of the Chinese Communist party in Peking, the Chinese paper *People's Daily* published a devastating attack on the offending Yugoslavs.[1] It described the Yugoslav programme as 'anti-Marxist', 'out-and-out revisionist', and 'a wild attempt to induce the working class to surrender to capitalism'. The *People's Daily* went on: 'Speaking like the reactionaries of all countries, and like the Chinese bourgeois rightists, the Yugoslav party leaders have violently slandered the dictatorship of the proletariat.' The Chinese article was reprinted in *Pravda* on 6 May, but the Soviet Comunist party's own article criticizing the Yugoslav programme in more restrained language was not printed until 9 May. When it appeared, it was seen to contain veiled threats of political action against Yugoslavia in the event of her continued intransigence. Two days later President Voroshilov cancelled his forthcoming state visit to Yugoslavia, and Yugoslav-Soviet trade talks were put off. On 28 May the Soviet Government postponed credits promised to Yugoslavia for five years, valued at \$285 million.

The fact that the Chinese attack on Yugoslavia preceded the Soviet one, and that the former was more sweeping and more bitter, suggested that China had seized the ideological initiative ahead of her Russian ally. The evidence, however, is conflicting on this point. The bitterness of the Chinese attack was particularly appropriate to the internal situation in China at that time and the party's struggle against 'bourgeois rightists'. Moreover, it was the Soviet Union which actually took practical measures against the Yugoslav State. And lastly, it is interesting to note that the

[1] 'Contemporary Revisionism', *People's Daily*, Peking, 5 May 1958.

Bulgarian comment, published in *Rabotnichesko Delo* on 15 May, came remarkably close to the Chinese accusation that the Yugoslav party programme was a general revision of Marxism; and the Bulgarians never stray from the strictest adherence to the Moscow directive without instant correction.[1] These points suggest that the anti-Yugoslav campaign was generally co-ordinated within the Communist alliance, and was launched by its smallest member, the Albanian Communist party. On the other hand, the Chinese contribution emerged as the most aggressive, partly because of the relevance of revisionism to China's internal situation, but also perhaps because the Chinese were anxious to press the Soviet Union and the bloc into a more forceful condemnation of the type of 'revisionism' of which Yugoslavia stood accused. Chinese recognition of the Algerian rebels as a government has been cited as evidence of a split on foreign policy between the two countries. However, this apparent discrepancy can be explained by the fact that France had not recognized Communist China, while the Soviet Union could hardly recognize the Algerian rebels without severely damaging her own relations with France.

If this interpretation of the Chinese attitude to the Yugoslav programme is accepted, it helps to clarify Mr. Khrushchev's anxiety to keep as firm a hand as possible on the Chinese party during the Middle East crisis of July and August 1958. It will be remembered that during this crisis Mr. Khrushchev began his tactical counter-measures to the Anglo-American move into Lebanon and Jordan by exaggerating the danger of war in the Middle East and at the same time tried to persuade the Western Powers to accept an emergency Summit meeting. In his eagerness to exploit the situation Mr. Khrushchev agreed to Mr. Macmillan's suggestion of a high-level meeting within the Security Council. Two days later, on 25 July, the Chinese Communists accepted Mr. Khrushchev's decision, in spite of the embarrassing fact that in the Security Council the delegate of President Chiang Kai-shek would be present. However, on the 28th, Mr. Khrushchev abandoned the plan for a meeting in the Security Council, and called instead for a Five-Power meeting outside the United Nations, and set off on a flying visit to China. It seems certain, therefore, that Mr. Khrushchev changed his mind about the

---

[1] A Bulgarian correspondent's incorrect description of a provincial amalgamation of co-operative farms in Bulgaria as a 'commune' was denied by the paper with humble apologies within twenty four hours.

Security Council *before* going to Peking, probably when his own advisers pointed out the right of the Nationalist representative on the Council to be present. In the event, the visit to Peking probably served to give Mao Tse-tung an opportunity to impress on Mr. Khrushchev the inadvisability of going to a Summit meeting on the background of an Anglo-American military success in the Middle East—and to acquaint him with a Chinese decision to reactivate the crisis in the Formosa Straits. For Mr. Khrushchev, who was accompanied by Marshal Malinovski, the main purpose must have been to make clear to Mao Tse-tung just how far the Soviet Government was prepared to go in support of Chinese foreign policy at that juncture, and to urge caution in the event of a direct challenge to the United States.

In the first week of September 1958 the Chinese Communists suddenly began to bombard the offshore islands of Quemoy and Matsu, to the accompaniment of a vigorous propaganda campaign calling for nationwide efforts to help the armed forces to capture the islands. It is probable that the decision to bombard these two Nationalist-held islands originated in the need to provide a motive for the mass mobilization of the people to fulfil new agricultural and industrial tasks in accordance with a recent resolution of the party leadership.[1] Perhaps also Mao Tse-tung was influenced in this decision by a belief that Soviet military power was now so great that risks could be taken by the Communist bloc which were unthinkable before the achievements in rocketry of 1957. In either case there was a danger, as the Soviet Union saw it, that the Americans, fresh from their success in the Middle East, might regard the bombardment as a *casus belli*. So during the crisis the Soviet Government apparently undertook to stand guard over the operation to deter the United States from taking this irrevocable step. On 7 September Mr. Khrushchev wrote to President Eisenhower warning him that an attack on China would mean war with Russia, and the whole Soviet propaganda machine swung round behind the Chinese claim to take Quemoy and Matsu by force, if necessary. Indeed, so heated became the Soviet support for the Chinese cause, that President Eisenhower felt unable to accept one of Mr. Khrushchev's letters because of its 'abusive' language.

[1] See below for the connexion with the Chinese Communes. On 30 September *N.C.N.A.* announced that 95 million militia members were already engaged on production work, a clear indication that those mobilized for the 'defence of the country' were really required as unpaid manpower on the land.

So far, Sino-Soviet relations had survived the tests of ideology and revisionism, a severe crisis in the Middle East, and renewed local fighting in the Formosa Straits. From mid-1958 onwards, however, the strains and stresses on the alliance multiplied, thanks largely to Chinese revolutionary fervour, particularly in ideology and the economics of Communism and her enthusiasm for Soviet military power. In the summer of 1957 the Chinese leaders had hastened to acknowledge Soviet ideological and political leadership. Yet less than a year later, with apparent indifference to their own experiences, they embarked on a plan for which they made an almost heretical claim: to be able to speed up the rate of advance towards Communism. This plan was the Chinese Commune.

At the second session of the Eighth Congress of the Chinese Communist party held in May 1958 the Chinese leaders announced the beginning of what they called their 'great leap forward'. Targets for the second Five-Year Plan from 1958 to 1962 were to be stepped up to surpass British production of steel and coal, and in order to achieve this the Chinese people would have to accept more austerity and lower wages. At the same time, the first Chinese Commune was set up in Honan province. According to official Chinese sources, the establishment of a Commune consisted of 'merging and transforming the smaller existing agricultural co-operatives into big people's communes, where industry, agriculture, exchange, culture, education, and defence merge into one, and the town and the Commune become one entity, with a higher level of collectivization'.[1] The Communes introduced a régime in which land, agricultural implements, factories, schools, and children's nurseries were all run communally. Thus, for example, all sewing and mending of clothes was done not in individual families, but by organized 'tailoring groups'; children were looked after in communal nurseries and house-cleaning was performed by regimented groups of cleaners. During the summer of 1958 the system spread from Honan into other provinces, and when the Politburo of the Chinese Communist party met from 17 to 30 August 1958 the party leaders were ready to launch a campaign to promote the establishment of Communes all over China and to give full publicity to their reported achievements.[2]

So vast a reorganization of Chinese life could be carried through

---

[1] *People's Daily*, 3 September 1958, and Peking Radio, 18 August 1958.
[2] On 11 August *People's Daily* attributed the Communes to Mao Tse-tung's personal initiative.

much more easily if the population of the provinces destined to be turned into Communes were mobilized in some form of para-military organization, such as the reserve militia. And, in fact, the rapid extension of the Commune system coincided with a widespread mobilization of the militia in Central and East China, where the Commune movement first got under way. It has already been suggested that the bombardment of Quemoy and Matsu provided an excuse for the mobilization of the population required for the establishment of the Communes. If this interpretation is correct, then in its opening stages the Soviet Union must have been aware of the real motive for the 'crisis' over Quemoy and Matsu and for reasons of its own was reluctant to use its influence to veto the Chinese experiment as long as the covering military activity did not lead to war with America. The Russians even allowed their party journals to write about the Chinese interpretation of the significance of the Commune, though they generally avoided the subject in the popular Press. In its issue No. 13, for 1958, *Kommunist* quoted the Chinese Communist party's claim that the realization of Communism was no longer something remote, and that the Communes must be used as the basis for finding a concrete path of transition to Communism.

During the same meeting of the Chinese Politburo new and more advanced targets were announced for the second Five-Year Plan: a bumper harvest was said to have allowed further progress in industry, and the target for steel production was raised from 7.1 million tons in May 1958 to 10.7 million tons—double the target for 1957. The whole resolution of the Politburo abounded with supreme confidence and self-assurance. Yet within a few months a different picture had emerged from within China itself. A plenary session of the Central Committee of the Chinese Communist party met from 28 November to 10 December 1958 to discuss the Communes, the economic plan, and the position of Mao Tse-tung himself, who had asked to be relieved of the post of Chairman of the Republic (the equivalent of President or Head of State) in order to concentrate on party affairs.[1] Discussing the Communes, the authors of the Central Committee's resolution admitted that they had aroused serious mis-

---

[1] Mao was later replaced by Liu Shao-chi, one of the leading theoreticians of the Chinese Communist party. It is possible that the widespread opposition to the Communes brought a right-wing group to the fore at this plenary session and forced the retirement of Mao Tse-tung from his post of Chairman.

givings all over the country, had caused disunity in the party, and were proving inefficient.[1] It described as 'utopian' any attempt to 'enter Communism by overreaching ourselves', and referred to 'over-eager people' who wanted to establish Communism too quickly. The resolution maintained that the building of a 'socialist' country—let alone Communism—would take perhaps more than twenty years.[2] As a result of this plenary session, the concept of a Commune as an advanced step towards Communism was formally abandoned by the Chinese, although the name and organization in part was retained as a type of Chinese collectivization.

What, then, occurred between August and November 1958? First of all, we can be sure that the Chinese spoke the truth when they admitted that the Communes were inefficient and widely re-sented. It seems almost certain, too, that as the Chinese campaign developed the Soviet Union became increasingly aware of the dangers in the Chinese claim to have found a short cut to Com-munism. Yet the Soviet party leaders appeared to have handled this deviation calmly, realizing no doubt that the Chinese were over-playing their hand, and that the Communes would arouse so much resentment as to be unworkable. In the interests of preserving the alliance, and preventing war with the United States the Russians probably agreed to stand guard over China during the mobilization of the militia for the Communes and the crisis provoked over the offshore islands for this purpose. They then stood by while the Chinese went ahead with their experiment, taking care that limited party circles in the Soviet Union were made aware of the extreme Chinese claim to have outstripped the Soviet Union in the advance towards Communism.

When the inevitable occurred, and the Chinese Commune move-ment began to totter, the Soviet Government had a firm foundation on which to build its objections to the Communes' ideological implications. Without serious damage to the alliance, the Soviet Government eased the Chinese party leaders out of their claims to have found the gateway to Communism, and then left them to re-build the Communes as best they could.

[1] See also *People's Daily*, 25 August 1958, for criticisms of the communes by the people.
[2] Six months after this plenary session of the Central Committee the Chinese revealed that the targets of the economic plan had not been reached; only 250 million tons of grain for 375 million; and only 8 million tons of steel instead of 10.7.

Since the Soviet experts were aware of the inherent shortcomings of the Communes, they knew that it would be far less damaging to the solidarity of the bloc if they came to grief on the opposition of the Chinese people than as a result of a direct Soviet reaction against their ideological significance.[1]

The whole incident of the Chinese Communes showed that at this stage Mr. Khrushchev certainly understood how to deal with his unwieldy, excitable, and sensitive ally in Peking. No doubt he hoped that his recent successes in bringing the Chinese round to his point of view—to which, no doubt, the Soviet grip on military, scientific, and industrial aid to China contributed—would put an end to Chinese-inspired deviations in matters which were of great importance to Soviet supremacy in the Communist world. Yet less than six months later the Soviet leader found himself face to face with another crisis provoked by the Chinese: the decision to challenge and perhaps humiliate India by creating a series of border incidents. These incidents were an indirect result of the rising of the Tibetan people against the Chinese Army of Occupation which had been going on sporadically since 1956, but burst into open flame in February and March 1959. By the end of 1958 Tibetan rebel forces, who controlled areas to the south and east of Lhasa, were closing in on the capital, and their presence gave courage to the anti-Chinese elements of the Tibetan Government. A Chinese attempt to kidnap the Dalai Lama was foiled, and armed Tibetan nationalists, encouraged by the Government, defied the Chinese garrison of Lhasa from fortified monasteries and official buildings. On 20 March 1959 the Chinese Army counter-attacked and drove the nationalists out of the city, and for many months ahead the Tibetans waged a bitter struggle to slow down or halt the relentless Chinese advance along the main valleys of the Tibetan massif. The flight of the Dalai Lama and many members of the Tibetan Government, as well as thousands of Tibetan refugees, to India during the rising turned official Chinese anger against India, and the tide of anti-Chinese feeling which swept through India and other Asian countries caused Peking to believe that Delhi had had a hand in the events in Tibet.[2] When the rebellion

---

[1] During Mr. Mikoyan's visit to the U.S.A. he told a Los Angeles audience on 12 January 1959 that Russia had tried Communes in 1918-19, but' soon found that they could not work without a developed economy'. *New York Times*, 14 January 1959.

[2] A Chinese Note of Protest to India in June 1959 used the phrase 'some kind kind of collusion with the Tibetan rebels'.

in Lhasa had been brought under control it was this Chinese anger
which probably led to the decision to punish or pillory India before
Asian public opinion for her 'support' for the Tibetan nationalists.
China had various territorial claims against India and, as a ruthless
military power, probably despised India's unmilitary outlook and her
small professional army. The Chinese Government sent troops over
the border in north-east India, seized a frontier post, and accused
India of violation of Chinese territory. When the Indian Government reacted firmly, the session of the Standing Committee of the
National People's Congress in Peking from 11 to 13 September 1959
was turned into a forum for abuse of India and Mr. Nehru personally.

The Soviet Government attempted to minimize the Sino-Indian
frontier clashes, but the impartiality of her comments gave grounds
for the belief that Mr. Khrushchev found the dispute embarrassing
in the extreme. A statement by *Tass* on 10 September 1959 for the
first time failed to give unqualified Soviet support to a Chinese case
in international affairs, and actually emphasized the close ties between India and the Soviet Union. The fact that in spite of this
scarcely-concealed admonition from the Soviet Union the Chinese
proceeded to extend their border dispute with India into the Ladakh
area of Kashmir[1] made it clear that the Chinese were sufficiently
roused to forget, even for a moment, the dangers inherent in a rift
between themselves and the Russians.

As the Sino-Indian dispute dragged on through 1959 and 1960 a
new element of disagreement between the Soviet Union and China
appeared in connexion with Mr. Khrushchev's policy of rapprochement with the United States and his eagerness to achieve a Summit
conference. Chinese comment at the time of Mr. Khrushchev's visit
to the United States in September 1959 was lukewarm, but the main
point at issue between Moscow and Peking appeared to be the Soviet
attitude to war and peace. When the Soviet leader visited Peking in
October 1959 he went out of his way to warn the Chinese of the
dangers of placing too much confidence in war and violence as a
short cut to Communism. 'We must not test the strength of the
imperialists,' he said. But the Chinese paid little heed to Mr. Khrushchev's remarks and when the ninetieth anniversary of Lenin's birth

---

[1] Subsequent information made it clear that the Chinese had 'occupied'
part of Ladakh for several years—sufficiently long to build a road connecting
Sinkiang with western Tibet.

came round in April 1960 their leading theoretical journal *Red Flag* published a series of articles in which Lenin was invoked to prove that war was inevitable as long as imperialism existed. 'We believe in the absolute correctness of Lenin's thinking,' the Chinese journal affirmed. 'War is an inevitable outcome of exploiting systems, and the source of modern wars is the imperialist system. Until the imperialist system and the exploiting classes come to an end, wars of one kind or another will always appear.[1]

This article, which contained many other passages in militant vein, appeared at the same time as the equivalent Soviet journal, *Party Life*, was discussing war and peace, but in quite different terms. The Soviet journal wrote: 'Our party, developing Lenin's teaching constructively, examined the problem of peace and war in modern conditions in a new light. On the basis of a realistic appraisal of the relationship of forces on the international scene, the Twentieth Congress of the C.P.S.U. drew the bold and tremendous conclusion that it is possible to exclude war from the life of society while capitalism still exists.'[2]

The Soviet Government, therefore, based its rejection of the traditional Communist view that war is inevitable on the deterrent value of weapons of mass destruction. But the Chinese challenged this view, too, in their journal *Red Flag*. On 19 April the journal wrote: 'Whichever way you look at it, none of the new techniques like atomic energy, rocketry and so on has changed the basic characteristics of the epoch of imperialism and proletarian revolution, as alleged by the modern revisionists.'

These quotations represented the first ideological disagreement between the Soviet Government and China to appear in the open, and suggested that the Soviet leaders were faced with a severe test in their relations with the Chinese Communist party. The Chinese Communists also challenged the Soviet view that war could not help to bring about a Communist Revolution more quickly. The Soviet journal *Kommunist* of September 1960 wrote: 'Modern nuclear war can in no way be a factor in speeding up or in hastening the victory of Socialism.' The Chinese adopted the opposite view, and *Red Flag* wrote: 'Socialism, far from being destroyed, would be achieved all the more quickly in the event of war. . . . The result of a nuclear war will certainly not be the annihilation of mankind.'

[1] *Red Flag* (Peking), April 1960.
[2] *Partiinaya Zhizn* (Party Life), April 1960.

There seems little doubt that the Chinese Communists maintained their right to have their say on matters of ideology and foreign policy, even if this meant open criticism of Soviet views and policies. The present stage of China's revolution makes her liable to outbursts of misdirected energy, nationalist pride, and unrealistic overconfidence. Up to the summer of 1960 most of these outbursts were controlled and channelled safely by Moscow, and thanks to Mr. Khrushchev's ability to handle the Chinese, did not interfere with the basis of the alliance. However, the evidence which came to light in the latter part of the year revealed a much more fundamental divergence. It concerned the use to which Soviet military strength ought to be put in the formulation of foreign strategy. Although the Chinese wrote irresponsibly about the effects of nuclear war, it would not be true to say that they advocated aggression by the Communist bloc. What they did believe was that at a time when Soviet military strength was so great, and her achievements in rocket propulsion and guided weapons so remarkable, more risks could be taken by the bloc as a whole in the pursuit of Communist objectives. The Chinese apparently felt so strongly that their position represented the only true interpretation of Marx-Leninism that they were, in the summer and autumn of 1960, prepared to face a showdown with the Soviet leaders on this issue.

Another point at issue between the Soviet and Chinese Communist parties was the value to be placed upon aid to neutralist national régimes in Africa and Asia. In the Soviet view aid to a Nasser or a Nehru helped to keep these régimes out of the Western camp, and even if they were not attracted into the Communist bloc, their independence of American power made such aid worth while. On the other hand, the Chinese believed that non-Communist national régimes with a neutralist foreign policy were worthless to the Communist cause and should be classified as allies of the 'imperialists'. Such aid as the Soviet Union could distribute should be reserved for Communist powers and for genuine revolutionary movements under the leadership of the Communist party. In practice, the Chinese demanded that Soviet aid now going to India or the United Arab Republic should be diverted to China, and the Russians' refusal to agree to this caused great resentment in Peking.

Whatever the outcome of the 1960 dispute, there can be little doubt that China will present a problem of great complexity for any future Soviet Government. China's population is over 600 million, and is growing at the rate of 15 million a year. The expansion of China's population into the sparsely inhabited outer provinces may not absorb the increase by the end of the century, and after that immigration into bordering territories may be inevitable.[1] Mr. Khrushchev's plan to populate Eastern Siberia, for example, may have been prompted by a far-sighted view of this danger. On the economic front, where for so long the Soviet Union has held the whip-hand, it has been noticed that the Chinese have made strenuous efforts to speed up their repayment of Soviet loans in order to free themselves from their financial indebtedness to the Soviet Union. Thus, from 1950 to 1955, China received $1,325 million in Soviet loans, to be repaid over long periods, and was obliged to pay for unspecified assets left over from Port Arthur in 1955. China's policy aimed at securing the means of repayment of these debts by austerity at home, restricting imports, and raising exports. The growth of the surplus of exports over imports in the interest of repayment since 1955 has been startling: in 1956 it was $30 million, in 1957 $200 million, and in 1958 the planned surplus was $300 million. Although a new economic agreement was signed in February 1959 to cover the period 1959–67—a sign that the Chinese still needed Soviet aid —it is clear that they are anxious to settle their Soviet debt as soon as possible, and ultimately to be completely independent of Soviet support.

Soviet strategy towards China must be directed towards one aim: to prevent the outbursts of revolutionary enthusiasm and nationalist arrogance characteristic of the present phase of the Chinese revolution from leading to war in the Far East, or to a situation in which Soviet attention would be unnecessarily diverted from target areas of great promise for Communist influence and expansion, to solve Sino-Soviet problems. Up to the middle of 1960 Mr. Khrushchev exhibited the expert knowledge, firmness, and tactical shrewdness required to handle most short-term problems provided by the Chinese Communists. Evidence has appeared, however, which suggests that the difference between the two parties became so acrimonious in 1960–61 that they spread to every aspect of Sino-Soviet

[1] According to an article by Klaus Mehnert in *International Affairs*, Vol. 35, No. 4, 'Soviet-Chinese Relations', about 10,000 Chinese had already emigrated as workers into Outer Mongolia by the end of 1957 (p. 419). Outer Mongolia was legally part of China until 1945, and Chinese maps still show its frontier with China as a dotted line (ibid).

~ relations and to a personal feud between Mr. Khrushchev and Mr. Mao Tse-tung.[1] How far the quarrel will develop remains to be seen, but since the root of the problem concerns Soviet reluctance to underwrite Peking's exercises in 'brinkmanship', it is possible that if a new Sino-Soviet relationship emerges from the 1960 crisis, one of its main features may be the abrogation of the existing Sino-Soviet military alliance, which commits the Soviet Union to go to China's help in the event of war. This could be, in fact, the Soviet Union's last and most effective instrument of control over China, for if the present Chinese leaders are made to realize that the Soviet military might on which they have placed so much reliance would not be used in their support in a Sino-American war, they may come to reconsider their whole opposition to Soviet foreign strategy and their potential challenge to Soviet leadership of the Communist bloc.

[1] *Observer*, 12 February 1961. The Chinese were particularly resentful at the sudden withdrawal of Soviet technicians from Peking in July 1960.

XX

THE LESSONS OF EXPERIENCE

THE chronological analysis of the strategy and tactics of Soviet foreign policy since the Second World War has reached the point where it must give way to an attempt to detect the main factors on which the Soviet Union's policy in the years ahead is likely to be based. Previous chapters in this book have shown that the Soviet Government is sufficiently devoted to the creation of a world which would acknowledge the rule of Communism to conduct a planned and active foreign policy, and there seems little doubt that any future leadership in Moscow would continue attempts to seize and maintain the initiative in foreign affairs. The present Soviet Government under Mr. Khrushchev inherited a tradition from Stalin which had led to the inclusion of several countries of Europe and Asia into a new 'Socialist camp', and nothing that happened after Stalin's death in 1953 gave any indication that Mr. Khrushchev or his colleagues were prepared to abandon this policy, to allow inhabitants of the 'Socialist camp' to opt out of it, or to forgo the recruitment of new members.

On the other hand, it is undeniable that after Stalin died some new strategic targets for the expansion of Soviet influence were chosen and new tactical methods adopted by his successors. Some of Stalin's methods were specifically rejected by the new leadership, others were approved in retrospect, and others again were continued in operation. On the basis of the evidence presented in previous chapters, we must now try to draw up a list of strategical and tactical decisions which, as seen from the Kremlin, have in the past brought success to the Soviet cause, and set aside those which have failed. In short, we must summarize and analyse the lessons of experience of Soviet foreign policy since 1944, in order to find the elements which, it is reasonable to assume, will be taken into account in Soviet planning in the future.

Let us, first of all, look back into the immediate post-war period. Here there can be no doubt that when an area in the world can, without danger or opposition, be occupied militarily by the Soviet Army, for any length of time, then its transfer to the Communist camp can be carried out swiftly and relatively efficiently, without regard for world public opinion. The social and administrative system of the area can be replaced by the one-party state with a party police or a militia. Leaders loyal to Communism can be supported, and parliamentary elections can sometimes be arranged so that the Communist party comes to power in an apparently legal fashion. Other parties can be faced with the alternative of joining a 'coalition' under Communist leadership or dissolution; and as soon as the Communist régime is in power all written and spoken opposition can be suppressed. The ideal preliminary, therefore, to the speedy expansion of the number of countries to the Communist camp is Soviet military occupation, generally recognized, willingly or unwillingly, by the rest of the world.

At once this raises the question of the readiness of the Soviet Government to use war and violence as a means of achieving its aims. Fortunately general war has not been tried by the Soviet Union to achieve its aims, although there were moments after the Second World War when Soviet acts of political and military expansion reached dangerous levels, very near to those at which American military counter-measures might have been invoked. The history of these years allows us, therefore, to conclude that no group of Soviet leaders successfully advocated all-out war as a means of attaining their objectives, although the present Government has not entirely ruled out the possibility that war might break out in certain circumstances.[1]

If general war was avoided by the Communist bloc, the same is not true of limited conventional warfare. In Stalin's day the North Korean Communist Army invaded South Korea after the United States Government had publicly declared the latter to be beyond America's vital defence perimeter. Since North Korea was a purely Soviet creation in 1950, this invasion must be regarded as a tactical decision of the Soviet Government, and the conclusions to be drawn from it are among the most important of the entire study. For the Soviet leadership cannot but regard this attempt to extend Communist power by a local war as a failure, in spite of the fact that the situation in the Korean peninsula was at the time favourable to the project. The area to be conquered was contiguous to the Communist land mass, and had been evacuated by American forces.

[1] See Ch. XXI for a discussion of the Soviet attitude to war.

With the American declaration on the defence of South Korea (as the Communists interpreted it) only South Korea's membership of the United Nations provided any protection and, in the Communist view, united military action was not likely to be authorized by a Security Council in which the Soviet member had the right of veto. Moreover, the South Korean Government was not firmly in power throughout the country: in the spring of 1950 pro-Communist guerillas were operating in several areas, and two or three of the South Korean Army's divisions were in action against them in the interior, leaving the northern frontier along the 38th parallel only weakly garrisoned.

Yet the attempt failed. Thanks largely to prompt United Nations action, the North Korean Army was defeated in the field, and collapsed so completely thereafter that the way was open for an advance into North Korea itself. Instead of gaining a new recruit for Communism, conventional warfare seemed likely to lose territory in which a Communist party had been firmly established in power. To prevent this, the mass intervention of the regular Chinese Army was organized, and although North Korea was saved for Communism, the Chinese and North Koreans failed to achieve the original aim: the extension of Communist power over the whole of the Korean peninsula.

When the post-Stalin leadership of the Soviet Union decided to use its influence to put an end to this unsuccessful project, we may assume that it resolved never to underestimate the ability of the United States, with the help of her many bases all over the world, to move effective military power to remote areas. The Soviet leaders no doubt also resolved not to accept Western public renunciation of their interests at their face value, and not to forget the very limited value of an auxiliary army. There can be no doubt that in 1950 the North Koreans possessed the best of the small armies in the Communist bloc. It fought well in the initial advance, with a mastery of tactical skill, and fiercely to begin with in defence, but its collapse in defeat was complete. The auxiliary army, therefore, should not be regarded as a reliable instrument for carrying out tasks in local conventional warfare. Today's Soviet leaders, when reflecting on Stalin's attempt to extend his power by his means, are likely to have reached the conclusion that war by proxy in the pursuit of new conquests is too risky in the modern world. There has been no repetition of the Korean war in Europe or Asia, and this prompts one to believe that the abandonment of this type of aggression is now a cardinal point in Soviet foreign policy.

Limited conventional warfare has, however, been used by the Soviet Union in a 'defensive' context—defensive, that is, from the Soviet point of view. In October and November 1956 the Communist régime in Hungary was overthrown by the spontaneous action of the Hungarian people; the local Soviet Army garrison of two divisions was paralysed, and forced to withdraw from Budapest. The choice before the Soviet Government was to accept the loss of Hungary as a Communist state and as a member of the Sino-Soviet bloc, or to reimpose Communism by force. Mr. Khrushchev after prolonged debate and hesitation—as he told a Hungarian audience —decided on the latter course, and sent the Soviet Army into Hungary in a conventional limited military campaign to restore the Communist party to power.[1] There can be no doubt that the Soviet action in Hungary was limited warfare. At least fourteen divisions were used, parachute troops were dropped, and the assault on Budapest on 4 November 1956 was carried out with infantry, armour, and artillery combining in accordance with modern battle techniques. In order to achieve better jumping-off positions for the Soviet troops, Czechoslovak territory was used for the deployment of the invading army.[2] The operation was successful; no outside interference was encountered or apparently expected. Although the Soviet Government was seriously embarrassed by the adverse publicity which the campaign against Hungary aroused, particularly in the West, in their own eyes resort to limited war was fully justified by the need to prevent Hungary from leaving the Communist camp. There can be no reasonable doubt, therefore, that the Soviet Government would use limited warfare again to defend or re-establish a Communist régime in an existing Soviet satellite which borders on the Soviet Union or is territorially part of the Soviet bloc.[3]

[1] N. S. Khrushchev in a speech to Hungarian workers at Csepel on 9 April 1958.

[2] *U.N. Report on Hungary*, Vol. I, p. 73, para. 182.

[3] An interesting case might arise in the event of an attack on Albania, which is a member of the Warsaw Pact, but has no common land frontier with the Soviet bloc. What would the Soviet Union do if an internal uprising threatened or overthrew the Communist régime in Tirana? Since there is no evidence on Soviet intentions in the text of the Warsaw Pact or of other Soviet-Albanian treaties, we can only speculate that the Soviet Government would formally fulfil its obligations to the Government by raising the issue in the United Nations. However, in view of the hostile attitude adopted by the Albanian Government to the

The Hungarian revolution also provided the Soviet Government with further evidence of the unreliability of an auxiliary army, and of the strains and stresses which Communist rule brings to a highly civilized and vigorous nation, leading, in extreme conditions, to a popular uprising. It was also significant in relation to the conception of disengagement in Europe. The events in Hungary showed how essential is a clear distinction between plans for disengagement which received Soviet blessing, such as the Rapacki Plan of 1958, envisaging nuclear-free zones, or a withdrawal of forces from Central Europe by both sides, and those put forward in the West, involving some hope of an end to Communist rule in East Germany, Poland, or Czechoslovakia through free elections. All available evidence strongly suggests that even in return for extensive concessions by the N.A.T.O. Alliance—perhaps even the dissolution of that organization—the Soviet Union would never allow an established Communist régime in Eastern Europe to be swept away in a popular vote. The Soviet leaders will not consider the replacement of a Communist régime by a neutralist one (on the Indian model) or a Social-Democratic one (as might have occurred in Hungary). To trade away voluntarily a Communist régime in anything more permanent than the shortest tactical retreat would imply nothing less than treachery to the Soviet leaders. While certain aspects of disengagement interest the Soviet leaders, they are prepared to resort to limited war to maintain the present Communist parties in power in Eastern Europe.

Another tactical means involving violence through which the number of Communist states might be increased is the action of a local Communist party in a foreign country taking over the leadership of an armed guerilla uprising against the established régime, either national or colonial. This occurred in Indo-China against the French and in Malaya against the British. It also occurred against the national Government in Burma and the Philippines and in Greece.[1] Soviet experience of these 'revolutionary' civil wars probably convinced the present leadership that this strategy can only be used in very limited circumstances. The Civil War in Greece, whether or not

---

Soviet Union during the Sino-Soviet dispute of 1960–61, it is possible that the present Albanian leadership might be left to fend for itself.

[1] The Communist armed rising in Indonesia at Madiun in 1948 was different in that it was a definite attempt at *coup d'état*, and was crushed so thoroughly by the Indonesian Government that there was no possibility of turning it into a civil war. See p. 55.

it was directly inspired by Soviet policy decisions, is a case in point. The situation of Greece in 1956 did possess some of the factors which aid Communist expansion. Greece had a common frontier in the north with the Soviet land bloc. Only two years had elapsed since a Communist-led rising had failed, largely due to armed intervention by Britain, and its suppression had aroused vocal criticism in many countries of the wartime coalition. Opposition had come from America and from the British Labour party, which in 1946 formed the British Government. A nucleus of Greek guerilla fighters already existed under Communist leadership, and this body could be kept in the field with help from Yugoslavia, Bulgaria, and Albania. Yet in spite of these advantages, the Communist rising failed, after causing great misery throughout northern Greece. There were three main reasons: United Nations' intervention through its Special Committee for the Balkans kept the salient facts of the Civil War before the public; and to a quite remarkable degree, by objective and persistent dissemination of the truth, neutralized Communist propaganda on the origins and conduct of the struggle. In particular, the Communist technique of abducting Greek children for indoctrination in East European countries aroused public opinion against the rebels. Secondly, American military and economic help for Greece under the Truman doctrine assisted the Greek Government more consistently and directly than anything that the Communist Governments could do for the guerillas. Thirdly, as it later transpired, the Soviet-Yugoslav dispute brought about the gradual withdrawal of Yugoslavia from the side of the rebels, and led to a split in the leadership of the rebels themselves. The factors operating against success in Greece from the Soviet point of view included, therefore, insufficiently tight methods of control by Moscow over the front-line fighters, the intervention of the United States, which was able to give direct and open help to the Greek Government, and the involvement of the United Nations. As a result, a civil war on the Greek pattern did not form part of Soviet foreign policy, strategically or tactically, after 1949.

All other examples of civil war took place in the Far East, and although several of them caused great damage, only one succeeded in bringing about a new Communist state—North Vietnam, in 1954. Stalin himself began to have doubts on the value of this policy of violence, and before he died he reversed his directives to Asian Communist parties, and some changes were made in the leadership of local parties concerned.[1] Nevertheless, guerilla warfare went on in Malaya, Indo-China, Burma, and in the Philippines, with decreasing chances of success as the local military authorities developed efficient methods of anti-terrorist campaigning, and the political hand-over of power to non-Communist nationalist forces proceeded. By 1960 civil war in the Philippines, Malaya, and Burma was to all intents and purposes over, and until perhaps the Soviet Union succeeds in extending its presence much farther and deeper into Africa and the Middle East it is not likely that this form of struggle will be applied to remote areas of the world. Soviet penetration will probably be confined to propaganda, economic aid, and political advice.

The one exception already mentioned was the successful carving of a new Communist state out of the northern part of French Indo-China at the end of a long guerilla campaign led by the Communist party. Many factors combined to favour the rebels in Indo-China, including their success in tying up large numbers of French troops, the unpopularity in France of the dispatch of national servicemen to Indo-China, the support given to the rebels by the French Communist party—at that time the largest political party in France—and rivalries within the anti-Communist camp in Saigon. But far more important than these factors was the impetus given to the rebellion by the victory of the Communists in China. From the autumn of 1949 to 1954 the guerilla movement in Indo-China possessed a direct link with one of the major Communist powers which was ready to provide supplies, arms and advisers.

Moving again down the scale of violence, an even more striking example of the effectiveness of a Western stand against Soviet pressure when a principle was at stake was the failure of the Soviet attempt to drive the Western Powers out of Berlin in 1948–49. The blockade of Berlin was unquestionably one of the greatest tactical defeats suffered by Soviet foreign policy since the Second World War. The Soviet Union failed to remove the Western civil and military authorities from the city, failed to prevent the population being supplied by air, ruined its reputation among West and East Berliners both on humanitarian and technical grounds (thanks to the success of the Western air-lift), and helped to prepare Western public opinion to accept the newly-created North Atlantic Treaty Organization signed on 4 April 1949. The reason for the Soviet failure was that

[1] See Ch. VI and Ch. VII. The change of leadership of the Indian Communist party is a case in point.

Stalin selected a battleground on which the key Western weapon—air power—could not be neutralized without world war, and allowed the West to stand firm materially and psychologically, to the point of presenting the Soviet Government with the alternative of war or withdrawal.[1]

So far this analysis of the lessons of post-war experience of Soviet strategy and tactics has dealt with limited war, civil strife, Communist-inspired rebellion, and the threat of force. With very few exceptions, all failed to bring the results for which they were planned and put into operation. Many did involve the threat of war, and nearly all played some part in influencing Western public opinion against Communism and against Soviet foreign policy. The majority took place during Stalin's lifetime, and it is a significant commentary on their value to the Soviet Union that these tactics were not re-employed by the post-Stalin Soviet leadership. The latter certainly resorted to violence and limited warfare to maintain its hold on Eastern Europe—specifically to restore Communist rule in Hungary, but otherwise concentrated on quite different strategies towards the non-Communist world. In the first place, Mr. Khrushchev and his colleagues selected India, Burma, the Arab Middle East, and Africa, which were neglected by Stalin, as their main target area; and secondly, they decided to pursue their objectives of ultimate Communist control by methods of political, economic, and social penetration, wherever possible avoiding involvement in violence.

Heralded by a change in the Stalinist propaganda line of approach to these nations, the Soviet Union began to offer economic aid to India, Burma, Afghanistan, Egypt, Syria and the Yemen, and to express public support for their national aspirations, or even some aspects of their political ideologies. After 1955 the Soviet Government began to build up its popularity in the Arab world, and sacrificed the Israeli Communist party in the interests of winning Arab public opinion. Soviet technicians and experts arrived in increasing numbers, more and more Soviet and East European Legations and Consulates were opened, and permanent trade missions were established all over the Middle East. Arab statesmen, Govern-

---

[1] There can be little doubt that the completeness of the Soviet defeat on Berlin in 1948–49 played a part in the automatic reaction of the entire Western camp to the Soviet return to this problem in 1958. The 1948 crisis convinced Governments and peoples that Berlin is one of the points of dispute between East and West on which the latter can really stand firm.

ment officials, and delegations were invited to tour the Soviet Union, students were accepted in Soviet universities, and every effort was made to extend cultural contacts between the Soviet Union and the target area. The few reliable details of Soviet loans and financial aid which became available gave the impression that the terms were designed to tie the economy and external trade of the Middle Eastern countries to the Soviet Union under the cover of support for Arab nationalism. Consignments of conventional obsolescent weapons sold to uncommitted countries were useful in raising Soviet prestige, in introducing specialists into Governmental and Service departments, and in controlling important sections of the recipient's foreign trade. By 1960 the Soviet Union had offered the United Arab Republic three times as much credit as to any other country except China. Had the Soviet planners been able to control the political situation in the Middle East, there can be little doubt that they would have firmly suppressed any unrest which showed signs of hindering their economic offensive.[1] For experience showed that every occasion on which violence, often inspired by uncritical acceptance of Soviet propaganda, appeared in the Middle East, Soviet economic penetration ran into unwelcome obstacles. The sale of Soviet and East European arms to Egypt, boldly proclaimed by the Egyptian Government, and reluctantly admitted first by the cover dealer, Czechoslovakia, and later by the Soviet Union, helped to awaken Western public opinion to Soviet activity in an area new to Soviet interests. The Suez Canal crisis of 1956, while it brought prestige to the Soviet Union as a champion of Arab rights and claims, exposed prematurely the extent of military equipment and aircraft already supplied to Egypt, and forced the Russians either to withdraw their aircraft from Egypt or to run the risk of using them against the Anglo-French armies. The flight of Soviet military advisers to the Sudan and the 'escape' of the Soviet jet-bombers during the crisis were certainly not parts of the Soviet plan. The whole Suez crisis focused attention on Soviet activity which Moscow would have preferred to remain undiscovered. Soviet prestige suffered, too, when the Egyptian attempt,

[1] The reaction to Soviet aid to India and to the Middle East presented contradicting dilemmas to the Soviet leaders. In India the prevailing political philosophy and the maturity of educated circles created a stability very helpful to Soviet economic penetration, but an unfavourable climate for the uncritical acceptance of Soviet propaganda. In the Arab countries admiration for Soviet achievements was enthusiastic, but unsettled conditions interfered with the smooth working of economic penetration.

supported by Communist propaganda, to overthrow the Government of Jordan failed, because one reason for the failure appeared to be the presence in the Eastern Mediterranean of American naval and military power.

Soviet lack of preparedness to deal with the political restlessness of the Middle East was most clearly shown in Mr. Khrushchev's reaction to the major crises of October 1957 and July 1958. In both cases the Soviet Government was unable to maintain a consistent policy and at some stages changed its tactics almost daily. In both crises it resorted to the unusual practice of announcing military manoeuvres and command postings in an attempt to retain prestige and to warn the Western Powers against interference in the troubled area. These measures were taken so hurriedly and were called off so quickly that they gave the impression of being tactical improvizations indicating loss of initiative on the part of the Soviet Government at a time of international tension.

It seems certain, therefore, that the lesson for the Soviet Government based on its experience in the Middle East since 1955 was that success is possible when economic and political penetration is undisturbed by local feuds or revolutions, but that whenever the area becomes disturbed and politically explosive Soviet prestige suffers and Soviet plans are retarded. When the disturbances reached international proportions Soviet reaction to American intervention appeared disjointed and improvised—in fact, the very opposite of a carefully planned campaign. Moreover, the revolution in Iraq presented the Soviet planners with an additional problem. For although the Iraqi Communist party was granted legal status by the new régime, and should have been a reliable instrument for Soviet political penetration of the country, many of its actions were so unruly and violent as to alienate General Kassem and the Iraqi Army. The self-criticism which the party was forced to make in August 1959 indicated that the Soviet Government was not always able to command prior assurances of obedience even from its political servants and allies in the temperamental and hot-blooded atmosphere of Arab politics.[1]

Whatever future decisions are taken in Moscow on the Middle East, there can be no doubt that increasing interest will be centred on the Continent of Africa. The peoples of Africa, both in the independent states and those emerging into some form of nationhood,

[1] In the Iraqi paper *Ittihad al Shaab*, 3 August 1959.

have been potentially receptive to anti-Western propaganda, which can in many countries be freely disseminated under the constitutions which states like Guinea and Ghana are in process of evolving. Radio broadcasts can reach those who cannot read, and in the more advanced states economic aid can be offered on favourable and even flattering terms.

The Soviet efforts aimed at Africa should be regarded as a deliberate move likely to play an ever greater part in Soviet foreign policy in the future, because successful ideological, political, and economic penetration of Africa could seriously threaten the interests of the Western Powers who have responsibilities there, and might help to drive wedges between Britain, France, and the United States. Provided that the African campaign is carried out skilfully, using radio propaganda, diplomatic contacts, Communist 'front' organizations aiming at the African trade unions, and East European trade missions, the possibilities for extending Soviet influence could in theory be considerable, while the cost in resources and risk to the Soviet Union would be negligible.

Moreover, a great effort has been made to attract the younger generation of African nationalists, some of whom have been educated in Moscow and other East European capitals, and it cannot be denied that Communist influence has been spread in these circles. A major part of the Soviet effort is to set these young men and women against the older generation of African nationalist politicians, many of whom learnt to appreciate the values of parliamentary democracy and the tactics of non-violence.

On the other hand, there are difficulties to be overcome. Communist theory and Soviet development played no part in the postwar upsurge of African nationalism, and the main differences in West and Central Africa have been over the pace of the move towards self-government, not over the goal itself. Secondly, as Professor Potekhin, the Soviet expert on Africa, himself noted, many of the African leaders are devout Christians, educated by missionaries, of whom even he wrote: 'They brought a certain benefit to the Africans by encouraging health services and education.'[1]

It seems clear, however, that opportunities for the spread of Soviet influence in Africa will be available in the years ahead; probably the most crucial question will be whether the Soviet planners, perhaps unnerved by their experience of Middle Eastern politics, will

[1] Professor I. Potekhin, in *Sovietskaya Etnografiya*, No. 2, 1959.

be able to plan and operate effectively at long range in conditions dominated by African nationalism.

Finally, we come to the lessons to be drawn from Sino-Soviet relations. The Soviet leadership has a record of instability of another kind to draw upon in its relations with Peking—the instability of a numerically powerful Communist ally which appeared to hunger for recognition of equality in industry, military strength, and, most embarrassing of all, in ideology. The Soviet Union is faced with a party and Government which regards the rest of the world as an enemy against which Communist pressure ought to be maintained relentlessly with the object of bringing down the capitalist system in the shortest possible time. The Soviet Union has tried to retain as much of its power to influence the Chinese as possible, both economic and military, and will no doubt work hard to keep this control, while acceding to Chinese requests for aid and political support. But the Soviet Union is now faced by a Chinese leadership which has rejected Soviet views on almost every important aspect of Communist policy —the use of war to further Communist aims, aid for non-Communist neutralist Governments, relations with the United States, the supply of nuclear weapons to China, and the leadership of the Communist movement. As far as can be ascertained, the Soviet Union still has a degree of ultimate control, particularly in the military field, and it may be that in the next few years this will suffice to keep the Chinese party in check. But a radical change in the relationship between the two great Communist powers cannot entirely be ruled out, and we may find advocates in Peking of a policy of 'going it alone', with all its hazards and dangers, rather than acceptance of a further period of Soviet tutelage and leadership.

When the Soviet leaders analyse the experience they have gained from the seventeen years from 1944 to 1961, one fact must stand out above all others: since the day, in 1946 or 1947, when Stalin decided that the United States had entered the lists against Soviet expansion and the spread of Communism in Europe and Asia, the United States could, in some form, be discerned behind almost every failure of a Soviet strategical or tactical plan. When such a plan succeeded or some event developed successfully for the Soviet Union it was usually because America was absent or disinterested. Soviet analysts would argue that Greece was saved from Communism in 1949 because the United States came to her aid. Without prompt American action and United Nations' intervention, South Korea would have collapsed under the blows of the Communist Army from the north. In the Middle East, the United States more than once brought its power to bear with effective speed, and, with Britain, upheld the régimes in Jordan and Lebanon in 1957–58. Conversely, no United States' influence was exerted in Iraq after the July revolution in 1958, and the new régime was able to consolidate its hold on the country. Returning to Europe, the blockade of Berlin was a failure because the Western Allies, led by the United States, were able to intervene directly with effective counter-measures, while Czechoslovakia fell into Communist hands because there was no way in which the United States could prevent the Communist *coup d'état*. In 1956 Mr. Khrushchev was able to take the decision to resort to conventional warfare against Hungary partly because of the serious practical difficulties in the way of intervention by the West or the United States. In Poland one of the factors which probably caused Mr. Khrushchev to hesitate over a full-scale reoccupation of the country was his appreciation of possible excuses for Western military intervention arising out of fighting between Poles and Russians in which the East Germans or Soviet troops based on East German soil were involved. And no Soviet analyst would forget that in the one case when two Western Powers—Britain and France—failed to force their policy through to a successful conclusion—the attack on Egypt in 1956—the U.S.A. was resolutely ranged in the opposite camp.

In the Soviet view, therefore, success is likely to depend on the Soviet ability to prevent American intervention in any plan aimed at increasing Soviet influence in the world. The Soviet leaders know that the existing world power of the United States of America must be removed or drastically reduced before the world can be brought to Communism. In Communist terms, 'experience has shown that the struggle in the main direction' is still against the United States of America, and the Soviet leadership's eternal question is how to paralyse American power and influence.

XXI

SOVIET THINKING ON WAR

THE material examined in previous chapters suggests that the basic task of Soviet foreign policy in the years ahead will be to neutralize the mobility of American power and influence, for while this exists in its present form the establishment of Communist rule over the greater part of the world will be an impossibility. It is now time to examine some of the methods which the Soviet Government might use to reach this goal in the next ten or twenty years. Before proceeding to this examination a word of caution must be entered against the possible invention by one side or the other of a scientific device which might bring about the elimination of its rival with little or no loss to itself. It is, one must suppose, theoretically possible that such a device or substance might be invented or discovered, and if the human leadership of the country making the discovery was of a character willing to make an all-out bid for world domination, it might indeed be used. But setting this possibility aside for lack of concrete evidence, there seem to be two possible ways in which the Soviet Union might try to neutralize American power in the years ahead.

The first is the use of war, either all-out nuclear war on a global scale or some form of conflict on a limited scale. In Lenin's and Stalin's day war between the Communist and non-Communist 'camps' was held to be inevitable and, even, in some circumstances, desirable as a short cut to the collapse of the 'capitalist' system. Towards the end of his life Stalin appeared to modify official doctrine on this point, and since the Twentieth Congress of the Soviet Communist party in 1956 the Soviet Government has maintained that war is not fatally inevitable even while 'capitalism' still exists.[1] This does not mean that the Russians believe that war has already been eliminated from human society, for a great deal of time and effort on their part has gone into an examination of the causes of modern war and the ways in which it might break out. According to the Communist thesis worked out in 1956, the Soviet leaders appeared to believe that global war could come about in three ways. First,

[1] For an up-to-date affirmation of this view see *Party Life*, No. 7, April 1960, as quoted on p. 257 above.

war could break out as the result of a preventive attack launched by the United States against the Soviet Union or her allies, perhaps as an act of desperation to recover markets and sources of raw materials gradually disappearing into an expanding Communist camp. Secondly, an act by a deranged pilot on air patrol, or some other example of human error or miscalculation could set off a nuclear war. Thirdly, a small-scale or civil war, in which one of the Great Powers interfered, could lead in certain circumstances to the use of weapons of mass destruction and thus to global nuclear war. There are of course, other dangerous possibilities on which the Soviet leaders remain silent. These include a preventive attack by the Soviet Union on America or her allies, and a call by the Chinese Government, arising out of a Sino-American clash, to the Soviet Union to honour its mutual defence treaty with China.

These five possibilities of global war must now be studied in greater detail to see whether any of them appears feasible to the Soviet Government in solving their main problem today. Take, for example, a Soviet preventive attack on the United States. No evidence has so far reached the West that the Soviet Government has concluded, or is likely to conclude, that the degree of destruction of American power necessary to make a preventive attack worth while could be achieved by existing Soviet forces, or by any expected in the foreseeable future. Soviet military and political planners realize that in modern conditions no preventive blow could achieve 100 per cent results, and even the smallest human or mechanical failure could bring disastrous consequences to the Soviet Union. The existing retaliatory capabilities of the American Strategic Air Command and British Bomber Command are certainly well understood in the Soviet Union. All the evidence available points to the conclusion that a deliberate planned all-out nuclear attack by the Soviet Union on the United States or her allies cannot be considered by any Soviet Government as a practical means of neutralizing American power.

The nearest approach which Soviet military thinkers ever made to the doctrine of 'first strike' occurred in the period 1955–57, when a group of leading Soviet soldiers put forward the theory of the 'pre-emptive blow'.[1] As one of its advocates, Major-General Talenski,

---

[1] See Ch. VIII. The main known protagonists of the 'pre-emptive blow' were Army-General P. A. Kurochkin, and Major-General N. A. Talenski, both concerned with the training of senior officers.

put it: 'Our task is to work out a solution seriously, paying particular attention to methods and systems of advance warning of a surprise aggression by an enemy, and of dealing him pre-emptive blows at all levels, strategic, tactical, and operational.' But the advocates of a pre-emptive blow were in no sense recommending a preventive war: the decision to launch a pre-emptive blow depended entirely on *the receipt of accurate intelligence* of an imminent attack against the Soviet Union, and it is relevant in the context of the type of warning which would be available to the Soviet Government in the event of an assault by manned bombers against Soviet bloc targets.

Then in 1957 came the first successful test-firing of a Soviet I.C.B.M. When I.C.B.M.s become available for operational use in significant quantities (perhaps in the mid-1960s), the period of warning given to the victim of a rocket attack might be cut as to as little as four minutes (for Western Europe) and twenty minutes (for the North American Continent). These critical minutes would, no doubt, allow the defenders to fire missiles, including those launched from Polaris-carrying submarines, and to send aircraft on long-distance flights towards their targets, but the action in which they would then be engaged would be retaliatory, and not pre-emptive. Only if, in the years, ahead, no agreement banning the use of space satellites for military purposes was reached, and vehicles were launched which could be relied upon to detect pre-launching activity, and transmit warnings of operational launchings allowing the defenders much greater latitude, would the pre-emptive strike come into its own again. Since space satellites may in the future be used for this purpose, a Soviet capability to strike a pre-emptive blow may be expected to keep pace with developments in this field.

The next possible cause of a war, in Soviet eyes, would be an American preventive attack on the Soviet Union. This possibility was for decades a standard theme in Soviet propaganda. But in 1959 the Soviet leadership began to modify its views on the likelihood of such an attack by the Americans. Mr. Khrushchev gave public expression to his view that the destructiveness of modern nuclear weapons, rendered greater by the latest means of delivery, could make war impossible, and thus rule out a deliberate preventive attack by the United States. In his speech to the Supreme Soviet in Moscow on 31 October 1959 Mr. Khrushchev said:

At last, ever broader circles . . . begin to understand that a war under present conditions, with the existence of nuclear and rocket weapons, threatens with unprecedented sacrifices and destruction primarily those countries which would venture to unleash a new world war. . . . In a few minutes the most powerful means of destruction could be delivered to any point on the globe. A new war would not spare anyone, and would cause mankind unprecedented sacrifice, devastation, and suffering.[1]

The Soviet leader made his point again in his speech to the same body on 14 January 1960:

> If the possibility is not excluded that some capitalist countries will draw level with us in the field of modern armaments, will they not, possibly, act perfidiously and attack us first, in order to make use of the factor of surprise, with such formidable weapons as rocket atomic weapons, and thus have an advantage for achieving victory? No. Modern means of waging war do not give any country such advantages.[2]

In April 1960 the Soviet Government gave this estimate of nuclear war theoretical backing in a speech by Mr. Kuusinen, delivered in Moscow on the occasion of the ninetieth anniversary of Lenin's birth:

> Lenin, according to the evidence of N. K. Krupskaya, even as long ago as 1918, said that 'modern science continually increases the destructiveness of war. The time will come when war will become so destructive that it will be altogether impossible.'[3]

It seems certain, therefore, that Mr. Khrushchev came to the conclusion that *the United States Government, to which he was ready to ascribe every other sin in the political calendar, could not obtain a decisive world victory as a result of an all-out nuclear attack on the Soviet Union, and has therefore given up the idea.* In addition, according to the Soviet thesis, many American 'business interests' are beginning to 'agree' with the Soviet and Chinese view that Communist society is in a better position to survive a nuclear war than 'capitalist' systems. By 1960 the Soviet Government had, in fact, come very near to accepting the existence of mutual deterrence based on nuclear armaments, but stopped short of complete agreement because of the possibility of war by mischance or miscalculation.

Soviet military and political doctrine envisages two dangers under this heading: first, that an irresponsible leader might come to power in a country possessing nuclear weapons and rockets, and second, that a misreading of intelligence, a faulty warning system, or even a temporarily deranged pilot on air patrol might be the cause of a

---

[1] *Pravda*, 1 November 1959.
[2] *Pravda*, 15 January 1960.
[3] *Red Star*, 23 April 1960.

nuclear war. As long ago as November 1957 Mr. Khrushchev spoke
of this danger:

> When planes with hydrogen bombs take off, that means that many
> people will be in the air piloting them. There is always the possibility of a
> mental blackout when the pilot may take the slightest signal as the sign
> for action, and fly to his intended target. Under such circumstances a war
> may start purely by chance, since retaliatory action would be taken immedi-
> ately. Does not this show that in such a case a war may start as a result of
> a sheer misunderstanding or of a derangement in the normal state of a
> person, and this may happen to anyone.[1]

In his speech to the Supreme Soviet on 14 January 1960 Mr.
Khrushchev raised the other point that 'irresponsible' leaders could
lead the world to war. After describing the military might of the
Soviet Union, and its ability to strike a retaliatory blow, he went on:

> All this is quite sufficient to exercise a sobering influence on any person
> of normal psychology. But naturally, one cannot speak for madmen . . .
> nations ought to take care that government, parliament, and other re-
> sponsible posts for ensuring peace are not penetrated by people who have
> mad and criminal aims.[2]

From these quotations it appears that Mr. Khrushchev transferred his fear of American military action against the Soviet Union
from a deliberate preventive attack to a mischance or miscalculation,
or to the elevation to supreme power of an 'irresponsible' politician.
This view, illogical though it may seem to those who understand the
way in which parliamentary democracy works and appreciate the
safeguards against the occurrence of accidents when issues of peace
and war are at stake, may well be the basis for the current Soviet
defence effort. It helps to explain Mr. Khrushchev's readiness to put
so much reliance on the long-range deterrent forces while cutting
down on Soviet conventional arms.[3] In Mr. Khrushchev's view, an
'irresponsible' Head of State who was inclined towards a war for the
destruction of Communism would be more likely to pay attention
to an impressive Soviet rocket and nuclear potential than to a large
conventional army. [4]

Although the present Soviet leaders have narrowed down the

---

[1] *Pravda*, 29 November 1957.
[2] ibid, 15 January 1960.
[3] The appointment of Marshal Nedelin on 6 April 1960 as Commander-in-
Chief Rocket Forces was an example of this.
[4] If the reductions in troop strength announced by Mr. Khrushchev in
January 1960 are carried through, the Soviet peacetime forces would by 1963

number of situations in which war might break out, there remain two more dangers: a Soviet entry into a war in support of Communist China and a limited or civil war in which the Great Powers intervened. If China and the United States became involved in hostilities in the Formosa Straits, the Chinese Government could call on the Soviet Union to honour its military obligations by initiating a nuclear strike against American bases in the Pacific, and perhaps even against the West Coast of the United States. The Soviet Government would then have to decide between launching a preventive war on China's behalf or refusing to uphold the Sino-Soviet defence treaty.

If this situation developed, it is very unlikely that the Russians would launch a nuclear war to cover China's involvement in war especially if the rift in Sino-Soviet relations continues. Generally speaking, even if the Chinese Government drifted into war with the United States, they would find it difficult to carry on a war without Soviet approval. Certainly up to 1960 the nature of Soviet military influence in China was strong enough to control Chinese military agressiveness. If, however, at some stage in the future the Chinese decided to try to 'go it alone' and to make a bid for the leadership of the world Communist movement, the Soviet Government might think it wise, as we have already noted, to abrogate their military alliance with China, in the hope that this might act as a deterrent to aggressive tendencies in Peking.

We now come to the possibility of a limited war initiated by the Soviet Army (as opposed to an auxiliary force), or a small war in which one or more nuclear powers intervened.[1] The Soviet view on limited wars is that they would almost certainly develop into global conflicts. An article in the Soviet Army journal, *Military Herald* in 1958 contained this passage: 'We must bear in mind that at the present time the world is indivisible, and each local, minor war has a tendency to become the prologue to a world war, and then turn into a world-wide military conflagration.'

---

probably consist of less than 100 operational divisions, backed by a tactical air force, and submarine navy, and a considerable array of rockets with ranges from 5,500 miles down to 650 miles, capable of attacking bases in the United States and her allies with nuclear weapons.

[1] In this context a 'limited war' is held to mean either a localized conflict between two national states, e.g. Israel and the United Arab Republic, or a civil war inside a country in which 'volunteer' or regular forces of one or more of the nuclear powers may intervene.

Limited wars in which either of the Great Powers have vital interests have become less likely in recent years, largely because of the network of alliances which have been set up. A glance at the map of the frontiers of the Soviet Union shows that the number of countries which could suffer non-nuclear invasion by a member of the Soviet bloc or where intervention by the Soviet Union in a local war could be restricted to the original zone of operations are very few. In the West, any attack on or intervention in Norway, Germany, Greece, or Turkey would immediately involve N.A.T.O.; a Soviet attack on or intervention in Persia would involve C.E.N.T.O., and Britain, a nuclear power; an attack on Afghanistan alone would be senseless except to cut a road through to Pakistan, a member of C.E.N.T.O. and S.E.A.T.O.; and the Soviet Far Eastern frontier runs exclusively with China. Any Western attempts to intervene militarily in member states of the Warsaw Alliance would also involve the Soviet Union in hostilities. There is, therefore, little geographical scope for limited wars which could remain limited while the Soviet bloc retains its existing frontiers. Perhaps the greatest risk in this connexion would be the outbreak of a civil war with ideological undertones in Persia, Iraq, or in south-east Asia, in which intervention by a Great Power became difficult to avoid.

We may assume, therefore, that policy planners in the Soviet Union concede that an all-out nuclear surprise attack, deliberately planned as an act of foreign policy, has no place in Soviet or American planning while the present complex of arms represents the ultimate in the means of mass destruction. Global war could, however, break out following the assumption of power by 'irresponsible' political leaders, as the result of a tragic accident of human error or mechanical failure, or possibly in the course of intervention in a civil war.

On the other hand, students of Soviet military thought are frequently struck by the amount of research published in the Soviet Union on the type of war which might have to be fought by the Soviet armed forces should hosilities break out. Soviet military theory still maintains that the exchange of nuclear strikes between the U.S.A. and the U.S.S.R., however severe, *might not* annihilate either power, and that military operations *could* continue on land, sea, and in the air, possibly for a long time, until one side or the other had destroyed the opponents' armed forces, and perhaps occupied his territory. As a Soviet military journal put it:

The defeat of the enemy will be achieved through the annihilation of his armed forces. Wars are won only when the enemy's will to resist is broken, and it can only be broken when the armed forces of the enemy are destroyed. Therfore, the directive of combat operations must be the destruction of the armed forces, and not the strategic bombing of targets in the rear.

And *Military Herald* expressed it like this in June 1958:

The armed forces of both sides and the territorial extent of armed struggles are so great under contemporary conditions that it is scarcely possible to conclude a war within a short period of time. Even the appearance of atomic and hydrogen weapons and long-range and medium rockets cannot ensure the swift destruction of massive armed forces, and consequently a swift conclusion to the war. In fact, the use of these weapons by both sides leads rather to the prolonging of a war, than to its speeding up. The appearance of atomic and hydrogen weapons alters the nature of war in many ways, but a war cannot and will not be fought with these weapons alone. It can hardly be doubted that if a third world war is unleashed, it may embrace the land and water surface of the whole globe.[1]

The military establishment which the Soviet Union maintains and the training which it undergoes conform to the conception that operations may go on after a nuclear strike. It is, for example, significant that the formal adoption of this theory by the Soviet Government—1954–55—coincided with the reorganization of the air defence forces of the Soviet Union. The anti-aircraft artillery, ground-to-air missiles, part of the interceptor fighter forces, and some element of civil defence, have since 1955 formed a united command under one man—Marshal Biryuzov—with the status of an arm of service equal to the ground, air or naval forces. The organization of this headquarters gives the impression that it is intended to carry on an independent struggle to lessen the effects of a nuclear blow on the U.S.S.R. without regard to the activities of the other three services, or to the success or failure of military operations elsewhere. This type of organization ties in with the measures of economic and industrial decentralization put into effect by Khrushchev in recent years, and one of the reasons for this move was to enable vast provinces of the Soviet Union to survive a nuclear strike and to continue to function independently of the central government, if necessary.[2]

---

[1] This view was reiterated in an article in *Red Star* on 16 February 1960 entitled 'On What the Manpower Strength of an Army Depends'.

[2] See N. S. Khrushchev's answers to H. Shapiro, *New York Times*, 19 November 1957.

Again, the type of training which the Soviet ground forces and tactical air force undergo is indicative of swift mobile land operations.[1]

This Soviet determination to train the Soviet armed forces to fight on after a nuclear strike appears to lead to one conclusion: if the war may have to continue until the final destruction of the enemy's armed forces has been achieved through a series of land, air, and sea engagements, perhaps extending all over the land and water surface of the globe, then *it is absolutely essential to ensure that the Soviet armed forces escape destruction during a nuclear strike against the Soviet Union, regardless of the damage done to centres of industry and population.* This can only be done on any large scale by a gigantic dispersal operation, and by removing the bulk of the Soviet Armed forces, either into remote areas of Central Asia and the Far East or by moving them *en masse* as far away from the Soviet Union as is practicable. Soviet territory, of course, would be extremely unhealthy after a nuclear blow had been struck, and the Soviet leaders probably envisage as their first priority exploiting the conventional superiority of the Soviet forces in Eastern Europe and Western Russia to force a passage away from the areas of radiation at all costs, even if this requires a full-scale invasion of Western Europe and perhaps selected areas of the Middle East. An additional argument in favour of this course would be that if Soviet forces, with or without employing tactical atomic weapons, succeeded in making a major penetration into the N.A.T.O. area, and crossed the Rhine into France, moving down also into Italy, the Western Allies would perhaps be less ready to use the hydrogen bomb against cities such as Paris or Rome and against the peoples of allied N.A.T.O. powers temporarily under Soviet military occupation.

The outbreak of nuclear war might well bring simultaneously *a major Soviet attempt to occupy as much of the N.A.T.O. bridgehead*

[1] An article on tank tactics which was broadcast in 1959 to Soviet troops in East Germany contained the following typical material: 'By using atomic weapons, large gaps can be made in the enemy's defences, and there will be whole areas which will not be occupied by his units in defence. Our tank units must find and use these gaps boldly and they must penetrate intelligently the enemy's defence swiftly in depth, and attack him from the flanks and the rear. However, in this penetration action, the tank company concerned may come under enemy fire from the flanks. It is advisable to use the echelon formation in the direction of the endangered flank. One platoon moving 150 to 300 metres behind in echelon formation towards the flank of the company will protect the rest of the company from the enemy flank action.'

in Western and Southern Europe as possible, and also parts of the Middle East. This would accomplish two tasks at the same time: the destruction, or at least the defeat, of the enemy's (N.A.T.O.'s) main forces in the European bridgehead, and the dispersal of the main elements of the Soviet armed forces in relative safely, away from the area of concentrated nuclear radiation inside the Soviet Union. There, Marshal Biryuzov's air defence organization would be struggling to produce some kind of order out of the destruction produced by a nuclear attack, and would be fully occupied by the need to keep essential services operating for civilian and military alike.

The practical application of this principle, logical though it is, faces the Soviet defence chiefs with a whole range of problems of logistics and of military security. Certainly it is significant that there was a large-scale reorganization of the logistic services of the Soviet Army after 1957; for the first time in the history of the U.S.S.R. these services are commanded by a Marshal of the Soviet Union—Marshal Bagramyan—who ranks as a Deputy Minister of Defence. An officer of his wide combat experience and high rank would certainly be required to deal with problems of the build-up of reserve supplies, the creation of new and imaginative methods of bringing food, fuel, and ammunition to the front line in conditions of atomic radiation, and the prevention of contamination of water supplies.

General Kurochkin, Head of one of the Soviet Military Academies, enlarged on this point in an article on military thought. 'In modern war', he wrote, 'When enormous armies operating over huge distances depend so much on being supplied uninterruptedly with enormous amounts of all kinds of war materials, it is essential to work out in great detail all problems of the organization of strategic, operational and tactical supply areas. Problems of transport, the defence of supply lines against destruction at their bases or during rail transport to the front line becomes of prime importance in view of the employment of the new weapons.'

The details of the military and air campaign to be fought by the invading Soviet Army cannot, of course, be accurately forecast. But Soviet military planners probably consider that they could in the last resort put the N.A.T.O. forces in the West European bridgehead out of action in a mobile land campaign with the forces now in East Germany and Western Russia, despite enormous losses. They would also expect, once they had reached the main centres of population, to set up some kind of civil administration through the local Communist parties, and be able, after the campaign was over, to begin to support themselves off the land, until clarification of the situation back in the Soviet Union—and of further Western intentions for the prosecution of the war—were forthcoming.

Let us now turn to look at the situation in the Middle and Far East. Here the Soviet incentive to move rapidly would be the same: to disperse the operational land and air forces, using, if necessary, foreign territory. Troops now stationed in the Transcaucasus and the Turkestan Military Districts might well disperse into Persia and Afghanistan. Probably the scope of the campaign here would be dictated more by the need to select a suitable area for 'settling' a considerable Soviet force—say up to twenty divisions—in which the problems of logistic support would not be unduly complicated; in fact, the Soviet aim would be to create a viable military 'camp' in the more fertile areas of the Middle East, rather than to add complete Middle Eastern states to the list of occupied territories.

In the case of the Far East, it would not be surprising if plans existed to disperse Soviet forces into remote areas away from potential targets for nuclear bombardment, possibly deploying some formations into Outer Mongolia.

At some stage after the opening of hostilities, varying according to the area of operations, we may expect the Soviet armed forces to be encamped in three major 'centres of escape': the West European bridgehead now held by N.A.T.O., parts of the Middle East, and in remote areas of Siberia and Outer Mongolia. Completion of this operation would probably bring to an end *phase one* of the global war, and with it most of the predictable—relatively speaking—strategic moves in the struggle. Very many unknown factors would then enter into any Soviet calculation of *phase two*. For example: the actual degree of destruction wrought in the Soviet Union, in North America, and in other overseas bases of the United States; the accuracy or otherwise of the Soviet prediction that both sides would be able to continue the war after phase one; and whether both sides, or only one would have any resources left for the continued use and production of atomic or nuclear weapons. And if neither side had this capability, what would be the relationship between the two sides in conventional forces and in trained manpower? It would be true, for example, to say that in occupying the N.A.T.O. bridgehead the best elements of the Soviet land and tactical air forces would probably have been engaged, and have suffered severe losses, while even if the existing N.A.T.O. forces were totally destroyed they would represent only a fraction of the potential land army of a fully-mobilized Western Alliance. And add to these uncertainties the actual degree of destruction wrought by the use of atomic and hydrogen weapons on the civilian population, water supplies, agricultural land and the disposal of waste, and the difficulties of any kind of forecast of further military operations mount alarmingly. Future Soviet moves would depend on whether the Soviet leadership had reliable intelligence about the West's continuing nuclear capability. Until this question was answered, the preservation of the armed forces would certainly be the primary aim of the Soviet High Command. The Russians might attempt raids with close air support; probing, frightening, and keeping on the move all the time, within, of course, the limits allowed by fuel and supplies. The Soviets would expect the West to carry out the same kind of long-range reconnaissance, facilitated by seapower, against which the Soviet Union would make maximum use of its submarine fleet. If, however, the Soviets came to believe that a certain strategic area had been written off by their opponents in the interests of an overall Western plan, they might be tempted to occupy it permanently, organizing it along Communist lines to serve their war effort. They would try to keep the main body of their forces intact until a final clarification of Western strength and Western morale and Western military capabilities had been achieved. That the Soviet High Command is thinking in terms of this kind of rapidly-executed combined operation can be guessed from the following quotation from *Military Thought*: 'The characteristics of the type of offensive strategy [for us to study] include: frontal attacks and counter attacks in the most complicated conditions, both day and night; independent air and sea operations, with coastal areas in conditions of great speed, and rapidly changing circumstances; mounting combined operations within a short time-limit.'

This reconstruction of possible strategy of the Soviet Union in the event of war is based on material published in the Soviet military Press. It shows that the Soviet High Command is well advanced in the study of the kind of war which might have to be fought. But it holds little hope to those who assumed that a general war could in certain circumstances provide a short-cut to Communism.[1]

[1] For example, those in China who wrote the article in *Hung Chi* (Red Flag), Peking, 19 April 1960.

For even if the Soviet Union emerged stronger than its opponents, and bodies of Soviet troops attempted to maintain themselves and some kind of Communist society in various areas of Europe, Africa, and Asia, the homeland of Communism would be uninhabitable for years to come, and the Soviet Union would be useless as the 'leader of the Socialist camp.' Soviet defence policy is, therefore, likely to be geared to some form of deterrent against a war beginning through miscalculation. Because of this, we are likely to see for some time to come a Soviet military establishment with a strong bias towards the long-range rocket, and conventional forces designed to prevent defection from the Communist camp and at the same time to be able to play an important part in operations on land, sea, and in the air should a general war break out.

As can be seen from the foregoing argument, the practical danger to the Soviet Union in the event of war (as seen in Moscow) would be a surprise attack with nuclear weapons delivered either as a result of a miscalculation by an 'irresponsible' politician or of a human or mechanical error. Soviet defence policy must therefore concentrate in the years ahead on reducing the number of bases from which a strike against Soviet territory could be launched. It is at this point that military necessity and foreign strategy combine. As seen from Moscow, each American or N.A.T.O. overseas base is both a potential launching site and a key factor in the mobility of American power. Their elimination, therefore, has become a fundamental element in Soviet political as well as military strategy, and it is in this field that Soviet disarmament policy has an important part to play.

Let us be quite clear about the Soviet attitude to disarmament. The Soviet Government, like the other Great Powers, would like to dispense with the burden of armaments, but is not prepared to consider any measures to this end which would endanger the existence of the Soviet bloc or would expose established Communist régimes to political dangers which could result in their collapse or gradual disappearance.

Soviet disarmament proposals have generally been based on the existing threat to the national security of the Soviet Union. Thus, when the United States had a monopoly or complete superiority in weapons of mass destruction, the abolition of these weapons was the basic demand of all Soviet disarmament plans. When, in 1955, the detection and prevention of a surprise attack on the Soviet Union became Moscow's main preoccupation in defence the Russians agreed to measures of inspection and control which would have given them some degree of supervision over the American Strategic Air Command, at the expense of their own less dangerous Long-Range Air Force. Under the Soviet plan put forward on 10 May 1955, conventional armed forces and military budgets were to remain at the level of 31 December 1954, and a control system approved by the Great Powers was to be introduced. The Soviet Union developed its proposals to include a two-year agreed time-limit for the destruction of nuclear weapons, the reduction of the forces of Russia, China, and America to between 1,000,000 and 1,500,000 men, and those of Britain and France to 650,000 men, and the abolition of all military bases on foreign soil.[1]

In the light of the Soviet view of Western Europe as an American-dominated bridgehead in what ought to be a Communist land mass, it is easy to see the advantages to the Soviet Union of a scheme similar to that put forward in May 1955. Soviet conventional armed forces could enjoy an effortless manpower superiority over any force in Western Europe, while the United States' inability to retaliate with nuclear weapons would leave Soviet territory invulnerable and American power immobile. The possession of nuclear weapons by Britain and American helped to prevent a Soviet land invasion of Western Europe from 1949 onwards, and we have just described how unrewarding the global war which would certainly follow from such an attack would be for the Soviet cause. But an attack from the East could become a real possibility if Soviet conventional forces faced a N.A.T.O. alliance incapable of inflicting severe damage on the Soviet Union itself.

If the Soviet outlook on disarmament continues to be based on the concepts of military responsibility for national security it is possible that in the years ahead the Soviet Government will find it to its advantage to conclude a limited agreement with the Western powers based on the protection of the Soviet Union from surprise attack. The problems of manpower, the Soviet economic plan, the danger of the spread of nuclear weapons and the hope that a disruption of the armaments industry in the West would seriously undermine the latter's economy are arguments in favour of such an agreement. Similarly it is possible that the Soviet Union will agree to a treaty banning the testing of nuclear weapons, since its leaders may

[1] For full details of the plan see Ch. VIII.

believe that such a treaty may harm American military-scientific progress more than its Soviet counterpart.

However, in 1959, Mr. Khrushchev undertook a remarkable step in the field of disarmament and foreign strategy. Addressing the General Assembly of the United Nations in New York, he combined disarmament with a comprehensive scheme to paralyse once and for all the mobility of American power. He offered the elimination of the armed forces and the General Staffs of all states within a four-year period, and their replacement by national 'militias', restricted to the territory of each country. No Government would be allowed to station a single soldier, ship or aircraft overseas. The effect of this proposal would be startlingly simple. By 1964 or soon afterwards Communist militias would be installed in Russia, East and Central Europe, sufficiently well organized and indoctrinated to go to the help of any West European Communist party engaged in subversion or armed rising. No British or American forces would be available to counter Communist infiltration or open intervention, and there would be no strategic air or rocket force to strike back at the Soviet Union or her allies. American power would have become completely immobile, and the elimination of the Western European bridgehead would only be a matter of time.

All the evidence suggests that the full weight of Soviet authority will be put behind these proposals for total disarmament in the years ahead, because they combine the goal of foreign strategy—the paralysation of American power, and the aims of the armed forces themselves—the invulnerability of the Soviet Union. Soviet soldiers, scientists, writers, and diplomats have been unanimous in their support of the total disarmament plan in discussions with their Western colleagues, and indeed the plan, if accepted by the West, would solve all Soviet military and diplomatic problems at one blow. In the meantime the Soviet leaders are likely to use every form of pressure to attack and reduce American mobility by trying to remove every existing American overseas air, land, or sea base, each of which has a part to play in maintaining the ability of the United States to strike with devastating power against the Soviet Union. In disarmament, as in foreign strategy, the guiding principal of the Soviet Government will be: for Russia, invulnerability; for America, paralysis.

The final conclusion to be drawn from this study of the Soviet attitude to war must be: at the present stage, neither global nor limited war offer sufficiently reliable guarantees of success to the Soviet leadership. The Soviet Union must, of course, guard against war by miscalculation, and must not forgo the prestige value of the possession of a mighty armoury of nuclear weapons and rockets.[1] But the best contribution which Soviet military power can make to foreign policy is in the field of skilful co-ordination of defence and disarmament policies. A total ban on nuclear weapons would greatly assist Soviet expansion, but short of this, Soviet strategy is likely to press for the abolition of as many American bases as possible. The Soviet Union will use every weapon of foreign policy, trade, defence, and disarmament, including its latest scheme for the abolition of regular armed forces, to compel the United States to give up base after base, and eventually to drive American power back to the North American Continent. Soviet policy aims at creating an America so static and so paralysed that a Soviet Union which had achieved parity in industrial production could ultimately impose its will on the United States by the exercise of economic power. Having rejected military means to achieve its aims, the Soviet Government appears to have concluded that in the nineteenth century Britain, and in the twentieth, the United States, came to dominate the world by mobility of power and economic pre-eminence. The Soviet leaders, who have always shown themselves to be skilful pupils, propose to advance Communism by the same methods.

[1] Mr. Khrushchev's reply to a question put by a visiting Japanese delegation representing the Asian Solidarity Committee on the possibility of the unilateral renunciation of nuclear tests by the Soviet Union was significant: 'This would delay the development of nuclear weapons, and might have serious effects on the forces of peace.' (Moscow Radio's Far Eastern Service, 19 March 1957.)

XXII

THE ROLE OF ECONOMIC POWER[1]

EVIDENCE drawn from the Soviet Union's experience in foreign affairs since 1944 and from Soviet military doctrine and planning has shown that in Soviet eyes the main obstacle to a successful foreign strategy has been the influence of the United States and the mobility of its political, military, and economic power. By a process of elimination the conclusion has been reached that neither global nor limited war offers realistic prospects of neutralizing American power, though certain aspects of foreign and defence policy, connected, for example, with disarmament, could help to reduce its mobility. There remains the possibility that success in foreign strategy could be achieved if economic and industrial pre-eminence over the United States was secured, so that the Soviet Union, using economic power to impose its will throughout the non-Communist world, could finally succeed to bring the United States to its knees.

There appear to be two sides to the Soviet plan to succeed the United States as the world's greatest economic and industrial power. One is to make the Soviet Union into an attractive example for the rest of the world, particularly for uncommitted nations and the new states emerging to nationhood in Africa and Asia, by displaying a high standard of living, brilliant scientific achievements, and the ability to produce goods of the best quality quickly and in a business-like manner. This aim was explained by Mr. Khrushchev in his speech to the Twenty-first Congress of the Soviet Communist party on 27 January 1959:

> Let us show our goods, and let the world decide which is the better system. Obviously the most progressive and lasting is the one which ensures to every man and woman the greater amount of material goods, the better working and living conditions, the more opportunities for their spiritual development. People everywhere will make the right choice, and they will do it without being forced by a new war and the use of nuclear weapons.[2]

---

[1] Mr. T. Zavalani, author of *How Strong is Russia?* provided the economic material for this chapter, and prepared the charts on pp. 294–297.

[2] *Pravda*, 28 January 1959.

This is a relatively simple objective, and, if the Soviet Government could supply the consumer goods necessary to create the high standard of living promised by Mr. Khrushchev, the Russians should have little difficulty in advertising the fact to the outside world. But belief in Soviet economic superiority, and goodwill towards the Soviet Union, cannot by themselves neutralize American power or obstruct its mobility especially when America's economic power will certainly not stand still in the years ahead. Therefore the other side of the plan is more ambitious and practical: in the words of Mr. Khrushchev at the Twenty-first Party Congress:

If we calculate per head of population, another five years will probably be needed after the fulfilment of the seven-year plan to catch up with and outstrip the United States in industrial output. By that time, or perhaps even sooner, the Soviet Union will advance to the first place in the world both in the absolute volume of production and in production per head of the population. This will be an historic world victory for socialism in peaceful competition in the international arena.[1]

It is clear from this claim that the Soviet leader equated the first place in the world in absolute volume of production per head of the population with the achievement of his political goal: the neutralization of American power. Mr. Khrushchev went on to list the factors which, in his view, would make the equation valid: the internal contradictions within the 'capitalist camp', the attractions of the new high Communist living standards, and the strength and unity of the Communist bloc.

Before examining the significance which a great increase in economic power in the Soviet Union could have for the country's foreign strategy, it is essential to obtain some idea of the motives behind the Soviet Seven-Year Plan, and to examine the priorities which it reveals in Soviet economic thought. Is the Plan intended, for example, to tackle the problem of economic strength by giving increased emphasis to the satisfaction of the demands of Soviet consumers, and by establishing the model for underdeveloped countries of which the Soviet Premier spoke? Or is the main emphasis still to be on heavy industry, defence, and the requirements of the space age? Or does the Plan indicate that the Soviet leaders believe that they can carry out both these tasks in one period of seven years? On the answers to these questions depends the part which

[1] *Pravda*, 28 January 1959.

economic power will be expected to play in Soviet foreign policy in the next two decades.[1]

The Seven-Year Plan itself was launched at the Twenty-first Congress of the Soviet Communist party on 27 January 1959 in the form of a long report by Mr. Khrushchev on what he called 'the control figures for the development of the national economy in the period 1959–65'. Mr. Khrushchev said nothing about the fate of the Five-Year Plan, laid down in 1956 at the Twentieth Party Congress, and which had two years still to run. One explanation for the abandonment of the previous plan was that the rate of annual increase of industrial output did not coincide with the Plan's targets. For example, the average rate of increase of gross industrial production was 10 per cent instead of the planned 13 per cent in 1956–57, and in 1959 had fallen as low as 7 per cent instead of the required 10–12 per cent. The cotton cloth industry had failed to reach its first year's target by 8 per cent in 1956, and had achieved a rate of increase of only 3–4 per cent in 1957–58.[2]

The new Plan may have owed its form and timing to Mr. Khrushchev's desire for a spectacular policy in the field of industry similar to his plan for the cultivation of the unploughed lands of Siberia and Kazakhstan, and to the massive Soviet programme of scientific research.

Let us look first, then, at the ideas behind the new Plan. Mr. Khrushchev's view that the control figures of the Seven-Year Plan would help to make a decisive contribution to the creation of the material and technical base upon which Communism could be constructed formed a central theme of his report to the Twenty-first Congress.[3] Soviet Press comment also emphasized that if the targets were reached by 1965 the economic potential of the Socialist camp and the fighting power of the Soviet armed forced would be strengthened. The U.S.S.R. and the Communist bloc would then produce more than half of the industrial commodities in the world. Of the targets themselves, the most important were the following: gross industrial production should rise by 80 per cent by 1965, that is, at an annual rate of 11.5 per cent. Heavy industry should maintain and strengthen its leading position through an increase of 85 per cent.

---

[1] The detailed targets of the Seven-Year Plan appear as Table I on p. 294.
[2] Calculations prepared by T. Zavalani.
[3] Mr. Khrushchev said that the day in which a worker who, in 1959, earned 30 roubles a day under Socialism earned *five times* that sum, he would have crossed the threshold of Communism.

TABLE I

U.S.S.R. SEVEN-YEAR PLAN 1959–65

Production Targets in Physical Quantities

Commodity	1965 Plan	Percentage of Increment 1959–65 per cent
Total industrial production	—	80
Heavy industry	—	85
Light industry	—	50
Coal (million metric tons)	600 – 612	20
Crude steel (,, ,, ,,)	86 – 91	57 / 66
Rolled steel (,, ,, ,,)	65 – 70	53/ 63
Pig iron (,, ,, ,,)	65 – 70	64/ 77
Oil (,, ,, ,,)	230	100
Electric power (billion kW)	500	110
Cement (million metric tons)	75 – 81	127/145
Forging and stamping machines	—	250
Locomotives	—	150
Chemical equipment (bil. rub.)	3.5	220
Timber (million cubic metres)	275	17
Cotton fabrics (billion metres)	77 – 78	33/ 38
Woollen fabrics (million metres]	500	65
Silk fabrics (billion metres)	1.5	76
Footwear (million pairs)	515	45
Sugar (million tons)	9.2 – 10	76/ 90
Meat (,, ,,)	6.1	114
Fish (,, ,,)	4.6	60
Motor cars ('000)	750 – 856	46/ 67
2 Buses		
2 Trucks		
Radio and television sets ('000)	9302	90
Television only (,,)	4550	70
Washing machines (,,)	2570	378
Refrigerators (,,)	1.450	300
Domestic sewing machines (,,)	4.550	117

Light industry's increase should be 50 per cent. When dealing with individual items, the Soviet planners took the precaution to use the form of control figures, or 'ranges', which allowed flexibility in the final targets.

Among the most significant trends in the new Plan was the proposal to build a new metallurgical centre—the third so far—based on the recently discovered iron-ore deposits in Siberia and Kazakhstan. The output of non-ferrous metals, it is interesting to note, remained a secret; all that the Plan revealed was that production should be increased thanks to exploitation of the abundant resources of Kazakhstan, the Urals, and Central Asia. The increases to be made in electric power should be boosted by the completion of several large hydro-electric power stations, and by the use of cheap coal in Siberia.

Great emphasis was laid on the expansion of the chemical industries, particularly in plastics and artificial fibres. The fuel policy outlined in the Plan aimed at increasing the share of oil and natural gas in the national fuel balance from 31 per cent in 1958 to 51 per cent in 1965. New oilfields should be opened in the Central Asian Soviet Republics, with six or seven refineries to service them on the construction list, using 15,000 kilometres of pipelines to carry the crude oil.

The new Plan aimed at progress in all branches of machine-building and engineering. New and better machinery would be needed to reach the targets in metallurgy, chemicals and fuel, and the use of atomic power in several branches of heavy industry would be extended. Automation and the use of electronic devices would be developed in all these industries, particularly in engineering.

To finance this tremendous programme, the Soviet Government planned to invest the sum of 1,940 billion roubles in the country's economy from 1959 to 1965. The main branches of heavy industry would receive 1,200 billion roubles, that is, 63 per cent of the total, and light industry, 85 billion roubles, or 4.5 per cent of the total. Agriculture would be given 500 billion roubles, partly from investments by the Government, and partly from the undivided capital of the collective farms. Taking the Soviet Union as a whole, housing and the building of communal 'cultural institutions' would account for 375 billion roubles, and investment in rail transport would be 100 billion roubles.

Various estimates have been made in Britain and America on the the likelihood of the targets of the Seven-Year Plan being reached by 1965. All agree that success would certainly depend on the Soviet Government's ability to increase the labour force, particularly through demobilization of serving soldiers, to modernize equipment, to raise the productivity per head of the working population, and to provide the right kinds of incentives to a managerial class with a rising standard of living, and increasingly expensive material and cultural tastes. With these problems solved, the targets are probably within reach of the Soviet Union. But one interesting comparison which can be made between the Soviet targets of 1965 and American achievements in 1957, shows something of the gap between some Soviet targets and the ultimate Soviet goal: to surpass American production, both in absolute volume and in production per head of population.[1]

Reckoned in percentages of the actual American production figures for 1957, the Soviet Seven-Year Plan's targets for 1965 would be, in sample, as follows:

TABLE II

SOVIET PLANNED PRODUCTION FOR 1965 IN PERCENTAGES OF AMERICAN ACTUAL PRODUCTION IN 1957

Items	per cent	Items	per cent
Coal	96	Cotton fabrics	65
Pig iron	65	Woollen fabrics	140
Steel	63	Meat	40
Oil	50	Butter	115
Electric power	50	Sugar	320

These figures would only be valid for 1965 if the United States failed to increase the production of any of these articles above the 1957 level. The calculations take into consideration the greater rate of growth of industrial production in the Soviet Union, as shown in the following table:

TABLE III

COMPARATIVE RATE OF GROWTH OF INDUSTRIAL PRODUCTION

	U.S.A.	U.S.S.R.
1953	100	100
1957	107	154

The difference between 7 per cent in America and 54 per cent in Russia was partly due to the fact that America in this period was an industrially saturated country, while Russia was in a state of industrial accumulation. In fact, even if American production stood still between 1959 and 1965, the Soviet Union would still produce less coal, pig iron, steel, oil, electric power, cotton fabrics, and meat than the United States, but more woollen fabrics, butter, and sugar.

[1] As the Soviet Seven-Year Plan dealt in 'ranges', it provided a maximum and minimum figure. For the purposes of this comparison, the minimum Soviet figure is used in each case. The differences between maximum and minimum target figures are rarely as much as 10 per cent.

The Soviet Plan as published in the Press did not give details about certain other consumer goods, of which it was recorded only that production would be continually increased. Some of these are included in the following table, which gives further data of the size of the gap between American and Soviet production of durable goods for personal consumption.

TABLE IV

INDEX OF DURABLE CONSUMER COMMODITIES RELATED TO THE NUMBER OF PEOPLE IN THE U.S.A. AND THE U.S.S.R. IN 1957

Commodities	One Unit per Number of People	
	U.S.A.	U.S.S.R.
Passenger cars	27	1,900
Radio sets	10	55
TV sets	25	300
Refrigerators	53	555
Washing machines	43	370

The Soviet leaders do not claim in this Plan to be able to overtake the United States in the production per head of the whole range of consumer goods and achieve a higher standard of living than in the United States. For that, Mr. Khrushchev would have to revert to the economic policies begun tentatively by Mr. Malenkov in 1953–54, and would probably have to persevere in them for a period of about twenty years in order to saturate the home market. In the words of the United Nations' *Economic Survey of Europe* in 1959: 'Little change is expected in the average rates of growth of personal material consumption foreseen in the Seven-Year Plan as compared with the recent past, but the available data are insufficient for firm conclusions to be drawn.' [1]

The logical conclusion, therefore, is that as in the case of previous Plans, the new programme is intended as a first priority to maintain and increase the military power of the U.S.S.R. It is significant that 63 per cent of the country's total investment goes to heavy industry, which has worked in the past for defence purposes. Further evidence pointing in this direction can be found in an examination of the Soviet defence budget. Officially, this stands at 12.9 per cent of the total expenditure for 1960, but it must be remembered that the Soviet budget carries many defence items under other headings. The official military budget covers the following: the upkeep of the armed forces,

[1] *Economic Survey of Europe*, 1959, Geneva, 1960, Ch. III, p. 61.

payment for arms and ammunition *delivered to the Defence Ministry*, maintenance of military academies and schools, and military intelligence. The Chief Political Directorate of the armed forces is probably maintained financially by by the Central Committee of the party, and the para-military organization D.O.S.A.A.F., which has 19 million members and a yearly budget of billions of roubles, is a charge on the local authorities. Pensions, which amounted to nearly 50 billion roubles in 1957 (and the bulk of them were for war veterans)—come under the heading of social insurance. The enormous sum spent on research and production of nuclear weapons and ballistic missiles is paid out of the budget of the Soviet Academy of Sciences and the various Research Institutes which are subordinate to it. In many Soviet educational establishments there is a department of military training, which is paid for out of the budget of the Ministry of Education of the Soviet Republic concerned. When these hidden expenditures are added to the official defence allocation of 12.9 per cent, the total military expenditure is raised to between 15 and 20 per cent of the Soviet national income.[1] To this figure should be added the 25 per cent of the national income, which goes into capital investment, and this means that the Soviet people are allowed to spend for themselves about 60 per cent of the new values which they create during the year. This is corroborated, with fair approximation, by the sum total of the wages and salaries bill, the income of collective farmers and of retired people. On Soviet evidence, therefore, it seems probable that two-fifths of the Soviet gross national product is used to maintain and improve the defence capabilities of the Soviet Union.

To sum up at this point: assuming that the relevant labour and managerial problems are solved, the chances that the heavy industrial targets of the Seven-Year Plan will be reached appear to be favourable.[2] But it will not be possible for the Soviet Union to over-

---

[1] A work published by the Soviet Academy of Sciences in 1958, *Political Economy*, writes on p. 297: 'Direct military expenditure reached a yearly average of 47 billion dollars in the U.S.A. in 1952–54, which is more than two-thirds of the total budget. In the same years, defence expenditure in the U.S.S.R. was equal to 16 per cent of State Revenue.' But the authors omitted to explain that the U.S. budget represents only 20 per cent of the gross national product, while the Soviet budget represents 67 per cent, and thus distorted the true proportions of defence allocations in the Soviet Union and the United States.

[2] It should be remembered that these targets were not directly related to estimates of American industrial production in 1965. Mr. Khrushchev relegated the task of surpassing America in industrial production to a later period. (See p. 292.)

take America in the production of all those consumer goods which go to make up a high standard of living in the modern world. In the Soviet Union's favour, however, it should be remembered that many of the newly emerging countries are more impressed by rate of industrial growth than by evidence of a high material standard of living.

Success in the Seven-Year Plan will, however, provide the Soviet Government, after its defence commitments have been satisfied, with greatly increased stocks of raw materials, machinery, plant, and other manufactured goods, available for export under a concerted drive to influence overseas markets in the interests of Soviet foreign policy. This is the point at which Soviet economic power and foreign strategy meet and raise one of the most interesting aspects of the Seven-Year Plan: the use of the increased economic and industrial power which it will provide to influence countries in Asia, Africa, the Caribbean, and Latin America. A particular target in this respect would be states which now lease bases to the United States or her allies. The question for the Soviet Government is, therefore: Can increased economic power, wielded through programmes of foreign aid and trade, induce a country to accept a pro-Soviet foreign policy, or close its markets to American goods and services?

The Soviet leaders appear to believe that experiments in this field are certainly worth while. After the death of Stalin in 1953, the Soviet Union gradually broke down the long-standing barriers between Russia and the smaller non-Communist nations of Asia, Africa, and Latin America, and made it possible for the Soviet Union to offer trade and economic aid as an alternative to the programmes emanating from traditional Western sources. By 1955 the new Soviet policy was in full swing, offering everything from outright financial or material grants to arms deals and barter agreements, and more than one Communist source has openly described it as an act of political strategy.[1] From the evidence so far available (for it must be remembered that the Soviet aid programme is still comparatively young) the Soviet planners argue as follows: a 'new' country is offered, and accepts, a Soviet loan at an interest rate considerably lower than that provided by Western or international agencies. Provision is made in the agreement that the country will use the credit for the purchase of Soviet goods, and that the Soviet

---

[1] For example, the Hungarian paper *Propagandist*, Budapest, for March 1955, quoted in Ch. XIII.

Union will accept repayment of the loan by means of imports from the country concerned. The administration of the loan may also allow considerable numbers of Soviet or East European officials and technicians to live and work in that country, especially if the projects for which the credit was extended are being constructed with Soviet technical advice. The Soviet Union thus acquires in some more remote part of Asia, Africa, or the Caribbean a physical presence which can be used to spread Soviet influence and activities in the interests of Soviet foreign policy.

Meanwhile, as the recipient draws on his Soviet credit his imports from the Soviet Union increase, and when the time comes for repayment his trade is steadily diverted to the Soviet Union. A point in time should therefore be reached when the Soviet Government would be able to use its position of economic domination to exercise political influence over the debtor country. In theory, it could try to compel the latter to adopt the Soviet point of view in a specific international situation, or it could close the doors of the debtor country as a market for Western trade. And if the country concerned had a defence agreement with a Western alliance, the Soviet Government could attempt to persuade the Government to reject it outright, or could use accumulated Soviet influence to make any base useless to the Western defence effort.

It is true that in the course of the last five years the Soviet trade and aid programme has not succeeded in dominating the economy or the politics of any country to which this kind of assistance has been offered. But Soviet aid programmes are still in their early stages, and the Seven-Year Plan may be expected in Moscow to increase the chances of success in this field. The pattern of Soviet exports confirms the assumption that the Soviet Government aims at using part of its heavy industry and mineral resources to supply machinery and equipment for the industrialization of the underdeveloped countries. In 1958, out of a total of exported goods valued at 17.4 billion roubles (at the official rate of exchange equal to £1,560 million), 4.2 billion roubles' worth was for machinery and industrial equipment. The value of coal, crude oil, petroleum products, iron ore, and timber exported amounted to 6.5 billion roubles. These products, therefore, accounted for 63 per cent of the Soviet Union's total exports during that year.[1] Furthermore, in 1958,

[1] T. Zavalani. Machinery and equipment represented 40 per cent of the total of Soviet exports to China in 1958.

exports absorbed only a small proportion of the total industrial output, the highest figures being those for oil (10 per cent), iron ore (13 per cent) and coal (4.6 per cent). Indeed, it has been estimated that the Soviet Union could have supported a larger economic aid programme even in 1958–59.[1] According to an American statement, the whole Communist bloc aid programme amounting to $2 billion between 1954 and 1957 constituted less than 1 per cent of the gross national product of the Soviet Union and the East European countries for one year.[2] A doubling or more of the programme of 1956–58 could be undertaken by the Soviet Government, providing that the goods to be exported under credit schemes could be spread out over a number of industries. The existence of this unused potential in the field of foreign trade inevitably draws attention to the experimental nature of a policy which represents a departure from established Soviet tradition. Soviet planners must ask themselves: is this type of aid programme likely to bring results in the pursuit of vital Soviet objectives? Initially, these programmes certainly enjoyed the advantage of novelty, and of presenting to the emerging countries an alternative source of aid and trade to those of the West. In contrast to the detailed information required by Western or international agencies on the economic soundness of the projects for which the aid was requested, the Soviet policy of asking no questions and offering no advice appealed to the Governments of Asia and Africa. Soviet loans carried lower interest rates than those of the International Bank: the Soviet Government asked for 2·2 per cent interest rate from India and for the Soviet-built Bhilai Steel Mill, while the Indian Iron and Steel Company is paying the International Bank an interest of $4\frac{3}{4}$ per cent.[3] The Soviet Government has frequently accepted repayment in the local money, a tremendous advantage for young countries with no reserves of hard currency. And so far the Soviet Government has, in the non-Communist world, divorced offers and acceptance of aid from political alignment, carefully leaving this aspect of its programme for the moment to the goodwill produced by these favourable terms in the country concerned.

[1] *Soviet Economic Aid*, by Joseph S. Berliner, Council of Foreign Relations, Frederick A. Praeger Inc., New York, 1958, pp. 185–6.

[2] Statement by Mr. C. Douglas Dillon, Deputy Under-Secretary of State for Economic Affairs, on Soviet Bloc Economic Activities, U.S.I.S., London, 5 March 1958, p. 7.

[3] Berliner, op. cit., p. 158.

On the debit side, the Soviet Union has run into adverse criticism for its handling of some of these programmes. Countries which have received Soviet construction materials have complained of poor quality, lack of durability, and serious delays in delivery schedules. One such delay caused a Soviet ship carrying cement to arrive in Burma during the monsoon season, and when unloading was completed (in spite of Burmese requests to the Russians to hold up delivery), the material congealed, and turned the Rangoon piers into blocks of cement. A delivery of cement to Egypt arrived so late that local factories had already made good the losses suffered during the Suez crisis.[1] Resentment has also been caused in smaller Asian countries by the practice of Chinese and Russian missions in charging their expenses against the credit offered by their Government. And, as a Soviet aid programme develops in scope, it brings with it those faults which plague Soviet economic planning at home, including the chronic tendency of industrial managers to fulfil their part of the overall plan—if necessary at the expense of other enterprises along the conveyor belt—which leads to bottlenecks and delays in delivery.

Perhaps the most serious difficulty facing the planners of Soviet strategy has been to judge correctly the optimum target in any given country. This presents a real dilemma for the Soviet Government: its aid is supplied to influence countries towards the Soviet point of view, but if no effort is made to exploit the initial goodwill created by the offer, the aid may have to be written off as wasted. On the other hand, any direct attempt to force a Government to accept the Soviet point of view through economic pressure, or a threat to terminate aid (as in the case of Yugoslavia), could cause an anti-Soviet revulsion of feeling in the debtor country, and sweep away all the value of previous transactions. So far, Soviet aid has not prevented recipients from adopting anti-Communist attitudes in world affairs. The United Arab Republic has received great quantities of Soviet aid, yet it has taken up an anti-Communist position at home, and often abroad, too. Cambodia followed an anti-Chinese policy in spite of a loan of $22 million obtained from Peking in 1957.[2]

In other words, no Soviet aid programme has so far succeeded in bringing a pro-Soviet Government to power in a foreign country, or in persuading an anti-Communist Government to adopt a pro-

[1] Berliner, op. cit., p. 174.
[2] *New York Times*, 12 January 1958.

Soviet policy in international affairs.[1] The one occasion on which a swift Soviet offer might have produced a position of domination for the Russians was the case of the Aswan Dam in Egypt in July 1956. But it was not taken up. Indeed, the Soviet planners may even have come to the conclusion that the major countries of non-Communist Asia and the Middle East, India, Pakistan, Burma, Indonesia, Iraq, and the United Arab Republic cannot be persuaded to change their alignment through even the most generous Soviet aid programme. This is probably one reason why the Soviet Union has shown such interest in the very new countries of West and Central Africa, including Guinea, Ghana, and Congo, where the need for aid is so fundamental, and the lack of experienced administrators so great that Soviet offers might be able to open doors to the real kind of control envisaged in the original Soviet blueprint of the foreign aid programmes.[2] It is in these very undeveloped areas that the most persistent Soviet economic penetration will probably be attempted in the years ahead.

The evidence for or against a rapid rise in the amount of foreign aid offered by the Soviet Union is difficult to assess, and any conclusion at this stage must be tentative. But it seems likely that the Soviet policy planners have not yet made up their own minds on the value to be placed on this type of foreign strategy. It is, of course, to be valued as a policy consistent with Communist theory, and the Soviet authorities may be ready to wait years for positive results. On the other hand, having begun the policy in a more optimistic frame of mind in 1955, they may soon feel themselves obliged to continue the aid programme because of the inability of war and direct political action to achieve their goal: the destruction first of the mobility of United States power, and later of that power itself. Economic penetration of the uncommitted world, influencing governments against Western bases and Western alliances, and gaining control of traditional and essential markets of Western trading nations, may come to appear in Moscow (though not necessarily in Peking), *as the only possible policy for the Soviet Union in the next two decades.*

[1] This appears to have been one of the points at issue between the Soviet and Chinese Communist parties in 1960–61.

[2] In view of the clashes which have occurred at sessions of Afro-Asian 'front' organizations between the Soviet and Chinese points of view on the correct path for the 'revolution' in newly-emerging African territories, another reason for Soviet haste in these areas is to stake a firm Soviet claim there before the Chinese arrive.

We may assume, therefore, that the Soviet aid programme will go on. Steel mills will be built in India, factories will be offered to Burma and Indonesia, assistance towards the building of the Aswan Dam will be provided (within reason), but no risky military commitments must be undertaken.[1] Until the Soviet Union has firm evidence that steel mills, loans, and high dams can change alignments and remove bases, the strategists in Moscow are likely to rely on a limited and controlled flow of aid, technicians, and agitators into the uncommitted world, and to await results.

This kind of programme would not exclude tactical sallies into areas where a quick and dramatic Soviet offer could do temporary damage to the Western cause. In 1954 the Soviet Union bought Burma's rice crop when the Burmese had failed to find a market in the West. When the crisis arose between Britain and Iceland over fishing rights the Sovet Union stepped in and bought Iceland's surplus fish. In June 1960, when Cuba took over the Anglo-American oil refineries in unilateral action, Soviet oil tankers were on the spot quickly to keep supplies of fuel available to the Cuban Government, and later offered to buy Cuba's sugar crop when the United States cut its import quota drastically. Whatever achievements are registered in the Seven-Year Plan, the Soviet Government will ensure that its capacity for taking short-term tactical decisions of this nature will be improved. And should a new state appear, or an older state break up in civil disturbance or secession, the Soviet economic planners will be expected to be ready with an immediate offer of economic aid in terms of goods or credit available almost at a moment's notice. Dramatic offers of this kind will from time to time attract the headlines of the world's Press. But they require a large reserve of up-to-date equipment and technology, the creation of which, no doubt, will be a vital target of the Seven-Year Plan.

As seen in 1960, the priorities of Soviet economic policy appear to be: first, defence and science; and second, the standard of living required to give the Soviet Union 'model' status, and the creation of a vast pool of exportable surpluses of technicians, material, and knowledge, to pursue the goal of economic domination of the uncommitted world and the destruction of Western influence. It should not be forgotten that these priorities depend to a certain extent on non-economic factors. On the one hand, pressure from below among the Soviet people for a higher standard of living may compel the

[1] The final agreement on this aid programme was signed on 26 August 1960.

Government to divert more resources to the production of consumer goods and correspondingly reduce the allocation of heavy industry, and later the foreign aid programme. This may, indeed, have happened already, for on 17 July 1960 *Pravda* announced that 25–30 billion roubles would be transferred to light industry for the production of textiles and footwear. There is also the unending problem of agriculture, with its claim on machinery and manpower.[1] On the other hand, an outstanding success in the penetration of the uncommitted world might raise the status of economic power in foreign policy in the scale of Soviet priorities. But until such a victory has been achieved, the role of economic power is likely to be one of patient erosion, coupled with a readiness to go over to the offensive quickly and smoothly anywhere in the world where the political or economic situation has deteriorated for the Western Powers.

[1] The problem of agriculture claimed Mr. Khrushchev's particular attention in 1961. He toured many of the grain-producing areas of the Soviet Union and dismissed a number of senior officials concerned with agricultural production.

XXIII

THE STRUGGLE ON THE MAIN FRONT

THE earlier chapters of this book attempted to trace the development of a Soviet foreign policy entirely dominated by the mind of Josef Stalin, one of the really formidable figures of the twentieth century. From his first years as dictator in Russia, Stalin thought in terms of direct action to encompass the destruction of the non-Communist world. Armed aggression, subversion, deceit, threats of force, menaces, and utter ruthlessness were the hall-marks of Stalin's foreign policy, but so much of it was rooted in his extraordinary ignorance of the outside world and of the men and women who he regarded as his 'enemies', that when he died the Soviet Union was more unfavourably situated internationally than it had been at any time since the war. Stalin's policy had provoked the United Nations Organization into mounting the world's first successful collective security operation, and driven the United States, Canada, and Western Europe into close alliance. The Soviet dictator had alienated moderate political parties all over the world, antagonized the Yugoslav Communist party, and ignored the new emerging countries of Asia and Africa. In 1953 the Soviet Union was an isolated armed camp, with declining prestige, a stagnant agriculture, unbalanced economy and a political system based largely on intrigue and fear.

Stalin's successors, of whom Mr. Khrushchev soon emerged as the most vigorous and forceful, realized that this policy could not be continued. Within weeks of Stalin's death they began to repair the bridges linking the Soviet Union to the outside world. They talked to the West in language which encouraged her statesmen to think once again of serious negotiations with the Soviet Union. They restored relations with Yugoslavia, and launched a new policy to win over the nationalist régimes of the Middle East and Asia whose governments were uncommitted in the struggle between East and West. True, the Soviet leaders quarrelled among themselves at home and on foreign policy, on defence and armaments, and over personalities in their own Communist hierarchy. But by 1956, guided by Mr. Khrushchev, they had developed a new challenge to the non-Communist world. They seemed to base their foreign policy on the maintenance of two permanent bastions, one in Europe and the other in the Far East with a broad expanse for manoeuvre between them. In the West, the Soviet Government presented a firm front to the Western bridge-head in the Eurasian Continent: Communist Europe made it clear that it would offer no major concessions unless the West agreed to American military evacuation of Europe, and the elimination of N.A.T.O. and all its bases. In the East, Soviet foreign policy rested on the Sino-Soviet alliance, backed by the emotional support of several anti-colonial Asian countries. Between these two bastions lay an area which the Soviet Union felt free to penetrate politically, economically, and militarily, employing what means it could to bring these countries under Soviet influence. This was in particular Mr. Khrushchev's conception of a dynamic foreign strategy.

In 1956, however, this ideal suffered a severe setback. Mr. Khrush-chev, in his zeal to refashion his own personal grip on the centre of power in the Soviet Union, denounced Stalin so vehemently that the Communist world was shaken to its very foundations. The European bastion of his strategy almost collapsed under the strain; Poland re-asserted her nationality, and for a few days Hungary broke away from the Communist bloc altogether. The situation was restored only by resort to limited conventional warfare within the bloc itself. In addition, the Soviet Union's operations in the uncommitted areas were prematurely exposed during the Suez war, and while Soviet prestige among the Arab countries rose during the crisis, the failure of the Russians to use their aircraft in defence of Egypt did weaken the credibility of the new Soviet posture in several of the uncom-mitted countries.

After 1956 came the struggle to recover lost ground—a campaign waged by Mr. Khrushchev at home and abroad with all the skill of his forceful personality. Communist China was called in to help, concessions were made to the small countries within the bloc, and diversionary counter-attacks were delivered against the West. But the events of 1956 taught Mr. Khrushchev to understand the weaknesses of the Soviet position as well as its strengths, and when the former were again underlined in the crisis in the Middle East of 1957 and 1958, the Soviet leaders began to adopt a new approach to their problems of foreign strategy. Undoubtedly, Mr. Khrushchev en-countered some opposition at home, for in 1957 he was driven to outlaw four leading Soviet statesmen and his famous Minister of

Defence, Marshal Zhukov. But the Middle Eastern crisis taught him that his inability to influence the course of events in the area of manoeuvre decisively lay in the fact that his opponents, particularly the United States, enjoyed a mobility of power denied to the Soviet Union. The Western Alliance, through its air and sea power, its political bases and centres of influence and its economic networks all over the world, could exercise effective power in those areas in which the Soviet Union wanted to operate, but was unable to do so without risk of war. During the Suez, Syrian, and Lebanese crises of 1956–58, Soviet propaganda tried to conceal the immobility of Soviet power, but the direction of emphasis in Soviet foreign strategy since 1958 has shown that the lesson was understood in Moscow.

The Soviet leaders quickly realized that two conditions were necessary to neutralize this Western mobility: redoubled efforts to reduce the number of political centres and military bases belonging to the West in Asia, Africa, and Latin America, and a relative decrease in American economic power. Operations against the first target included sustained propaganda to oust the Americans from Europe, offers of far-reaching disarmament concessions in exchange for the elimination of military bases on foreign soil, and encouragement for all the dependent peoples in Africa and Asia to assert their right to immediate political independence. This campaign against bases also involved, on the diplomatic level, meetings at the Summit between the Heads of Government.[1] There is, therefore, one certainty about Soviet foreign policy in the next decade: it will be directed towards the elimination of every Western base or centre of influence which can threaten the military security of the Soviet Union, serve as a political or economic obstacle to Soviet penetration of the uncommitted world, or play a part in the mobility of Western power.

The second Soviet campaign—that directed to the relative weakening of American economic power—was initiated by Mr. Khrushchev at the Twenty-first Congress of the Soviet Communist party in January 1959. Its declared purpose was to give the Soviet people a

[1] The abortive Summit meeting in Paris in May 1960 was intended to dispose of one of the most unwelcome political bases of the Western Alliance—West Berlin. One of the reasons for the failure of the Conference to meet—and some of these were to be found in Soviet internal affairs—was that Mr. Khrushchev had come to the conclusion that the West was not prepared to make the necessary concessions on the issue of the city as a *political* base, and as a 'shop window' of the Western way of life.

standard of living which would attract underdeveloped countries to the Communist system, and to reach certain industrial levels of production from which an ultimate attempt could be made to overtake those of the United States, perhaps as early as the mid-1970s. The Soviet aim was, in fact, to make the same use of its economic power in foreign policy as in Soviet eyes the Western Alliance made of theirs. The available evidence suggests that the Seven-Year Economic Plan 1959-65 will not be able to approach the American levels in the production of consumer goods. The Plan's emphasis remains as in previous programmes on heavy industry and defence, but out of the greatly increased quantities of raw materials, machinery, and equipment produced under the Plan, a vast pool of exportable commodities could be made available for a foreign aid programme on a grand scale. The Soviet leaders want to be able to influence the policy of foreign governments both by their readiness to make tactical grants of aid in emergency conditions and by their ability to dominate the market in certain of their target areas to the exclusion of Western trade or aid.

The need to rely on economic and political means to keep the dynamism of Soviet foreign policy alive grew out of the great advances in nuclear physics and those in rocket-propulsion which led to the Soviet Intercontinental Ballistic Missile and the American and Soviet space research programmes. Indeed, one of Mr. Khrushchev's most striking adaptations of classical Marx-Leninism was his assertion, first made in 1956, that war is no longer inevitable between the Communist and non-Communist worlds. In 1960 the Soviet leaders went farther, and stated that the existence of weapons of mass-destruction could make war impossible. If Mr. Khrushchev continues in this belief, we may expect him to rule out nuclear war as a deliberate act of foreign policy, while retaining the capacity of the Soviet Union to fight one, should a world-wide conflict break out in other ways. Since the world system of alliances has restricted the areas in which direct political action can be carried on without risk of war, the choice of methods before any Soviet Government inspired by missionary zeal has been reduced to political subversion and economic penetration. Attempts at subversion there will always be, but possibly with diminishing returns as governments increase their vigilance and write conditions against it into their treaties of alliance. In most parts of the world, therefore, the Soviet policy planners are left with economic penetration—the last weapon in their hands which they can wield without restriction, and the last barrier before inactivity and loss of initiative.

Finally, the potential influence on foreign strategy of the situation inside the Communist bloc itself must not be forgotten. At the Twenty-first Congress of the Soviet Communist party in January 1959 Mr. Khrushchev included 'the unity of the Socialist camp' as one of the advantages enjoyed by the Soviet Union in its struggle to overtake the United States in economic power. It is true that since 1956 there has been no attempt on the part of any European member of the Soviet bloc to break away, nor is there likely to be in the foreseeable future. The Soviet readiness to use its conventional army to keep its smaller allies inside the bloc is certain to prevent a new split occurring either on the Yugoslav or the Hungarian model.

The question arises more realistically in connexion with China, a country with a population three times greater than that of the Soviet Union, and an economy and military power expanding at a revolutionary rate. China has received considerable amounts of aid from the Soviet Union, and has recently made strenuous efforts to pay off her debts and to stand on her feet economically.[1] It is believed that China may have the capacity to make a small-yield atomic weapon (largely for prestige purposes) early in 1963, and by then will be supplying her own armed forces with all except the heaviest weapons and the most modern aircraft. China could be a future contender for the leadership of the whole Communist camp, and any premature bid on her part for pre-eminence might lead to a split between the bloc's European and Asian members. Contemporary China exposes a more vigorous and revolutionary face to the outside world than Soviet Russia; on various points Soviet and Chinese policies and beliefs are at variance. The Chinese leaders have challenged Mr. Khrushchev's views on the inevitability of war, and incurred Soviet displeasure over their policy towards India. Sino-Soviet differences have appeared in the Communist approach to the newly-emerging states of Africa, and over aid to non-Communist nationalist régimes. The Chinese act as they do because that is how they interpret Marx-Leninism, and their interpretation differs from that of Mr. Khrushchev. How important is this likely to be in the realm of Soviet foreign policy?

On the one hand, for two states which acknowledge Marx-

[1] See *Communist China and Asia*, by A. Doak Barnett, Council on Foreign Relations, Harper & Brothers, New York, 1960, p. 376.

Leninism as their guiding principle, ideology would seem to be all-important. If they diverge, one must appear to be a revisionist party, and one the true interpreter of Leninist doctrine, and this also involves the formal leadership of the Communist world. In theory, there can be no compromise. But on the other hand, both states benefit from the maintenance of the closest alliance in international affairs, and both realize that a final break between them would seriously weaken and perhaps irreparably damage the structure of the 'Socialist camp'. What is likely to happen is a continuation of differences on the interpretation of correct Marx-Leninist doctrine on a basis of public 'non-recognition' of the existence of a dispute—rather like the refusal of pre-revolutionary Russian Governments to recognize the existence of a Polish nation within the boundaries of the Empire. Those who draw attention to the divergences in public or who try to exploit it will be denounced by both participants—but the dispute will go on, and from time to time proof of its continued existence will appear.[1] It may even be necessary for the Soviet Union to adjust its formal commitments to China, including its military alliance, in order to deter the Chinese from provoking a world war. It would be unwise either to deny or to exaggerate the Sino-Soviet dispute's ability to influence Soviet foreign policy, for one very simple reason. Both party leaderships will watch the second generations in their respective Communist parties, each hoping that the youth of the other country will adopt their interpretation, with the result that the divergence will disappear. No doubt the Russians calculate that Mao Tse-tung, Liu Shao-chi, and Chou En-lai will be replaced in the course of the next decade by men more in tune with the Soviet view of the world, based on advanced technological and scientific achievements; the Chinese probably hope equally fervently that the next generation of Russian Communists will be more revolutionary than the existing leadership. In so important a matter it may be that both sides are content to wait. Unless the Chinese, in particular, are ruled only by extreme arrogance, both Moscow and Peking must realize that the cost of settling the issue now would be too great for either contestant to bear.

In the final analysis, the Soviet leaders probably hope that their own victory over the United States through a successful campaign to neutralize America's mobility of power and to overtake America in

[1] For example, the documents quoted in the London *Observer*, 12 and 19 February 1961, and the Soviet criticism of Albania in October 1961.

industrial and economic strength may precede any critical breaking-point in Sino-Soviet ideological relations. With the United States and Europe unable to resist Soviet pressure, the Soviet Union would be so immeasurably stronger than China that the dispute on doctrine would fade into insignificance. *Unless, therefore, either side forces the issue in some entirely unpredictable way, the Sino-Soviet dispute is not likely to cause the Soviet Union to abandon her main struggle against Europe and America in the West.* This will be the 'struggle on the main sector', to use the politico-military language of the Communists, and it may be that by 1965, the end of the Soviet Seven-Year Plan, both the West and the Soviet leaders will know how it will be won and lost. The Soviet Union is ahead of the West in recognition that the struggle is for the world, and in concentration of effort to win it. The West's existing resources are considerably greater, and unless a major part of them are allowed to disappear by default, the West can meet and defeat the Communist challenge, directed by the strategy and tactics of the Soviet Government.

POSTSCRIPT

THE SOVIET CHALLENGE IN 1961

THE year 1961 was dominated in the field of Soviet foreign policy by two issues: the trial of strength within the Communist bloc between the Soviet Union and China, mainly visible to the outside world in the Soviet dispute with Albania, and the apparently suspended offensive launched by the Soviet Government against the Western Powers in Germany. Sino-Soviet relations had reached a critical point in 1960, and while the conference of the eighty-one Communist Parties held in Moscow in November strove to restore the outward façade of unity, it became increasingly clear that the basic problems had not been solved at the Moscow meeting. The Chinese were not prepared to reconsider their interpretation of Communist doctrine along Soviet lines, and the Russians declined to resume technical, economic, and military aid to China on the scale of earlier years, even though China was passing through a severe agricultural crisis resulting in widespread food shortages and economic difficulties. Soviet reluctance to make any practical concessions to China at a time of great need was all the more galling in the light of the cordial relations fostered by Mr. Khrushchev with the Indian Government, and the Soviet Government's supply of advanced weapons to Indonesia under an agreement signed in Moscow on 7 January 1961.

This was the background against which Mr. Khrushchev embarked on a new challenge to the West which, in its earlier stages at least, threatened to lead to a direct confrontation of American and Soviet military power.

On 3 March the Soviet news agency *Tass* released the text of a Soviet Government memorandum to Dr. Adenauer's Government on Berlin and a German Peace Treaty which appeared to be the opening shots of a new Soviet offensive on this subject. The Russians announced their intention of signing a Peace Treaty with the two German States, or if their overtures were rejected by West Germany, with the East Germans alone. This Treaty would, in the words of the memorandum, 'automatically end the occupation régime in West Berlin, with all its attendant consequences,' and the city would become a demilitarized free city. These proposals were taken up by the Press of the Soviet bloc in a general co-ordinated offensive against the status quo in the former German capital.

This challenge to the West on Germany was accompanied by tougher Soviet tactics in many fields. For example, when the Nuclear Test Ban Conference resumed its sessions in Geneva on 21 March, the Soviet delegate accused the West of benefiting from France's nuclear tests in the Sahara, restricted the number of annual inspections of nuclear testing sites under the proposed agreement to three, and demanded the replacement of the administrator of a test ban control organization by a Committee of Three, or 'troika', each member of which should have a veto. Since these proposals were obviously unacceptable to the West, it seems very likely that the Soviet Government wanted to put an end to the negotiations in circumstances in which the Western Powers could be blamed for their disruption. Indeed, as far as timing is concerned, it is probable that the Soviet Government had by March already decided in principle to resume the testing of nuclear weapons in the atmosphere, and that the period from April to the end of August, when the resumption of tests was announced, represented the time required by the military authorities to prepare the testing sites in Central Asia and the Arctic.

On 28 March the Consultative Committee of the Warsaw Pact organization met in Warsaw, presumably to hear details of the new Soviet offensive on Germany, and from the beginning of April the Communists began to demand a German settlement by the end of 1961—a dangerous move, verging on an ultimatum to the West. In May, President Kennedy paid his first official visit to Europe, and on 4 June he met Mr. Khrushchev in Vienna for discussions on the world situation. The two leaders restricted themselves to defining their respective positions on the German question, and emphasized the issues on which they could make no major concessions—including, on the Western side, freedom of access to West Berlin and the rights of the population in the three Western sectors. Within a week of the Vienna meeting, a Soviet memorandum which had been handed to Mr. Kennedy was published; it confirmed that the Soviet Union demanded a German Peace Treaty in 1961, with provisions handing over control of access to Berlin to the East German authorities. Mr. Khrushchev explained his position to the Soviet people in a long radio and television broadcast on 15 June: he suggested that after a Treaty had been signed, West Berlin's independence could be guaranteed by the presence of token contingents of Four Power troops, or by the United Nations, acting, in all likelihood, under the Soviet 'troika' system. But he added the warning that if Russia signed a treaty with East Germany alone, all Western rights in Berlin would cease, including rights of access, and that if East Germany's sovereignty was violated, those who did so would have to assume full responsibility for 'aggression'.

By mid-June, therefore, the Western Powers were faced by a Soviet threat to sign a treaty with East Germany within six months, under which Allied rights would be illegally subjected to East German control. Among the first to see the full implications of the situation were the East German people, and the stream of refugees into West Berlin rapidly mounted to 20,000 in June and to over 30,000 in July.

The next move in the Soviet offensive took the form of a calculated introduction of a Soviet military threat into the German crisis. On 21 June the Soviet Defence Minister, Marshal Malinovski, boasted of the strength of the Soviet armed forces, and one of his deputies, Marshal Chuikov, declared that the West had no rights in Berlin since they had not captured the city. The military challenge was reiterated on 8 July by Mr. Khrushchev, in a speech to graduates of the Military Academies in Moscow. After re-stating his demands on Berlin, the Soviet Premier announced the temporary cancellation of the programme of reductions in the armed forces, an increase in the defence budget of from 9,250 million roubles to 12,300 million roubles, and—most significantly—returned to the view that nuclear war would lead, not to mutual annihilation, but to the total destruction of 'imperialism'.[1]

The Western reaction to this threat took the form of military counter-measures, particularly in the United States, where President Kennedy ordered the despatch of more aircraft and troops to the European theatre, and the reactivation of reserve units and ships. At the same time the Western Powers re-emphasized their willingness to negotiate on Germany, while reserving their essential rights on the Berlin question. Meanwhile, throughout July and August Soviet military moves designed to influence and intimidate the West

---

[1] This view had been publicly supported by Mr. Khrushchev up to mid-1959, but had been replaced in his speeches on defence policy in the spring of 1960 by references to the universal nature of the destructiveness of nuclear weapons.

continued. On 9 August, at a reception for the second Soviet space-man, Major Titov, Mr. Khrushchev declared that the Soviet Union possessed a 100-megaton nuclear device, and on the same day it was announced that Marshal Konev, who had been on the retired list since July 1960, would take over command of the Soviet troops in East Germany.[1]

As tension mounted, observers noted that the East German Communist leader, Herr Ulbricht, paid a sudden visit to Moscow, and twenty-four hours after his return on 11 August, during the night of 12–13, the East Germans began to seal off their sector of the city by building a wall along its perimeter, under the protection of Soviet and East German Army units. At first the West seemed taken by surprise, and no counter-action was taken, but as the wall grew, and crossing-places were cut down to two or three, it became clear that the Soviet authorities, alarmed at the flight of 20,000–30,000 East Germans a month to the West, had decided to close down this escape channel once and for all. Soon refugees were reduced to jumping from windows or swimming canals under the machine-gun fire of East German guards; Allied contingents in the city were strengthened, and for a time Soviet and American tanks faced each other across one of the few official crossing places. However, while incidents continued to occur between Allied and East German officials, no further violent action was taken by the Russians in Berlin; the withdrawal in late September of the major Soviet Army units which had surrounded Berlin during the building of the wall suggested that by halting the stream of refugees without arousing the West to counter-action, the Soviet Government had achieved its immediate aim in Germany. In other words, in order to carry out its overall campaign to intimidate the West and exhibit Soviet power in Central Europe, it became necessary to stop the flow of refugees to West Berlin; this is exactly what the East Germans' wall achieved.

This campaign continued throughout the summer and autumn of 1961. On 23 August the Russians sent a Note to the West complaining of misuse of the air corridors to Berlin, couched in terms which aroused fears of early Soviet action to close them down. On the 29th

[1] Marshal Konev's appointment was in all probability a measure in the campaign to impress the West rather than a purely military posting. After the 22nd Congress of the CPSU in October 1961, Konev's predecessor and deputy, General Yakubovski, was given full membership of the Central Committee, an indication that Konev's position in Germany was not intended to be permanent.

the Soviet Government issued a warning that submarines which entered Soviet territorial waters would be destroyed. But the climax of the whole campaign came on 30 August: the Soviet Government announced its intention to resume the testing of nuclear weapons in the atmosphere.

There can be little doubt that many factors contributed to this decision. Certainly Mr. Khrushchev and his military advisers must have agreed that if tactics of intimidating the West were to be used in foreign policy, then the Soviet nuclear armoury must be brought up to date. The technical efficiency of the series in which between thirty and forty nuclear explosions were carried out in two months, was probably calculated to contribute to Western alarm, and to frighten outright some non-aligned countries. It is possible also that Mr. Khrushchev had his eyes on the effect which so impressive a series of nuclear tests might have in Peking. At all events, the successful discharge of so many nuclear devices, one of them with a yield of over fifty megatons, to which the United States replied by ordering small-scale underground tests in Nevada, undoubtedly improved the Soviet Union's military capabilities and played an important part in impressing the outside world with Russia's power and her readiness to act in total disregard of world public opinion.

While the Soviet Union was testing nuclear weapons in the atmosphere, the Warsaw Pact countries held a military conference on 10 September, and on the 25th large-scale manoeuvres covering East Germany, Poland, and Czechoslovakia were announced. Tension in October switched to north-western Europe, when the Soviet Government suddenly turned on Finland, where a Presidential election was approaching, and suggested military staff talks between Russia and Finland in view of the West German threat in the Baltic area. Fears were widespread that the Soviet Union was about to move in the Baltic, but after the Finnish President, Dr. Kekkonen, had paid a visit to Mr. Khrushchev in Novosibirsk on 25 November, the Soviet leader apparently lost interest in Finland, and abandoned his call for joint staff talks.

Mr. Khrushchev's failure to press home his military demands on Finland was symptomatic of a switch in Soviet tactics which appeared to coincide with the opening of the twenty-second Congress of the Soviet Communist party on 17 October. While tension over Germany remained high, incidents between the two sides in Berlin became less frequent, and the attitude of the Soviet authorities in the city became less rigid. Mr. Khrushchev quickly dropped the time limit of 31 December 1961 for the conclusion of a Peace Treaty with Germany, much to the distress of Herr Ulbricht and the East German Communist leadership. Indeed, a harsh speech made by Ulbricht on 23 November found no echo in the Soviet press. In fact, by mid-November it became fairly clear that Mr. Khrushchev had altered his timetable on the German question. Perhaps he decided that no further measures of 'brinkmanship' against West Berlin could be safely undertaken in the light of Allied military counter-preparations. It is possible, too, that having halted the mass exodus of East Germans through the West Berlin loophole, and demonstrated the military might of the Soviet Union to the world at large (and achieved an all-round improvement in Soviet military capabilities), Mr. Khrushchev felt that his Western flank was now relatively secure, and that he could safely turn his attention to his other major problem: Communist China.[1]

On the opening day of the twenty-second Congress of the Soviet Communist party, 17 October 1961 the world was taken aback when Mr. Khrushchev launched a bitter attack on the Albanian Communist party, and particularly on its leader, Enver Hoxha, whom he described as a Stalinist and an upholder of the cult of personality. Relations between Albania and the Soviet Union had been deteriorating ever since 1960, when the Albanians sided with the Chinese against Mr. Khrushchev in the series of conferences held to try to settle the ideological and other issues between Moscow and Peking. In 1961, the Russians closed down their submarine base at Valona in Albania, withdrew their military and economic advisers and cut down their contacts with the Albanian Government to a minimum.[2] But an open attack on the Albanian party at a Congress which had been generally expected to deal with past achievements and with the German problem was completely unexpected, and was immediately understood by the Chinese delegation, led by Chou En-lai, as an attack on the Chinese Communist party. Two days later, Chou En-lai spoke slightingly of the 'one-sided criticism of a fraternal party in public', and went on to say: 'to lay bare a dispute

---

[1] It is of some importance to note that one of the December issues of *Kommunist* (No. 18) carried an article which re-affirmed Mr. Khrushchev's thesis that nuclear war would destroy everything, and tacitly abandoned the more belligerent views he had adopted for tactical purposes in July.

[2] On 10 December the Soviet Union broke off diplomatic relations with Albania.

between fraternal parties or fraternal countries cannot be regarded as a serious Marxist-Leninist approach.' On 20 October the Albanian press reacted strongly to Mr. Khrushchev's remarks, and published a personal attack on him as 'an anti-Marxist liar'. On the 23rd Chou En-lai, after laying a wreath on Stalin's tomb, left for Peking, where he was met at the airport by Mao Tse-tung—a sign of the Chinese leader's confidence in his emissary's conduct in Moscow. Three days after Chou's return, the Chinese press printed side by side some passages from Mr. Khrushchev's speech and the full text of the Albanian reply, including the personal criticism of the Soviet leader. This procedure was repeated on 6 and 16 November, coupled with an enthusiastic Chinese greeting to the Albanian party on the twentieth anniversary of its foundation.

Publication of both sides of the dispute seems to have been the directive on which the Chinese press acted during the last months of 1961. The Chinese did, however, receive an Albanian economic delegation in Peking on 17 November, and after five weeks' negotiation, the Chinese announced the granting of credits and technical and material aid to Albania. At the same time both the Soviet and Chinese press published increasingly violent criticisms of each other's party policies and interpretations of Marxism, without actually mentioning their opponents by name. While the Soviet Union re-affirmed its belief in the universal destructiveness of nuclear war, a Chinese contribution to the clash on 10 December included references to the attractive possibilities of re-building the world after 'imperialism' had been destroyed in a nuclear war.

The events of the final weeks of 1961 showed, therefore, that a major shift in Soviet tactics occurred when Mr. Khrushchev deliberately brought the Sino-Soviet dispute out into the open in public and bitter criticism of China's closest friend in the Communist bloc, Albania. Albania's defiance by itself represented no serious threat to Soviet leadership of the bloc, and Mr. Khrushchev's decision to attack the Albanian leaders reads very like a deliberate provocation of the Chinese. By attacking Albania, Mr. Khrushchev probably hoped to force the Chinese either to disavow Albania's political stand, and be publicly humiliated within the Communist movement as an unreliable friend and ally, or by an act of open defiance in support of the Stalinist Albanian régime shoulder the responsibility for causing a split in the bloc. Mr. Khrushchev possibly believed that China's economic difficulties might cause her to value a resumption of Soviet aid (which had been gradually reduced since early in 1960) more highly than loyalty to small and distant Albania, and that there was a good chance that Mao Tse-tung would bow to Soviet pressure on this issue.

At the moment of writing, Mr. Khrushchev's calculations appear to have been based on false assumptions about the Chinese. The Chinese have neither capitulated under Soviet pressure nor reacted to his provocations by causing an open split in the Communist camp. They seem to have seen through the Soviet leader's plans, and have striven to give adequate material and political support to Albania without taking an irrevocable step towards a formal breach between the Soviet Union and China. It remains to be seen whether Mr. Khrushchev, faced by a continued refusal on the part of Mao Tse-tung to capitulate or formalize a breach, will feel it necessary to make the break himself. For although this would be an extremely serious step for him to take, and could have incalculable consequences for the Communist movement, it would not be without advantages for the Soviet Union. It would enable the Soviet Government to present itself to the West in negotiations over Europe as a moderate force, disassociated from the warlike and irresponsible Chinese. It would enable the Russians to win support from the Yugoslav-orientated states of Asia and Africa who frequently warn that Mr. Khrushchev is under severe pressure from elements in the Soviet party hierarchy demanding a more militant foreign policy. And it would allow the Soviet Government to take early and probably successful action to suppress the pro-Chinese factions in certain non-bloc Communist parties, such as the Indian, Burmese, and Indonesian parties, and restrict the spread of Chinese influence in extreme left-wing political groups in Africa.

Looking at Soviet strategy and tactics during 1961 in perspective, therefore, it is possible to trace further the development of the two themes which dominated the previous two years. The first was the Soviet desire to secure a safe and stable flank in Europe through a solution of the Berlin and German questions favourable to the Soviet Union. Such a settlement would allow Mr. Khrushchev to pursue his positive strategy of undermining the Western position in the Middle East, Asia, and Africa without undue anxiety about the position of the Bloc in Europe. In 1959 and early 1960 (until the U-2 incident) he believed he could achieve a European settlement by extracting voluntary concessions from the United States and Britain.

In 1961, he apparently came to the conclusion that there was more chance of success by intimidation. It seems, however, that by the autumn of 1961, the challenge of China loomed so large on the Soviet horizon that he felt it necessary to suspend his operations against the West in Europe temporarily while he attempted to solve the Chinese problem. While the future cannot be predicted, it is possible that 1962 may witness a similar division of Soviet effort between these two problems. We in the West must expect a varied programme of threats and conciliation to come from Mr. Khrushchev, as he himself calculates the relative urgency of the creation of a stable European bastion, and a favourable settlement of the future relationship between his country and its giant but as yet underdeveloped Eastern neighbour, China.

INDEX

Abakumov, General, 73
Abdul Illah, Crown Prince, 234
Acheson, Dean, Secretary of State, 44
Aden Protectorate, 126
Adenauer, Konrad, 107, 206, 312
Africa: China and, 243; Nationalism, 271; Soviet policy in, 203, 221–44, 271; Soviet propaganda, 118, 243, 270–2
Africa, North: anti-colonial struggle, 117
Afro-Asian Solidarity Committee, 243
Agriculture, improvement of, 88
Aidit, D. N., 137
Albania: China and, 317–18; Corfu Channel dispute, 66; Greece and, 11, 12; included in Warsaw Pact, 103; Soviet financial and economic assistance, 195; Soviet policy towards, 264n, 312, 317–18
Algeria: Government of, 250
Amer, General, 229
American Mutual Defence Assistance Programme, 1949, 28
Anglo-French-American meeting, Bermuda, 76
Annam, 52
Arab countries: Communism and, 240; nationalism, 118, 179; Soviet approach to, 119; build up of popularity, 268; economic and political penetration, 119; trade to absorb exports, 179; Soviet prestige, 191; supply of arms to, 179
Arab League, Soviet attack on, 118
Arab League Collective Security Pact, 121
Army, Soviet: reorganization of, 96n, 102–3, 315; manpower cuts, 104
Asia: Communist parties, exhaustion of, 56; policy of violence, 55, 57, 128; Soviet policy in, 128–40
Asia, South-East: Soviet policy in, 1945–53, 51, 139
Asian and Pacific Peace Congress, 57, 70
Aswan Dam proposal, 181n, 240, 302–3
Atlantic Treaty Headquarters, 28
Atomic bomb, 5, 35, 199; Soviet Union and, 68, 90, 95; U.S.A. and, 60, 90

Atomic energy: control of, Soviet attitude, 67; U.S.A. and, 67
Atomic weapons: Soviet Union's policy, 90n, 92
Aung San, 134
Austria, 81; Austrian State Treaty, 105; Negotiations for State Treaty, 74; deadlock in discussions, 79, 80n; signed, 1955, 106; Conference at Lugano proposed, 78; at Berlin, 78; Discussions in Moscow, 1955, 105; neutrality, declaration of, 106; Soviet troops withdrawn from, 104, 106
Azerbaijan: abandonment of Soviet régime, 50n; Communist zone, 39; Soviet attempts at separation, 9, 10, 39; detachment from Persia, 59, 118; United Nations and Soviet policy, 66

Baghdad Pact, 122–5, 127, 237
Bagramyan, Marshal I. K., 92, 284
Bakarić, 23
Balance of power, 204
Balkan Federation, 23
Balkan, zone of peace proposed, 207
Balkans, United Nations special commission on, 11, 12
Baltic, Soviet move in, 316
Bandung Conference, 123, 143
Bandung Powers, 187
Baruch, H. B., 67
Bases, military, 307
Belgium, Communist coalition, 16; Government, non-Communist, 21
Benediktov, Min. of State farms, 107; in Ghana, 242
Beneš, President, 24–25
Bengal, Communist party outlawed, 56
Beria, L. P., 72; indictment of, 108; trial and execution, 73
Berkovitsa, 11n
Berlin: blockade of, Soviet defeated, 267–8; Cominform and, 22; currency proposals, 26; Foreign Ministers' Conference at Geneva, 215; Four-Powers' meeting in Paris, 213; Soviet action in, 60; Soviet failure in, 47; Soviet proposals for East and West Berlin, 212; Peace Treaty, 313; Western

*Printed in Great Britain
by W. & J. Mackay & Co Ltd
Chatham*